MY HERO ACADEMIA

Writer / Letterer
Hideyuki Furuhashi

Penciller / Colorist
Betten Court

Original Concept
Kohei Horikoshi

【catastrophe】

noun | ca • tas • tro • phe
: a large-scale disaster in nature or human society;
or : the denouement of a tragedy, in the classical
tradition of storytelling

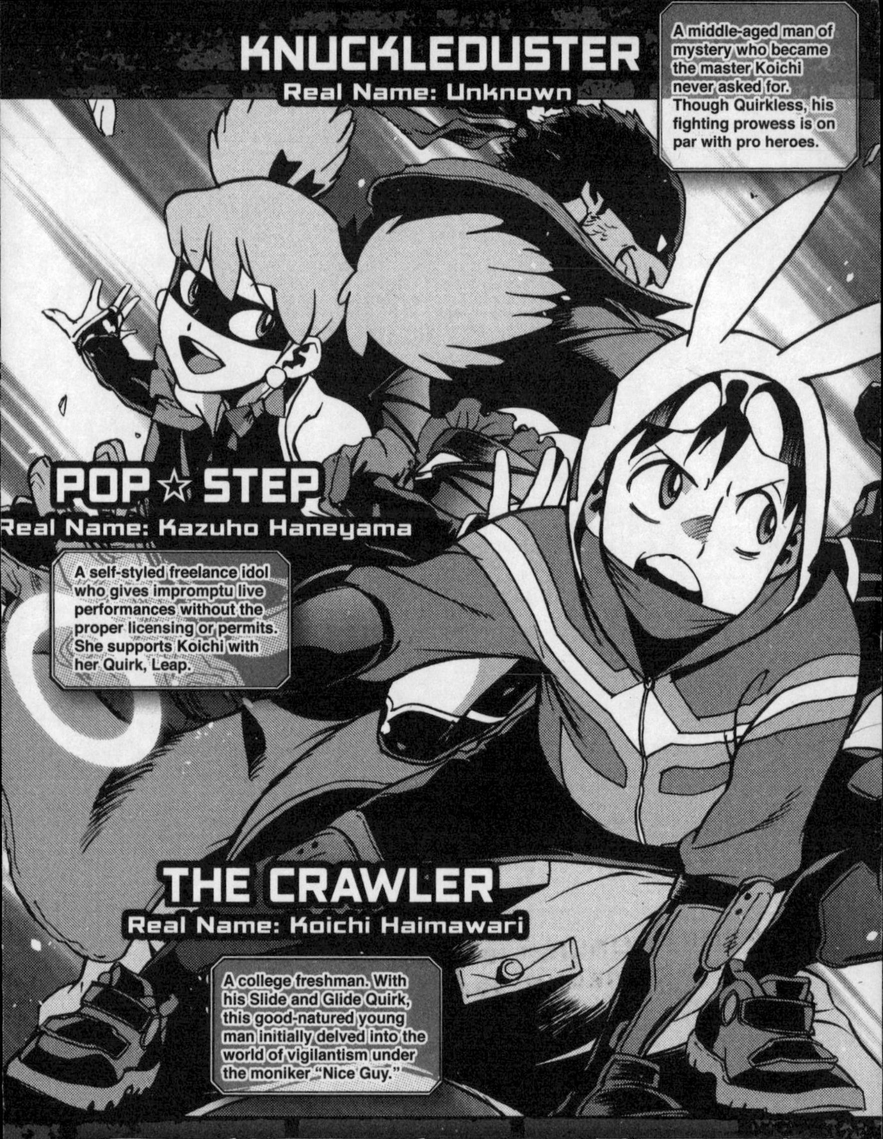
KNUCKLEDUSTER
Real Name: Unknown
A middle-aged man of mystery who became the master Koichi never asked for. Though Quirkless, his fighting prowess is on par with pro heroes.
POP☆STEP
Real Name: Kazuho Haneyama
A self-styled freelance idol who gives impromptu live performances without the proper licensing or permits. She supports Koichi with her Quirk, Leap.
THE CRAWLER
Real Name: Koichi Haimawari
A college freshman. With his Slide and Glide Quirk, this good-natured young man initially delved into the world of vigilantism under the moniker "Nice Guy."

STORY

What is "justice" anyway? Get ready for a PLUS ULTRA spin-off set in the world of *My Hero Academia*!!

Heroes. The chosen ones who, with explicit government permission, use their natural talents, or Quirks, to aid society. However, not everyone can be chosen, and some take action of their own accord, becoming illegal heroes. What does justice mean to them? And can we really call them heroes? This story takes to the streets in order to follow the exploits of those known as *vigilantes*.

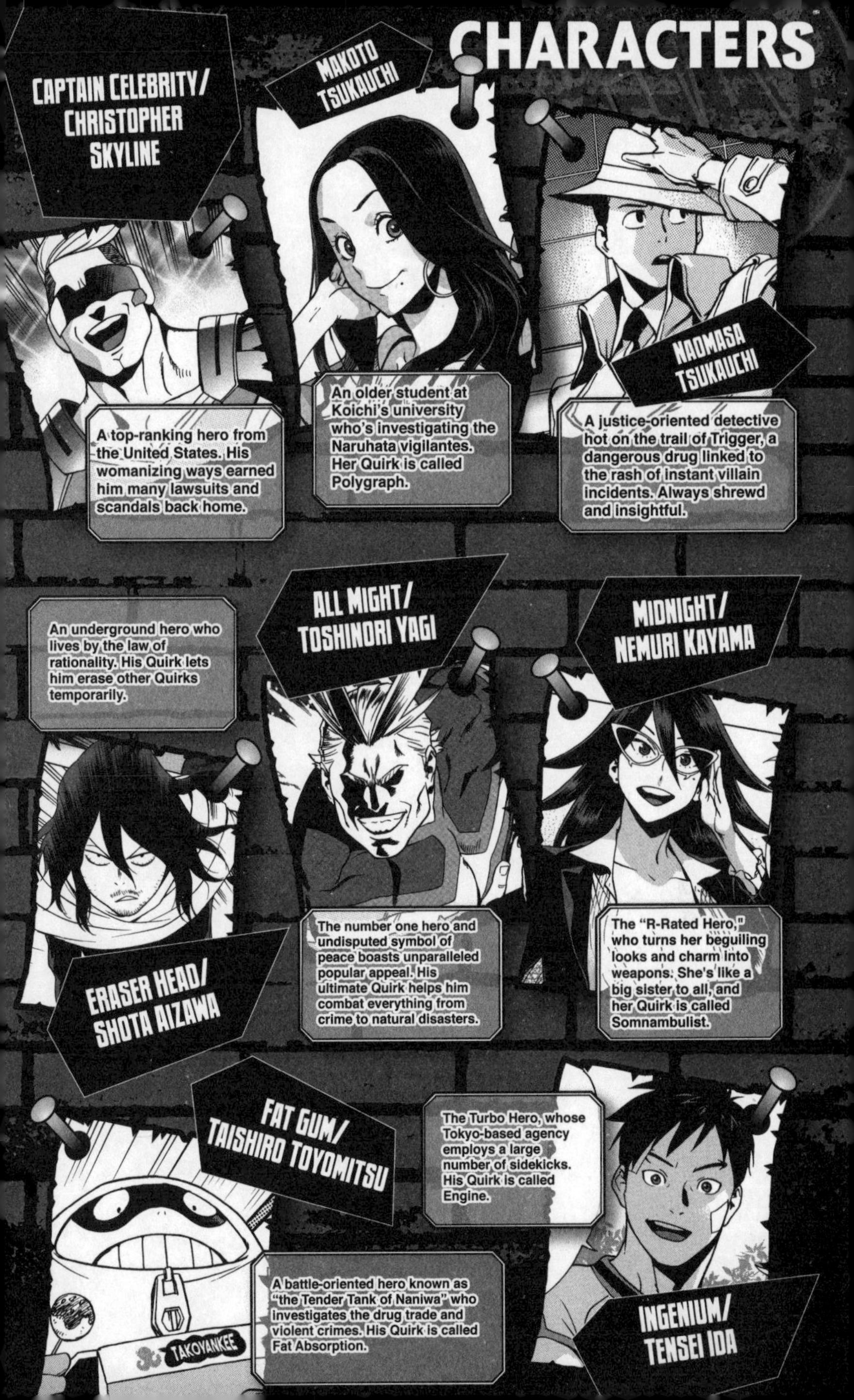
CHARACTERS
CAPTAIN CELEBRITY/ CHRISTOPHER SKYLINE
A top-ranking hero from the United States. His womanizing ways earned him many lawsuits and scandals back home.
MAKOTO TSUKAUCHI
An older student at Koichi's university who's investigating the Naruhata vigilantes. Her Quirk is called Polygraph.
NAOMASA TSUKAUCHI
A justice-oriented detective hot on the trail of Trigger, a dangerous drug linked to the rash of instant villain incidents. Always shrewd and insightful.
ERASER HEAD/ SHOTA AIZAWA
An underground hero who lives by the law of rationality. His Quirk lets him erase other Quirks temporarily.
ALL MIGHT/ TOSHINORI YAGI
The number one hero and undisputed symbol of peace boasts unparalleled popular appeal. His ultimate Quirk helps him combat everything from crime to natural disasters.
MIDNIGHT/ NEMURI KAYAMA
The "R-Rated Hero," who turns her beguiling looks and charm into weapons. She's like a big sister to all, and her Quirk is called Somnambulist.
FAT GUM/ TAISHIRO TOYOMITSU
A battle-oriented hero known as "the Tender Tank of Naniwa" who investigates the drug trade and violent crimes. His Quirk is called Fat Absorption.
TAKOYANKEE
INGENIUM/ TENSEI IDA
The Turbo Hero, whose Tokyo-based agency employs a large number of sidekicks. His Quirk is called Engine.

MY HERO ACADEMIA VIGILANTES

7

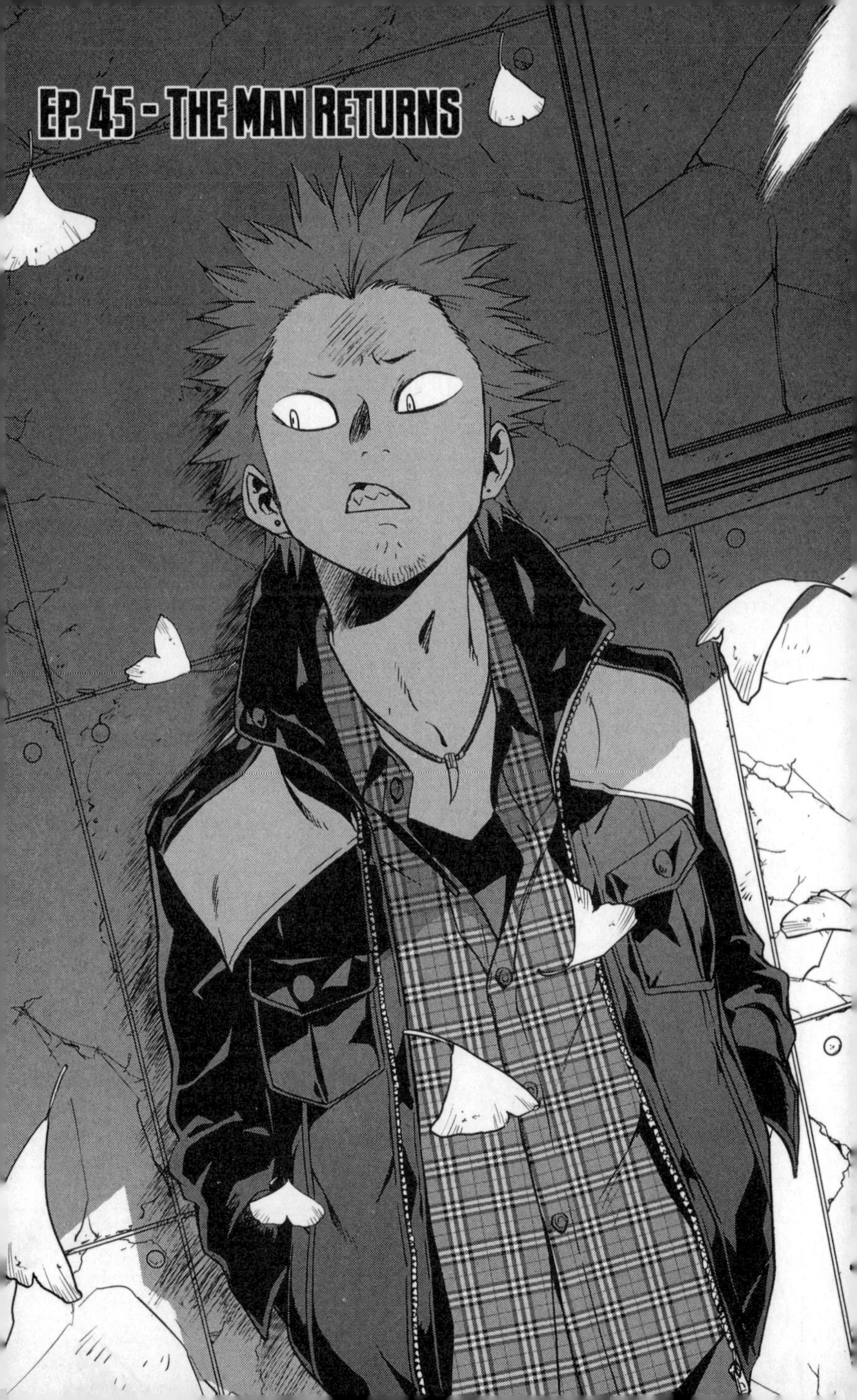
Ep. 45 - The Man Returns

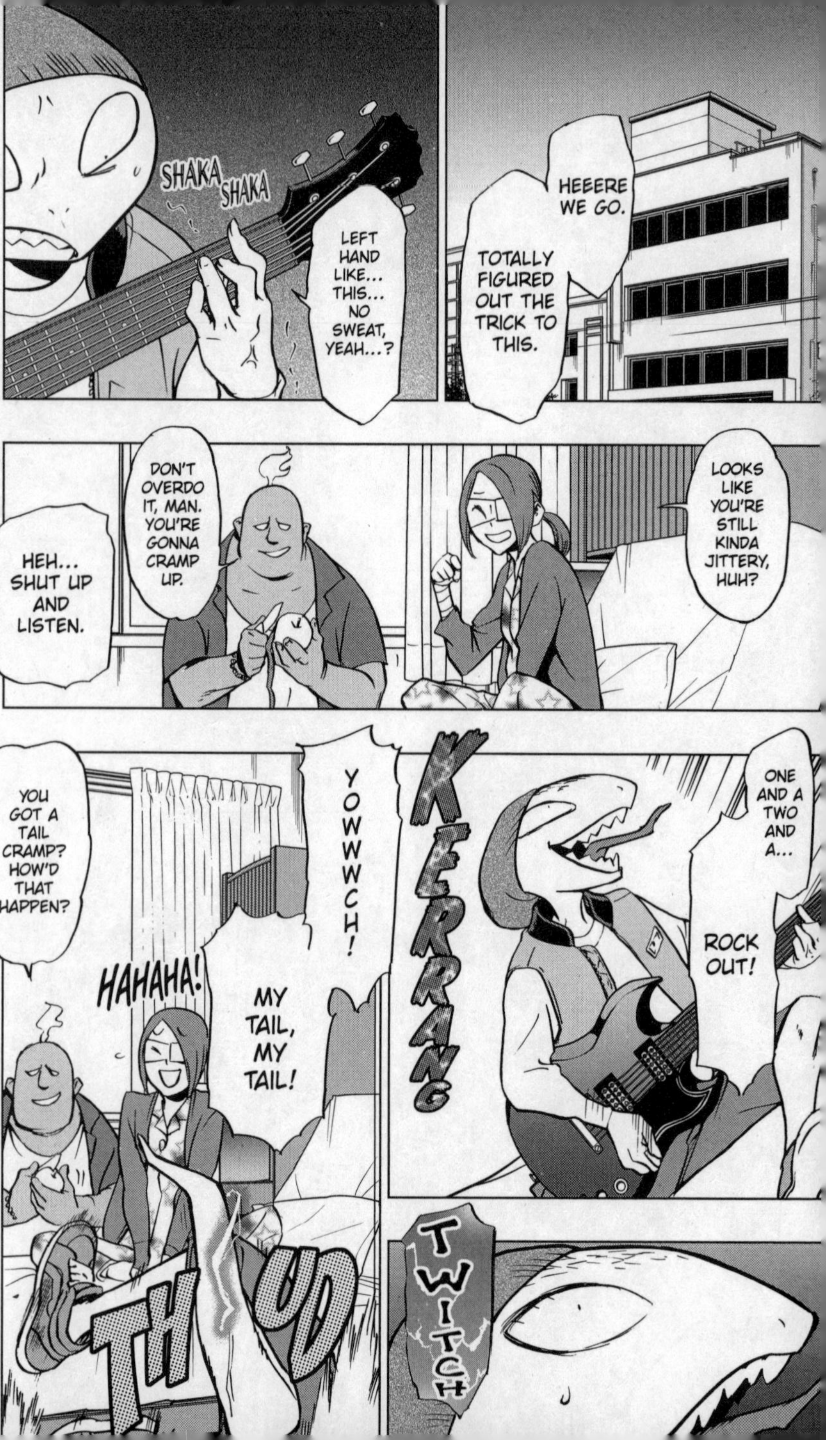
HEEERE WE GO.
TOTALLY FIGURED OUT THE TRICK TO THIS.
SHAKA SHAKA
LEFT HAND LIKE... THIS... NO SWEAT, YEAH...?
LOOKS LIKE YOU'RE STILL KINDA JITTERY, HUH?
DON'T OVERDO IT, MAN. YOU'RE GONNA CRAMP UP.
HEH... SHUT UP AND LISTEN.
ONE AND A TWO AND A...
ROCK OUT!
KERRANG
TWITCH
YOWWWCH!
YOU GOT A TAIL CRAMP? HOW'D THAT HAPPEN?
MY TAIL, MY TAIL!
HAHAHA!
THUD

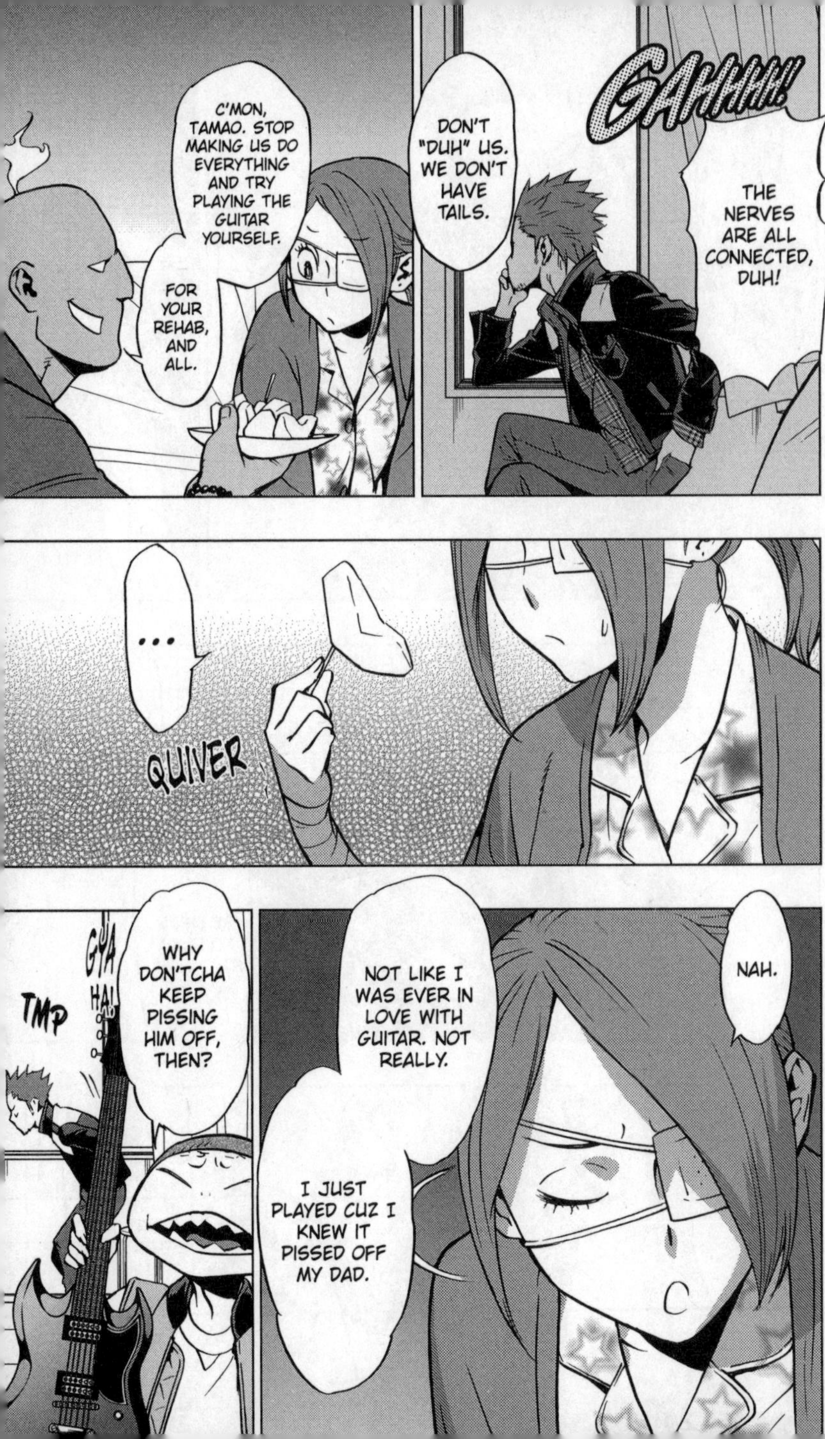
GAHHHH!!
THE NERVES ARE ALL CONNECTED, DUH!
DON'T "DUH" US. WE DON'T HAVE TAILS.
C'MON, TAMAO. STOP MAKING US DO EVERYTHING AND TRY PLAYING THE GUITAR YOURSELF.
FOR YOUR REHAB, AND ALL.
...
QUIVER
NAH.
NOT LIKE I WAS EVER IN LOVE WITH GUITAR. NOT REALLY.
I JUST PLAYED CUZ I KNEW IT PISSED OFF MY DAD.
WHY DON'TCHA KEEP PISSING HIM OFF, THEN?
GYA HA!
TMP

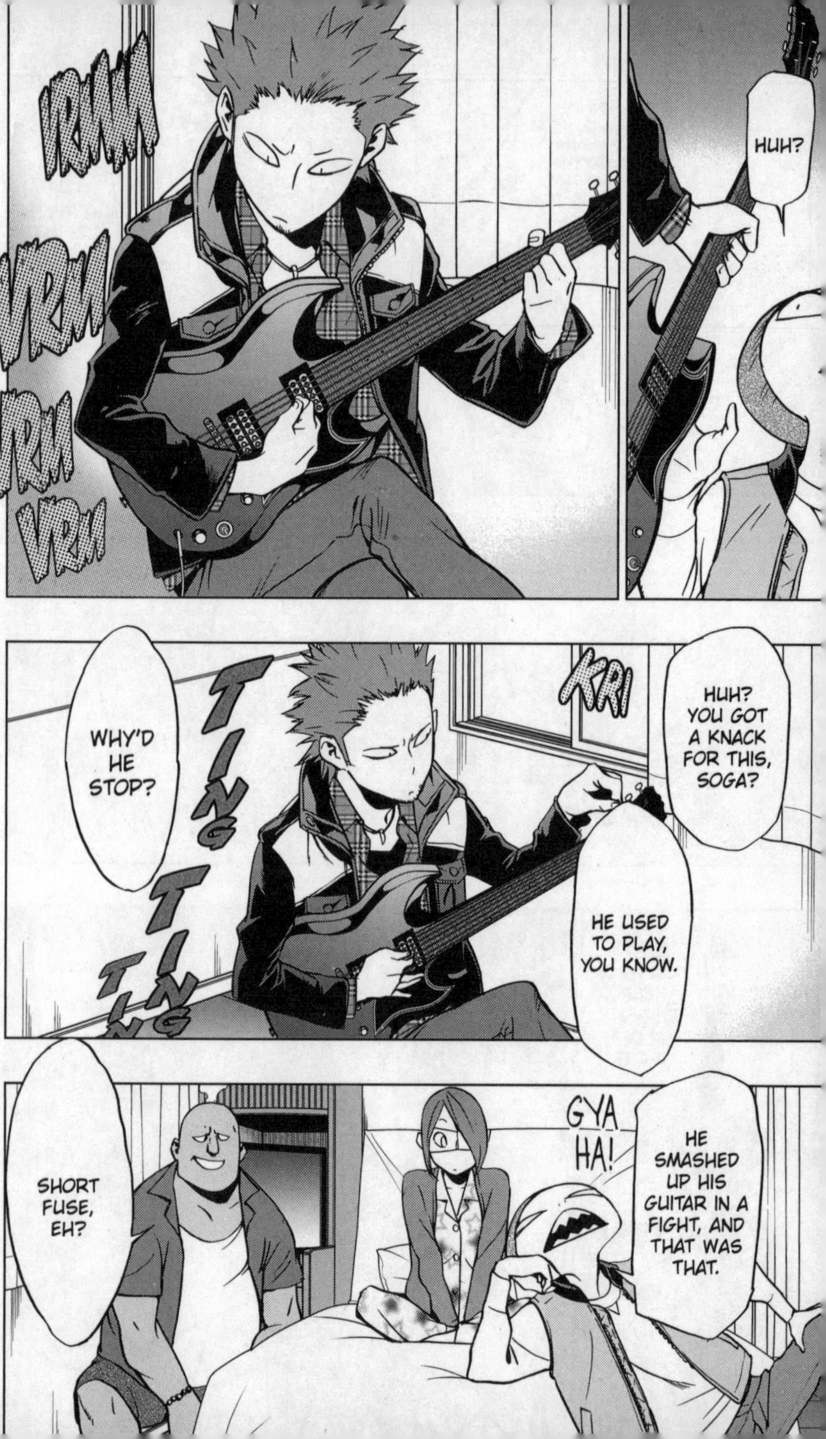
HUH?
VRMM
VRM
VRM
VRM
KRI
HUH? YOU GOT A KNACK FOR THIS, SOGA?
HE USED TO PLAY, YOU KNOW.
WHY'D HE STOP?
TING
TING
TING
HE SMASHED UP HIS GUITAR IN A FIGHT, AND THAT WAS THAT.
GYA HA!
SHORT FUSE, EH?

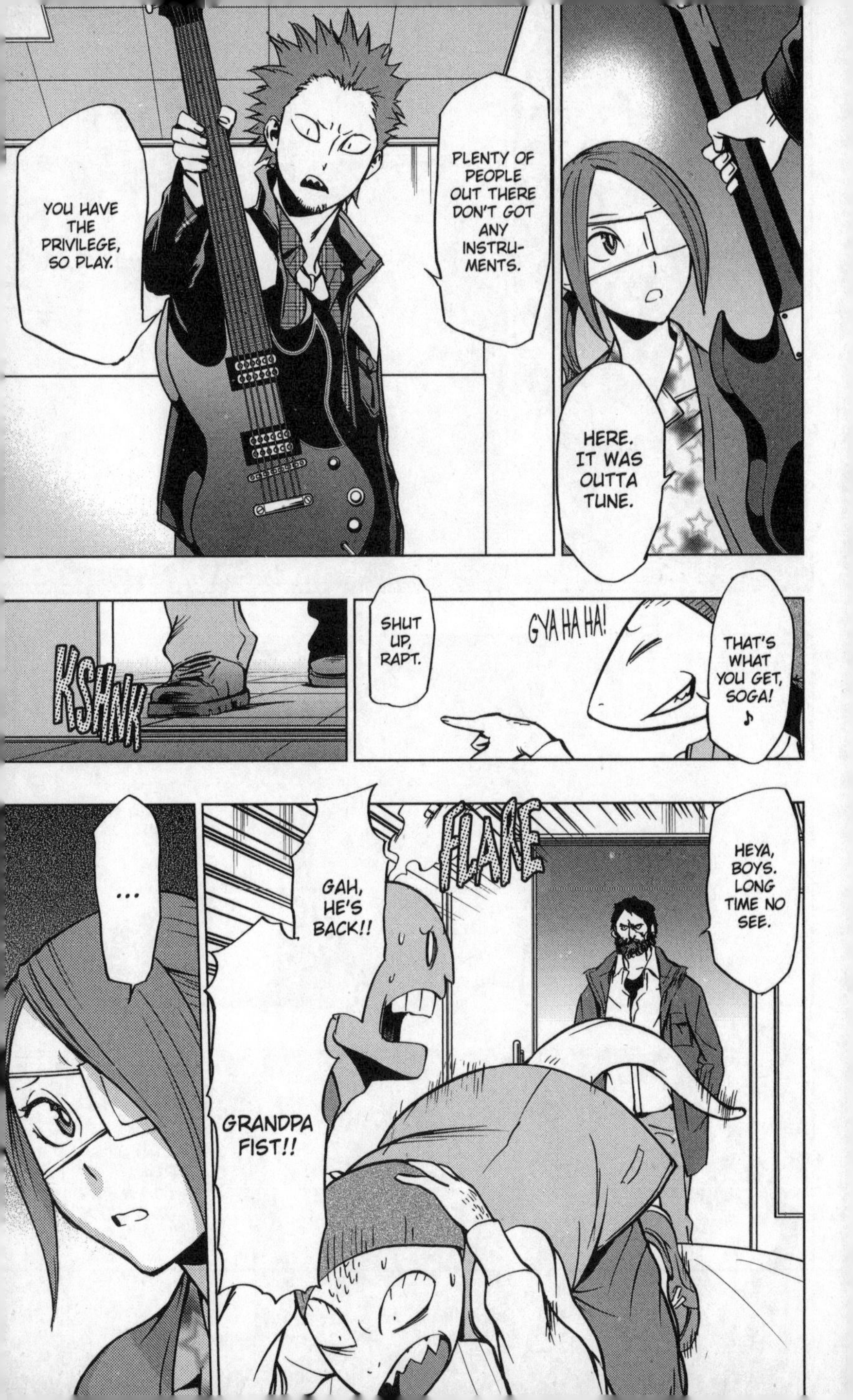
HERE. IT WAS OUTTA TUNE.
PLENTY OF PEOPLE OUT THERE DON'T GOT ANY INSTRU- MENTS.
YOU HAVE THE PRIVILEGE, SO PLAY.
THAT'S WHAT YOU GET, SOGA! ♪
GYA HA HA!
SHUT UP, RAPT.
KSHNK
HEYA, BOYS. LONG TIME NO SEE.
FLAKE
GAH, HE'S BACK!!
GRANDPA FIST!!
...

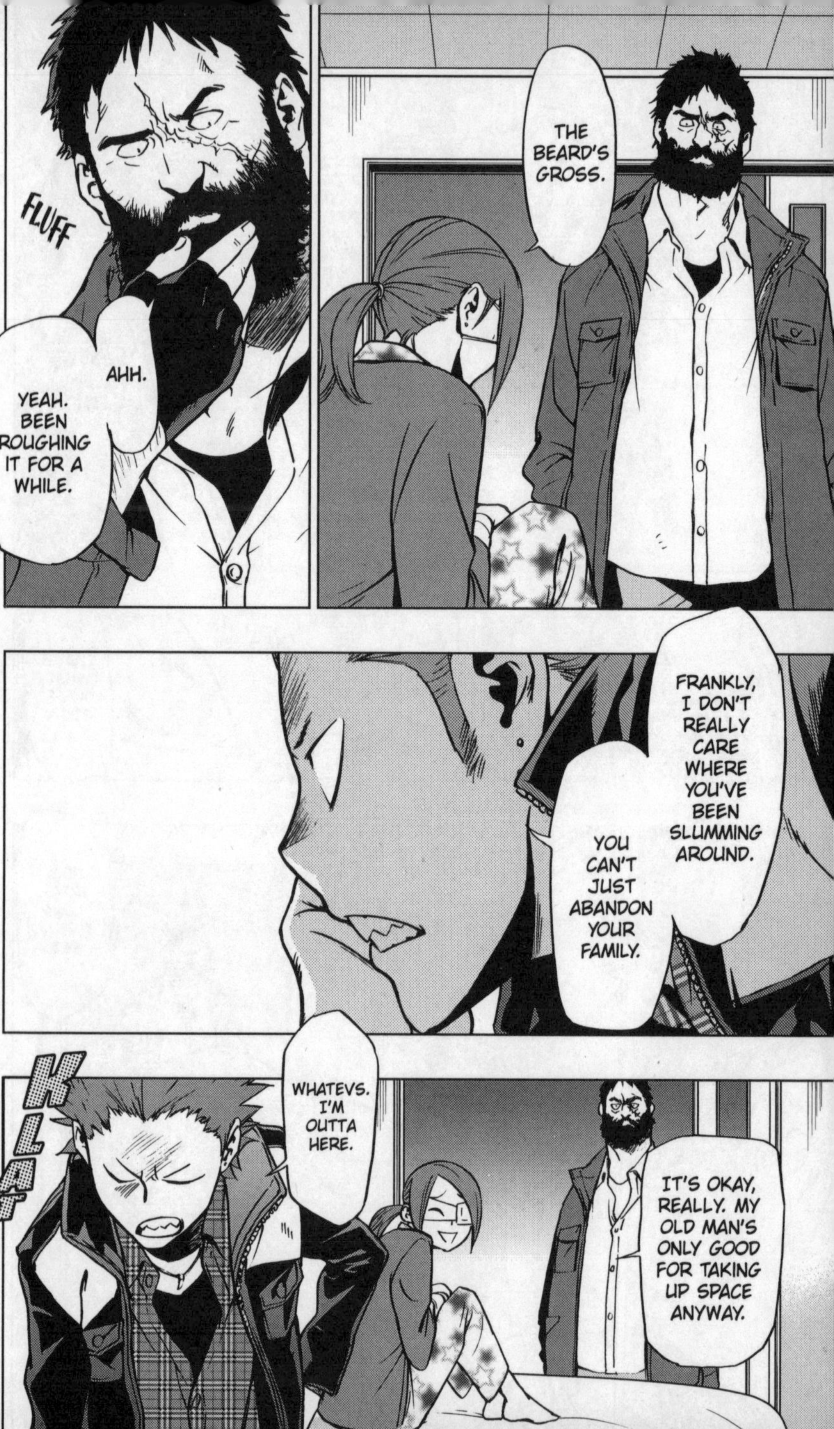
THE BEARD'S GROSS.
FLUFF
AHH.
YEAH. BEEN ROUGHING IT FOR A WHILE.
FRANKLY, I DON'T REALLY CARE WHERE YOU'VE BEEN SLUMMING AROUND.
YOU CAN'T JUST ABANDON YOUR FAMILY.
IT'S OKAY, REALLY. MY OLD MAN'S ONLY GOOD FOR TAKING UP SPACE ANYWAY.
WHATEVS. I'M OUTTA HERE.
KLAT

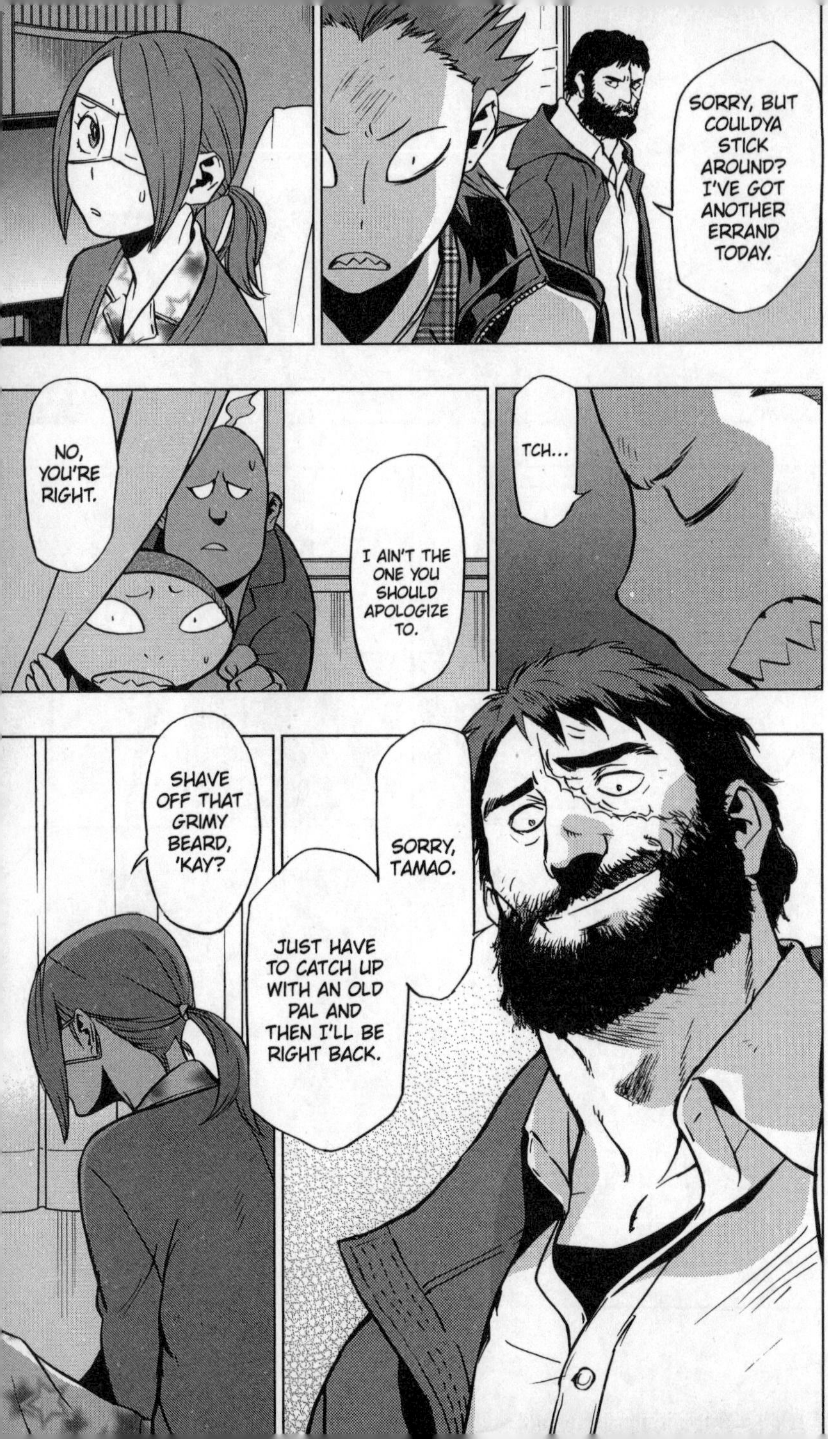
SORRY, BUT COULDYA STICK AROUND? I'VE GOT ANOTHER ERRAND TODAY.
TCH...
I AIN'T THE ONE YOU SHOULD APOLOGIZE TO.
NO, YOU'RE RIGHT.
SORRY, TAMAO.
JUST HAVE TO CATCH UP WITH AN OLD PAL AND THEN I'LL BE RIGHT BACK.
SHAVE OFF THAT GRIMY BEARD, 'KAY?

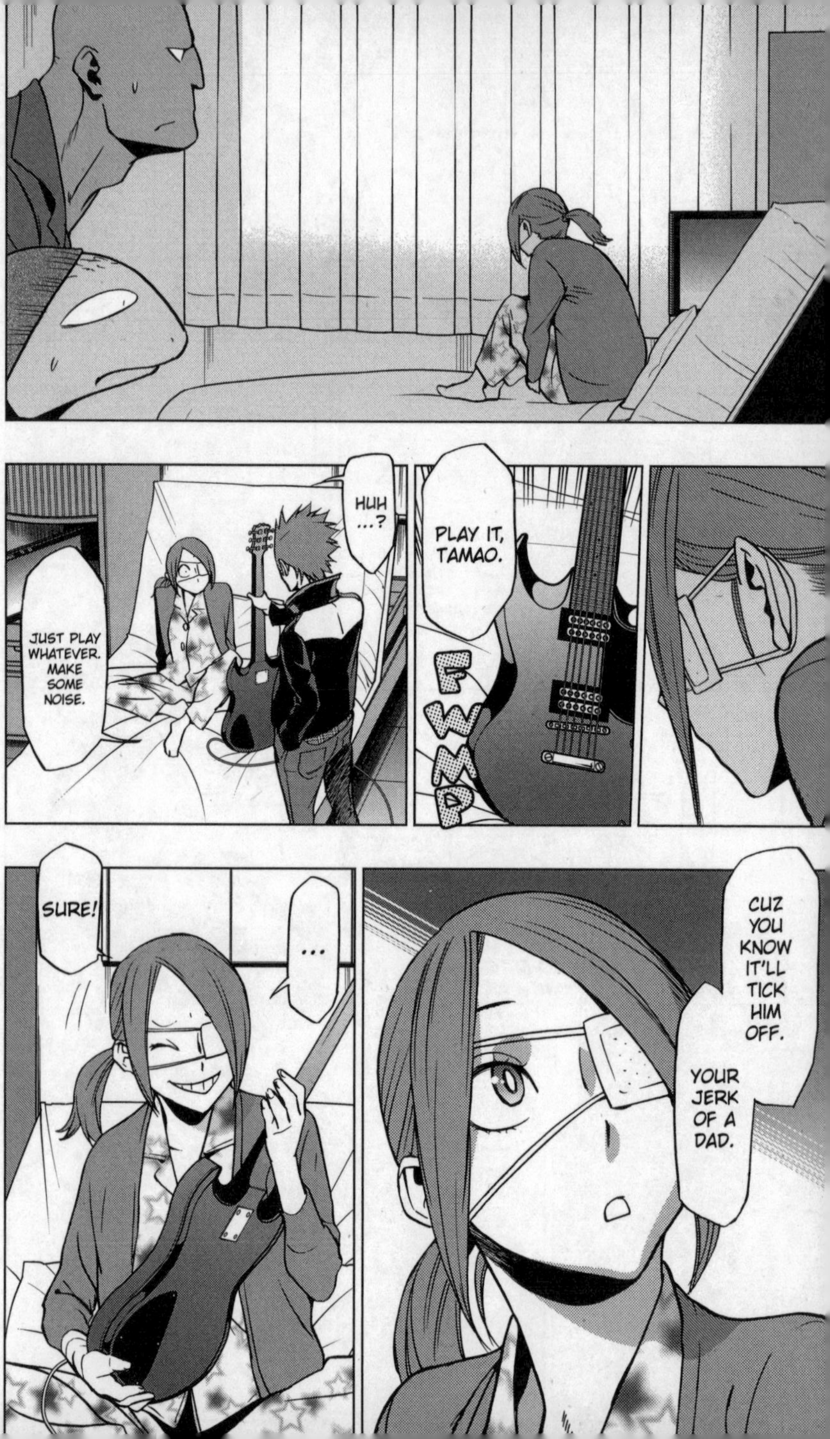
PLAY IT, TAMAO.
FWMP
HUH ...?
JUST PLAY WHATEVER. MAKE SOME NOISE.
CUZ YOU KNOW IT'LL TICK HIM OFF.
YOUR JERK OF A DAD.
...
SURE!

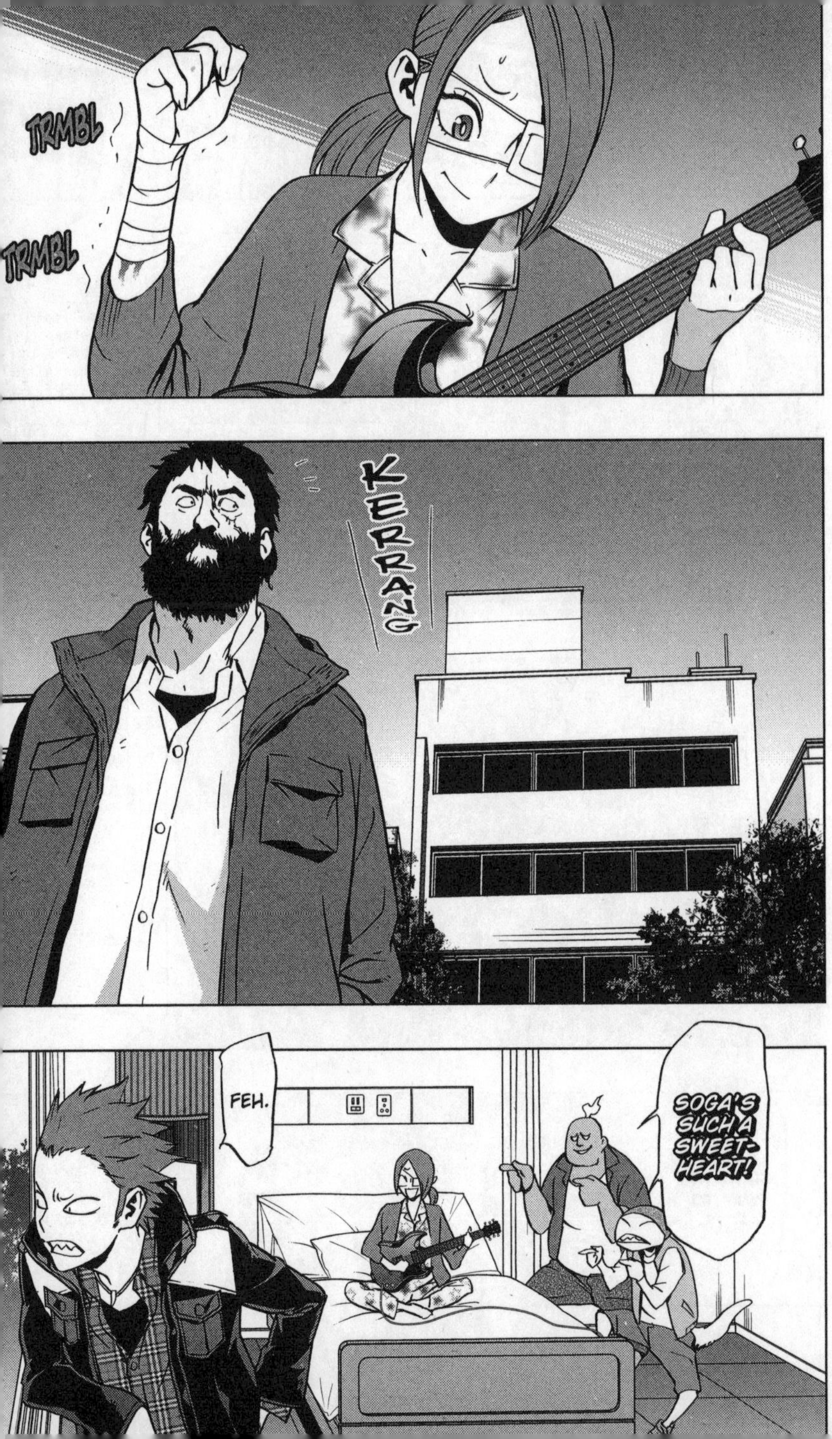
TRMBL
TRMBL
KERRANG
SOGA'S SUCH A SWEET-HEART!
FEH.

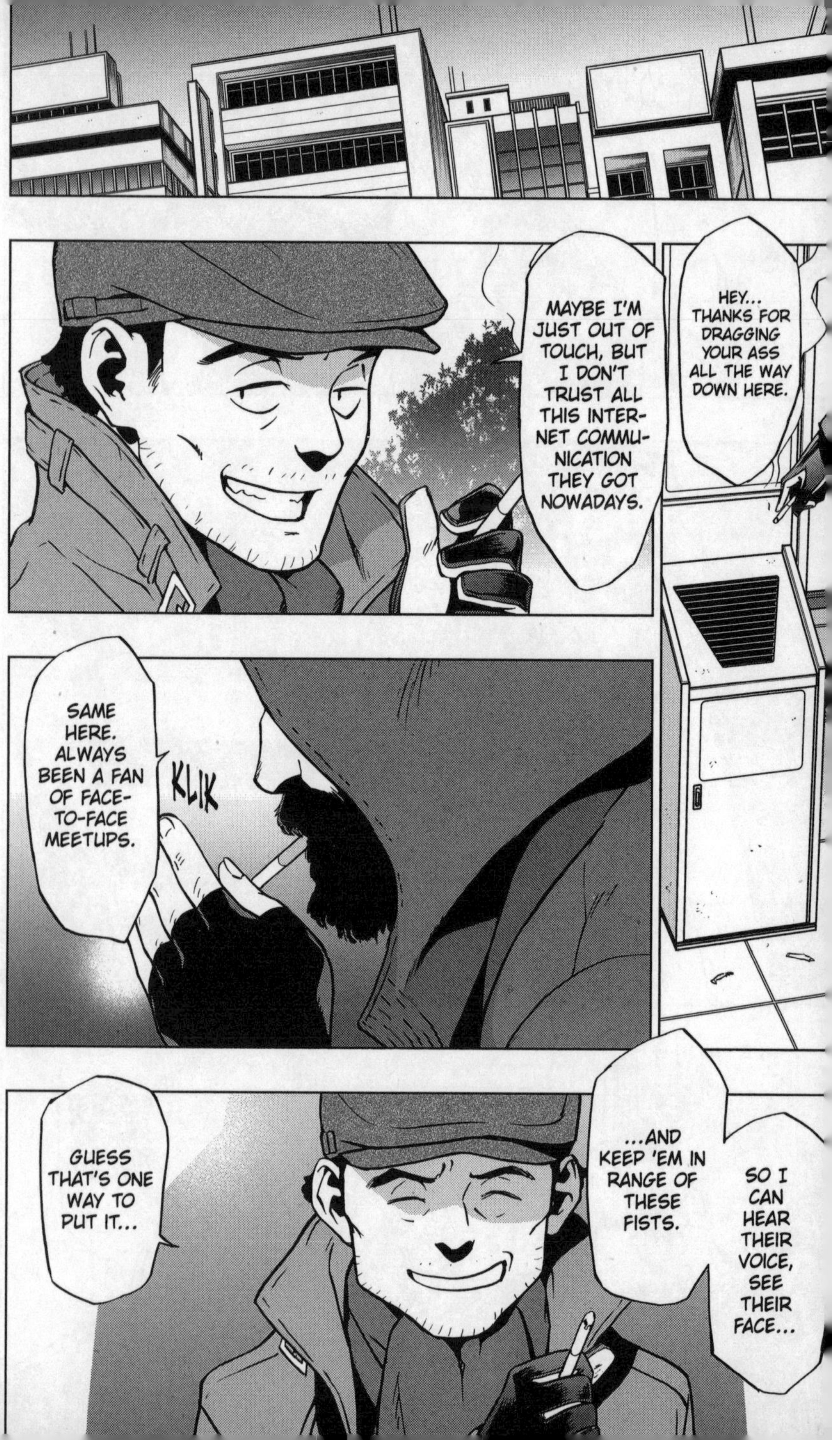
HEY... THANKS FOR DRAGGING YOUR ASS ALL THE WAY DOWN HERE.
MAYBE I'M JUST OUT OF TOUCH, BUT I DON'T TRUST ALL THIS INTER-NET COMMU-NICATION THEY GOT NOWADAYS.
SAME HERE. ALWAYS BEEN A FAN OF FACE-TO-FACE MEETUPS.
KLIK
SO I CAN HEAR THEIR VOICE, SEE THEIR FACE...
...AND KEEP 'EM IN RANGE OF THESE FISTS.
GUESS THAT'S ONE WAY TO PUT IT...

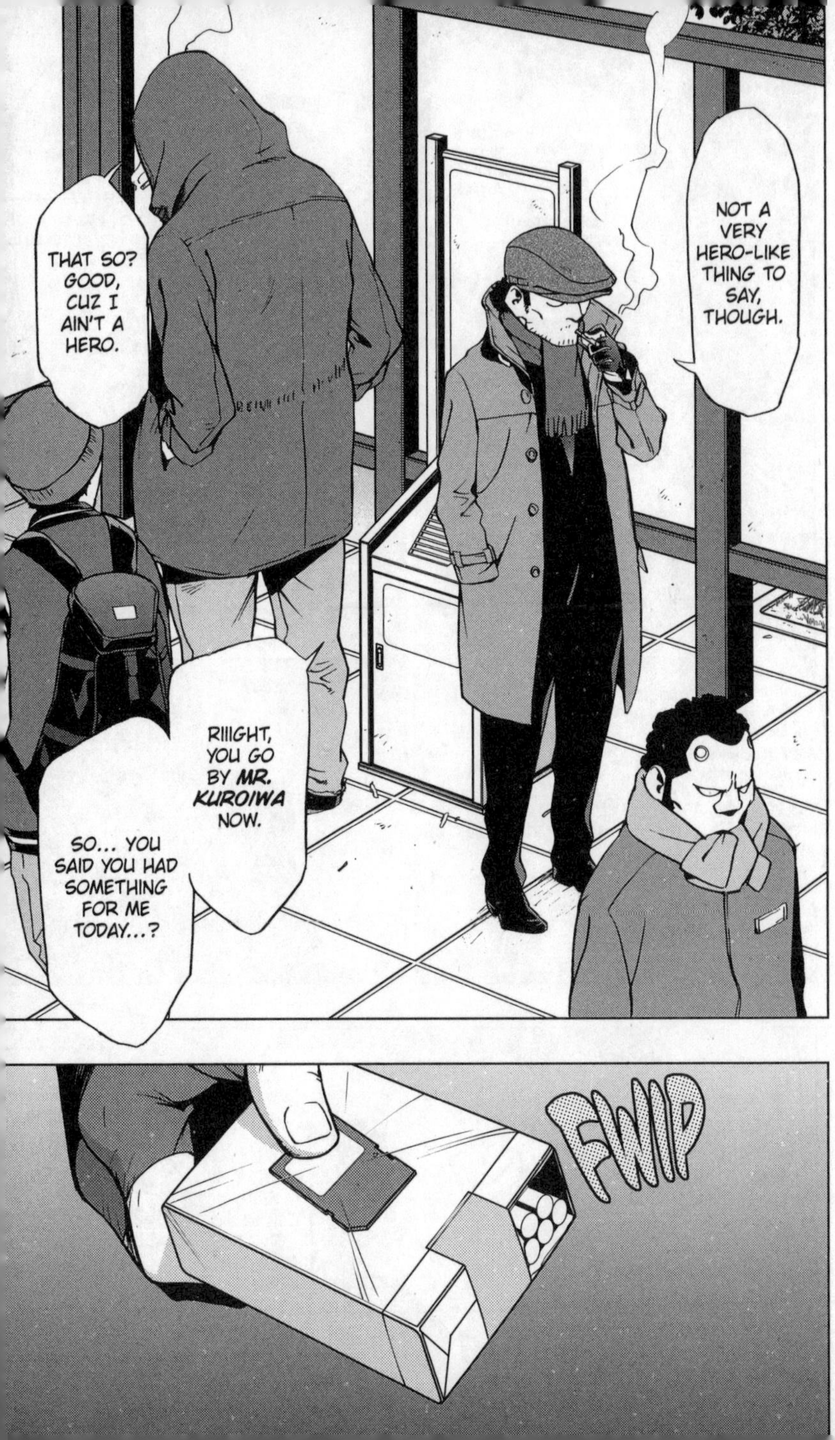
NOT A VERY HERO-LIKE THING TO SAY, THOUGH.
THAT SO? GOOD, CUZ I AIN'T A HERO.
RIIIGHT, YOU GO BY **MR. KUROIWA** NOW.
SO... YOU SAID YOU HAD SOMETHING FOR ME TODAY...?
FWIP

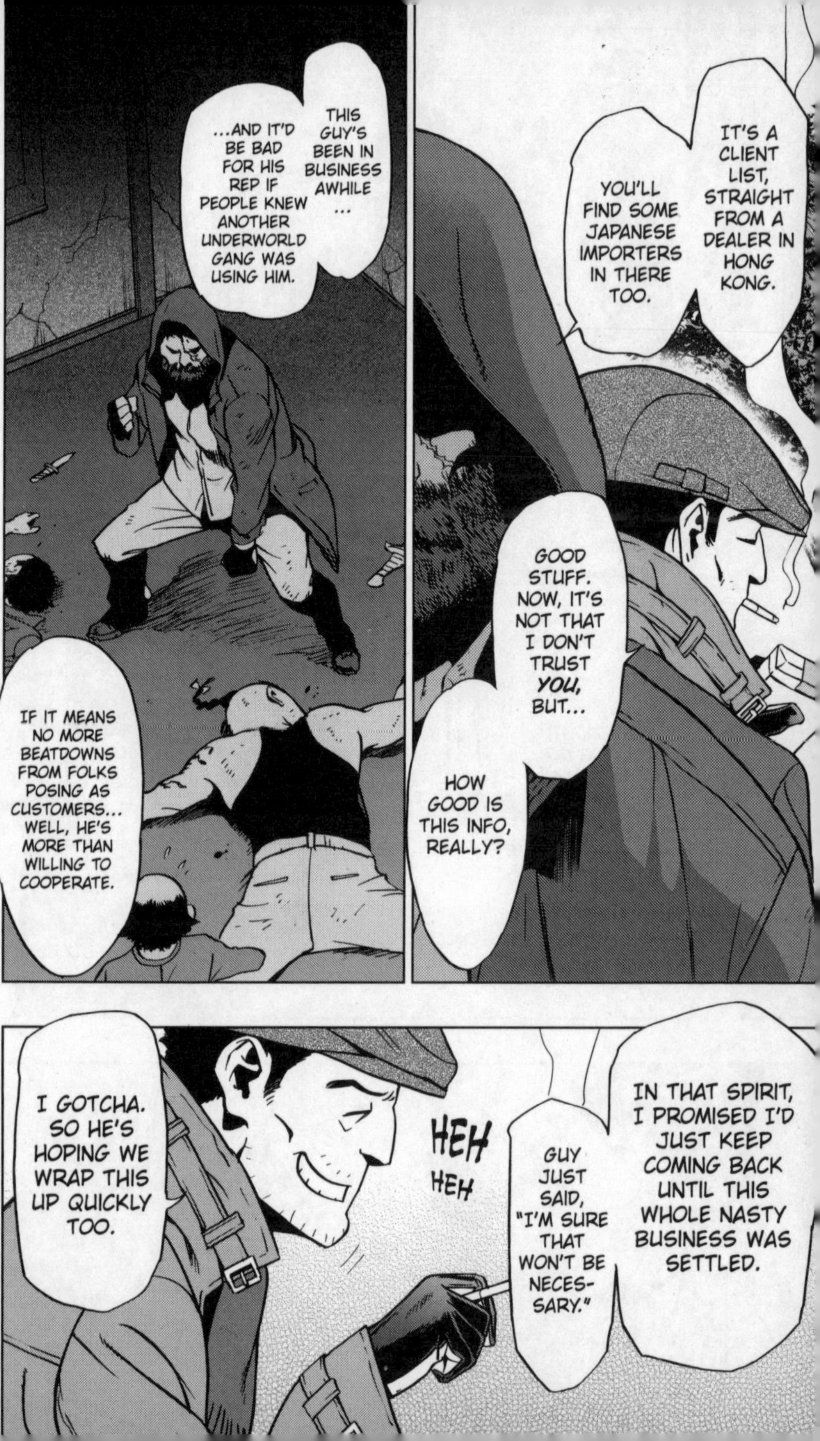

IT'S A CLIENT LIST, STRAIGHT FROM A DEALER IN HONG KONG.
YOU'LL FIND SOME JAPANESE IMPORTERS IN THERE TOO.
GOOD STUFF. NOW, IT'S NOT THAT I DON'T TRUST *YOU,* BUT...
HOW GOOD IS THIS INFO, REALLY?
THIS GUY'S BEEN IN BUSINESS AWHILE...
...AND IT'D BE BAD FOR HIS REP IF PEOPLE KNEW ANOTHER UNDERWORLD GANG WAS USING HIM.
IF IT MEANS NO MORE BEATDOWNS FROM FOLKS POSING AS CUSTOMERS... WELL, HE'S MORE THAN WILLING TO COOPERATE.
IN THAT SPIRIT, I PROMISED I'D JUST KEEP COMING BACK UNTIL THIS WHOLE NASTY BUSINESS WAS SETTLED.
GUY JUST SAID, "I'M SURE THAT WON'T BE NECES-SARY."
HEH HEH
I GOTCHA. SO HE'S HOPING WE WRAP THIS UP QUICKLY TOO.

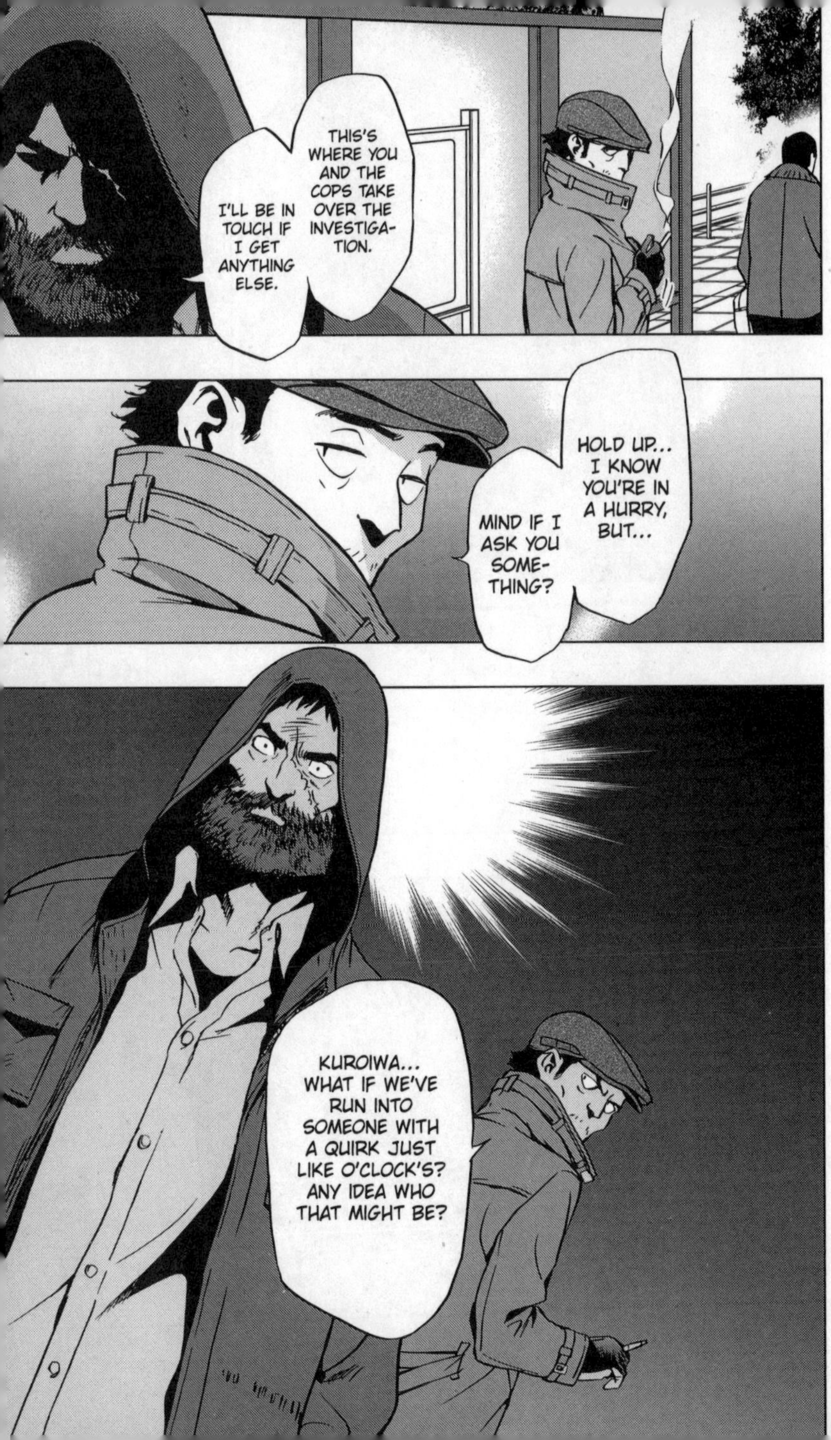
THIS'S WHERE YOU AND THE COPS TAKE OVER THE INVESTIGA-TION.
I'LL BE IN TOUCH IF I GET ANYTHING ELSE.
HOLD UP... I KNOW YOU'RE IN A HURRY, BUT...
MIND IF I ASK YOU SOME-THING?
KUROIWA... WHAT IF WE'VE RUN INTO SOMEONE WITH A QUIRK JUST LIKE O'CLOCK'S? ANY IDEA WHO THAT MIGHT BE?

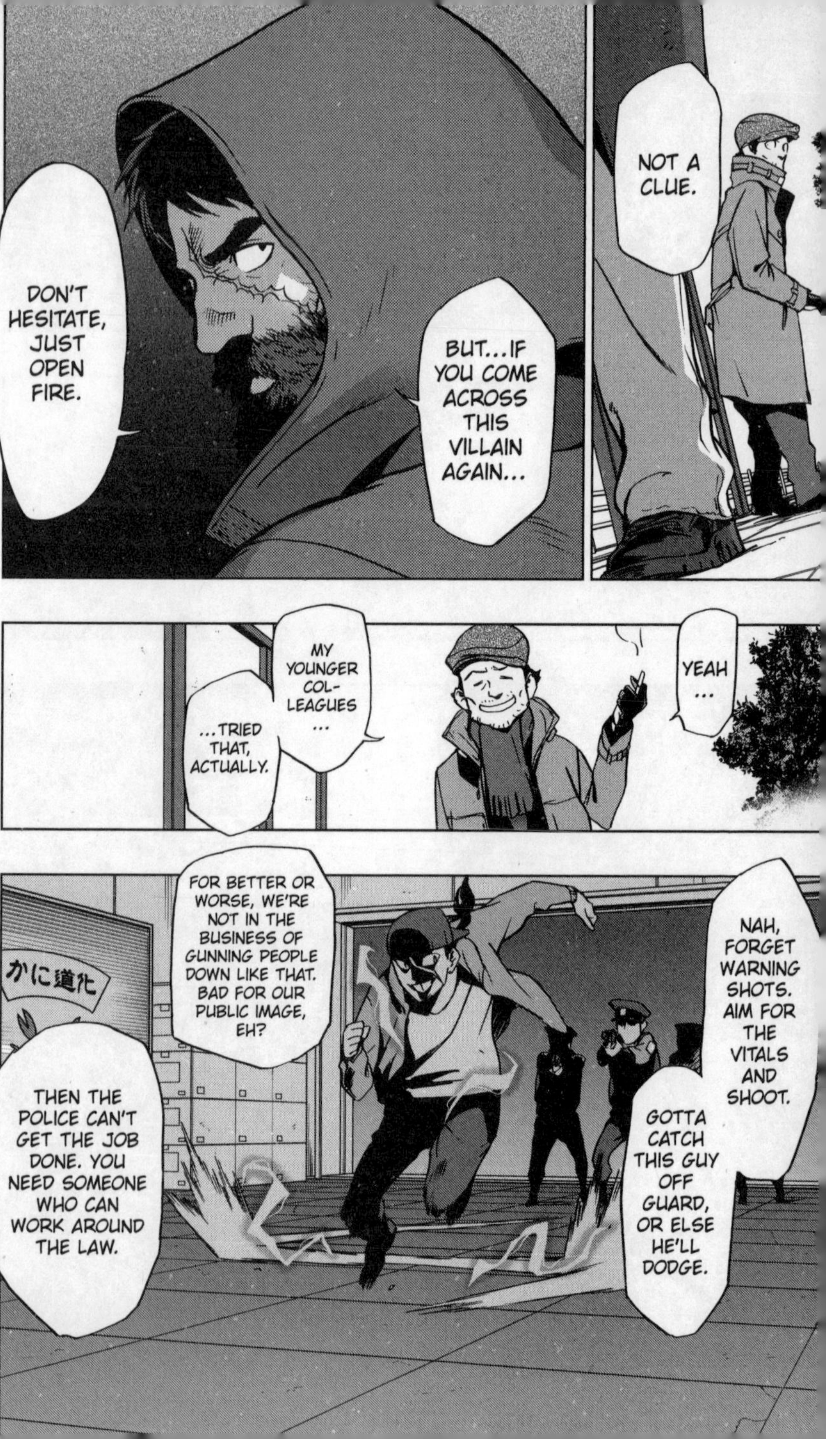
NOT A CLUE.
BUT...IF YOU COME ACROSS THIS VILLAIN AGAIN...
DON'T HESITATE, JUST OPEN FIRE.
YEAH...
MY YOUNGER COL-LEAGUES...
...TRIED THAT, ACTUALLY.
NAH, FORGET WARNING SHOTS. AIM FOR THE VITALS AND SHOOT.
GOTTA CATCH THIS GUY OFF GUARD, OR ELSE HE'LL DODGE.
FOR BETTER OR WORSE, WE'RE NOT IN THE BUSINESS OF GUNNING PEOPLE DOWN LIKE THAT. BAD FOR OUR PUBLIC IMAGE, EH?
かに道化
THEN THE POLICE CAN'T GET THE JOB DONE. YOU NEED SOMEONE WHO CAN WORK AROUND THE LAW.

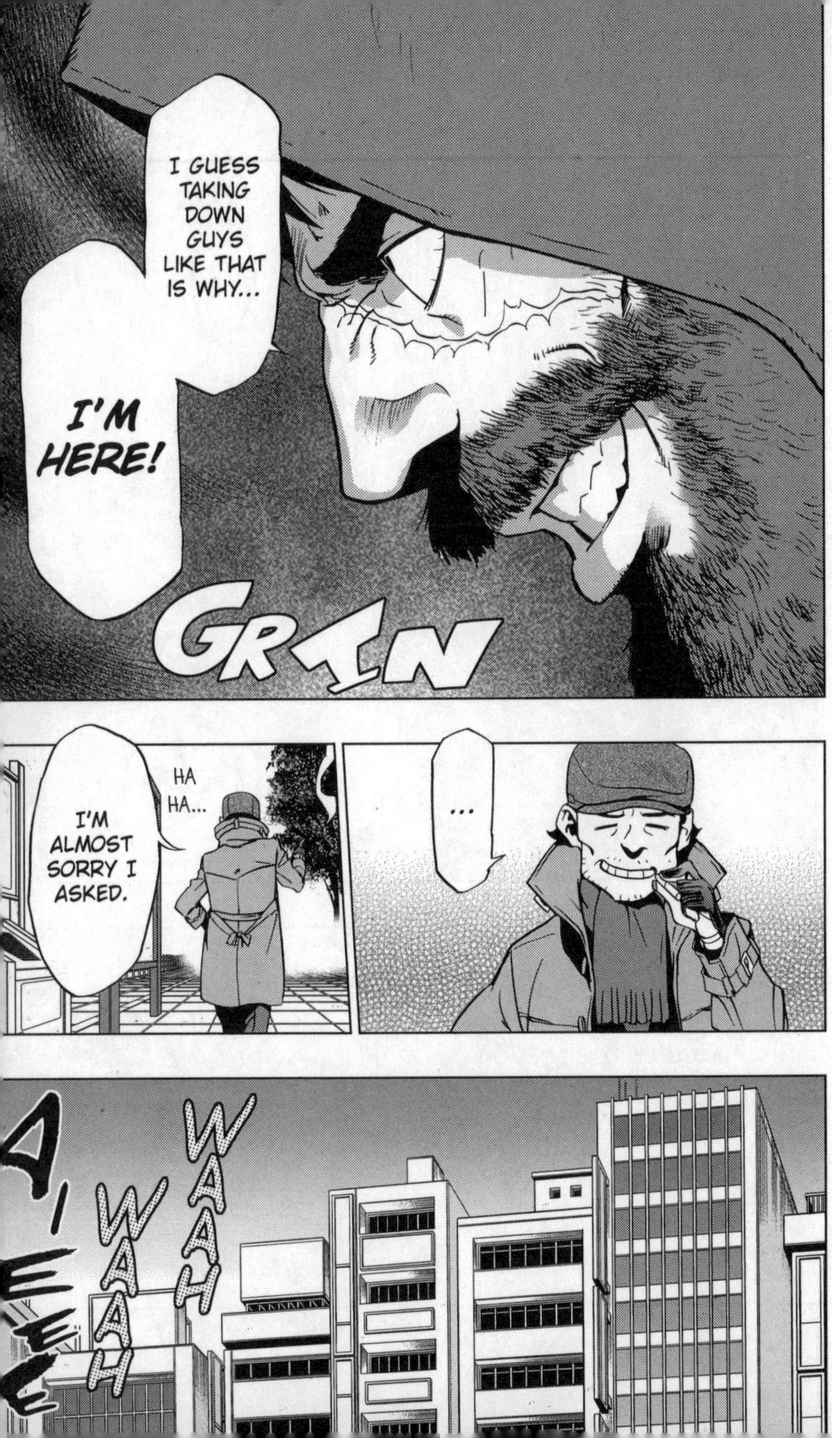
I GUESS TAKING DOWN GUYS LIKE THAT IS WHY...
I'M HERE!
GRIN
...
HA HA...
I'M ALMOST SORRY I ASKED.
WAAAH
WAAAH
AIEEEE

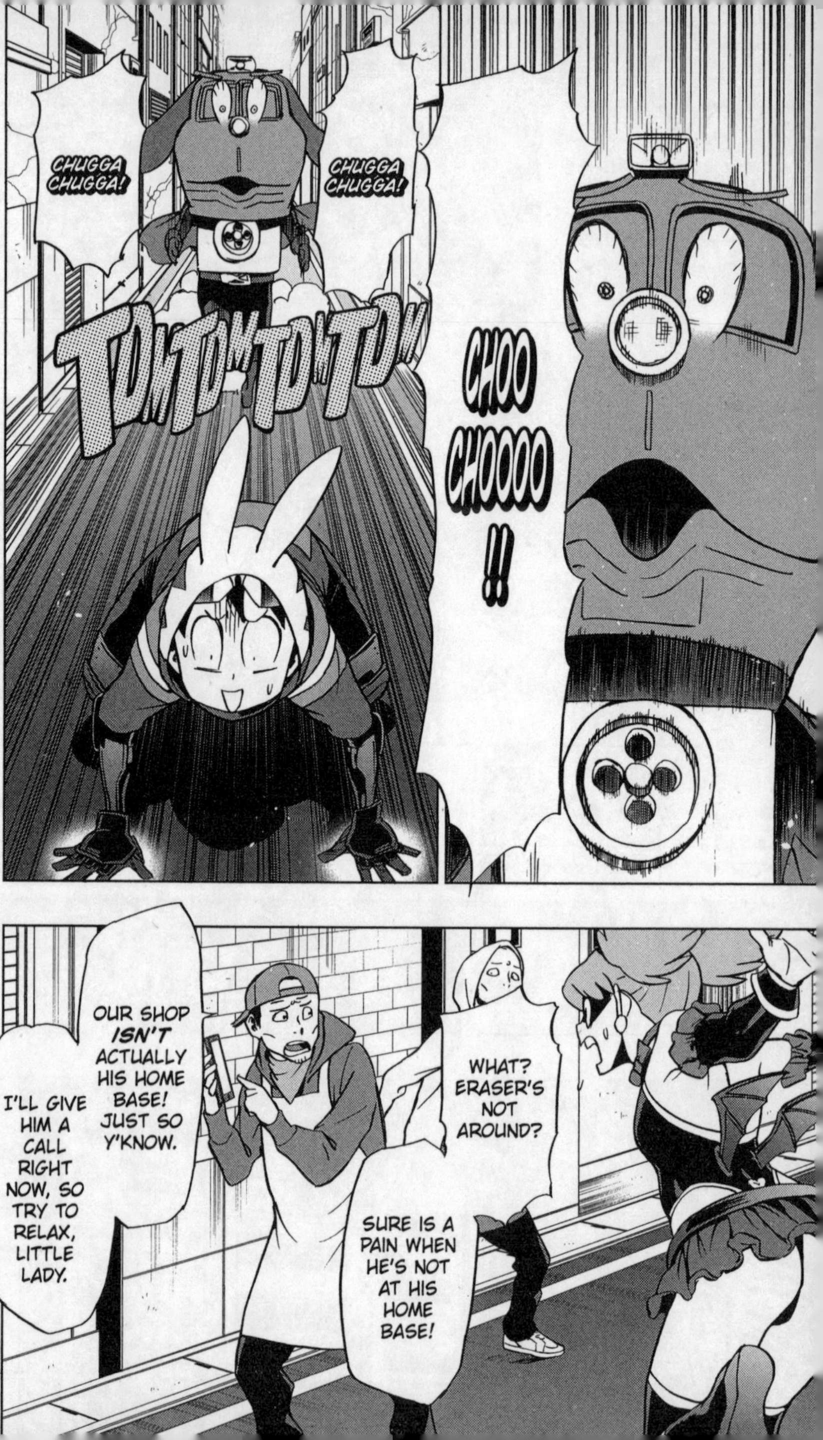
CHOO CHOOOO!!
CHUGGA CHUGGA!
CHUGGA CHUGGA!
TOMTOMTOMTOM
WHAT? ERASER'S NOT AROUND?
SURE IS A PAIN WHEN HE'S NOT AT HIS HOME BASE!
OUR SHOP *ISN'T* ACTUALLY HIS HOME BASE! JUST SO Y'KNOW.
I'LL GIVE HIM A CALL RIGHT NOW, SO TRY TO RELAX, LITTLE LADY.

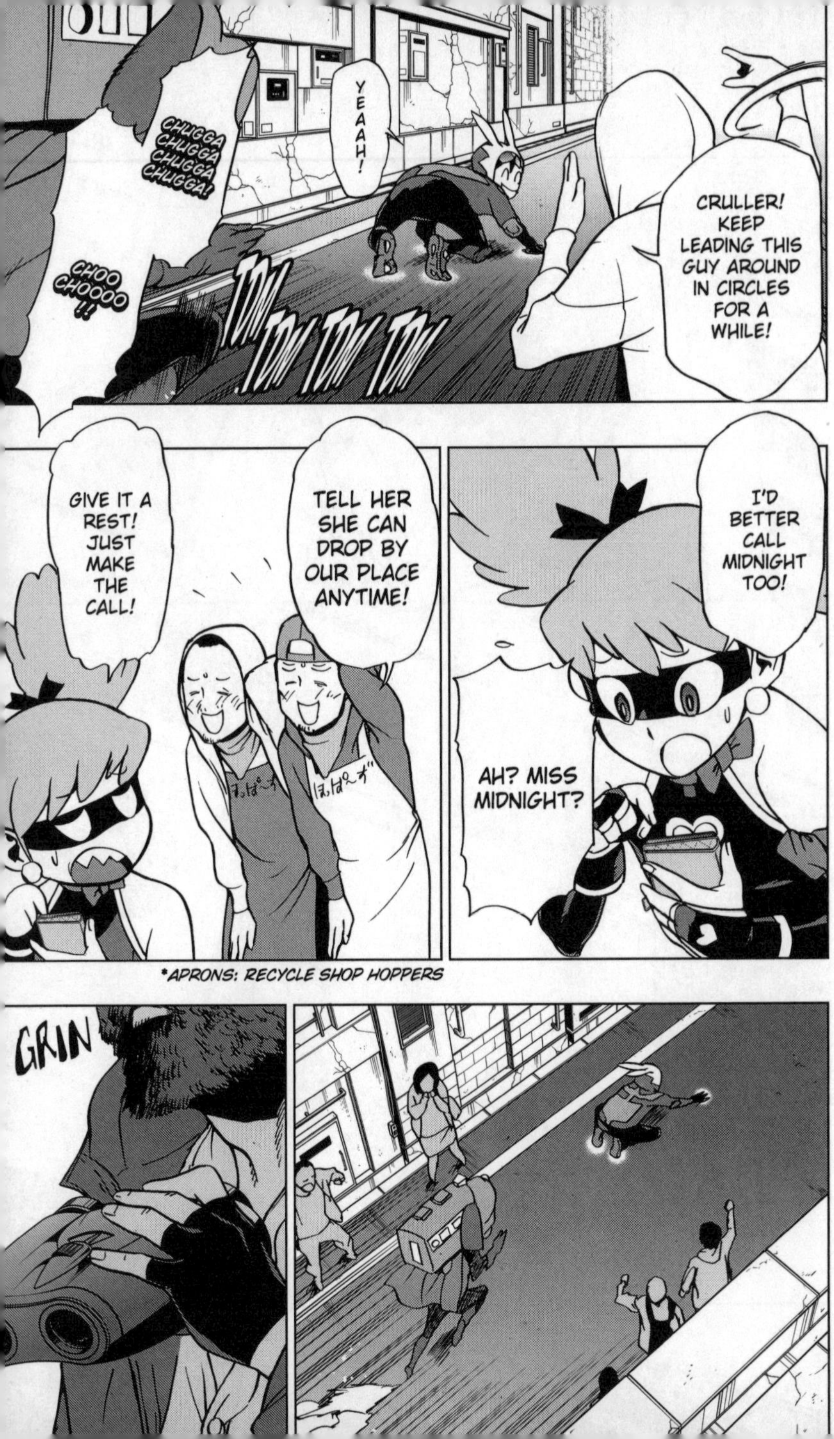
CRULLER! KEEP LEADING THIS GUY AROUND IN CIRCLES FOR A WHILE!
YEAAAH!
CHUGGA CHUGGA CHUGGA CHUGGA!
CHOO CHOOOO!!
TON TON TON TON
I'D BETTER CALL MIDNIGHT TOO!
AH? MISS MIDNIGHT?
TELL HER SHE CAN DROP BY OUR PLACE ANYTIME!
GIVE IT A REST! JUST MAKE THE CALL!
*APRONS: RECYCLE SHOP HOPPERS
GRIN

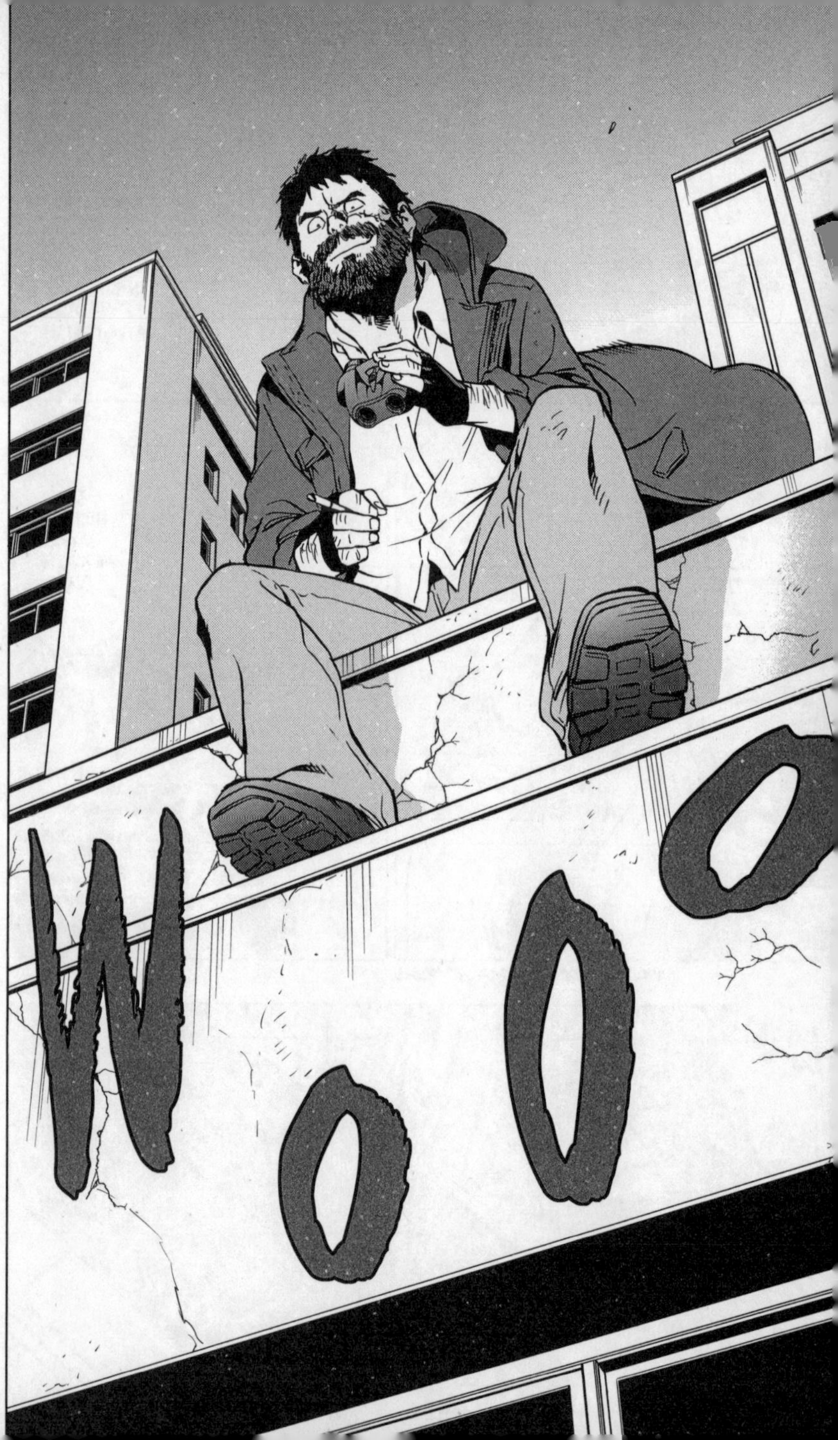
WoOO

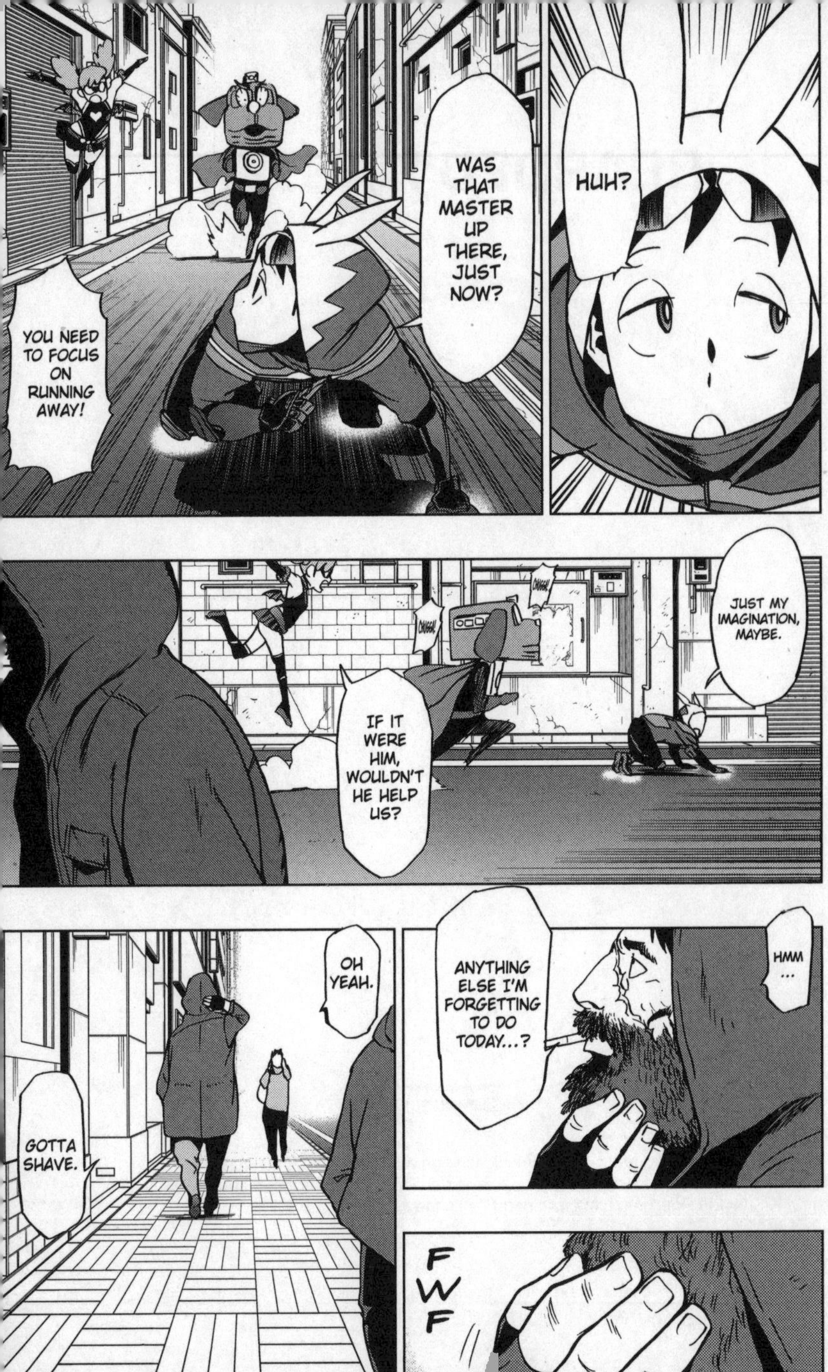
HUH?
WAS THAT MASTER UP THERE, JUST NOW?
YOU NEED TO FOCUS ON RUNNING AWAY!
JUST MY IMAGINATION, MAYBE.
IF IT WERE HIM, WOULDN'T HE HELP US?
HMM...
ANYTHING ELSE I'M FORGETTING TO DO TODAY...?
FWF
OH YEAH.
GOTTA SHAVE.

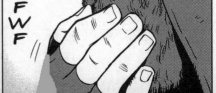

THE COLUMN

BEARDED MASTER

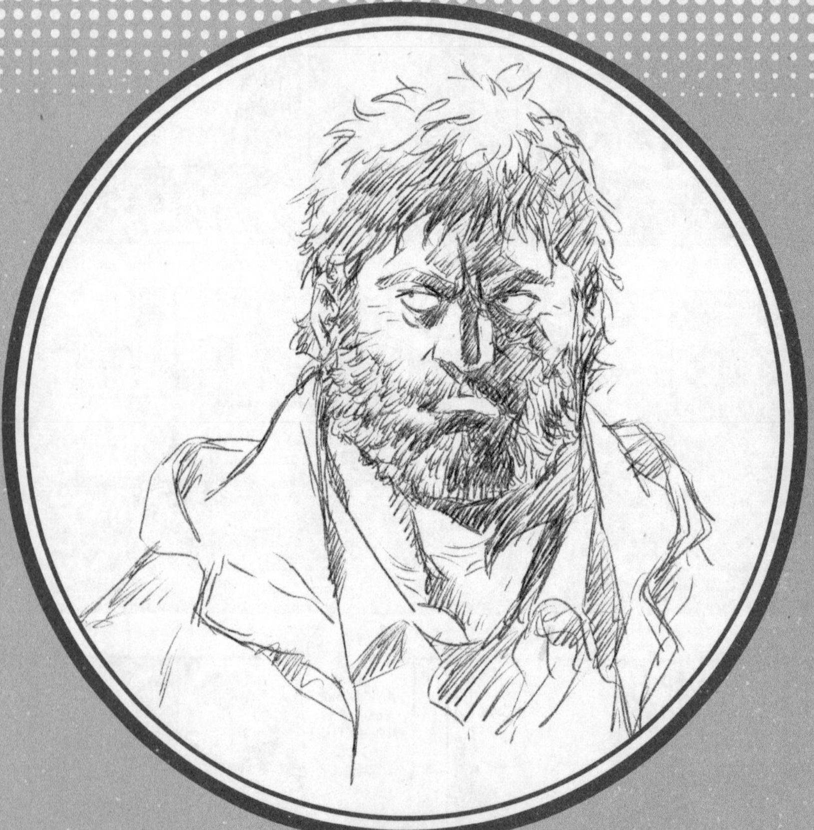

Beards are cool. They're great for communicating an apathetic, devil-may-care attitude.
Master is a character who easily could've headed down a bloodthirsty path, but the presence of his family, Koichi and Pop keep him grounded. That's the idea here.

—Furuhashi

Bearded Master is all well and good when I'm drawing rough sketches, but when it comes down to inking everything in? He becomes a real pain in the butt. (LOL)

—Betten

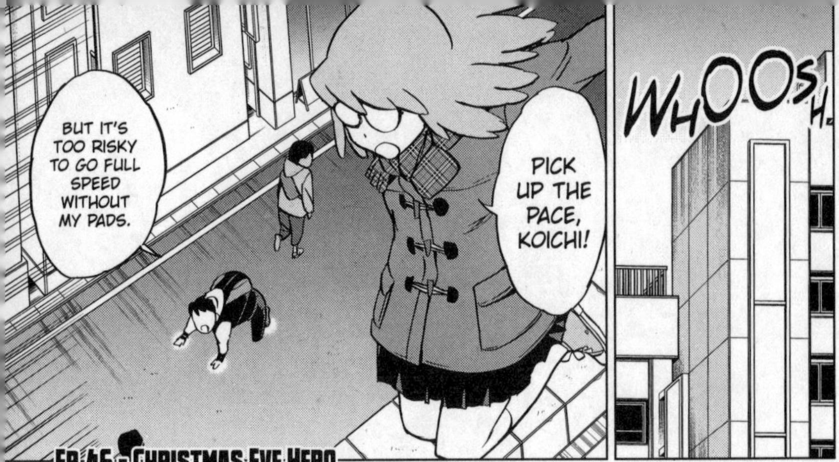
WHOOSH
PICK UP THE PACE, KOICHI!
BUT IT'S TOO RISKY TO GO FULL SPEED WITHOUT MY PADS.

EP. 46 – CHRISTMAS EVE HERO

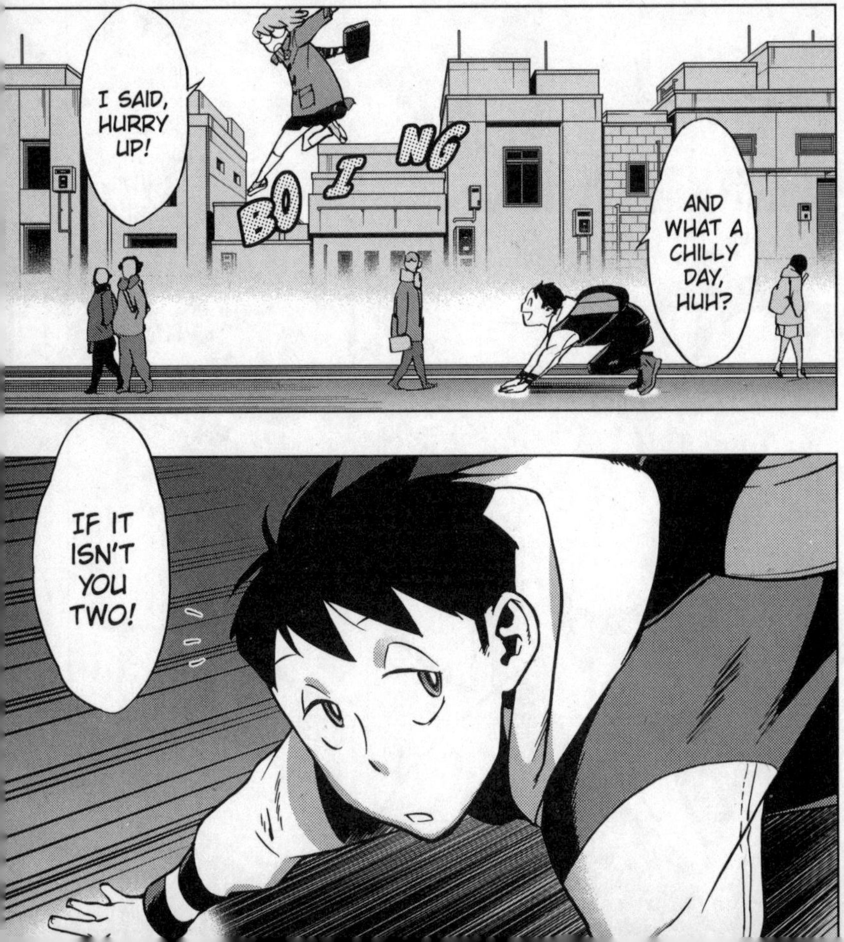
I SAID, HURRY UP!
BOING
AND WHAT A CHILLY DAY, HUH?
IF IT ISN'T YOU TWO!

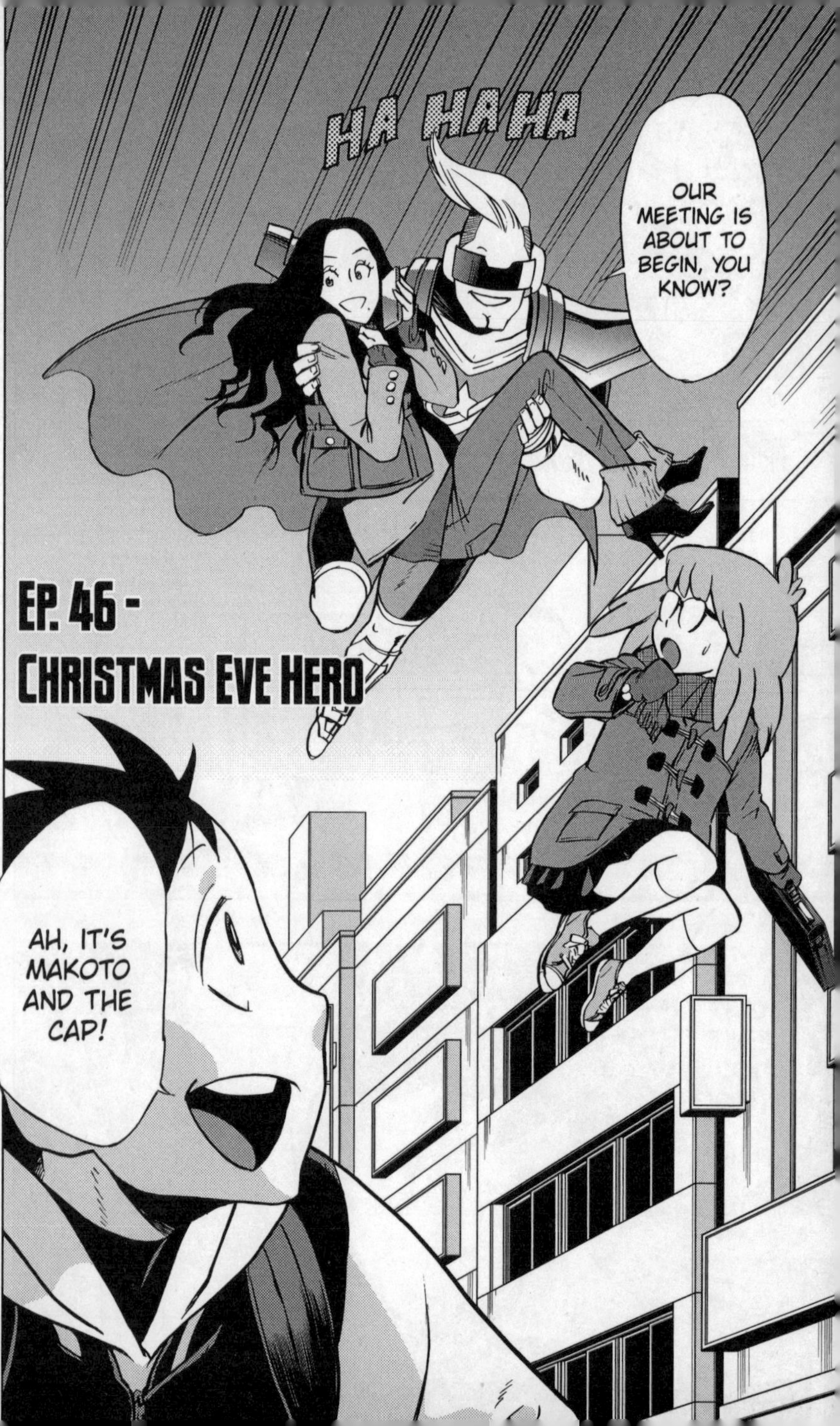
OUR MEETING IS ABOUT TO BEGIN, YOU KNOW?
HA HAHA
EP. 46 - CHRISTMAS EVE HERO
AH, IT'S MAKOTO AND THE CAP!

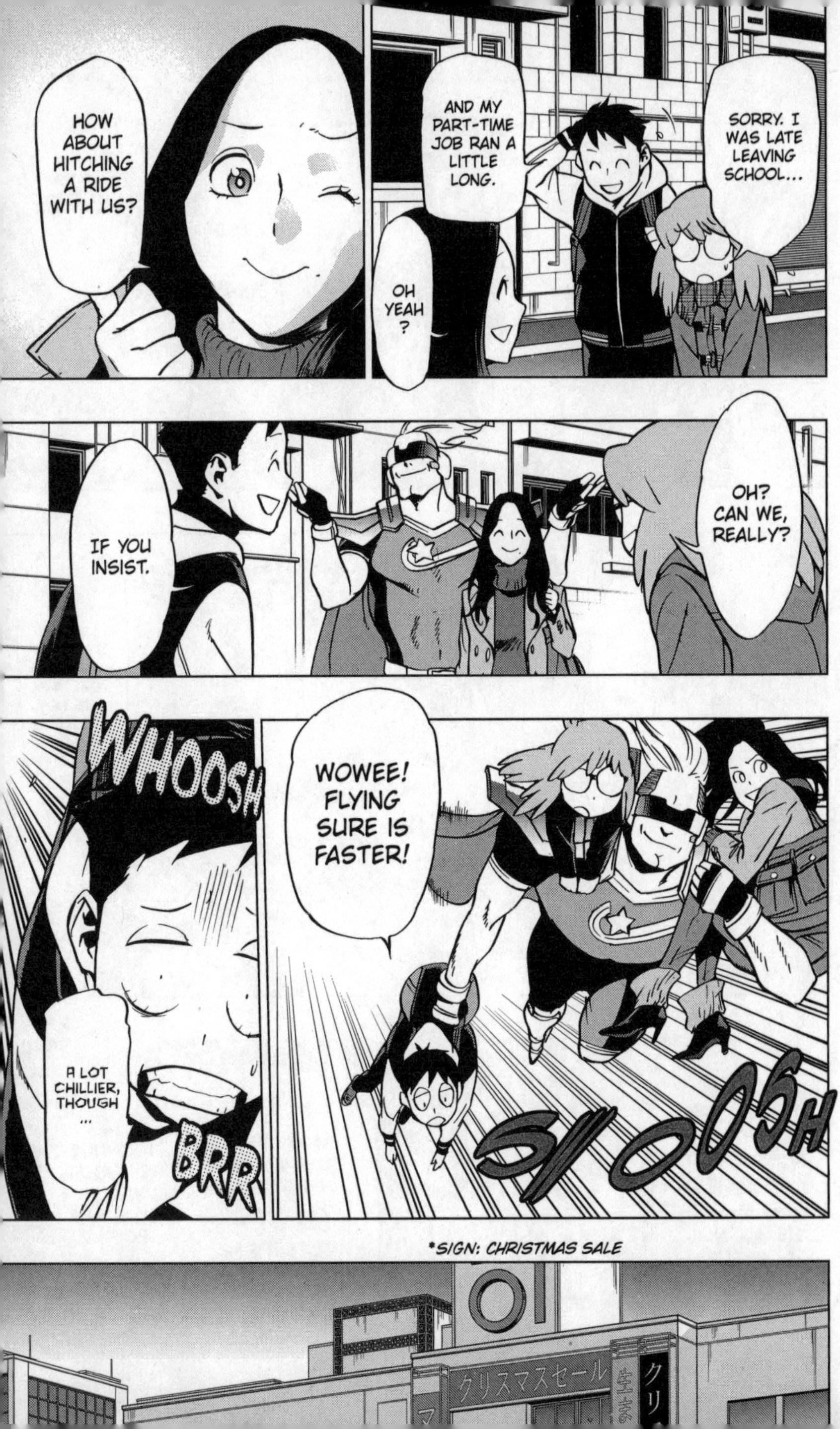
SORRY. I WAS LATE LEAVING SCHOOL...
AND MY PART-TIME JOB RAN A LITTLE LONG.
OH YEAH?
HOW ABOUT HITCHING A RIDE WITH US?
OH? CAN WE, REALLY?
IF YOU INSIST.
WOWEE! FLYING SURE IS FASTER!
SWOOSH
WHOOSH
A LOT CHILLIER, THOUGH...
BRR
*SIGN: CHRISTMAS SALE
クリスマスセール

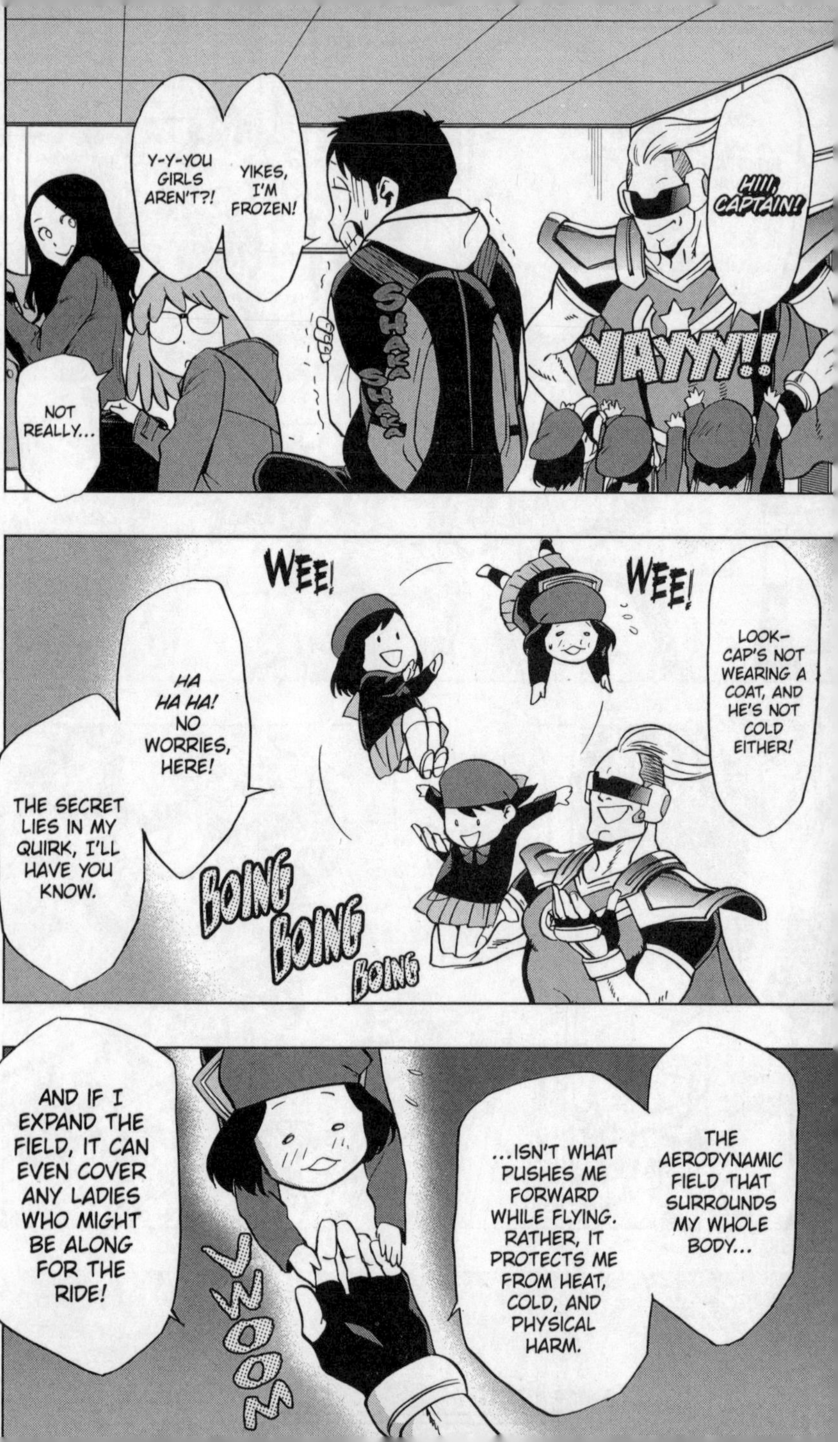
HIII, CAPTAIN!
YAYYY!!
YIKES, I'M FROZEN!
Y-Y-YOU GIRLS AREN'T?!
NOT REALLY...
LOOK—CAP'S NOT WEARING A COAT, AND HE'S NOT COLD EITHER!
WEE!
WEE!
HA HA HA! NO WORRIES, HERE!
THE SECRET LIES IN MY QUIRK, I'LL HAVE YOU KNOW.
BOING BOING BOING
THE AERODYNAMIC FIELD THAT SURROUNDS MY WHOLE BODY...
...ISN'T WHAT PUSHES ME FORWARD WHILE FLYING. RATHER, IT PROTECTS ME FROM HEAT, COLD, AND PHYSICAL HARM.
AND IF I EXPAND THE FIELD, IT CAN EVEN COVER ANY LADIES WHO MIGHT BE ALONG FOR THE RIDE!

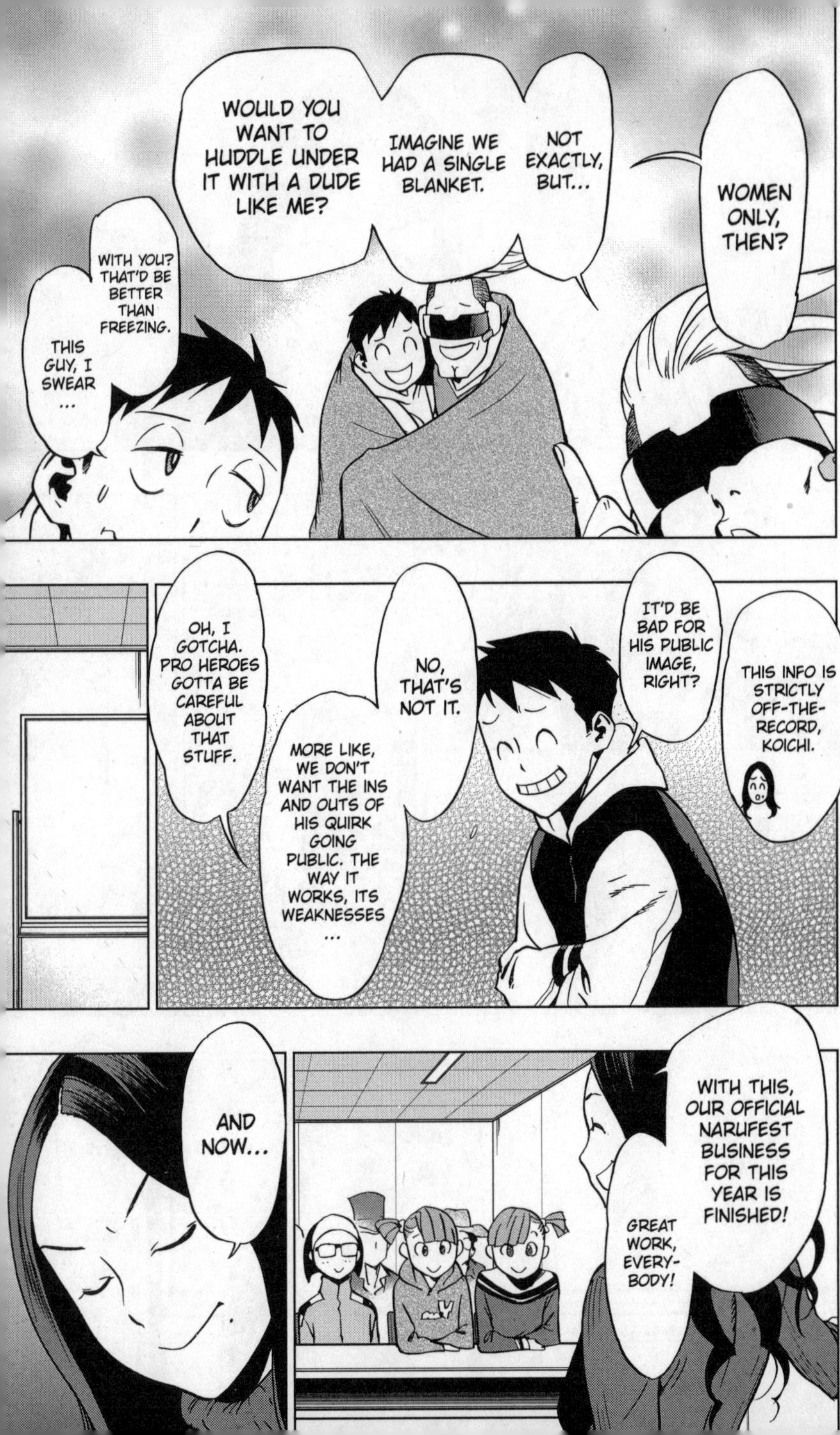
WOMEN ONLY, THEN?
NOT EXACTLY, BUT...
IMAGINE WE HAD A SINGLE BLANKET.
WOULD YOU WANT TO HUDDLE UNDER IT WITH A DUDE LIKE ME?
WITH YOU? THAT'D BE BETTER THAN FREEZING.
THIS GUY, I SWEAR ...
THIS INFO IS STRICTLY OFF-THE-RECORD, KOICHI.
IT'D BE BAD FOR HIS PUBLIC IMAGE, RIGHT?
NO, THAT'S NOT IT.
MORE LIKE, WE DON'T WANT THE INS AND OUTS OF HIS QUIRK GOING PUBLIC. THE WAY IT WORKS, ITS WEAKNESSES ...
OH, I GOTCHA. PRO HEROES GOTTA BE CAREFUL ABOUT THAT STUFF.
WITH THIS, OUR OFFICIAL NARUFEST BUSINESS FOR THIS YEAR IS FINISHED!
GREAT WORK, EVERY-BODY!
AND NOW...

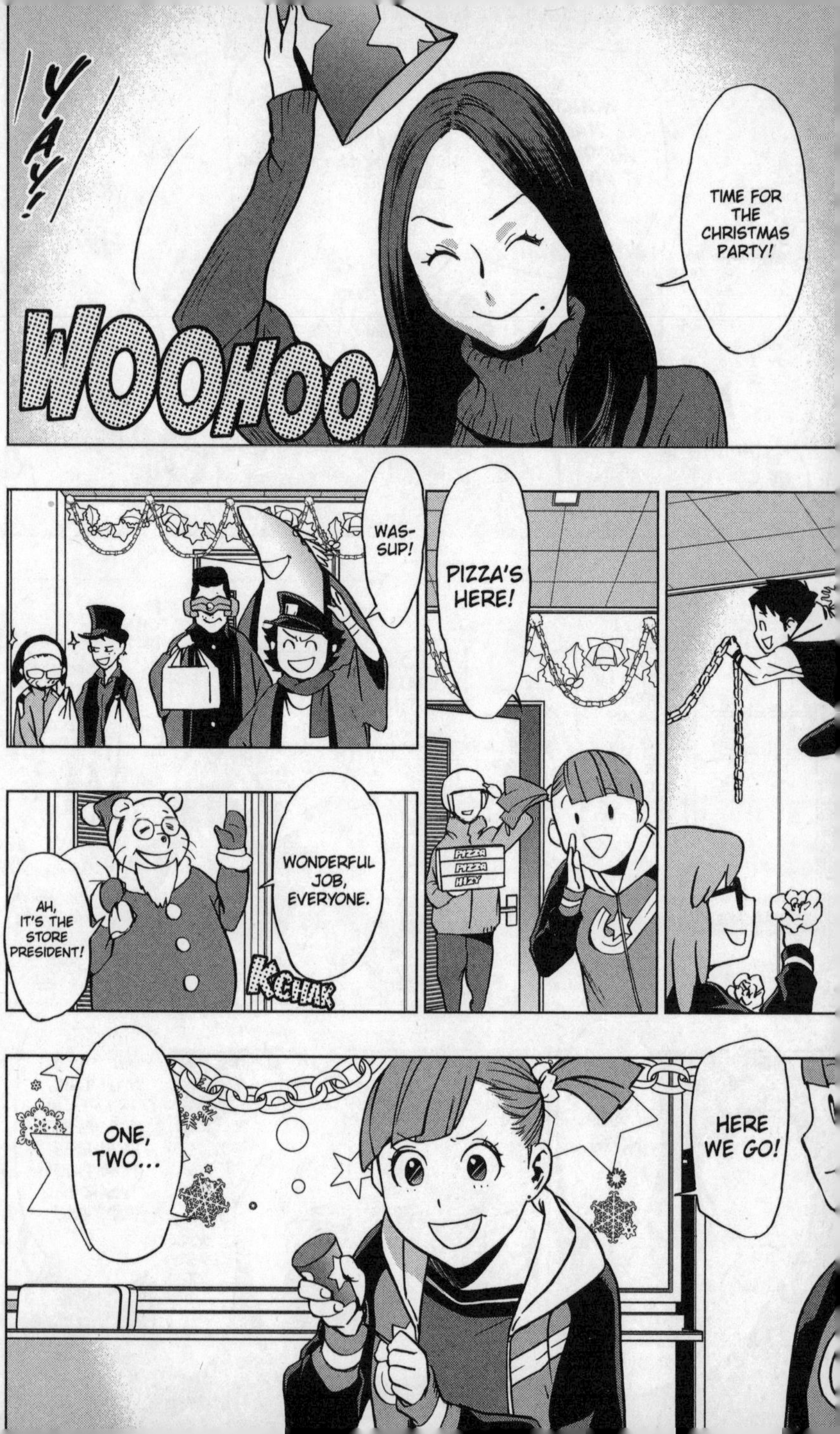
TIME FOR THE CHRISTMAS PARTY!
YAY!
WOOHOO
PIZZA'S HERE!
PIZZA
PIZZA
WAS-SUP!
WONDERFUL JOB, EVERYONE.
AH, IT'S THE STORE PRESIDENT!
KCHAK
HERE WE GO!
ONE, TWO...

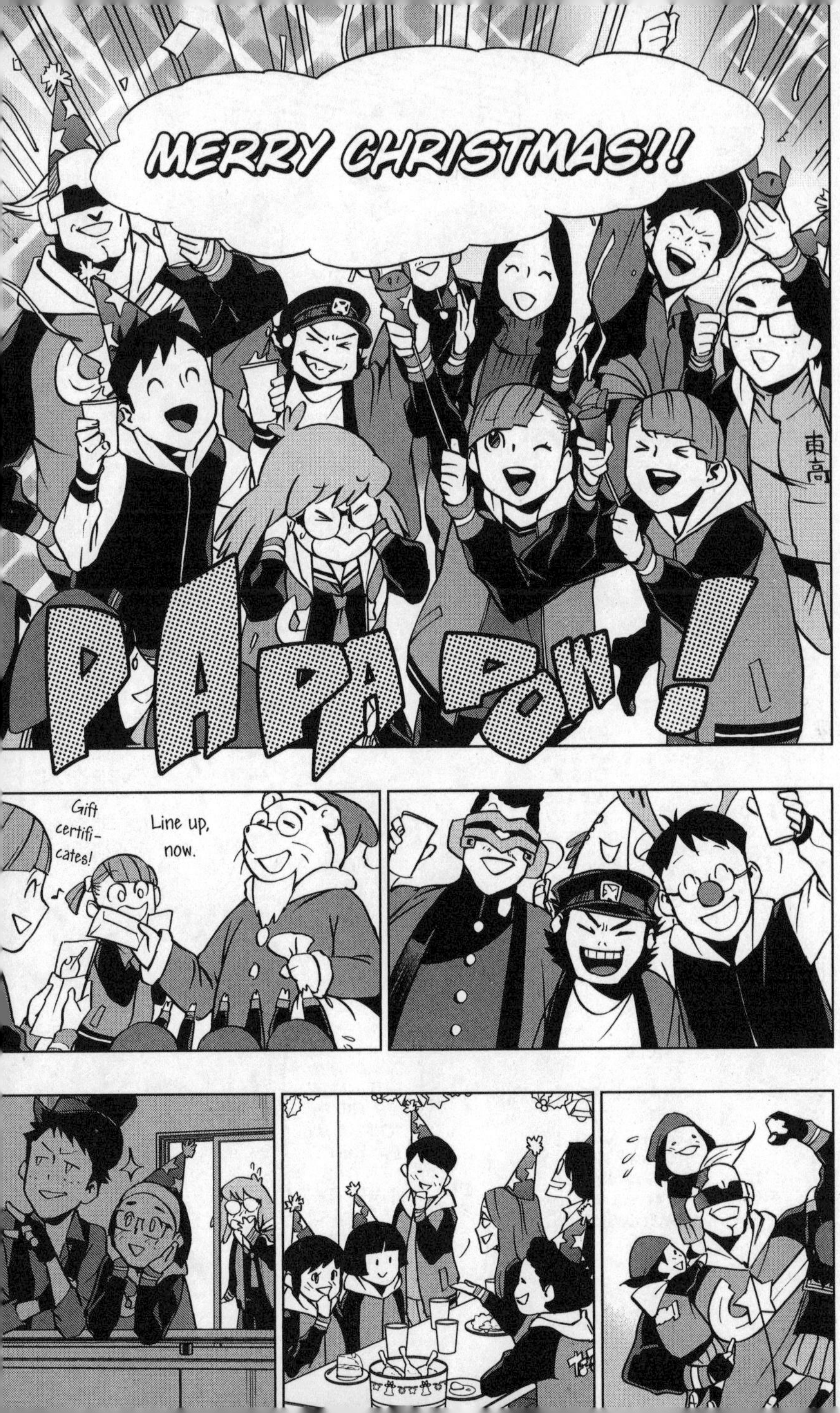
MERRY CHRISTMAS!!
東高
PA PA POW!
Line up, now.
Gift certifi-cates!

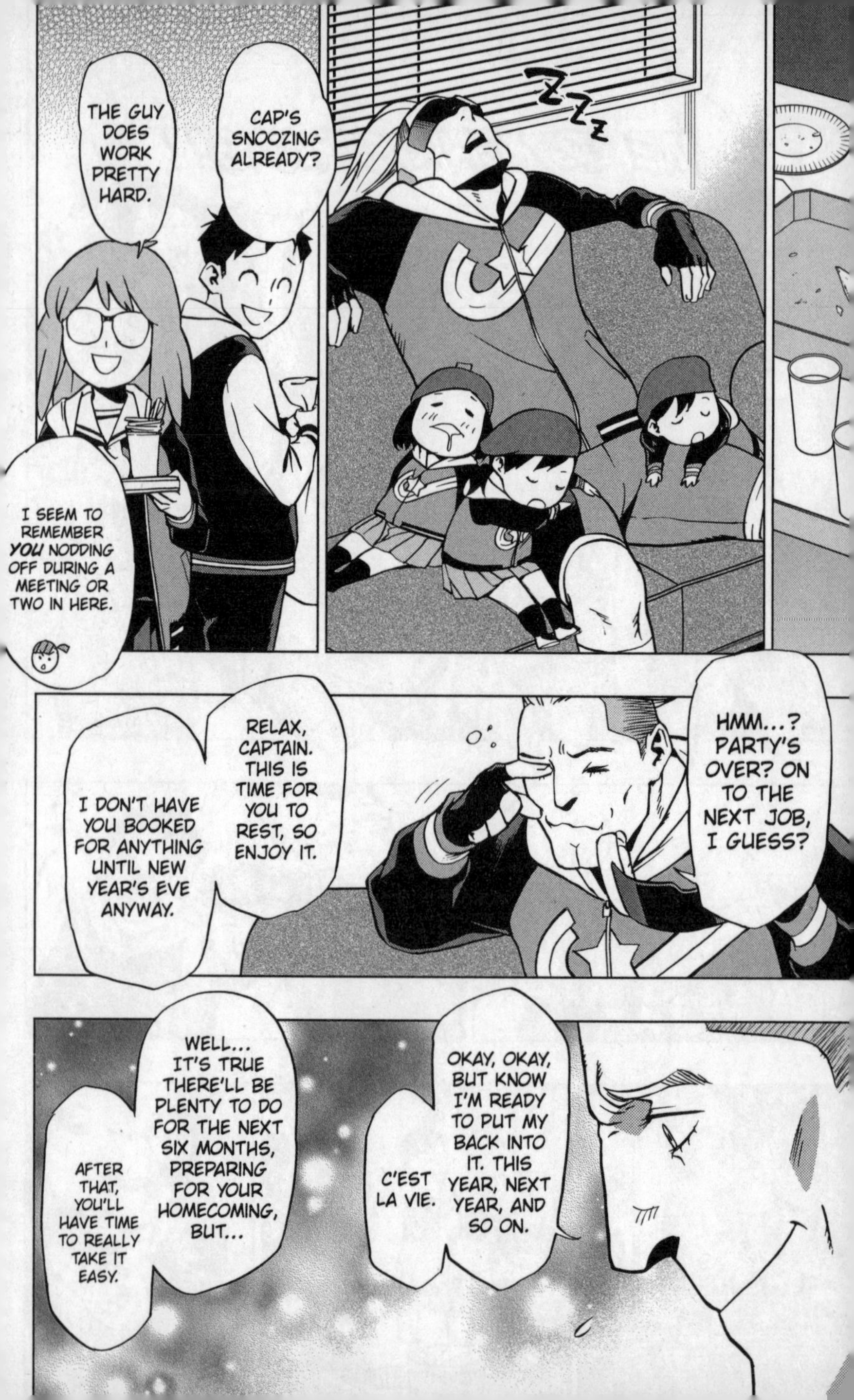
ZZZ
CAP'S SNOOZING ALREADY?
THE GUY DOES WORK PRETTY HARD.
I SEEM TO REMEMBER *YOU* NODDING OFF DURING A MEETING OR TWO IN HERE.
HMM...? PARTY'S OVER? ON TO THE NEXT JOB, I GUESS?
RELAX, CAPTAIN. THIS IS TIME FOR YOU TO REST, SO ENJOY IT.
I DON'T HAVE YOU BOOKED FOR ANYTHING UNTIL NEW YEAR'S EVE ANYWAY.
OKAY, OKAY, BUT KNOW I'M READY TO PUT MY BACK INTO IT. THIS YEAR, NEXT YEAR, AND SO ON.
C'EST LA VIE.
WELL... IT'S TRUE THERE'LL BE PLENTY TO DO FOR THE NEXT SIX MONTHS, PREPARING FOR YOUR HOMECOMING, BUT...
AFTER THAT, YOU'LL HAVE TIME TO REALLY TAKE IT EASY.

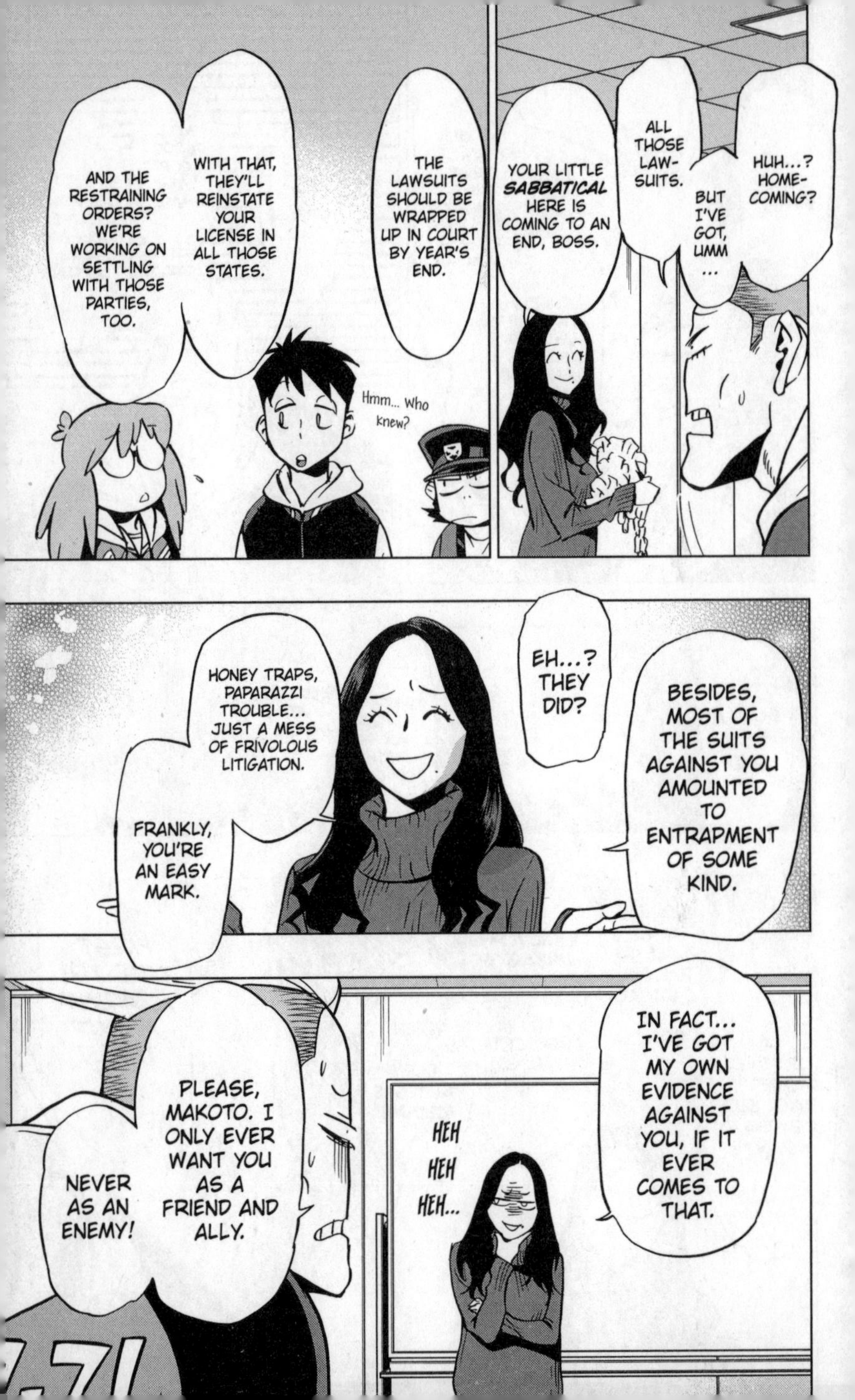
HUH...? HOME-COMING?
BUT I'VE GOT, UMM...
ALL THOSE LAW-SUITS.
YOUR LITTLE ***SABBATICAL*** HERE IS COMING TO AN END, BOSS.
THE LAWSUITS SHOULD BE WRAPPED UP IN COURT BY YEAR'S END.
WITH THAT, THEY'LL REINSTATE YOUR LICENSE IN ALL THOSE STATES.
AND THE RESTRAINING ORDERS? WE'RE WORKING ON SETTLING WITH THOSE PARTIES, TOO.
Hmm... Who knew?
BESIDES, MOST OF THE SUITS AGAINST YOU AMOUNTED TO ENTRAPMENT OF SOME KIND.
EH...? THEY DID?
HONEY TRAPS, PAPARAZZI TROUBLE... JUST A MESS OF FRIVOLOUS LITIGATION.
FRANKLY, YOU'RE AN EASY MARK.
IN FACT... I'VE GOT MY OWN EVIDENCE AGAINST YOU, IF IT EVER COMES TO THAT.
HEH HEH HEH...
PLEASE, MAKOTO. I ONLY EVER WANT YOU AS A FRIEND AND ALLY.
NEVER AS AN ENEMY!

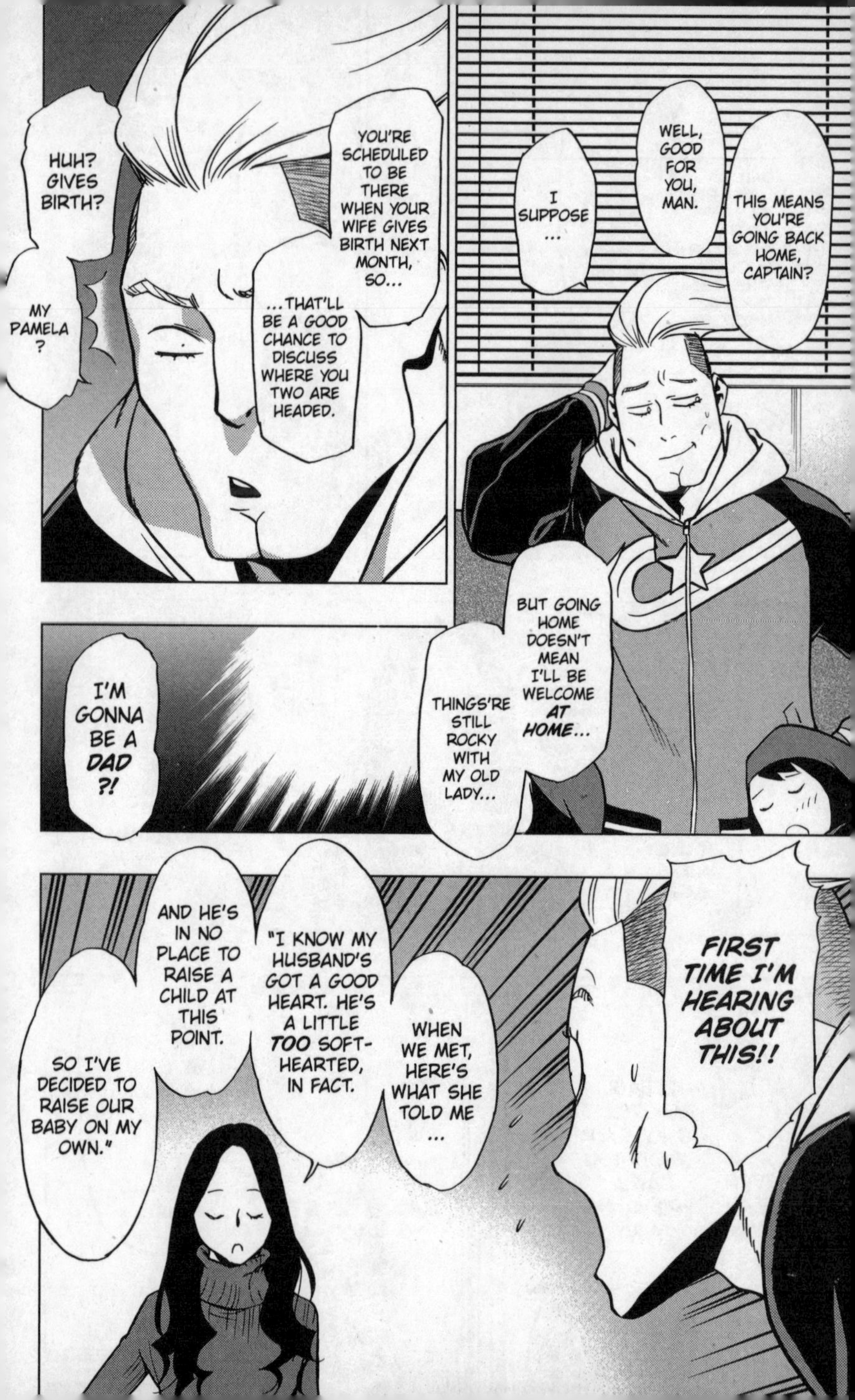
THIS MEANS YOU'RE GOING BACK HOME, CAPTAIN?
WELL, GOOD FOR YOU, MAN.
I SUPPOSE...
BUT GOING HOME DOESN'T MEAN I'LL BE WELCOME *AT HOME*...
THINGS'RE STILL ROCKY WITH MY OLD LADY...
YOU'RE SCHEDULED TO BE THERE WHEN YOUR WIFE GIVES BIRTH NEXT MONTH, SO...
...THAT'LL BE A GOOD CHANCE TO DISCUSS WHERE YOU TWO ARE HEADED.
HUH? GIVES BIRTH?
MY PAMELA?
I'M GONNA BE A *DAD* ?!
FIRST TIME I'M HEARING ABOUT THIS!!
WHEN WE MET, HERE'S WHAT SHE TOLD ME...
"I KNOW MY HUSBAND'S GOT A GOOD HEART. HE'S A LITTLE *TOO* SOFT-HEARTED, IN FACT.
AND HE'S IN NO PLACE TO RAISE A CHILD AT THIS POINT.
SO I'VE DECIDED TO RAISE OUR BABY ON MY OWN."

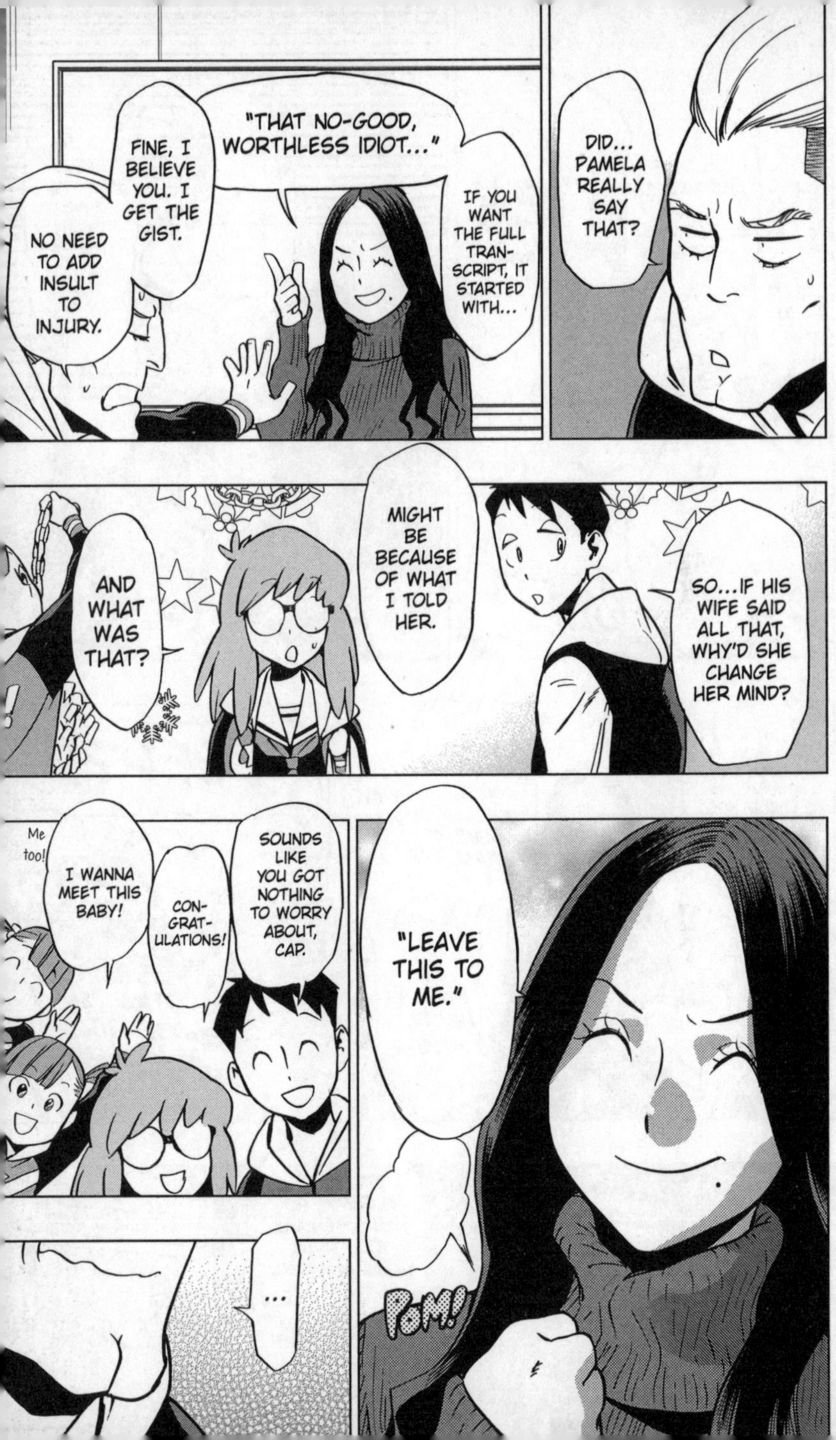
DID... PAMELA REALLY SAY THAT?
IF YOU WANT THE FULL TRAN-SCRIPT, IT STARTED WITH...
"THAT NO-GOOD, WORTHLESS IDIOT..."
FINE, I BELIEVE YOU. I GET THE GIST.
NO NEED TO ADD INSULT TO INJURY.
SO...IF HIS WIFE SAID ALL THAT, WHY'D SHE CHANGE HER MIND?
MIGHT BE BECAUSE OF WHAT I TOLD HER.
AND WHAT WAS THAT?
"LEAVE THIS TO ME."
POM!
SOUNDS LIKE YOU GOT NOTHING TO WORRY ABOUT, CAP.
CON-GRAT-ULATIONS!
I WANNA MEET THIS BABY!
Me too!
...

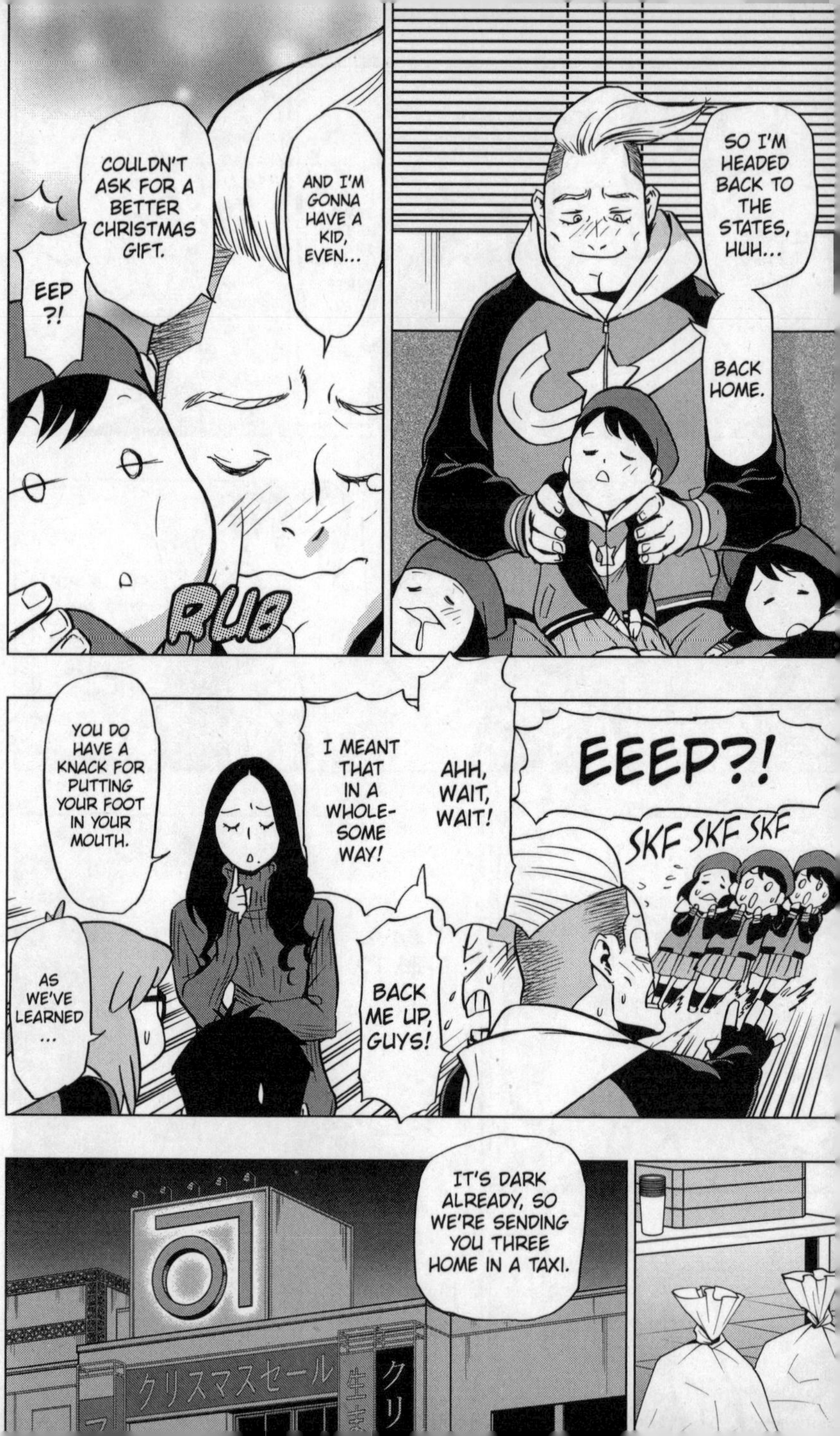

SO I'M HEADED BACK TO THE STATES, HUH...
BACK HOME.
AND I'M GONNA HAVE A KID, EVEN...
COULDN'T ASK FOR A BETTER CHRISTMAS GIFT.
EEP?!
RUB
EEEP?!
SKF SKF SKF
AHH, WAIT, WAIT!
I MEANT THAT IN A WHOLE-SOME WAY!
BACK ME UP, GUYS!
YOU DO HAVE A KNACK FOR PUTTING YOUR FOOT IN YOUR MOUTH.
AS WE'VE LEARNED...
IT'S DARK ALREADY, SO WE'RE SENDING YOU THREE HOME IN A TAXI.
クリスマスセール

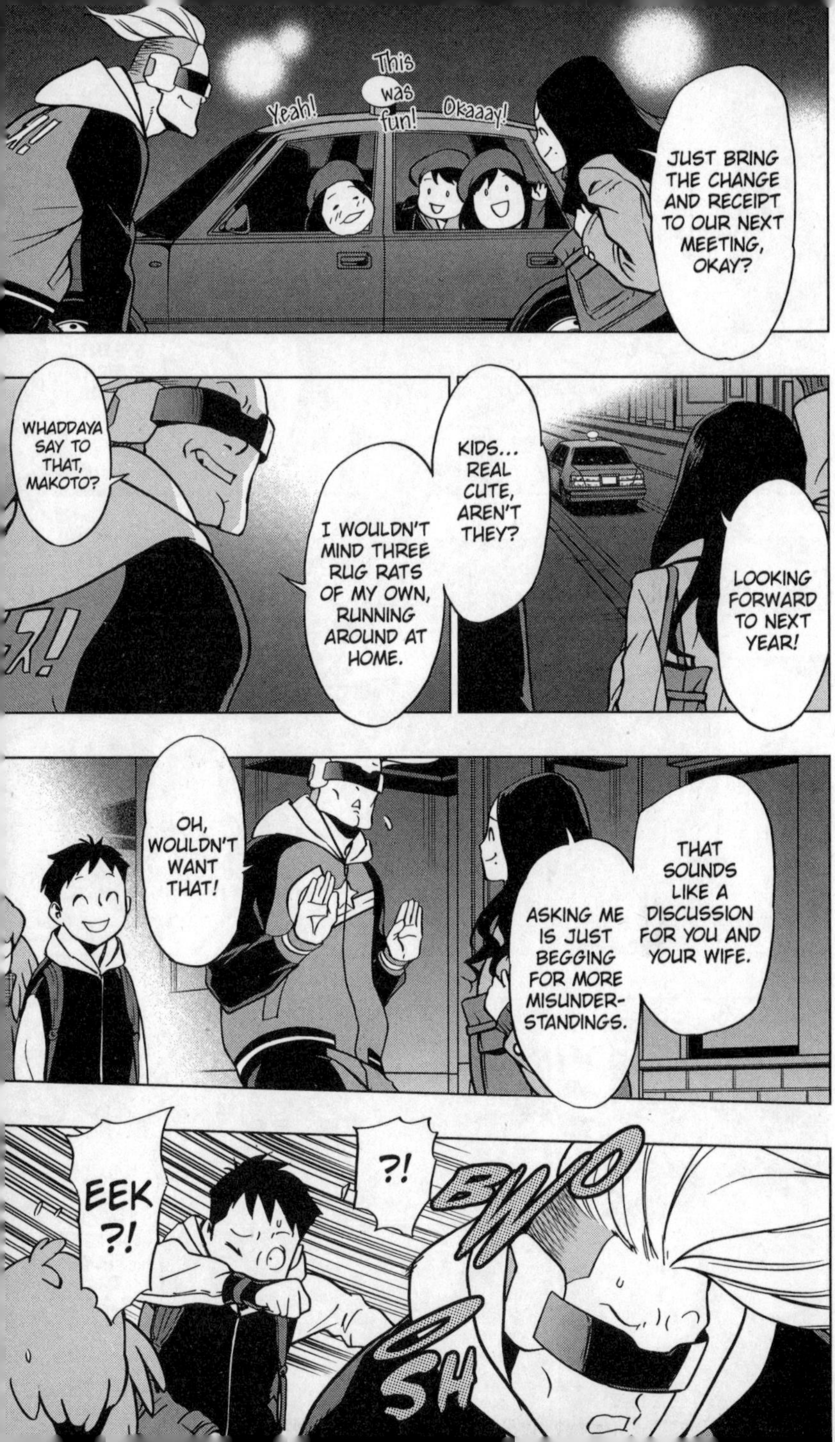
JUST BRING THE CHANGE AND RECEIPT TO OUR NEXT MEETING, OKAY?
Okaaay!
This was fun!
Yeah!
LOOKING FORWARD TO NEXT YEAR!
KIDS... REAL CUTE, AREN'T THEY?
I WOULDN'T MIND THREE RUG RATS OF MY OWN, RUNNING AROUND AT HOME.
WHADDAYA SAY TO THAT, MAKOTO?
THAT SOUNDS LIKE A DISCUSSION FOR YOU AND YOUR WIFE.
ASKING ME IS JUST BEGGING FOR MORE MISUNDER-STANDINGS.
OH, WOULDN'T WANT THAT!
WHOOSH
?!
EEK ?!

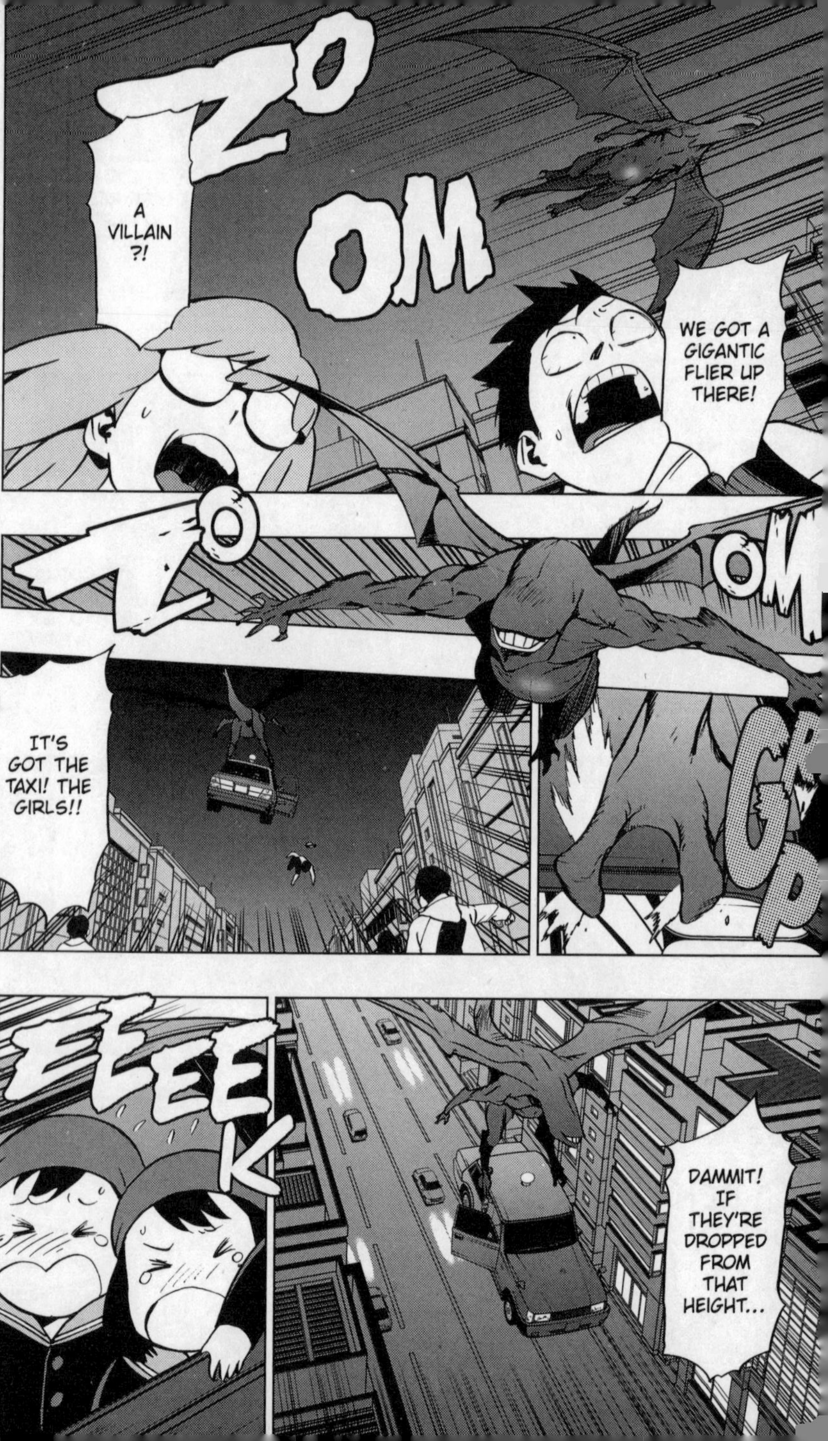
WE GOT A GIGANTIC FLIER UP THERE!
ZO
OM
A VILLAIN ?!
ZO
OM
IT'S GOT THE TAXI! THE GIRLS!!
DAMMIT! IF THEY'RE DROPPED FROM THAT HEIGHT...
EEEE
K

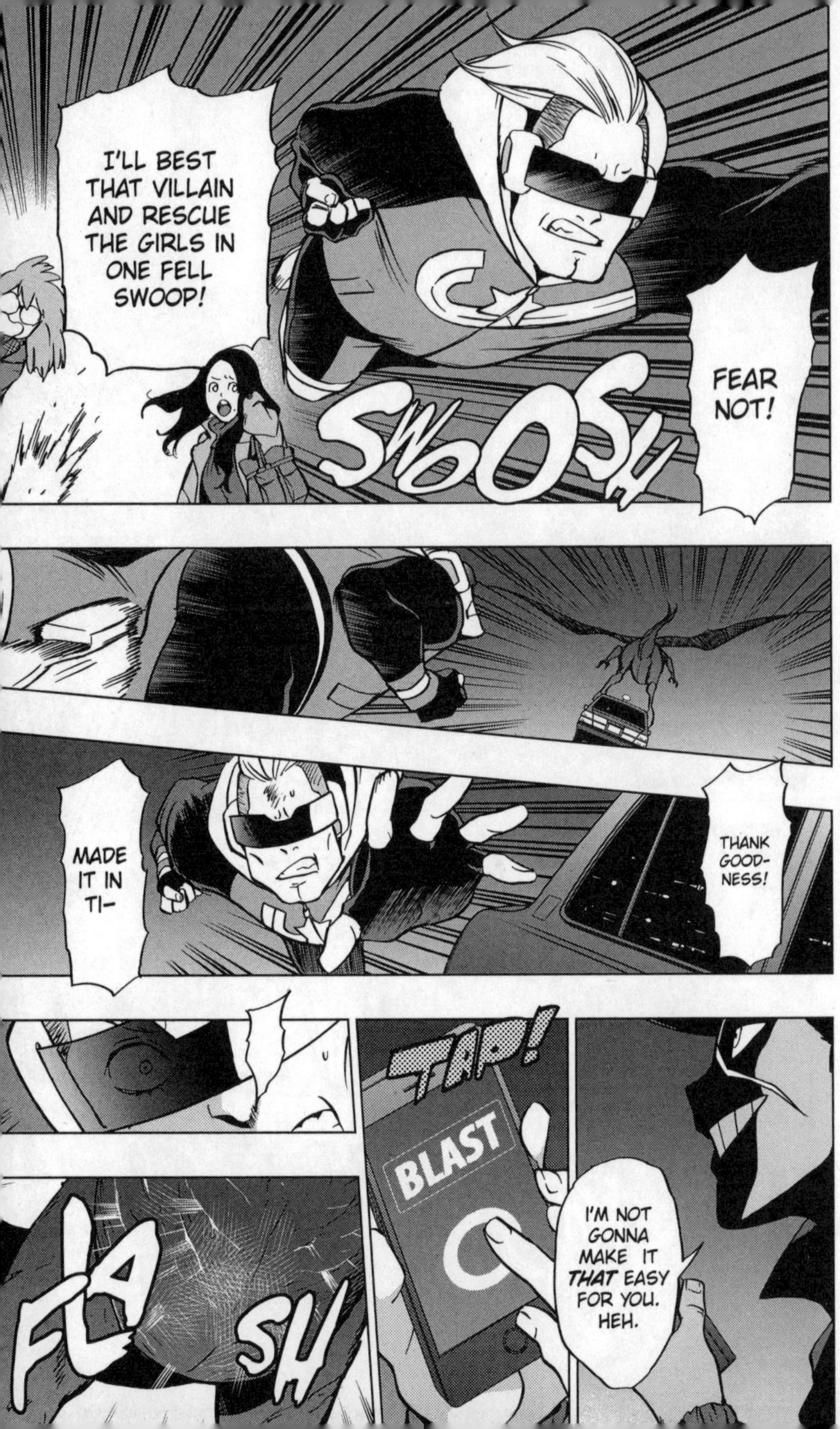
FEAR NOT!
SWOOSH
I'LL BEST THAT VILLAIN AND RESCUE THE GIRLS IN ONE FELL SWOOP!
THANK GOOD-NESS!
MADE IT IN TI-
I'M NOT GONNA MAKE IT *THAT* EASY FOR YOU. HEH.
TAP!
BLAST
FLASH

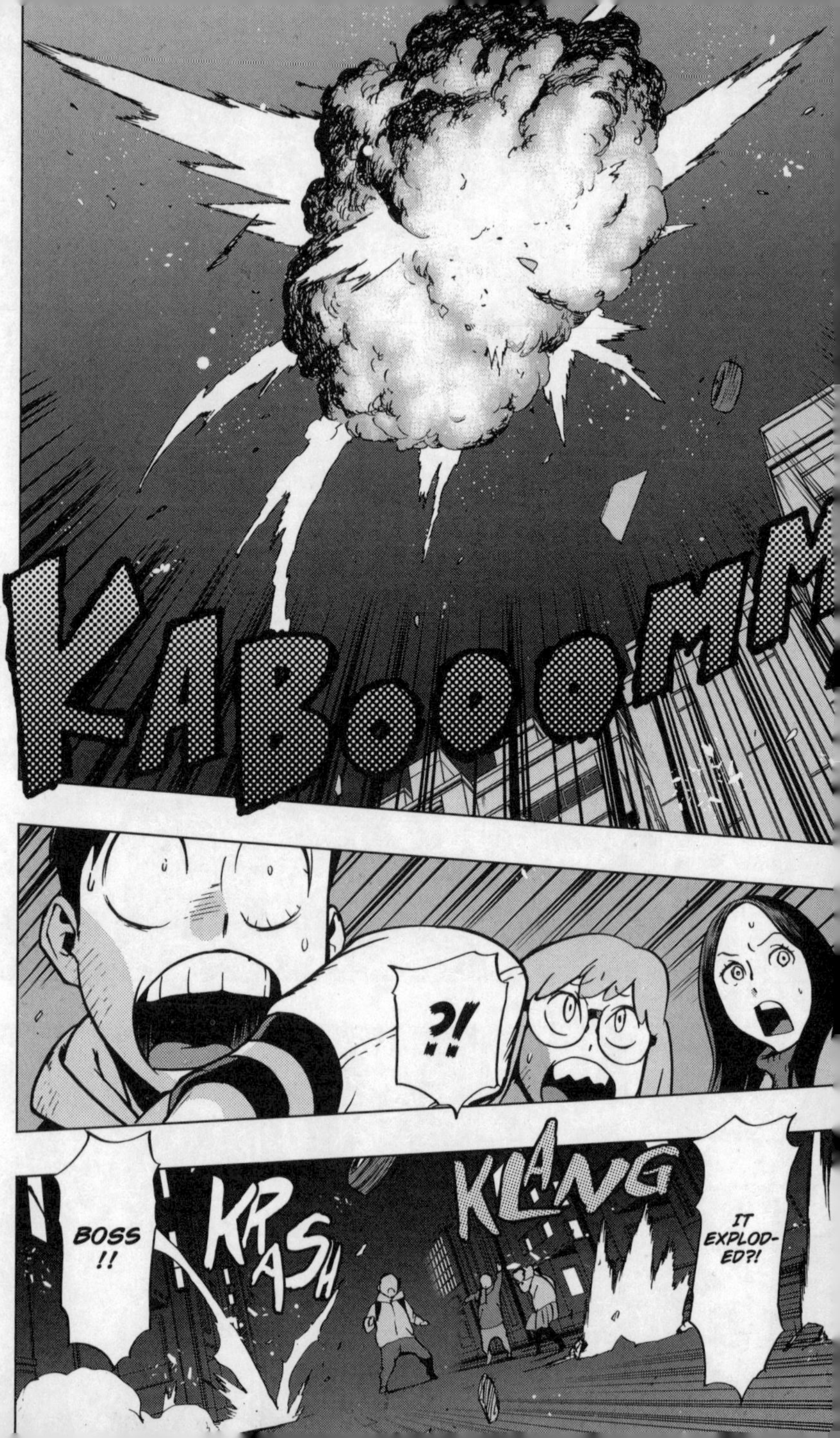
KABOOOMM
?!
IT EXPLODED?!
KLANG
KRASH
BOSS !!

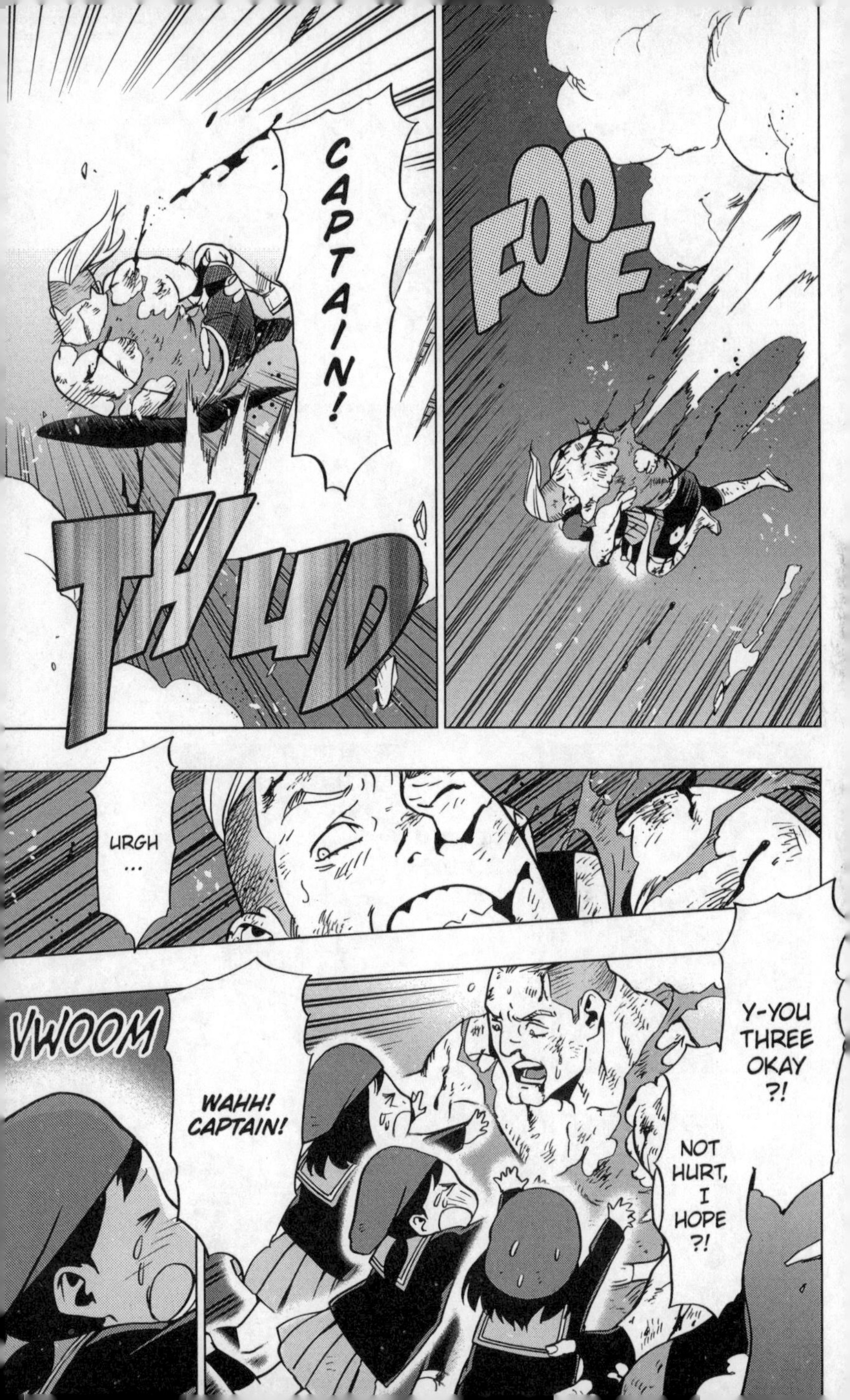
FOOF
CAPTAIN!
THUD
URGH ...
Y-YOU THREE OKAY ?!
NOT HURT, I HOPE ?!
WAHH! CAPTAIN!
VWOOM

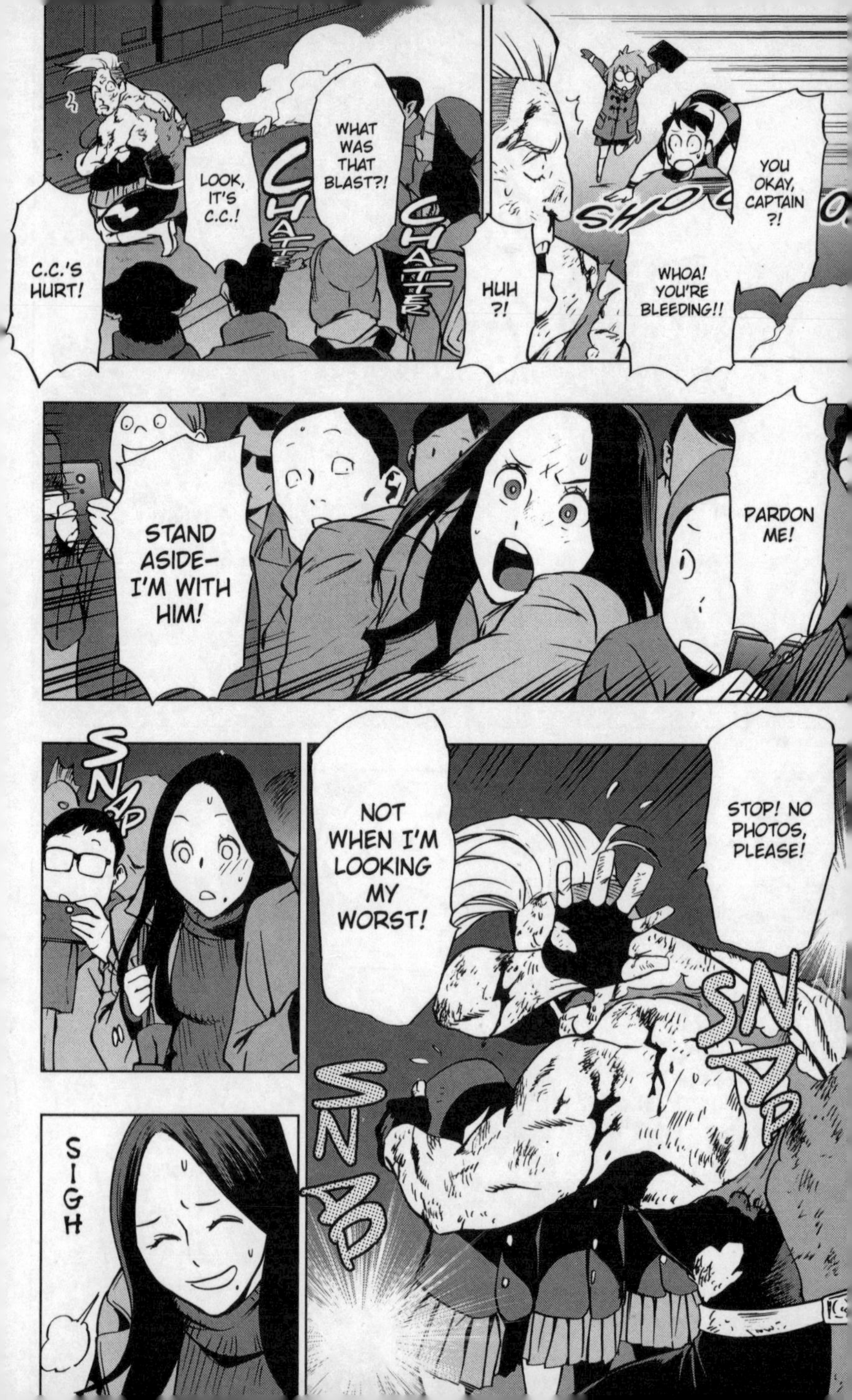
YOU OKAY, CAPTAIN?!
SHOO
WHOA! YOU'RE BLEEDING!!
HUH?!
WHAT WAS THAT BLAST?!
CHATTER
CHATTER
LOOK, IT'S C.C.!
C.C.'S HURT!
PARDON ME!
STAND ASIDE— I'M WITH HIM!
STOP! NO PHOTOS, PLEASE!
SNAP
NOT WHEN I'M LOOKING MY WORST!
SNAP
SNAP
SIGH

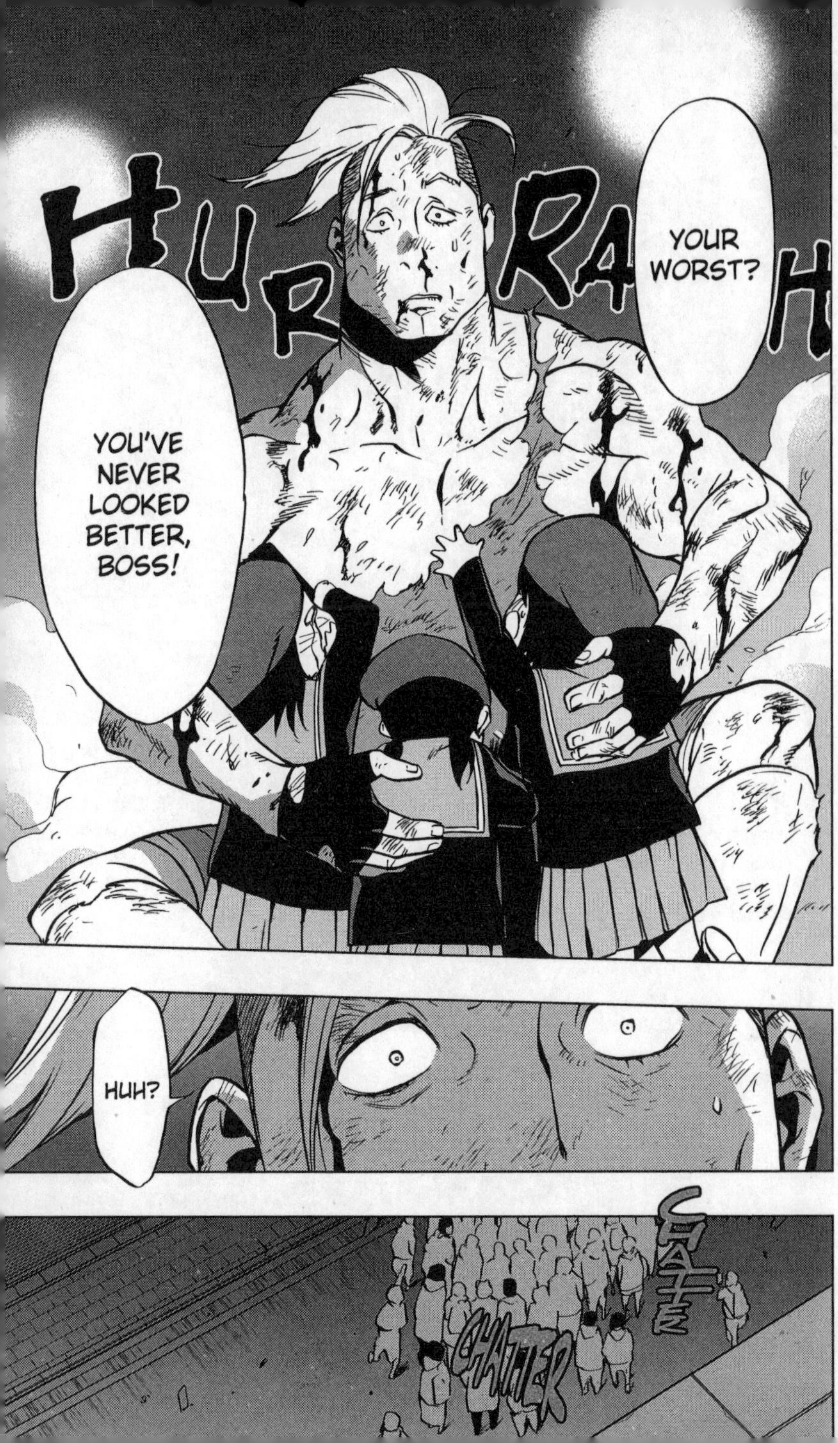
HURRAH
YOUR WORST?
YOU'VE NEVER LOOKED BETTER, BOSS!
HUH?
CHATTER
CHATTER

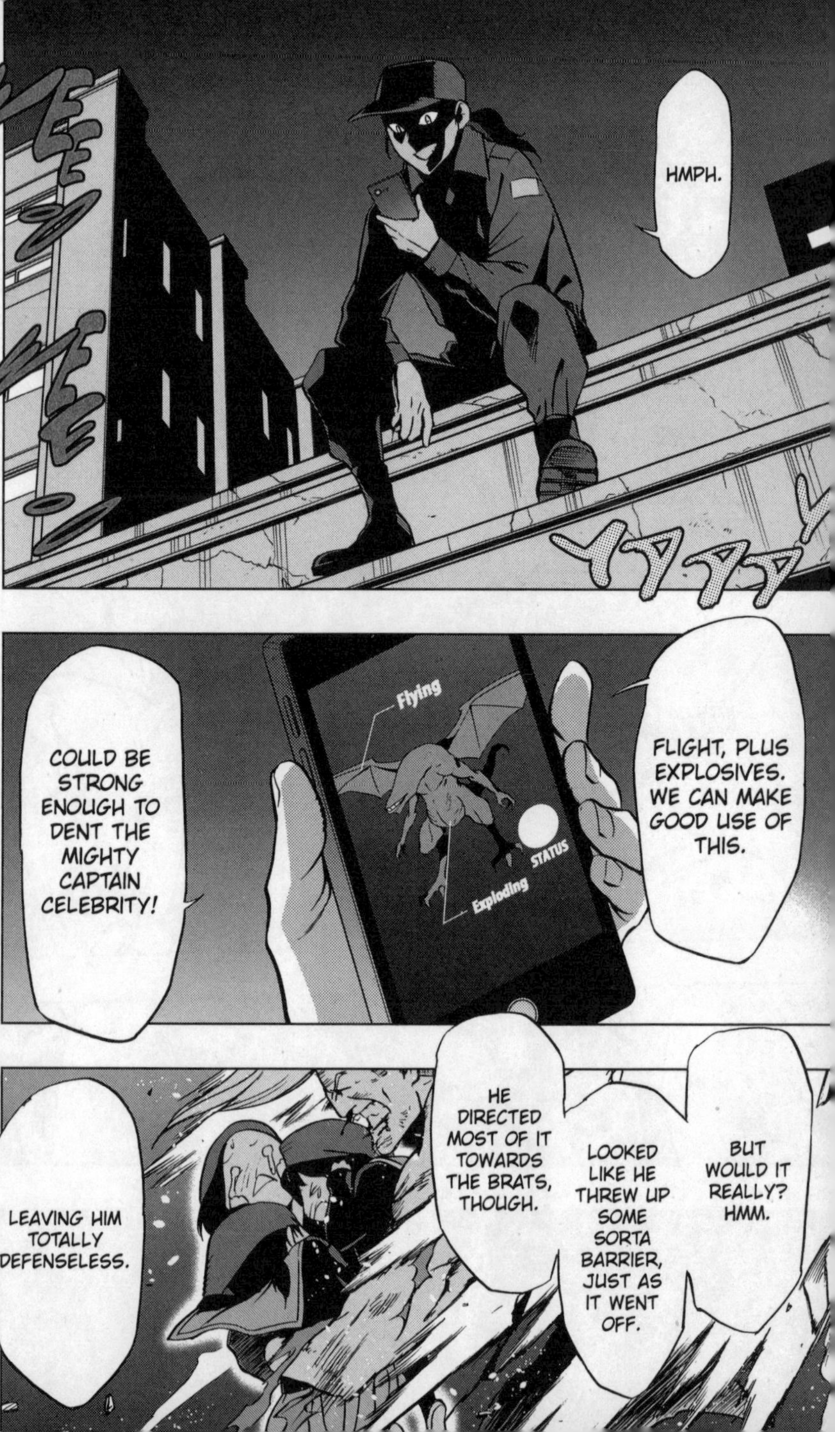
HMPH.
WEEOO WEEOO
YAAAY
FLIGHT, PLUS EXPLOSIVES. WE CAN MAKE GOOD USE OF THIS.
Flying
STATUS
Exploding
COULD BE STRONG ENOUGH TO DENT THE MIGHTY CAPTAIN CELEBRITY!
BUT WOULD IT REALLY? HMM.
LOOKED LIKE HE THREW UP SOME SORTA BARRIER, JUST AS IT WENT OFF.
HE DIRECTED MOST OF IT TOWARDS THE BRATS, THOUGH.
LEAVING HIM TOTALLY DEFENSELESS.

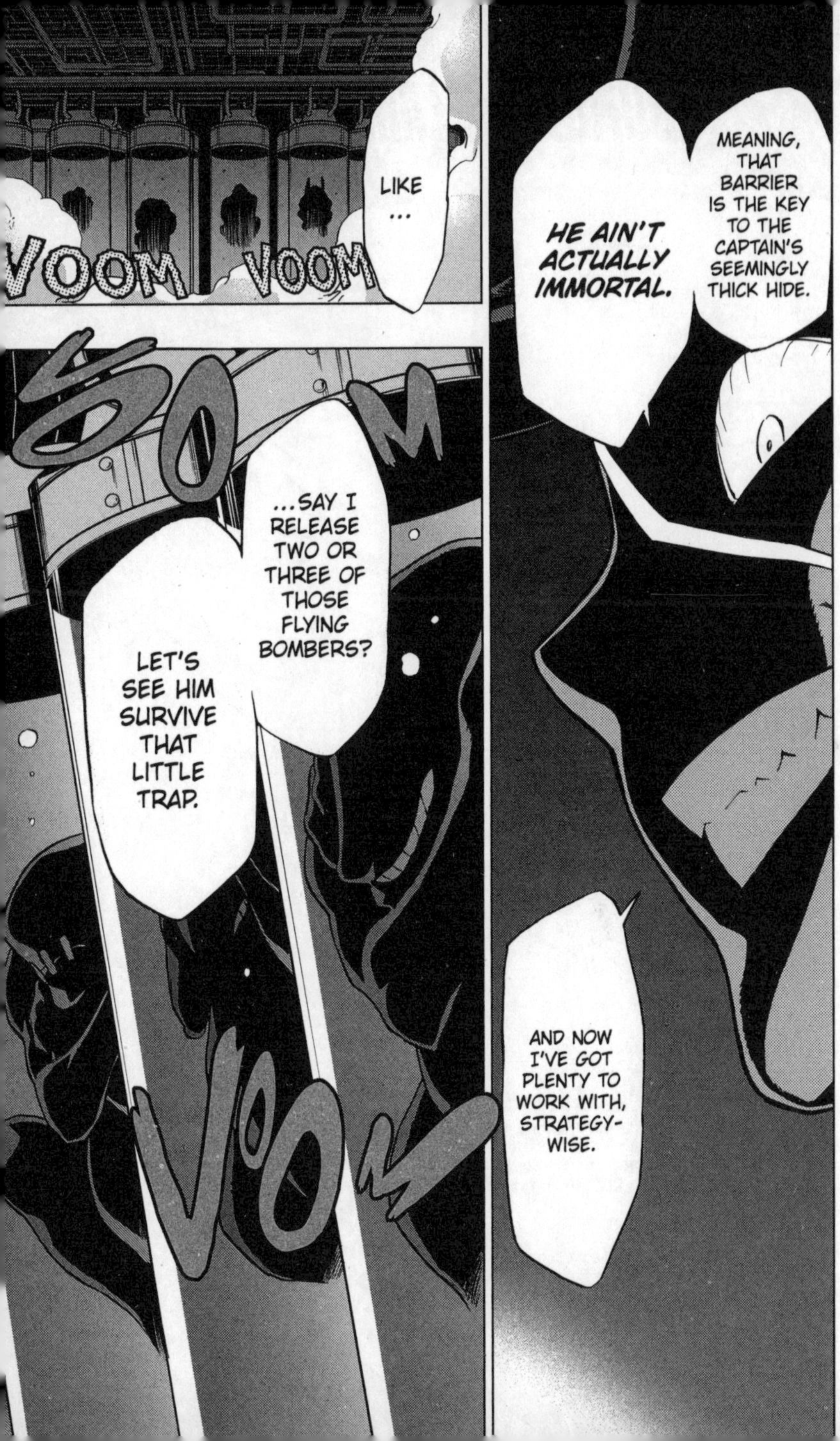
MEANING, THAT BARRIER IS THE KEY TO THE CAPTAIN'S SEEMINGLY THICK HIDE.
HE AIN'T ACTUALLY IMMORTAL.
AND NOW I'VE GOT PLENTY TO WORK WITH, STRATEGY-WISE.
LIKE ...
VOOM
VOOM
...SAY I RELEASE TWO OR THREE OF THOSE FLYING BOMBERS?
VOOM
LET'S SEE HIM SURVIVE THAT LITTLE TRAP.
VOOM

BOMBER VILLAIN

THE ROUGH DESIGN

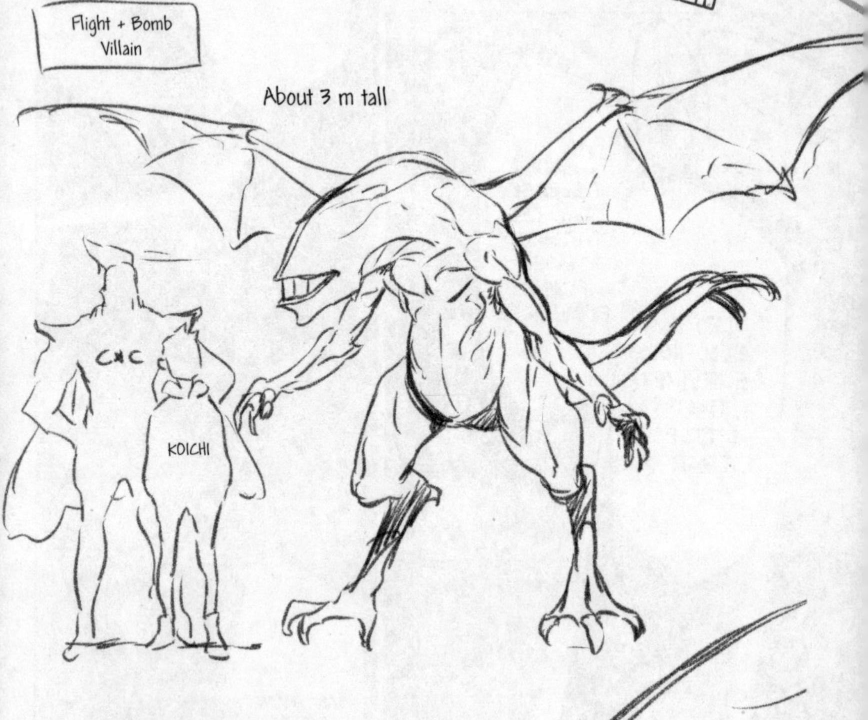
Flight + Bomb Villain
About 3 m tall
C&C
KOICHI

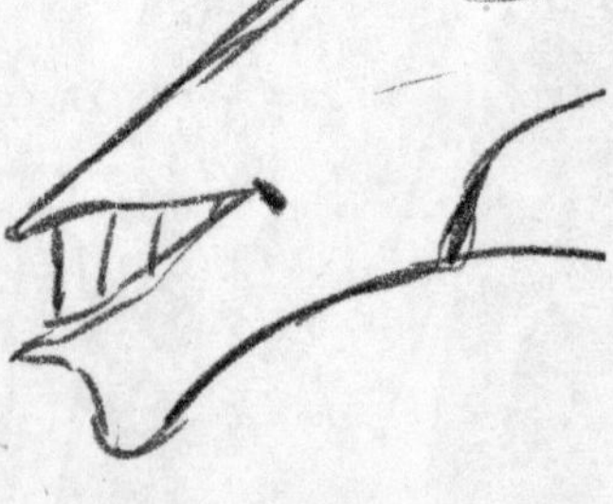

BEHIND THE SCENES

I came up with this enemy for the Christmas party chapter, but then I thought this thing is totally suited to terrorism, so it ended up getting mass-produced. The bombers really upped the stakes in the Sky Egg part of the story.

—Furuhashi

The design ended up looking like the cousin of Khezu (from *Monster Hunter*) and Mass Production Eva models (from *Neon Genesis Evangelion*). They're relatively fun to draw.

—Betten

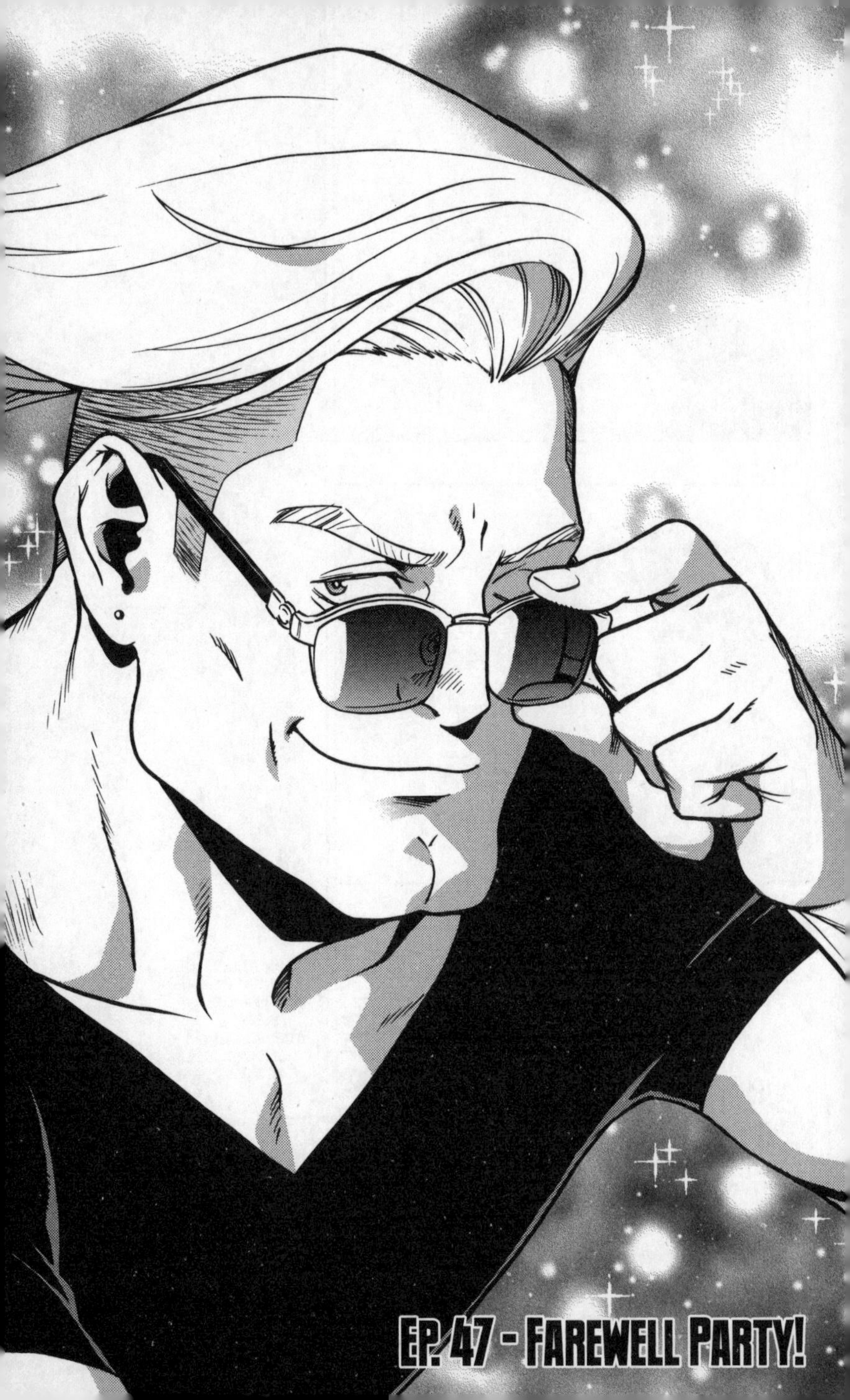
Ep. 47 - Farewell Party!

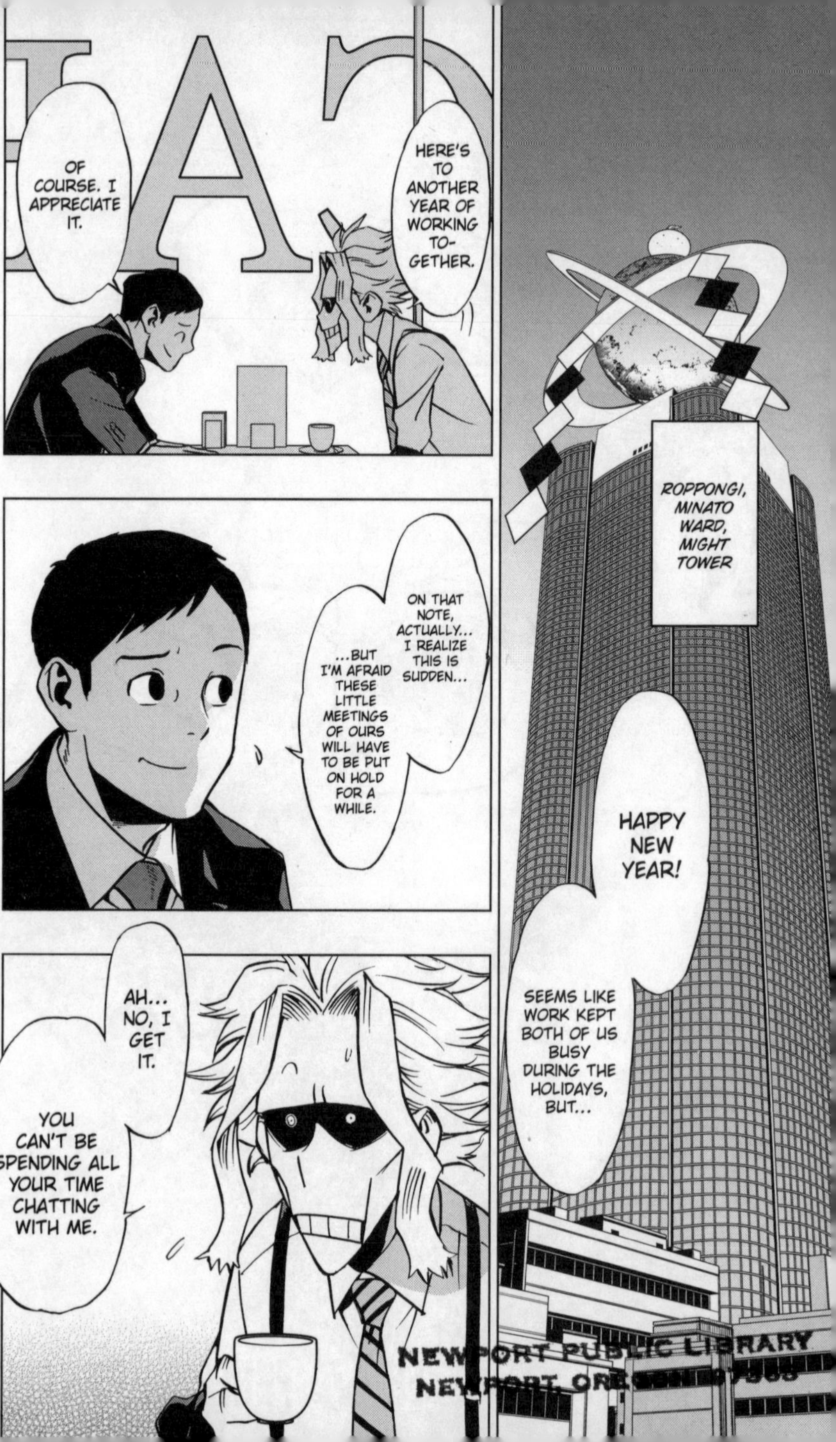
ROPPONGI, MINATO WARD, MIGHT TOWER
HAPPY NEW YEAR!
SEEMS LIKE WORK KEPT BOTH OF US BUSY DURING THE HOLIDAYS, BUT...
HERE'S TO ANOTHER YEAR OF WORKING TO-GETHER.
OF COURSE. I APPRECIATE IT.
ON THAT NOTE, ACTUALLY... I REALIZE THIS IS SUDDEN...
...BUT I'M AFRAID THESE LITTLE MEETINGS OF OURS WILL HAVE TO BE PUT ON HOLD FOR A WHILE.
AH... NO, I GET IT.
YOU CAN'T BE SPENDING ALL YOUR TIME CHATTING WITH ME.

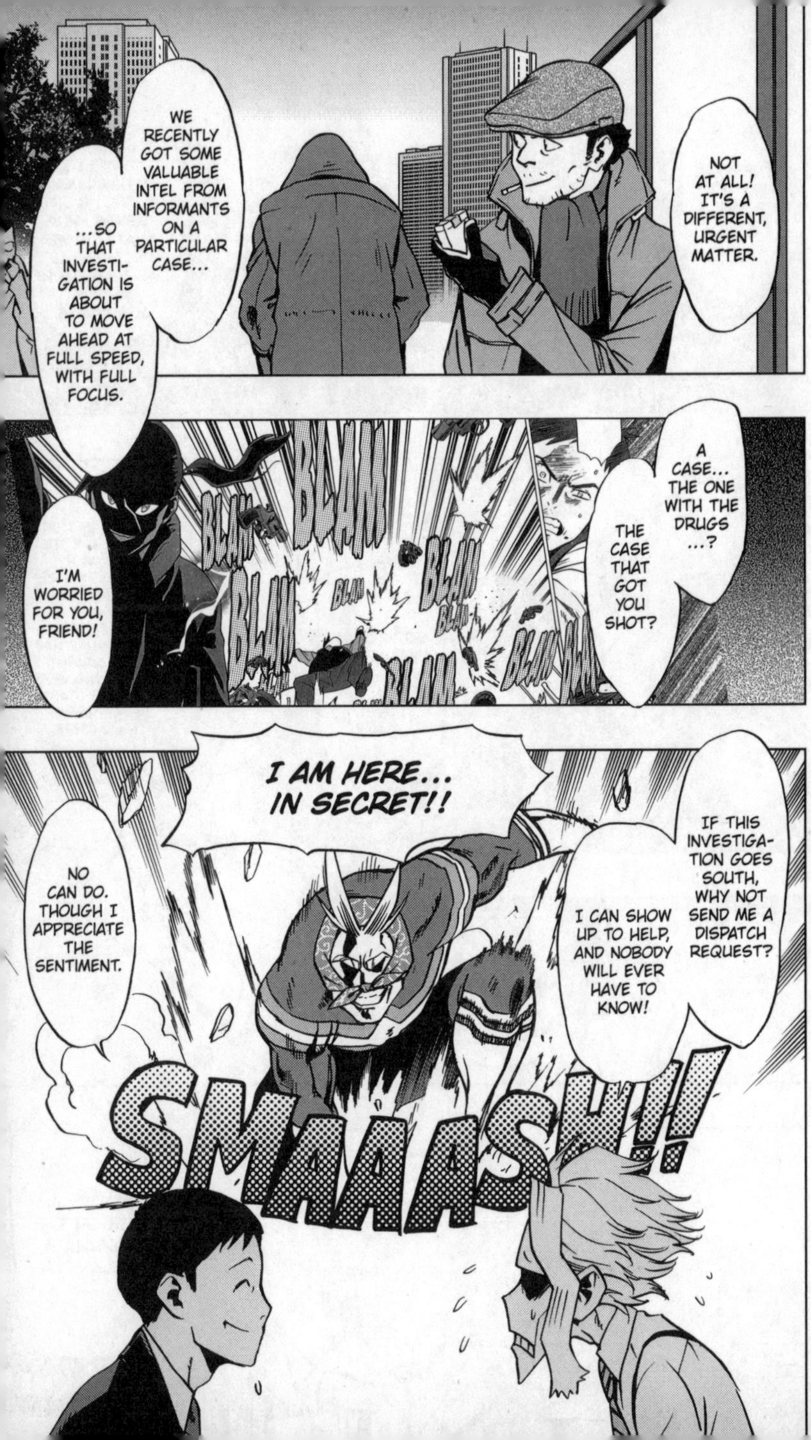
NOT AT ALL! IT'S A DIFFERENT, URGENT MATTER.
WE RECENTLY GOT SOME VALUABLE INTEL FROM INFORMANTS ON A PARTICULAR CASE...
...SO THAT INVESTIGATION IS ABOUT TO MOVE AHEAD AT FULL SPEED, WITH FULL FOCUS.
A CASE... THE ONE WITH THE DRUGS ...?
THE CASE THAT GOT YOU SHOT?
BLAM BLAM BLAM BLAM
I'M WORRIED FOR YOU, FRIEND!
IF THIS INVESTIGATION GOES SOUTH, WHY NOT SEND ME A DISPATCH REQUEST?
I CAN SHOW UP TO HELP, AND NOBODY WILL EVER HAVE TO KNOW!
I AM HERE... IN SECRET!!
SMAAASH!!
NO CAN DO. THOUGH I APPRECIATE THE SENTIMENT.

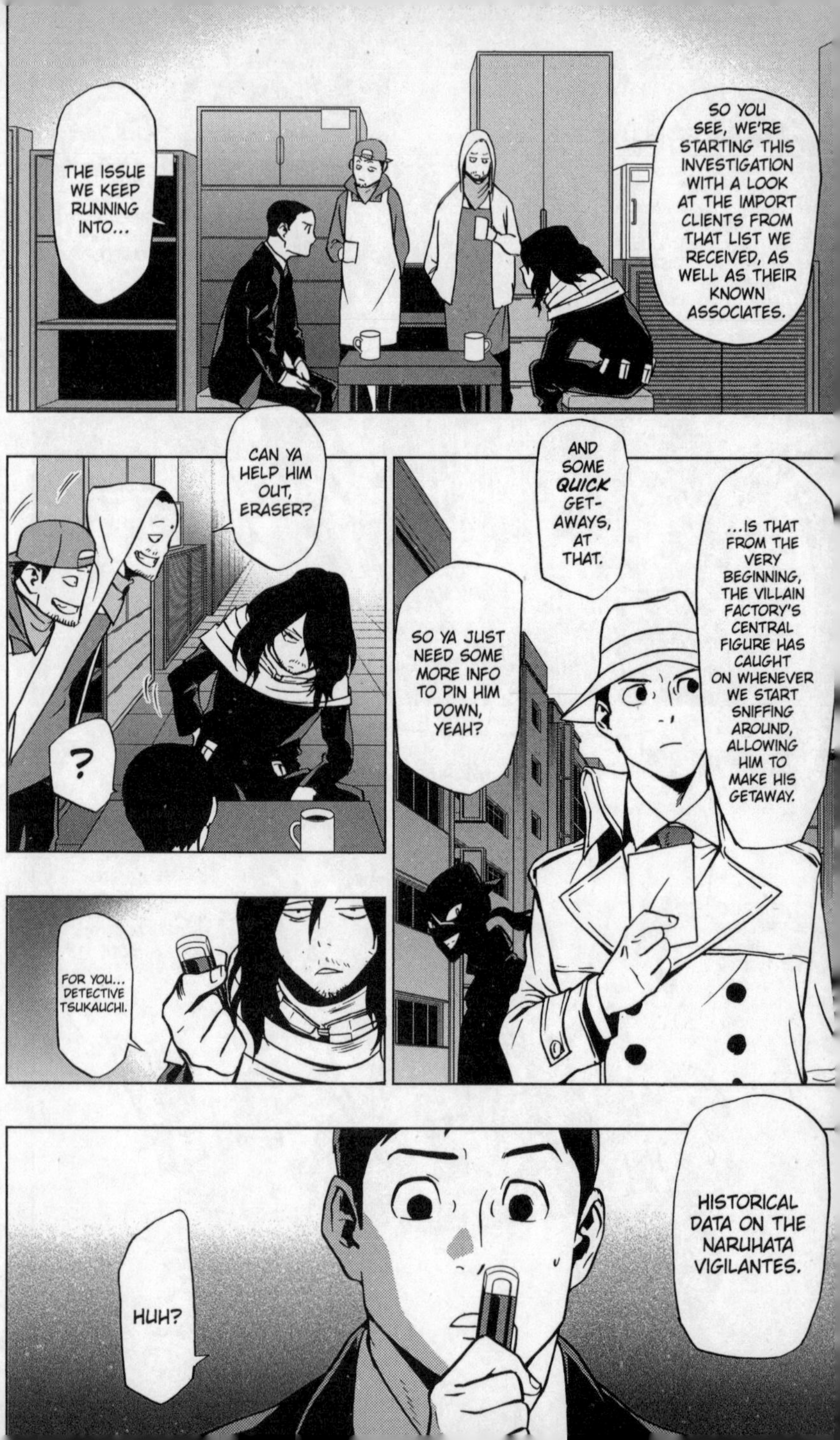

SO YOU SEE, WE'RE STARTING THIS INVESTIGATION WITH A LOOK AT THE IMPORT CLIENTS FROM THAT LIST WE RECEIVED, AS WELL AS THEIR KNOWN ASSOCIATES.
THE ISSUE WE KEEP RUNNING INTO...
...IS THAT FROM THE VERY BEGINNING, THE VILLAIN FACTORY'S CENTRAL FIGURE HAS CAUGHT ON WHENEVER WE START SNIFFING AROUND, ALLOWING HIM TO MAKE HIS GETAWAY.
AND SOME QUICK GET-AWAYS, AT THAT.
SO YA JUST NEED SOME MORE INFO TO PIN HIM DOWN, YEAH?
CAN YA HELP HIM OUT, ERASER?
?
FOR YOU... DETECTIVE TSUKAUCHI.
HISTORICAL DATA ON THE NARUHATA VIGILANTES.
HUH?

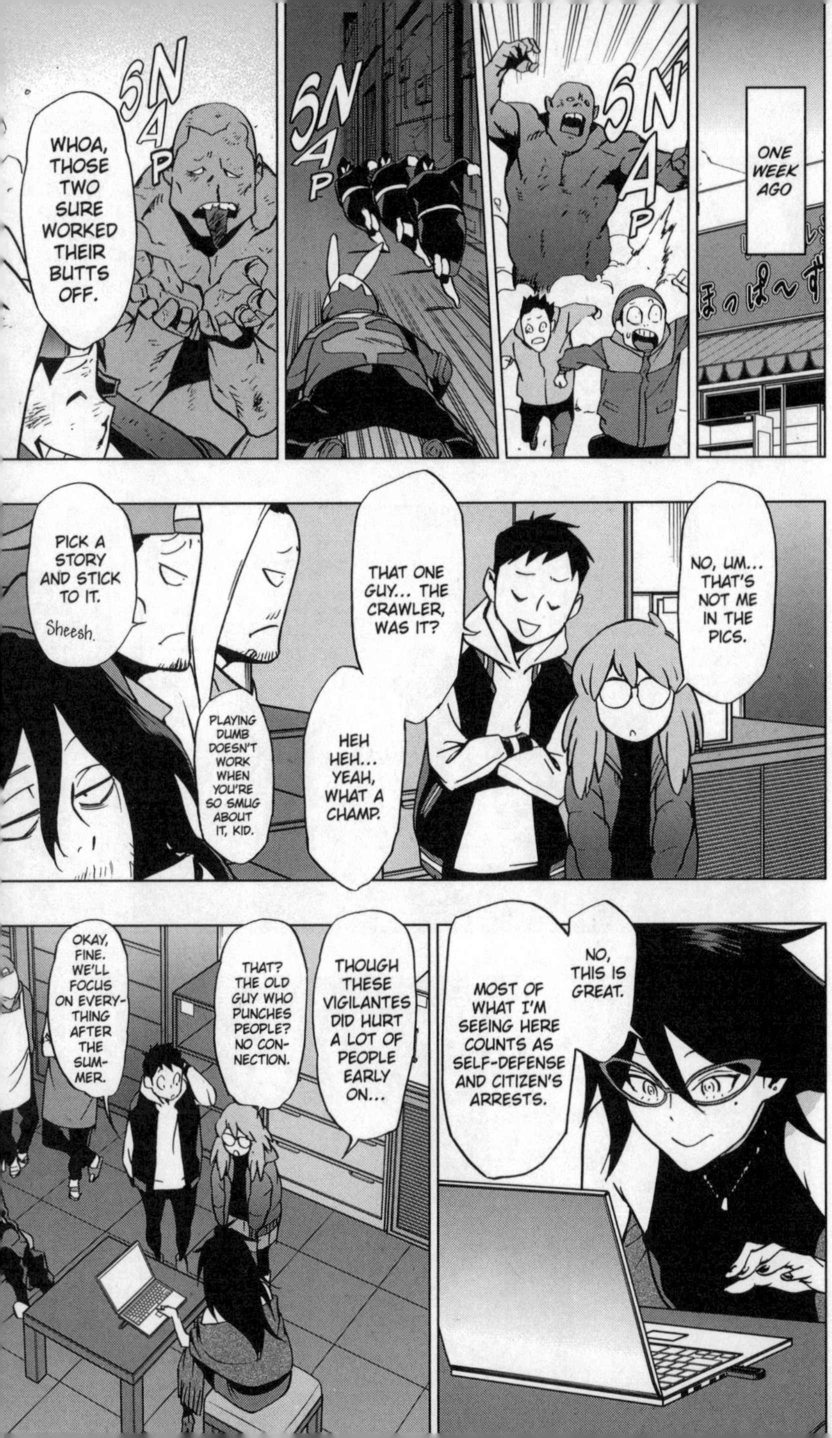
ONE WEEK AGO
ほっぱ〜ず
SNAP
SNAP
SNAP
WHOA, THOSE TWO SURE WORKED THEIR BUTTS OFF.
NO, UM... THAT'S NOT ME IN THE PICS.
THAT ONE GUY... THE CRAWLER, WAS IT?
HEH HEH... YEAH, WHAT A CHAMP.
PICK A STORY AND STICK TO IT.
Sheesh.
PLAYING DUMB DOESN'T WORK WHEN YOU'RE SO SMUG ABOUT IT, KID.
NO, THIS IS GREAT.
MOST OF WHAT I'M SEEING HERE COUNTS AS SELF-DEFENSE AND CITIZEN'S ARRESTS.
THOUGH THESE VIGILANTES DID HURT A LOT OF PEOPLE EARLY ON...
THAT? THE OLD GUY WHO PUNCHES PEOPLE? NO CONNECTION.
OKAY, FINE. WE'LL FOCUS ON EVERY-THING AFTER THE SUM-MER.

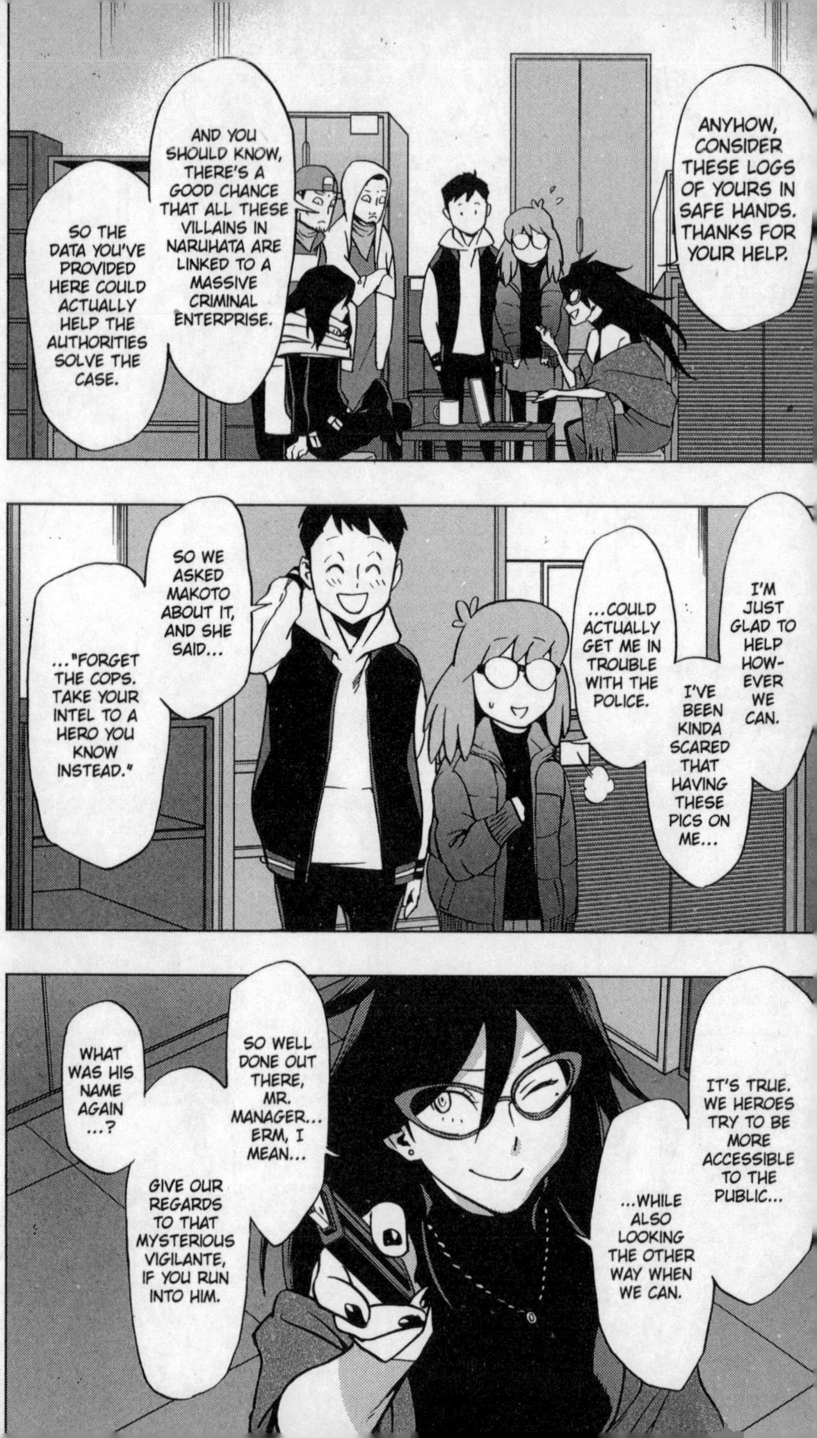
ANYHOW, CONSIDER THESE LOGS OF YOURS IN SAFE HANDS. THANKS FOR YOUR HELP.
AND YOU SHOULD KNOW, THERE'S A GOOD CHANCE THAT ALL THESE VILLAINS IN NARUHATA ARE LINKED TO A MASSIVE CRIMINAL ENTERPRISE.
SO THE DATA YOU'VE PROVIDED HERE COULD ACTUALLY HELP THE AUTHORITIES SOLVE THE CASE.
I'M JUST GLAD TO HELP HOW-EVER WE CAN.
I'VE BEEN KINDA SCARED THAT HAVING THESE PICS ON ME...
...COULD ACTUALLY GET ME IN TROUBLE WITH THE POLICE.
SO WE ASKED MAKOTO ABOUT IT, AND SHE SAID...
..."FORGET THE COPS. TAKE YOUR INTEL TO A HERO YOU KNOW INSTEAD."
IT'S TRUE. WE HEROES TRY TO BE MORE ACCESSIBLE TO THE PUBLIC...
...WHILE ALSO LOOKING THE OTHER WAY WHEN WE CAN.
SO WELL DONE OUT THERE, MR. MANAGER... ERM, I MEAN...
WHAT WAS HIS NAME AGAIN ...?
GIVE OUR REGARDS TO THAT MYSTERIOUS VIGILANTE, IF YOU RUN INTO HIM.

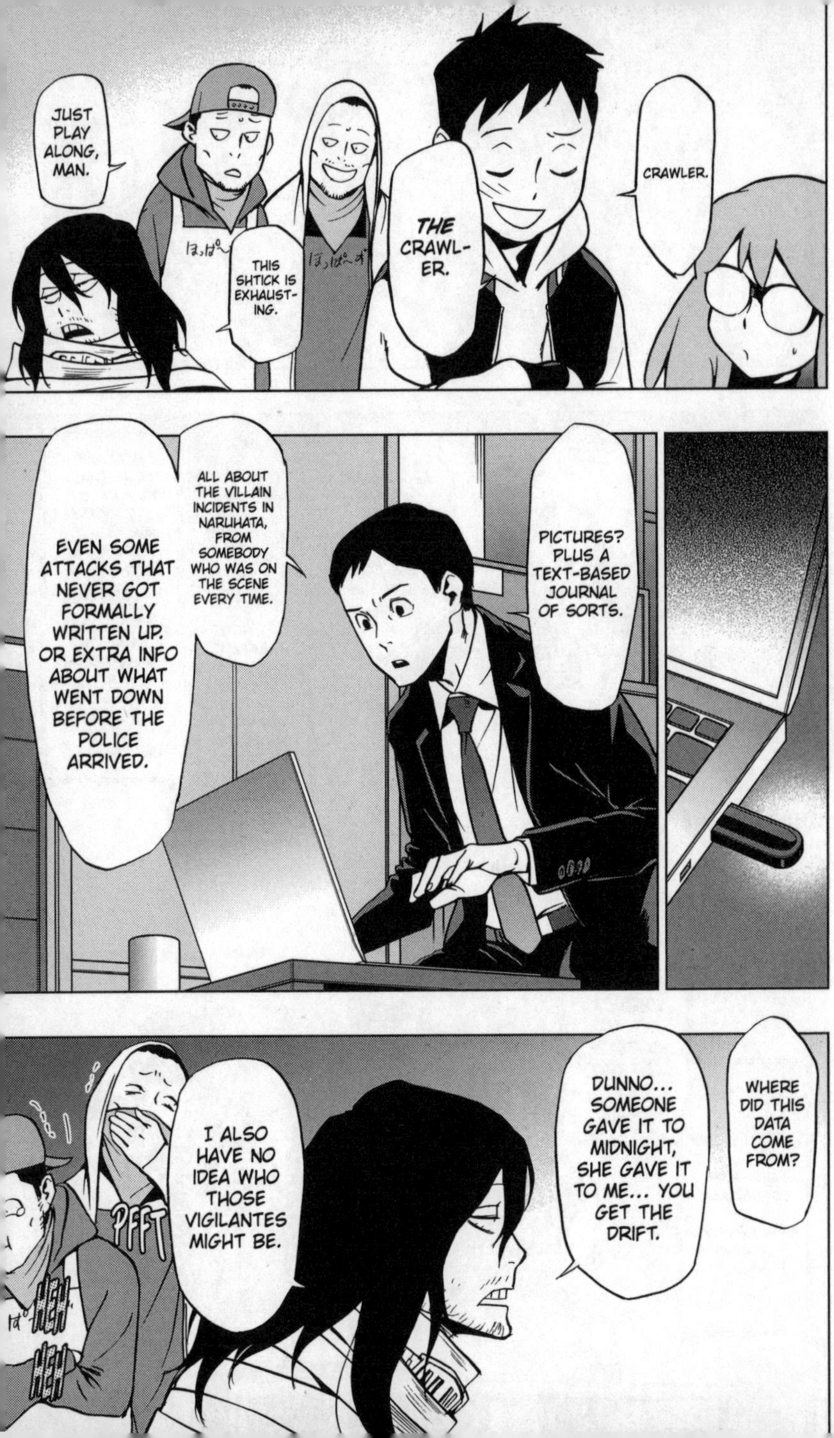
CRAWLER.
THE CRAWLER.
THIS SHTICK IS EXHAUSTING.
JUST PLAY ALONG, MAN.
PICTURES? PLUS A TEXT-BASED JOURNAL OF SORTS.
ALL ABOUT THE VILLAIN INCIDENTS IN NARUHATA, FROM SOMEBODY WHO WAS ON THE SCENE EVERY TIME.
EVEN SOME ATTACKS THAT NEVER GOT FORMALLY WRITTEN UP. OR EXTRA INFO ABOUT WHAT WENT DOWN BEFORE THE POLICE ARRIVED.
WHERE DID THIS DATA COME FROM?
DUNNO... SOMEONE GAVE IT TO MIDNIGHT, SHE GAVE IT TO ME... YOU GET THE DRIFT.
I ALSO HAVE NO IDEA WHO THOSE VIGILANTES MIGHT BE.
PFFT
HEH HEH

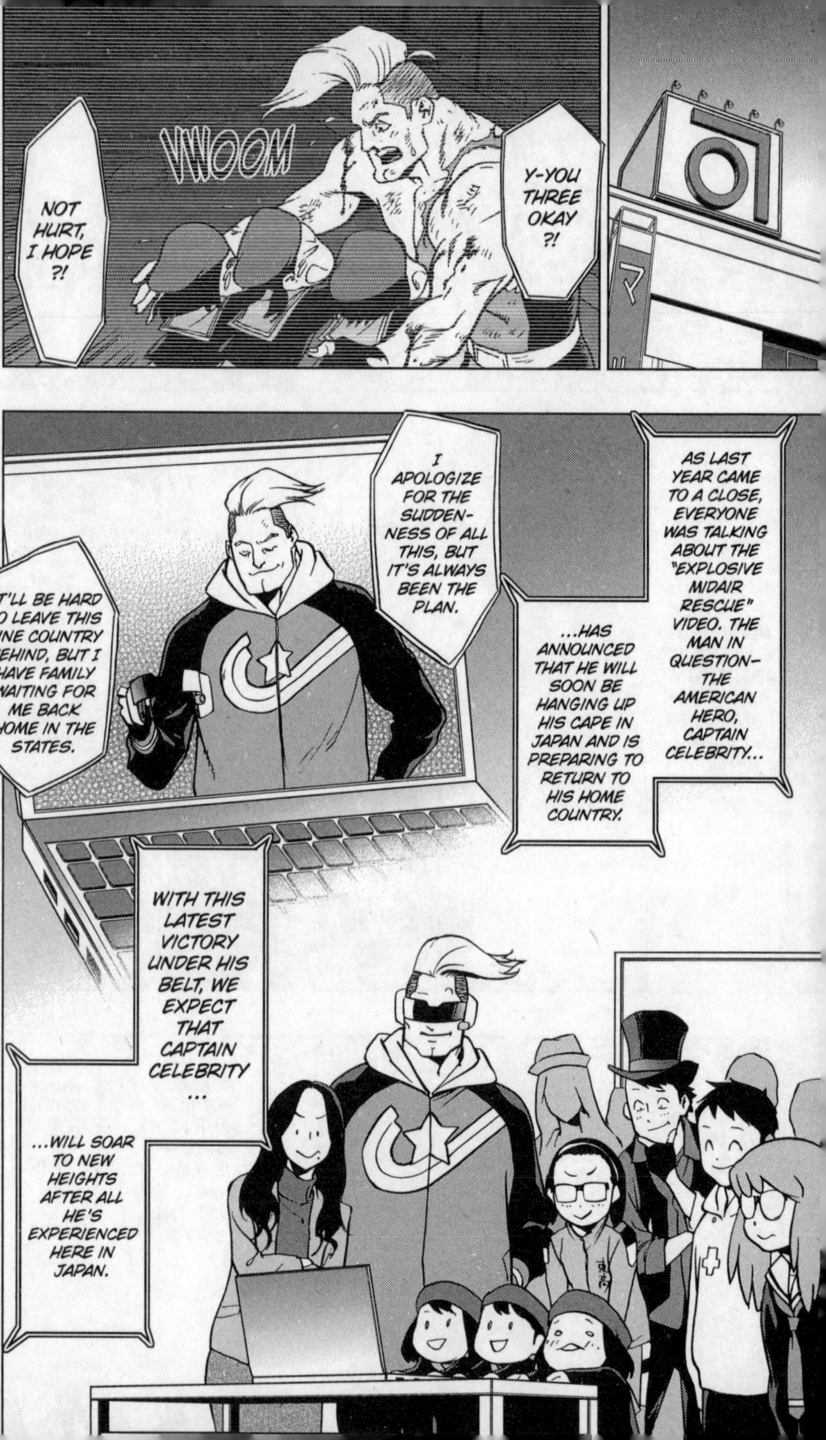
Y-YOU THREE OKAY ?!
VWOOM
NOT HURT, I HOPE ?!
AS LAST YEAR CAME TO A CLOSE, EVERYONE WAS TALKING ABOUT THE "EXPLOSIVE MIDAIR RESCUE" VIDEO. THE MAN IN QUESTION—THE AMERICAN HERO, CAPTAIN CELEBRITY...
...HAS ANNOUNCED THAT HE WILL SOON BE HANGING UP HIS CAPE IN JAPAN AND IS PREPARING TO RETURN TO HIS HOME COUNTRY.
I APOLOGIZE FOR THE SUDDENNESS OF ALL THIS, BUT IT'S ALWAYS BEEN THE PLAN.
IT'LL BE HARD TO LEAVE THIS FINE COUNTRY BEHIND, BUT I HAVE FAMILY WAITING FOR ME BACK HOME IN THE STATES.
WITH THIS LATEST VICTORY UNDER HIS BELT, WE EXPECT THAT CAPTAIN CELEBRITY...
...WILL SOAR TO NEW HEIGHTS AFTER ALL HE'S EXPERIENCED HERE IN JAPAN.

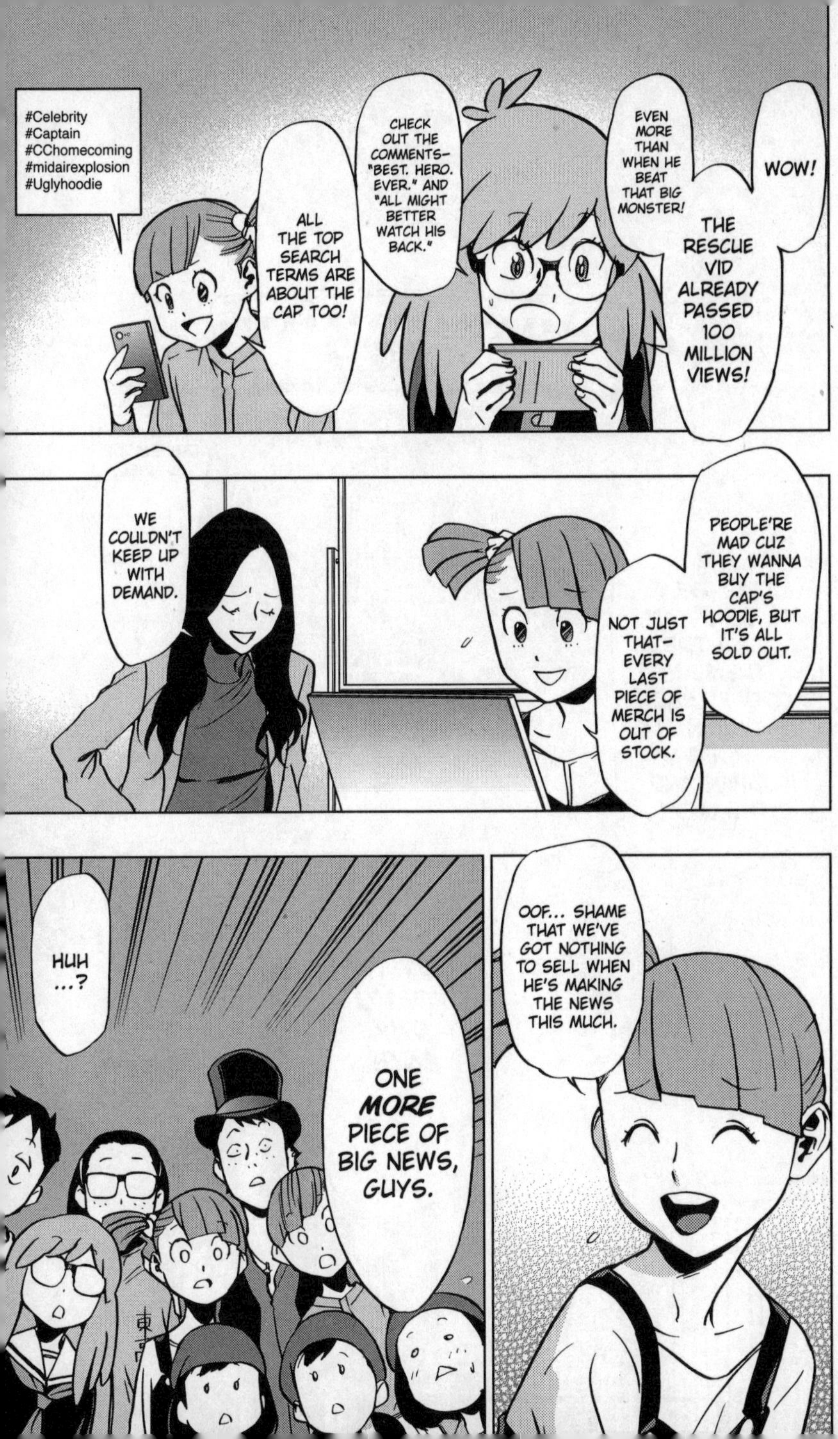
WOW!
THE RESCUE VID ALREADY PASSED 100 MILLION VIEWS!
EVEN MORE THAN WHEN HE BEAT THAT BIG MONSTER!
CHECK OUT THE COMMENTS— "BEST. HERO. EVER." AND "ALL MIGHT BETTER WATCH HIS BACK."
ALL THE TOP SEARCH TERMS ARE ABOUT THE CAP TOO!
#Celebrity #Captain #CChomecoming #midairexplosion #Uglyhoodie
PEOPLE'RE MAD CUZ THEY WANNA BUY THE CAP'S HOODIE, BUT IT'S ALL SOLD OUT.
NOT JUST THAT— EVERY LAST PIECE OF MERCH IS OUT OF STOCK.
WE COULDN'T KEEP UP WITH DEMAND.
OOF... SHAME THAT WE'VE GOT NOTHING TO SELL WHEN HE'S MAKING THE NEWS THIS MUCH.
ONE *MORE* PIECE OF BIG NEWS, GUYS.
HUH ...?

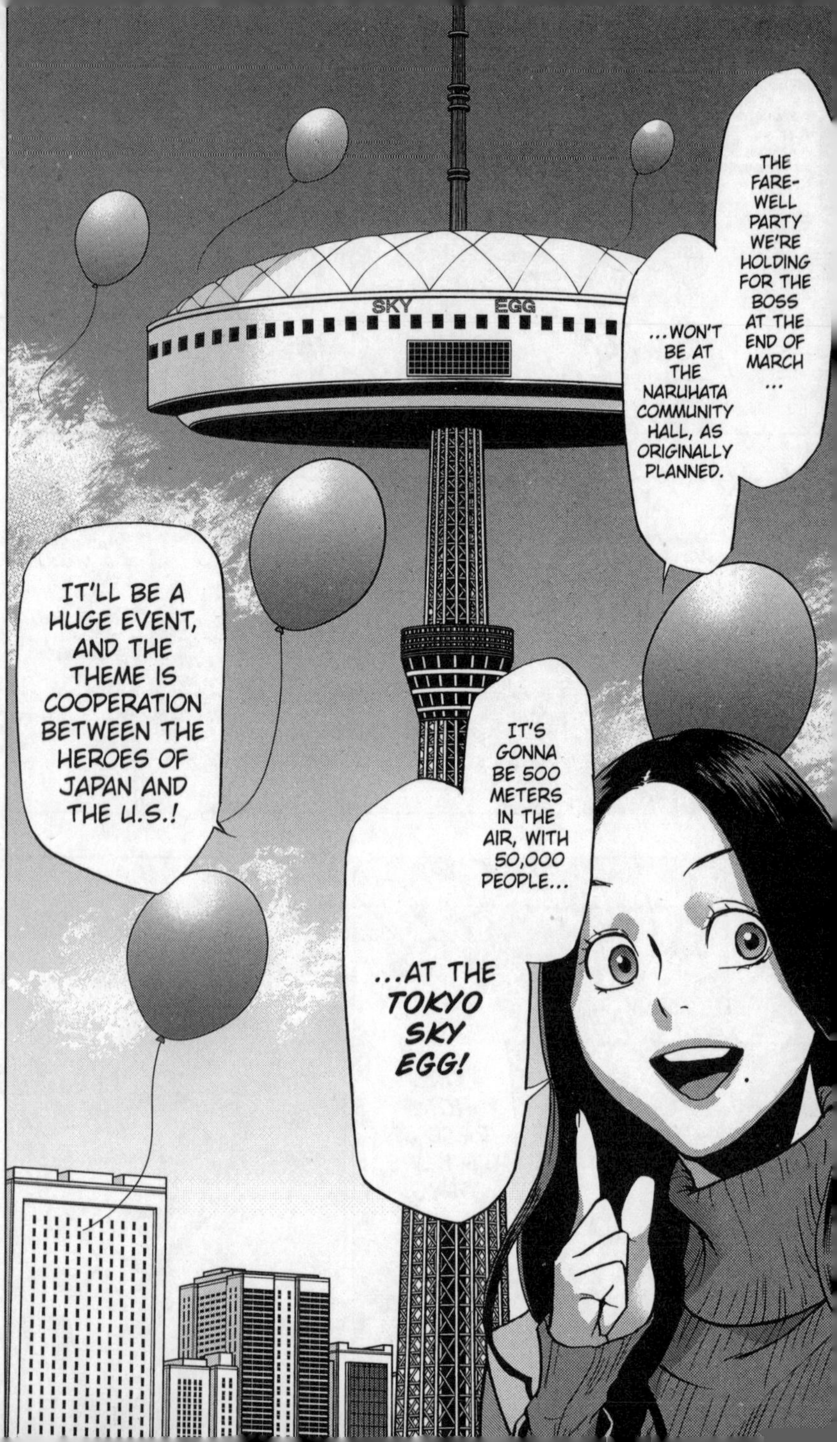
SKY EGG
THE FAREWELL PARTY WE'RE HOLDING FOR THE BOSS AT THE END OF MARCH...
...WON'T BE AT THE NARUHATA COMMUNITY HALL, AS ORIGINALLY PLANNED.
IT'S GONNA BE 500 METERS IN THE AIR, WITH 50,000 PEOPLE...
...AT THE *TOKYO SKY EGG!*
IT'LL BE A HUGE EVENT, AND THE THEME IS COOPERATION BETWEEN THE HEROES OF JAPAN AND THE U.S.!

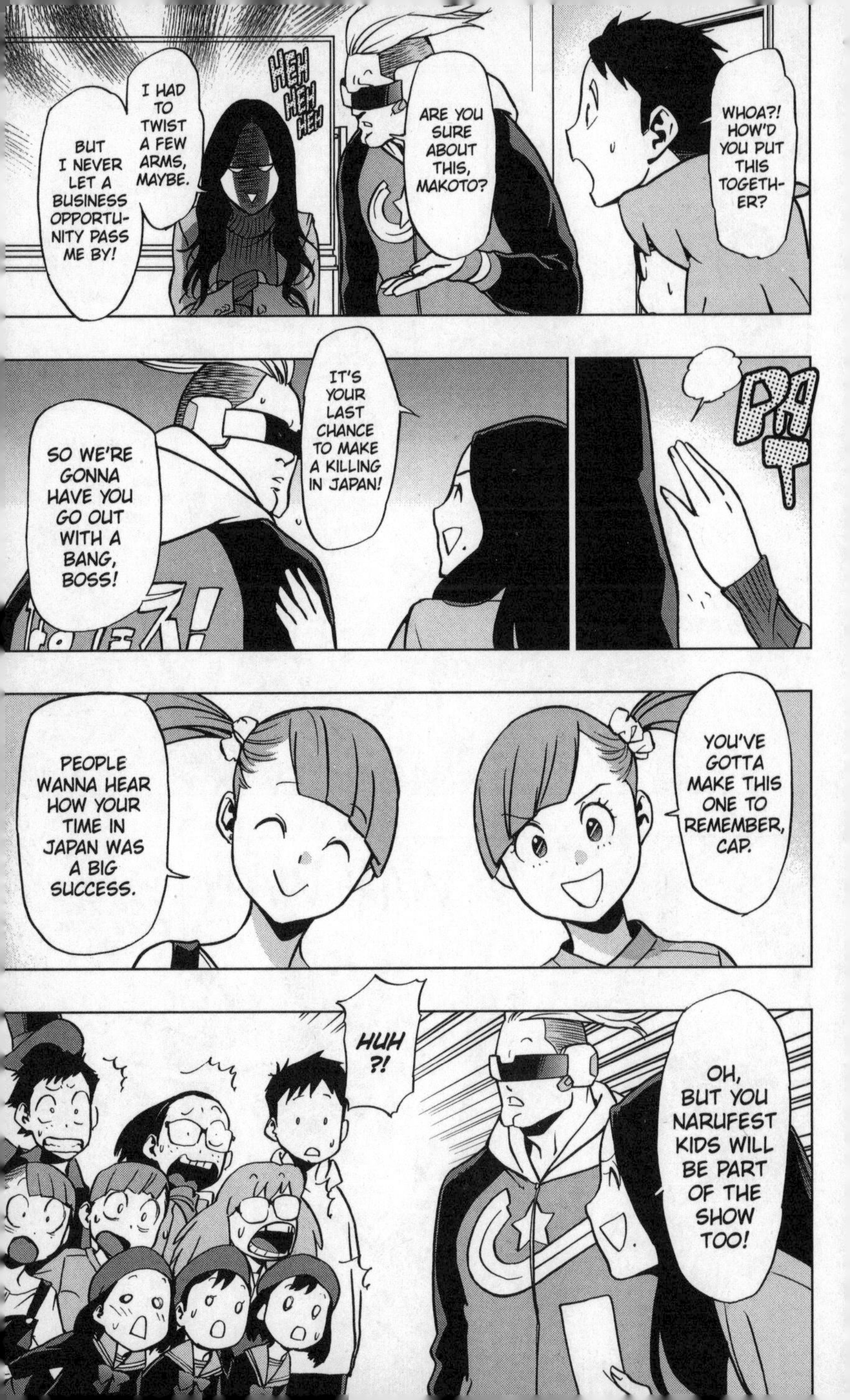
WHOA?! HOW'D YOU PUT THIS TOGETHER?
ARE YOU SURE ABOUT THIS, MAKOTO?
HEH HEH HEH
I HAD TO TWIST A FEW ARMS, MAYBE.
BUT I NEVER LET A BUSINESS OPPORTUNITY PASS ME BY!
PAT
IT'S YOUR LAST CHANCE TO MAKE A KILLING IN JAPAN!
SO WE'RE GONNA HAVE YOU GO OUT WITH A BANG, BOSS!
YOU'VE GOTTA MAKE THIS ONE TO REMEMBER, CAP.
PEOPLE WANNA HEAR HOW YOUR TIME IN JAPAN WAS A BIG SUCCESS.
OH, BUT YOU NARUFEST KIDS WILL BE PART OF THE SHOW TOO!
HUH?!

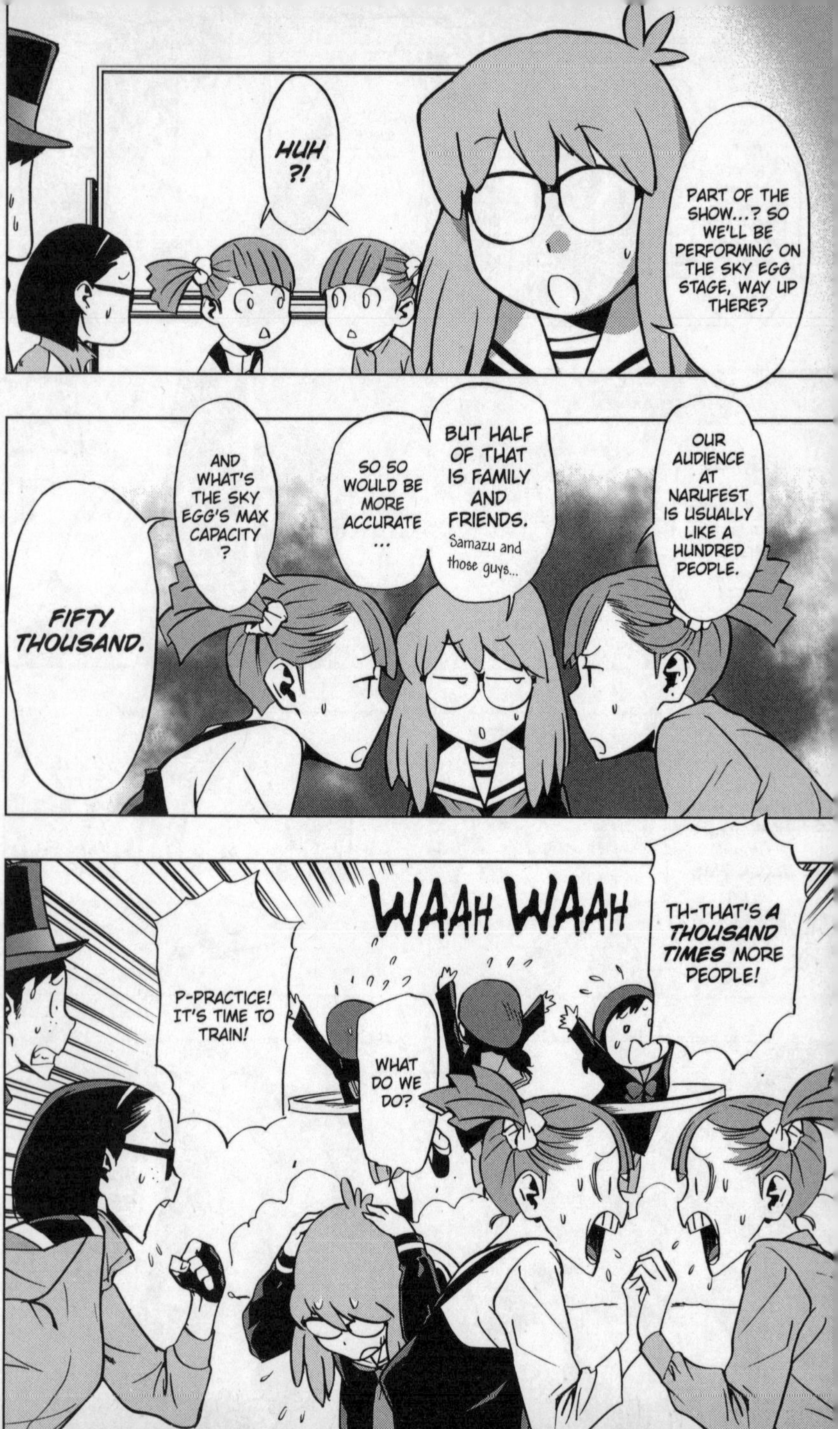
PART OF THE SHOW...? SO WE'LL BE PERFORMING ON THE SKY EGG STAGE, WAY UP THERE?
HUH ?!
OUR AUDIENCE AT NARUFEST IS USUALLY LIKE A HUNDRED PEOPLE.
BUT HALF OF THAT IS FAMILY AND FRIENDS.
Samazu and those guys...
SO 50 WOULD BE MORE ACCURATE...
AND WHAT'S THE SKY EGG'S MAX CAPACITY?
FIFTY THOUSAND.
TH-THAT'S A THOUSAND TIMES MORE PEOPLE!
WAAH WAAH
WHAT DO WE DO?
P-PRACTICE! IT'S TIME TO TRAIN!

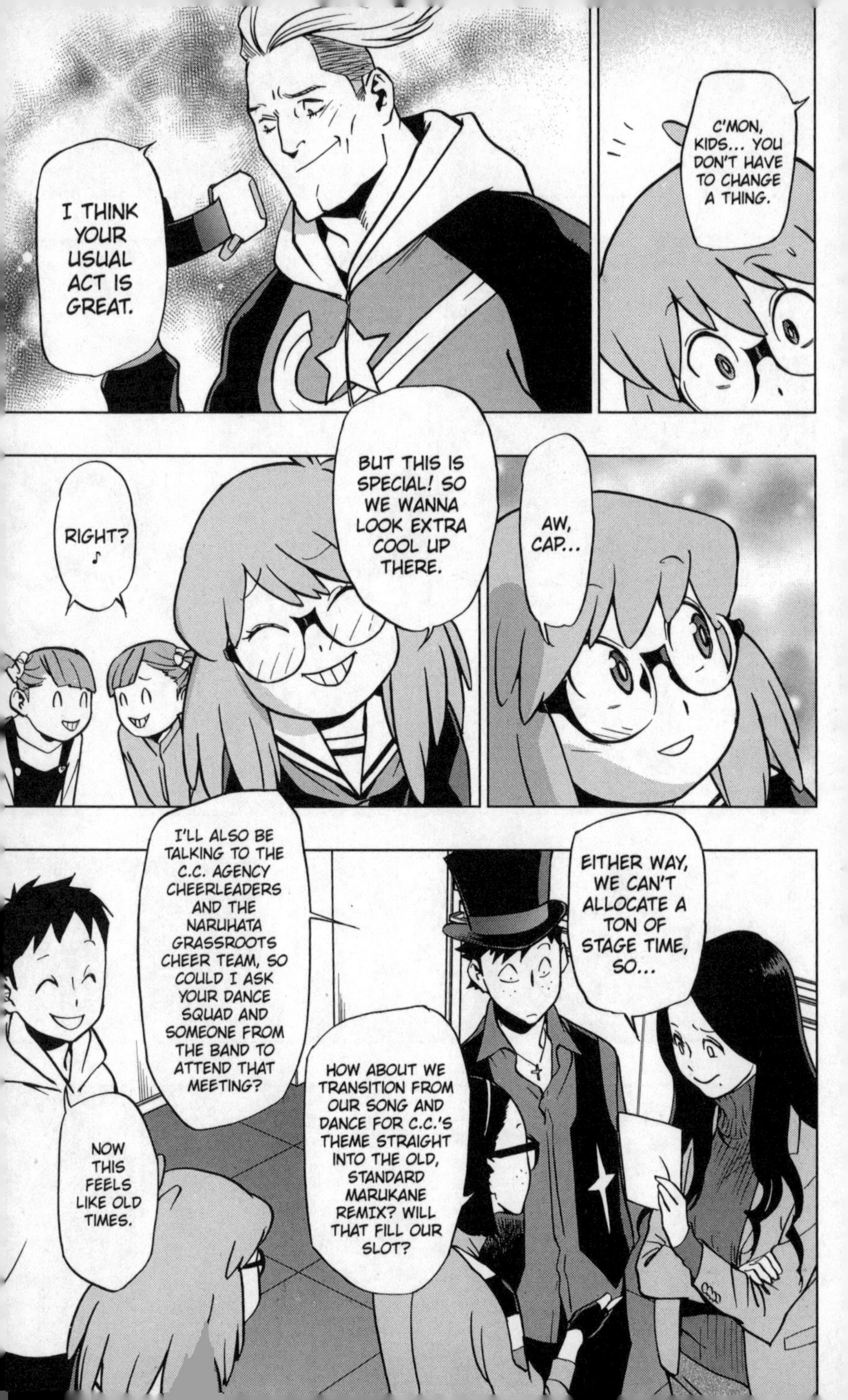
C'MON, KIDS... YOU DON'T HAVE TO CHANGE A THING.
I THINK YOUR USUAL ACT IS GREAT.
AW, CAP...
BUT THIS IS SPECIAL! SO WE WANNA LOOK EXTRA COOL UP THERE.
RIGHT? ♪
EITHER WAY, WE CAN'T ALLOCATE A TON OF STAGE TIME, SO...
HOW ABOUT WE TRANSITION FROM OUR SONG AND DANCE FOR C.C.'S THEME STRAIGHT INTO THE OLD, STANDARD MARUKANE REMIX? WILL THAT FILL OUR SLOT?
I'LL ALSO BE TALKING TO THE C.C. AGENCY CHEERLEADERS AND THE NARUHATA GRASSROOTS CHEER TEAM, SO COULD I ASK YOUR DANCE SQUAD AND SOMEONE FROM THE BAND TO ATTEND THAT MEETING?
NOW THIS FEELS LIKE OLD TIMES.

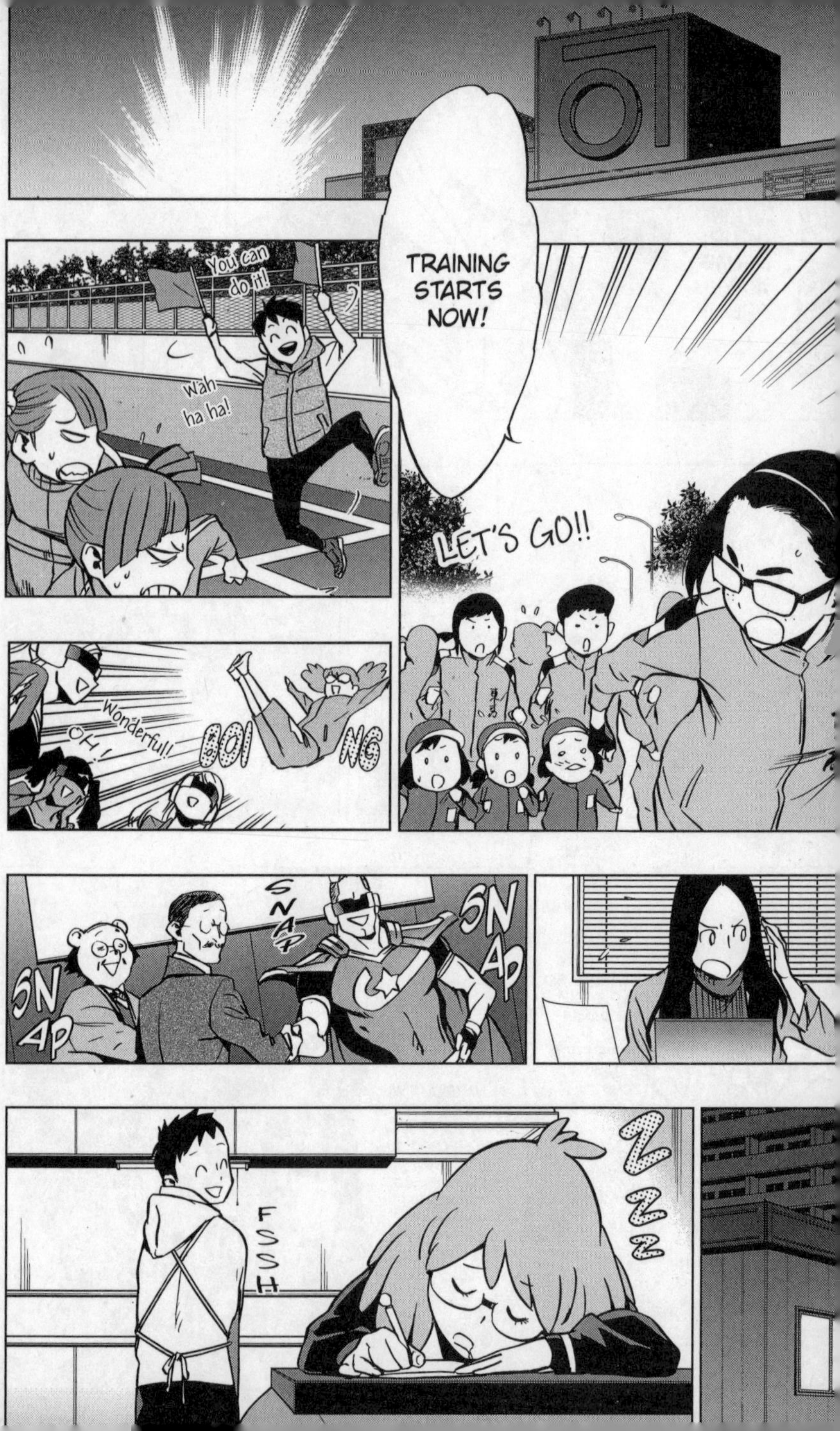
TRAINING STARTS NOW!
LET'S GO!!
You can do it!
Wah ha ha!
BOING
Wonderful!
OH!
SNAP
SNAP
SNAP
ZZZ
FSSH

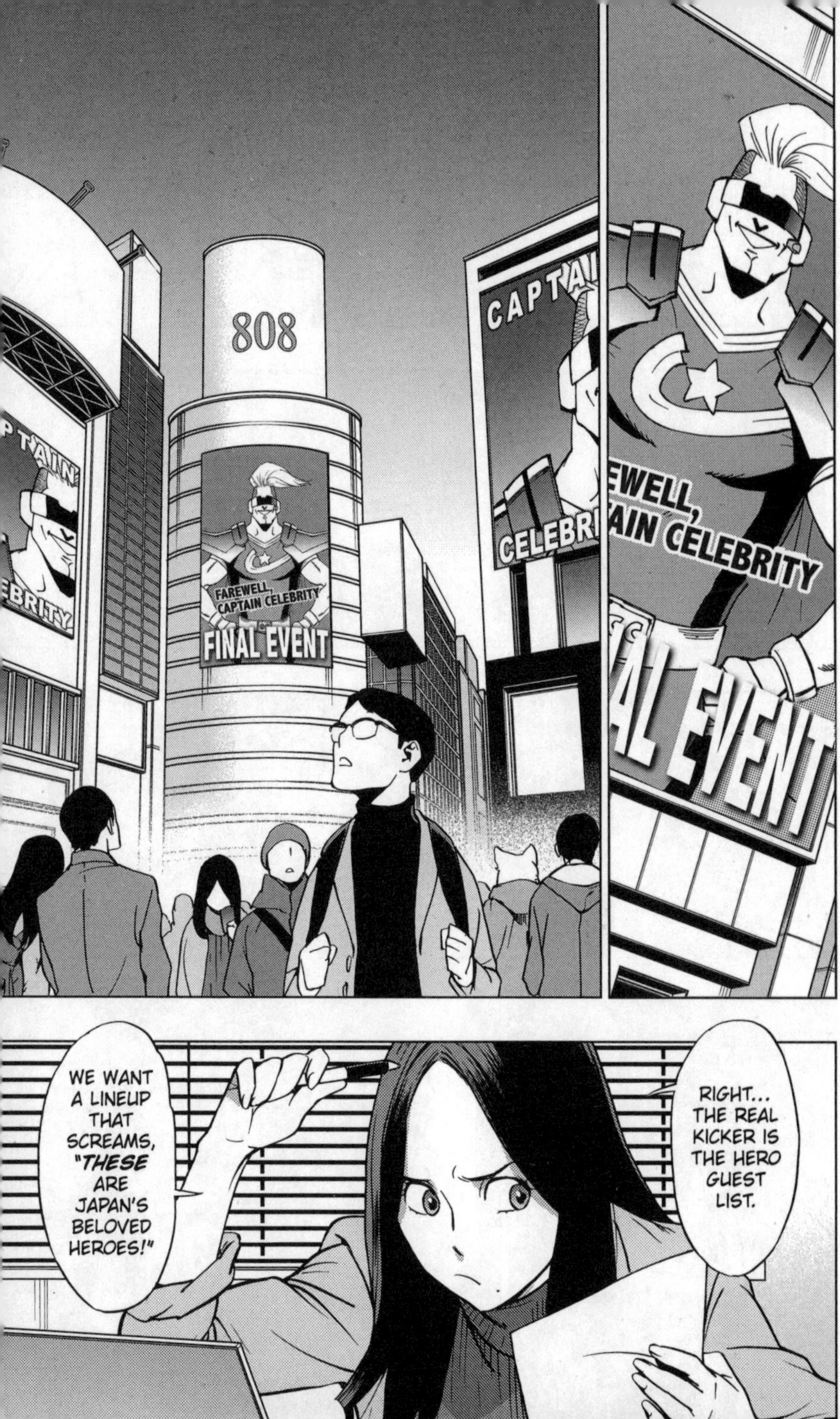
EWELL,
AIN CELEBRITY
AL EVENT
CAPTAI
CELEBRI
808
FAREWELL,
CAPTAIN CELEBRITY
FINAL EVENT
PTAIN
EBRITY
RIGHT... THE REAL KICKER IS THE HERO GUEST LIST.
WE WANT A LINEUP THAT SCREAMS, "*THESE* ARE JAPAN'S BELOVED HEROES!"

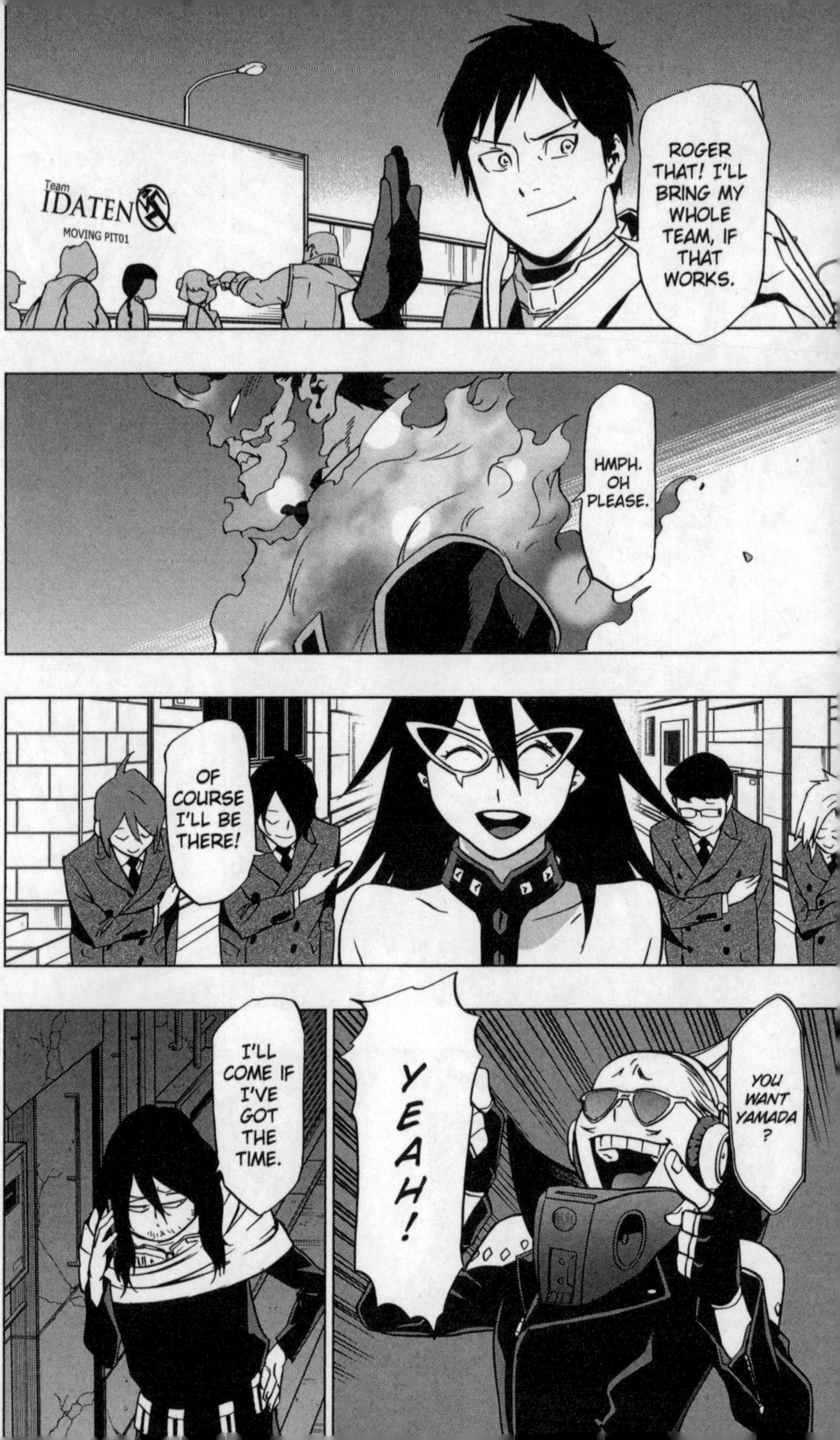
ROGER THAT! I'LL BRING MY WHOLE TEAM, IF THAT WORKS.
Team IDATEN
MOVING PIT01
HMPH. OH PLEASE.
OF COURSE I'LL BE THERE!
YOU WANT YAMADA?
YEAH!
I'LL COME IF I'VE GOT THE TIME.

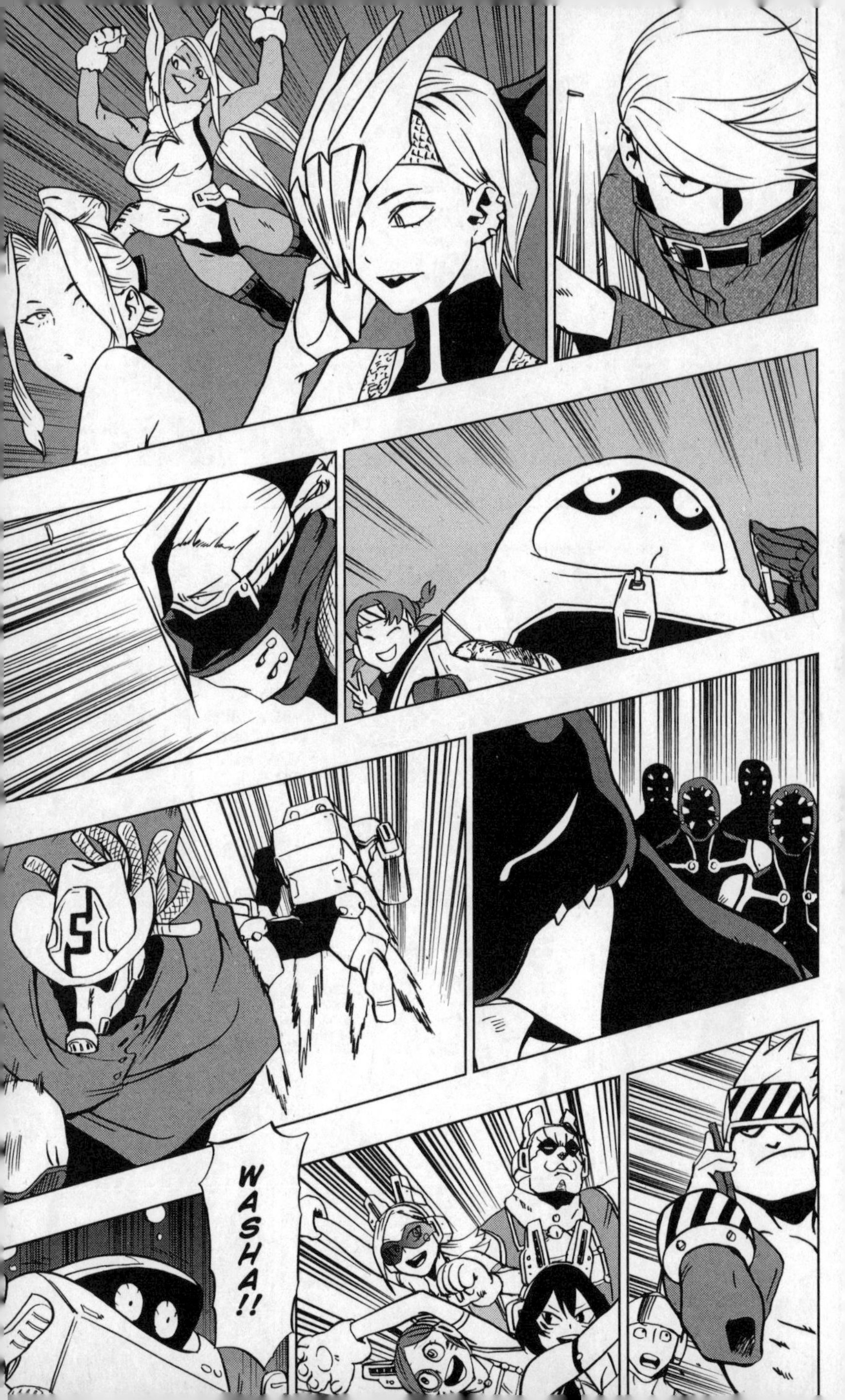
WASHA!!

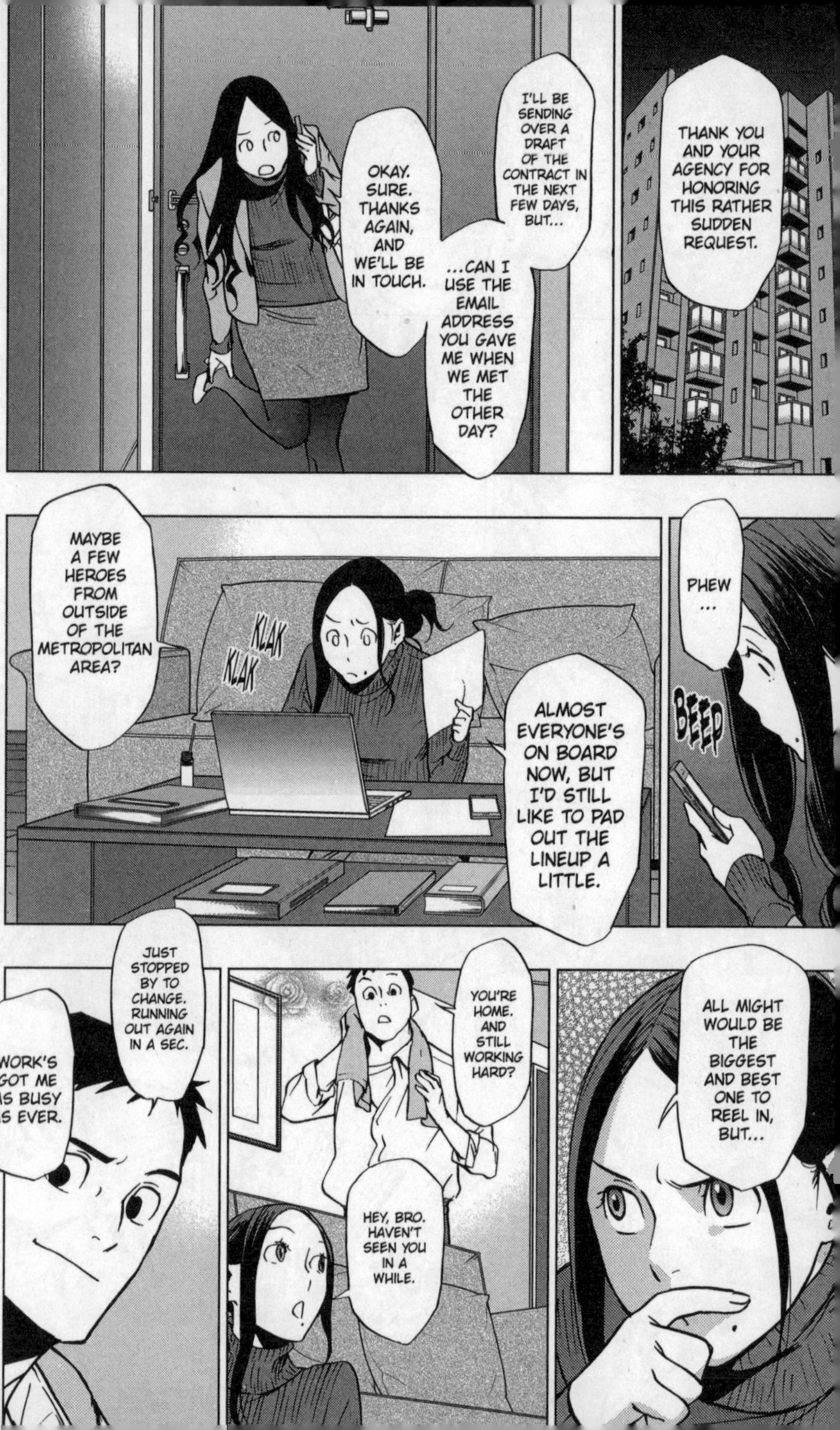
THANK YOU AND YOUR AGENCY FOR HONORING THIS RATHER SUDDEN REQUEST.
I'LL BE SENDING OVER A DRAFT OF THE CONTRACT IN THE NEXT FEW DAYS, BUT...
...CAN I USE THE EMAIL ADDRESS YOU GAVE ME WHEN WE MET THE OTHER DAY?
OKAY. SURE. THANKS AGAIN, AND WE'LL BE IN TOUCH.
PHEW...
BEEP
ALMOST EVERYONE'S ON BOARD NOW, BUT I'D STILL LIKE TO PAD OUT THE LINEUP A LITTLE.
MAYBE A FEW HEROES FROM OUTSIDE OF THE METROPOLITAN AREA?
KLAK KLAK
ALL MIGHT WOULD BE THE BIGGEST AND BEST ONE TO REEL IN, BUT...
YOU'RE HOME. AND STILL WORKING HARD?
HEY, BRO. HAVEN'T SEEN YOU IN A WHILE.
JUST STOPPED BY TO CHANGE. RUNNING OUT AGAIN IN A SEC.
WORK'S GOT ME AS BUSY AS EVER.

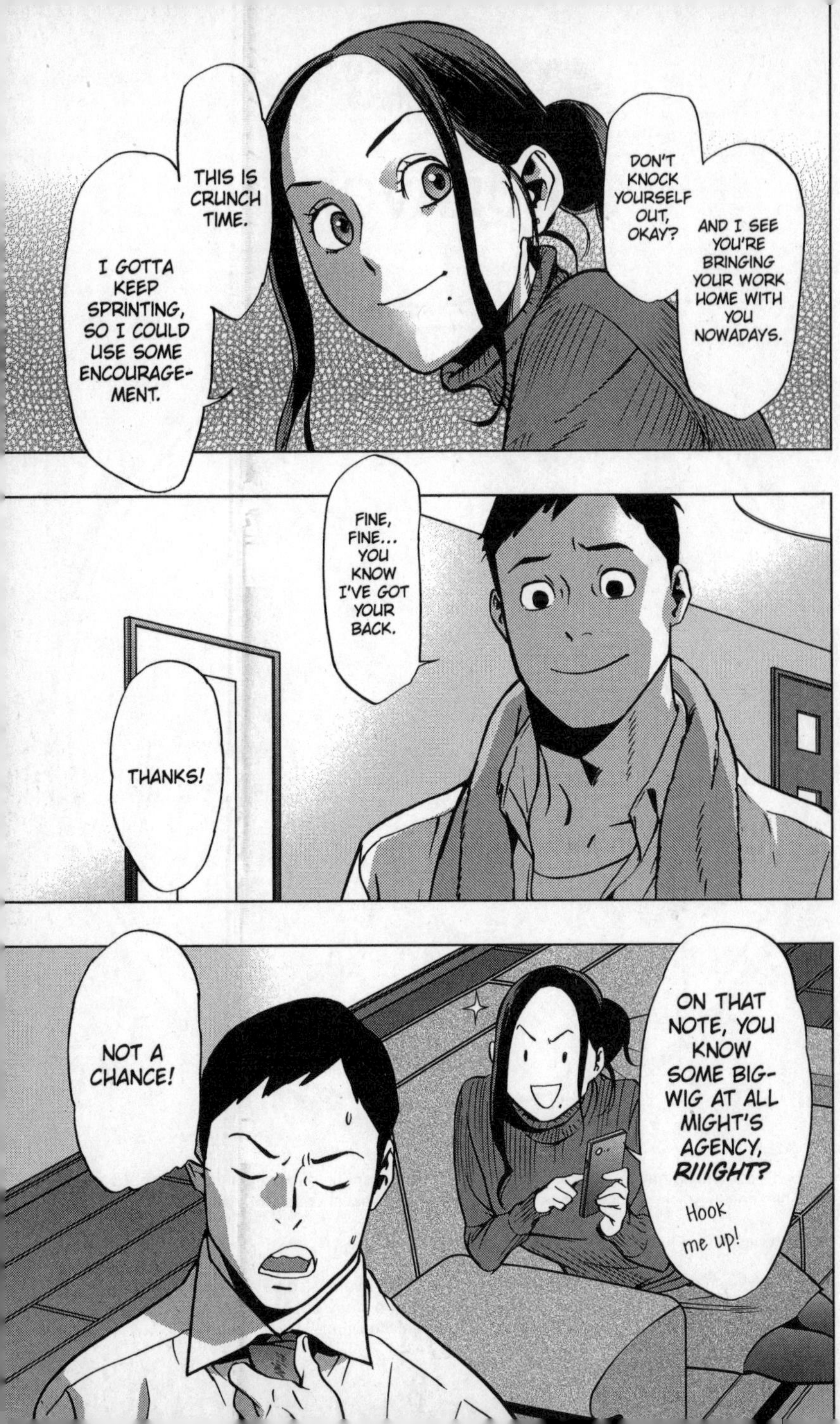
DON'T KNOCK YOURSELF OUT, OKAY?
AND I SEE YOU'RE BRINGING YOUR WORK HOME WITH YOU NOWADAYS.
THIS IS CRUNCH TIME.
I GOTTA KEEP SPRINTING, SO I COULD USE SOME ENCOURAGE-MENT.
FINE, FINE... YOU KNOW I'VE GOT YOUR BACK.
THANKS!
ON THAT NOTE, YOU KNOW SOME BIG-WIG AT ALL MIGHT'S AGENCY, *RIIIGHT?*
Hook me up!
NOT A CHANCE!

THE COLUMN

ENDEAVOR

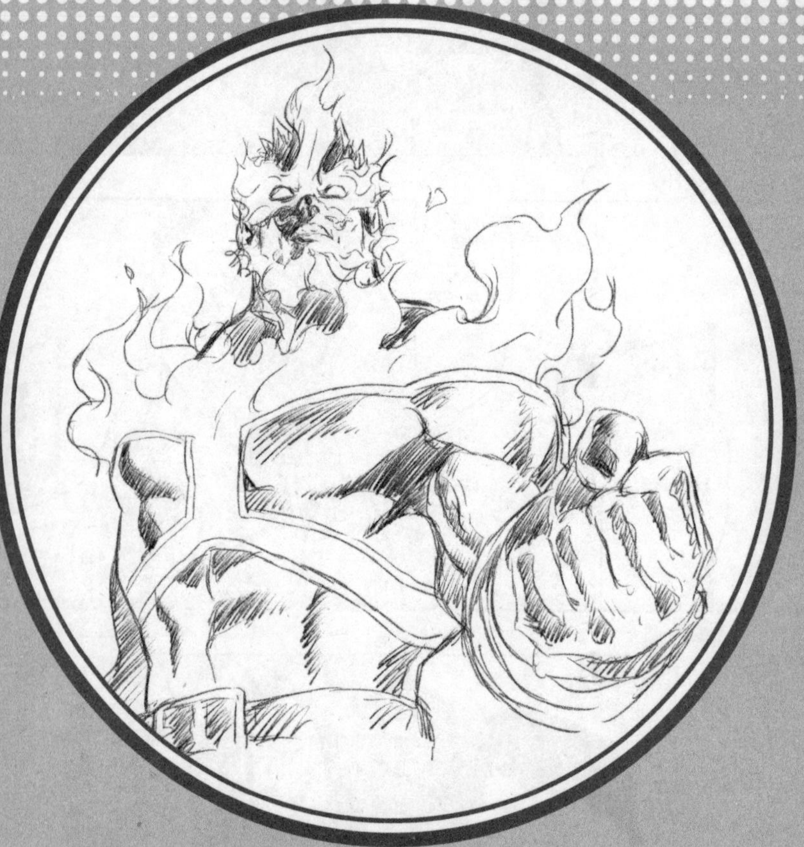

I think it's interesting how Endeavor plays the role of the scary hero. If we get the chance, I'd love to have him chase Koichi around and treat him like a villain. That sounds terrifying.

—Furuhashi

Endeavor doesn't seem like the type to enjoy appearing at events. It'd be a whole different sort of party if he showed up. Not that anyone asked, but while trying to figure out how to digitally create the texture on his flames, I resorted to copy-pasting pictures of real-life clouds. Trade secret.

—Betten

Ep. 48 - Investigation Start! Steamy Romance Spotted?!

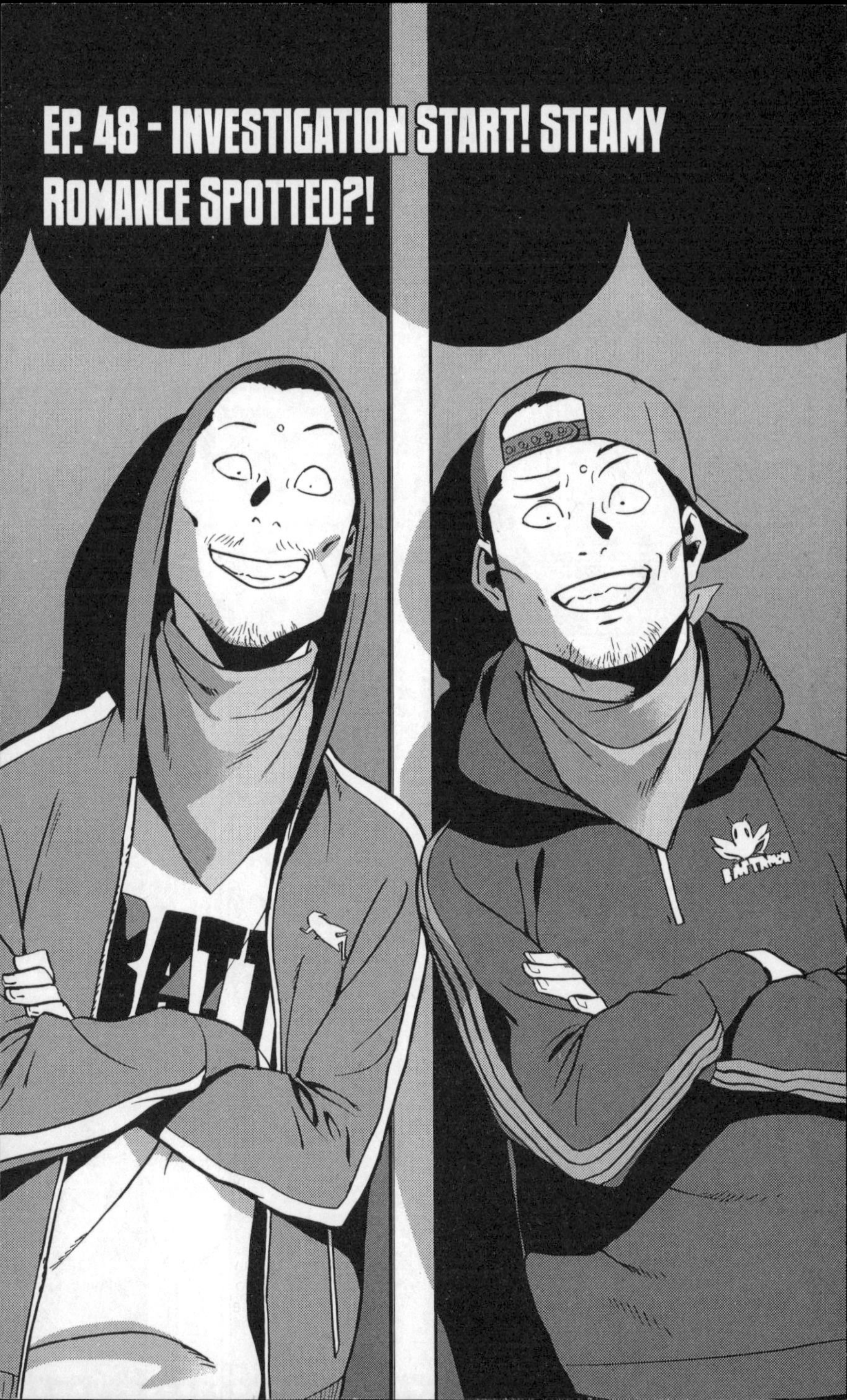

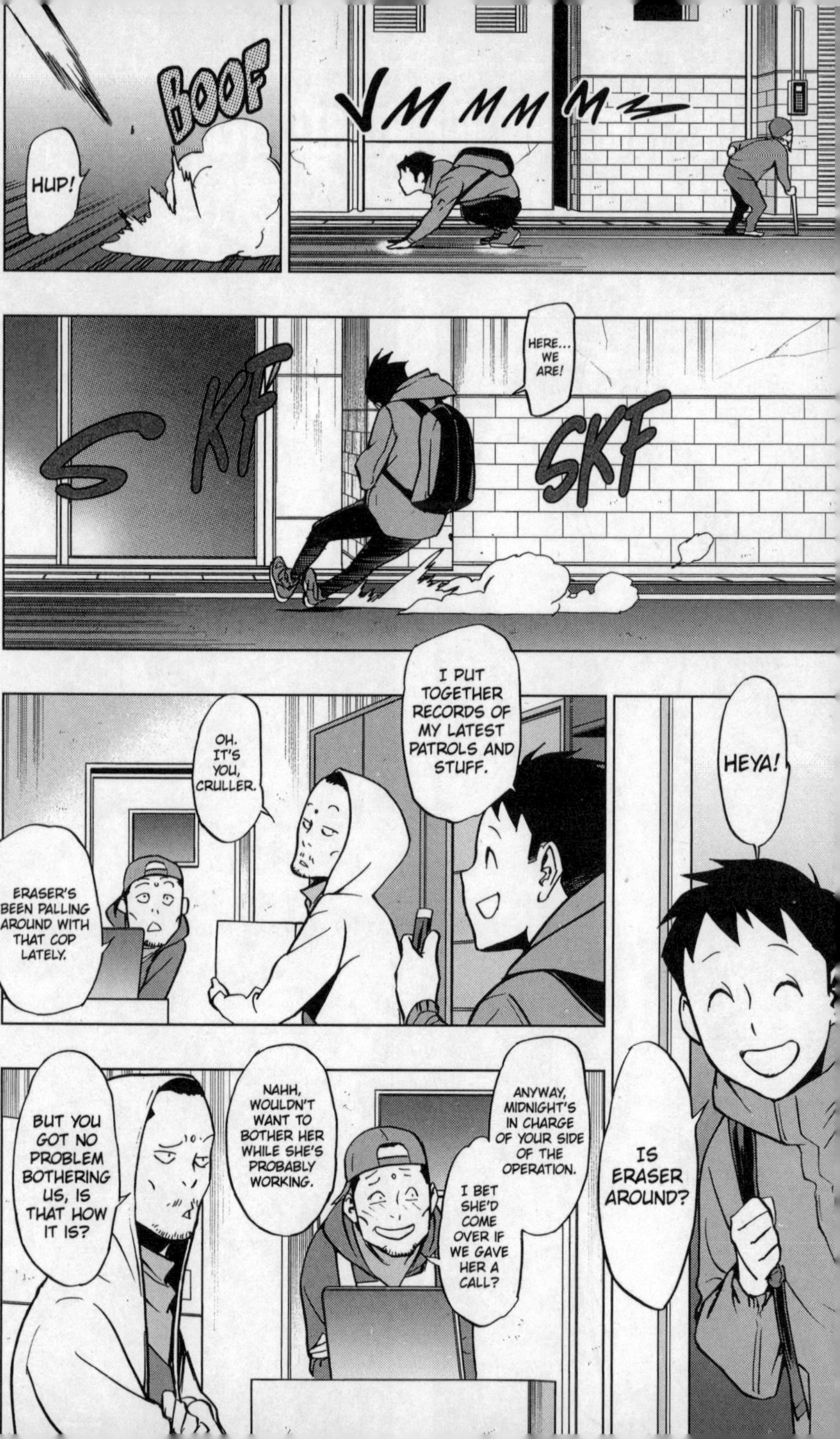
VMMMMM
BOOF
HUP!
HERE... WE ARE!
SKF
SKF
HEYA!
I PUT TOGETHER RECORDS OF MY LATEST PATROLS AND STUFF.
OH. IT'S YOU, CRULLER.
ERASER'S BEEN PALLING AROUND WITH THAT COP LATELY.
IS ERASER AROUND?
ANYWAY, MIDNIGHT'S IN CHARGE OF YOUR SIDE OF THE OPERATION.
I BET SHE'D COME OVER IF WE GAVE HER A CALL?
NAHH, WOULDN'T WANT TO BOTHER HER WHILE SHE'S PROBABLY WORKING.
BUT YOU GOT NO PROBLEM BOTHERING US, IS THAT HOW IT IS?

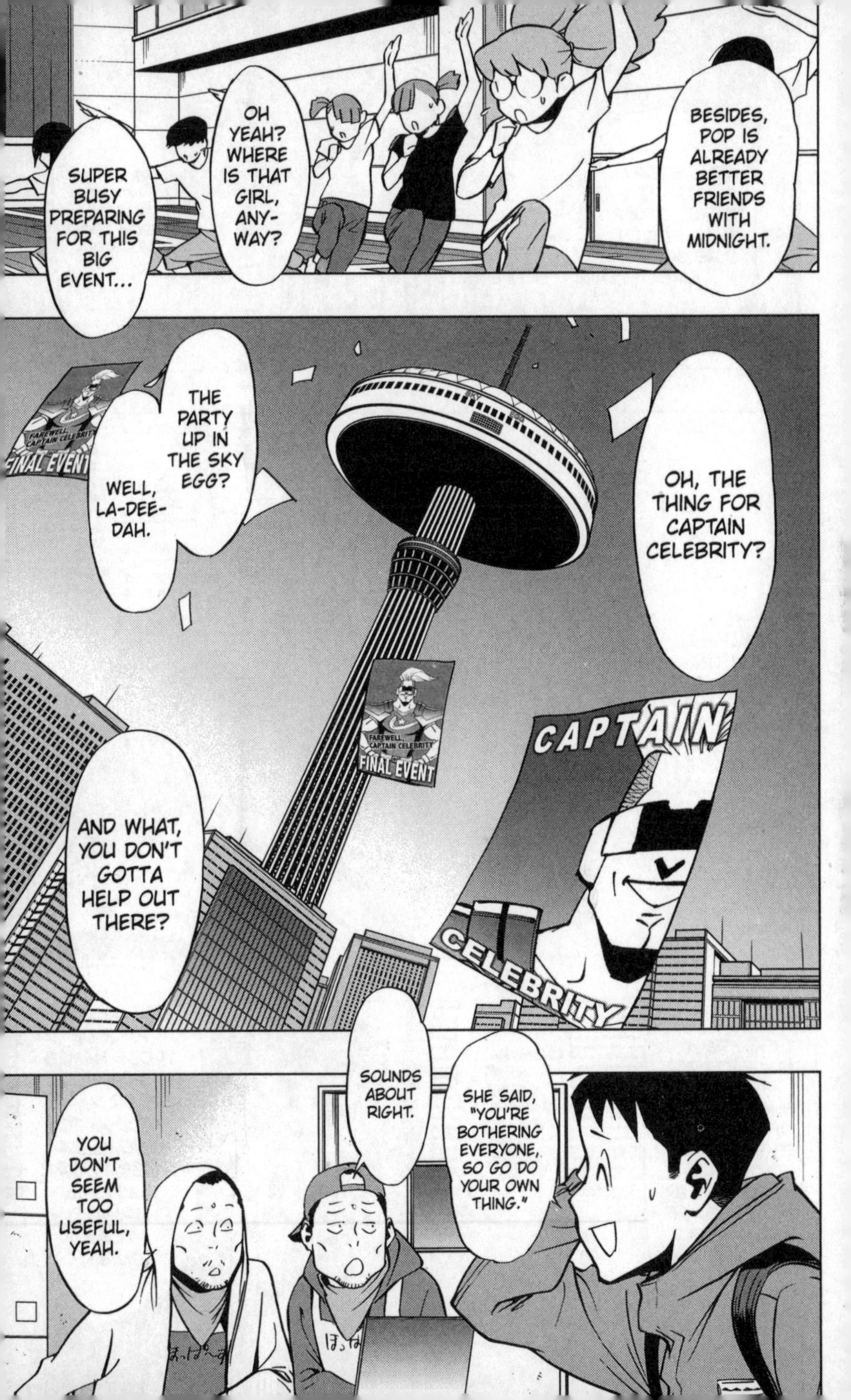
BESIDES, POP IS ALREADY BETTER FRIENDS WITH MIDNIGHT.
OH YEAH? WHERE IS THAT GIRL, ANYWAY?
SUPER BUSY PREPARING FOR THIS BIG EVENT...
OH, THE THING FOR CAPTAIN CELEBRITY?
THE PARTY UP IN THE SKY EGG?
WELL, LA-DEE-DAH.
FAREWELL, CAPTAIN CELEBRITY
FINAL EVENT
FAREWELL, CAPTAIN CELEBRITY
FINAL EVENT
CAPTAIN CELEBRITY
AND WHAT, YOU DON'T GOTTA HELP OUT THERE?
SHE SAID, "YOU'RE BOTHERING EVERYONE, SO GO DO YOUR OWN THING."
SOUNDS ABOUT RIGHT.
YOU DON'T SEEM TOO USEFUL, YEAH.

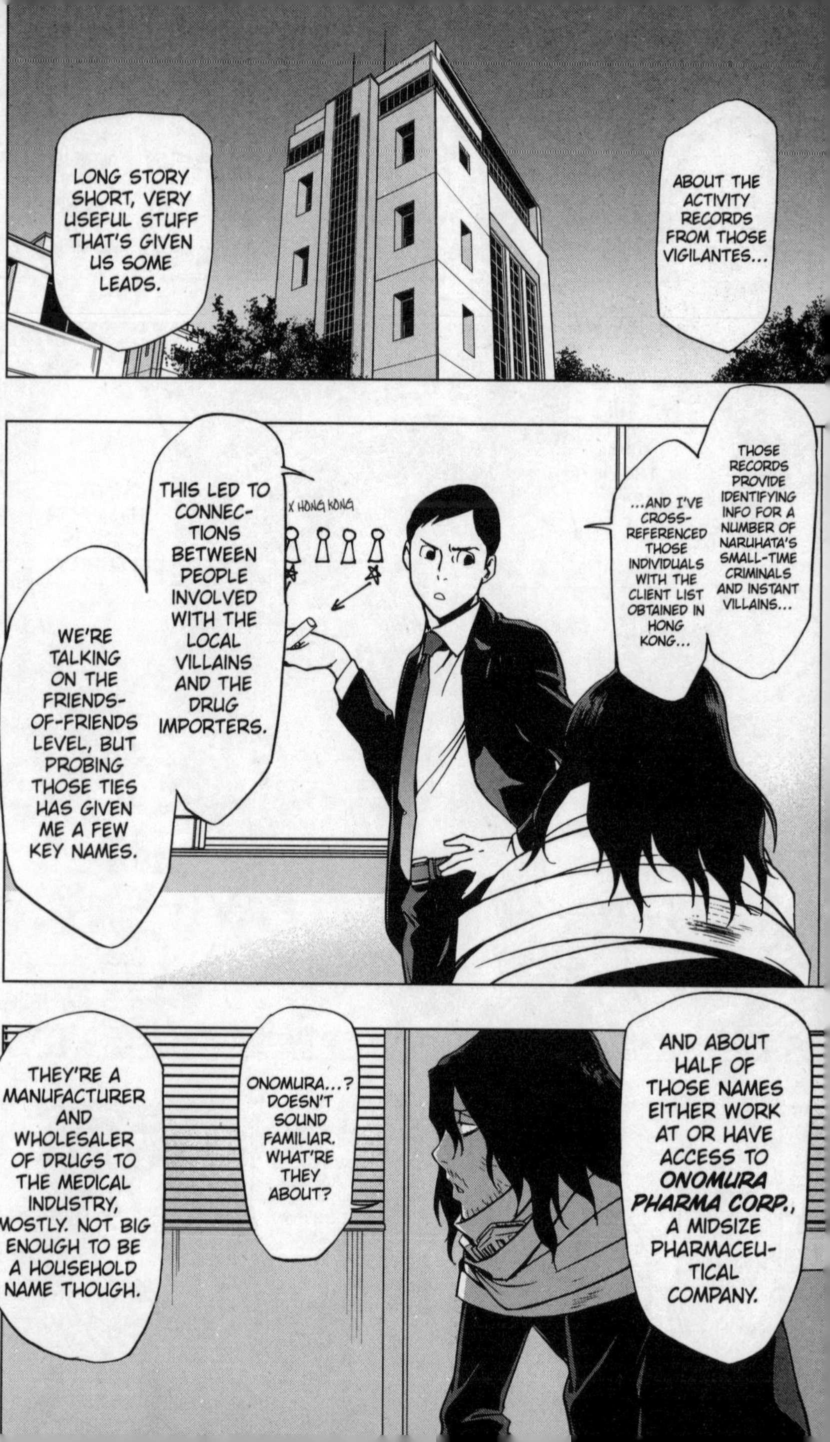
ABOUT THE ACTIVITY RECORDS FROM THOSE VIGILANTES...
LONG STORY SHORT, VERY USEFUL STUFF THAT'S GIVEN US SOME LEADS.
THOSE RECORDS PROVIDE IDENTIFYING INFO FOR A NUMBER OF NARUHATA'S SMALL-TIME CRIMINALS AND INSTANT VILLAINS...
...AND I'VE CROSS-REFERENCED THOSE INDIVIDUALS WITH THE CLIENT LIST OBTAINED IN HONG KONG...
X HONG KONG
THIS LED TO CONNEC-TIONS BETWEEN PEOPLE INVOLVED WITH THE LOCAL VILLAINS AND THE DRUG IMPORTERS.
WE'RE TALKING ON THE FRIENDS-OF-FRIENDS LEVEL, BUT PROBING THOSE TIES HAS GIVEN ME A FEW KEY NAMES.
AND ABOUT HALF OF THOSE NAMES EITHER WORK AT OR HAVE ACCESS TO *ONOMURA PHARMA CORP.*, A MIDSIZE PHARMACEU-TICAL COMPANY.
ONOMURA...? DOESN'T SOUND FAMILIAR. WHAT'RE THEY ABOUT?
THEY'RE A MANUFACTURER AND WHOLESALER OF DRUGS TO THE MEDICAL INDUSTRY, MOSTLY. NOT BIG ENOUGH TO BE A HOUSEHOLD NAME THOUGH.

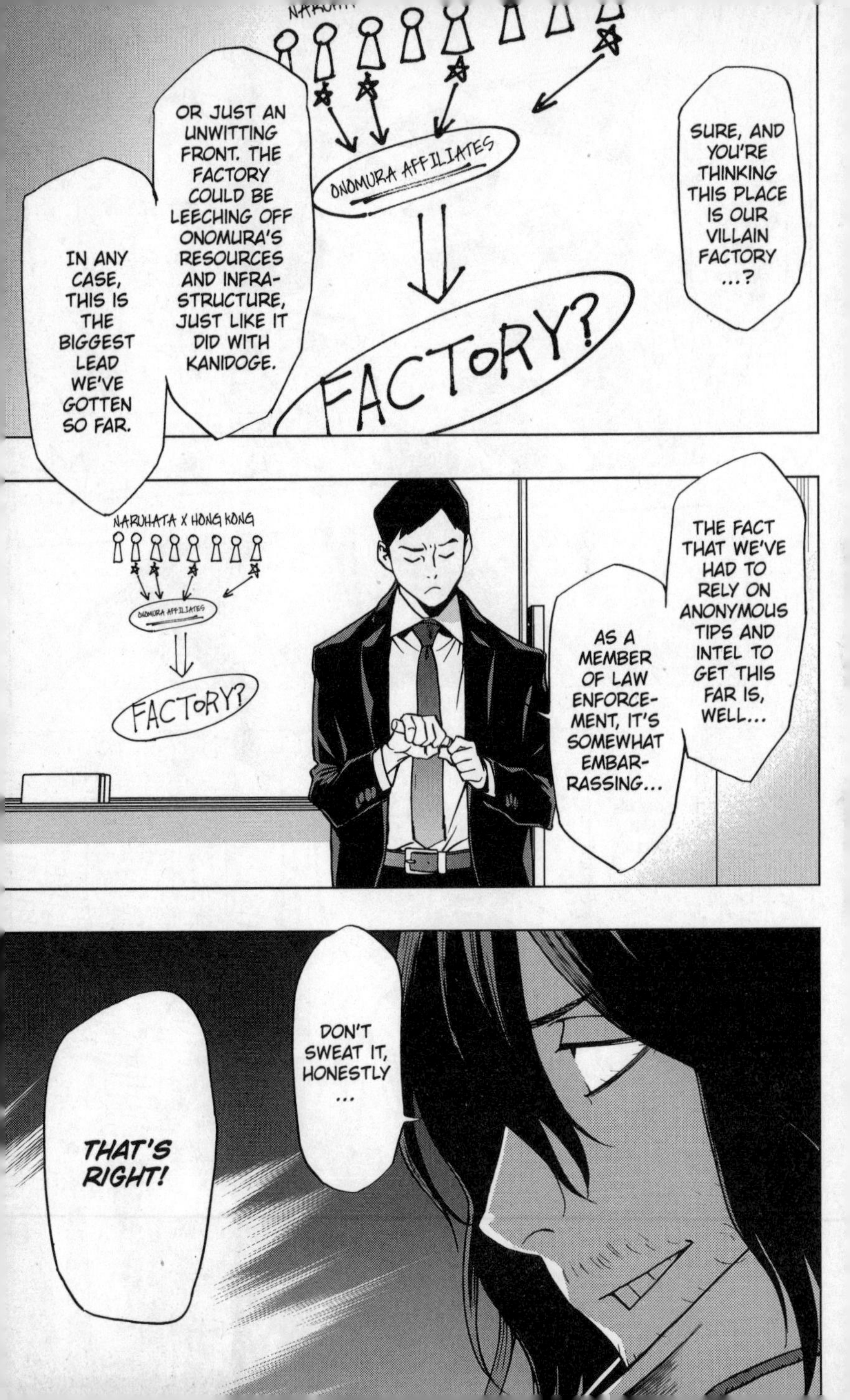
SURE, AND YOU'RE THINKING THIS PLACE IS OUR VILLAIN FACTORY ...?
ONOMURA AFFILIATES
FACTORY?
OR JUST AN UNWITTING FRONT. THE FACTORY COULD BE LEECHING OFF ONOMURA'S RESOURCES AND INFRA-STRUCTURE, JUST LIKE IT DID WITH KANIDOGE.
IN ANY CASE, THIS IS THE BIGGEST LEAD WE'VE GOTTEN SO FAR.
THE FACT THAT WE'VE HAD TO RELY ON ANONYMOUS TIPS AND INTEL TO GET THIS FAR IS, WELL...
AS A MEMBER OF LAW ENFORCE-MENT, IT'S SOMEWHAT EMBAR-RASSING...
NARUHATA X HONG KONG
ONOMURA AFFILIATES
FACTORY?
DON'T SWEAT IT, HONESTLY ...
THAT'S RIGHT!

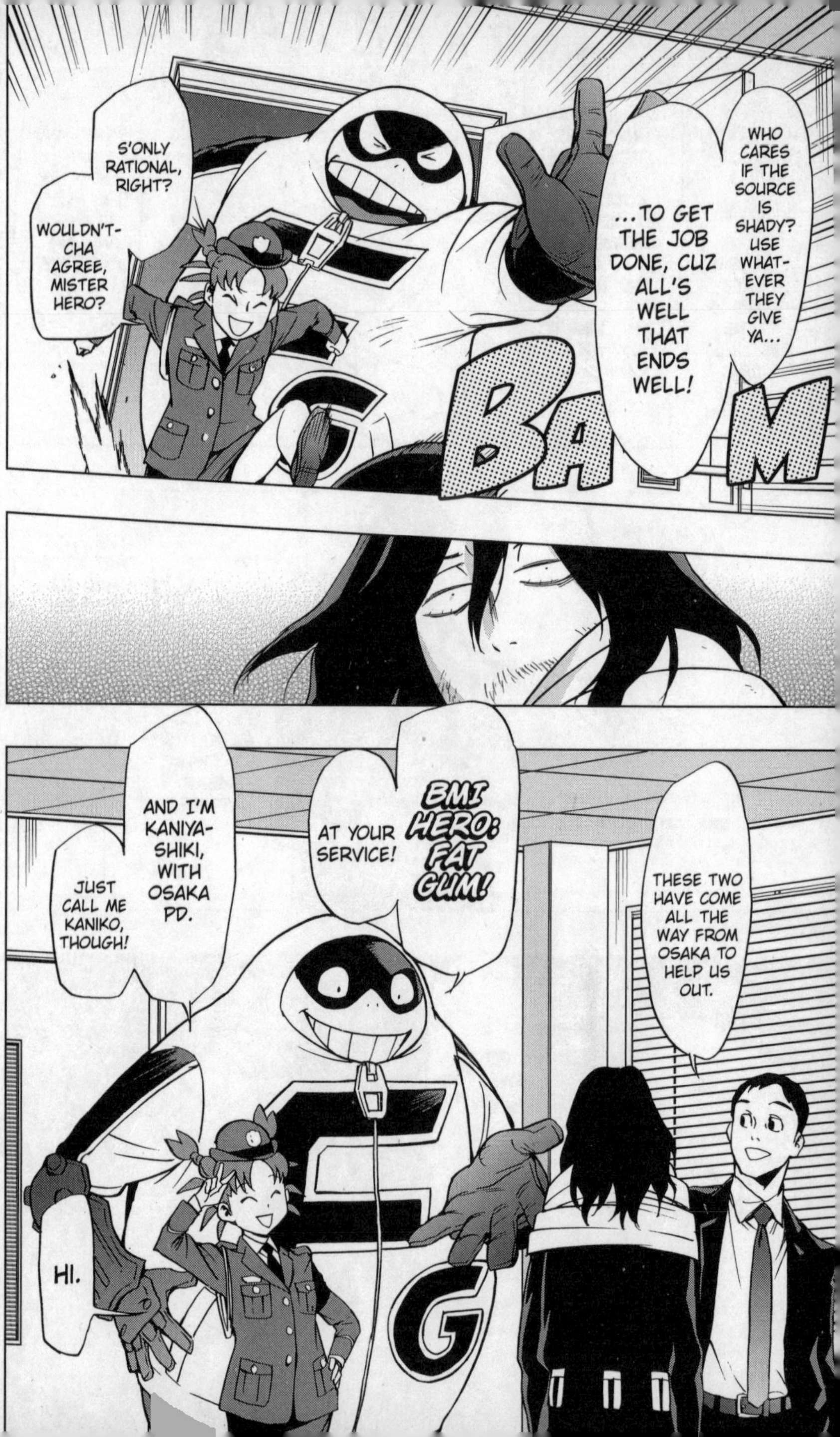
WHO CARES IF THE SOURCE IS SHADY? USE WHATEVER THEY GIVE YA...
...TO GET THE JOB DONE, CUZ ALL'S WELL THAT ENDS WELL!
BAM
S'ONLY RATIONAL, RIGHT?
WOULDN'T-CHA AGREE, MISTER HERO?
THESE TWO HAVE COME ALL THE WAY FROM OSAKA TO HELP US OUT.
BMI HERO: FAT GUM!
AT YOUR SERVICE!
AND I'M KANIYASHIKI, WITH OSAKA PD.
JUST CALL ME KANIKO, THOUGH!
HI.

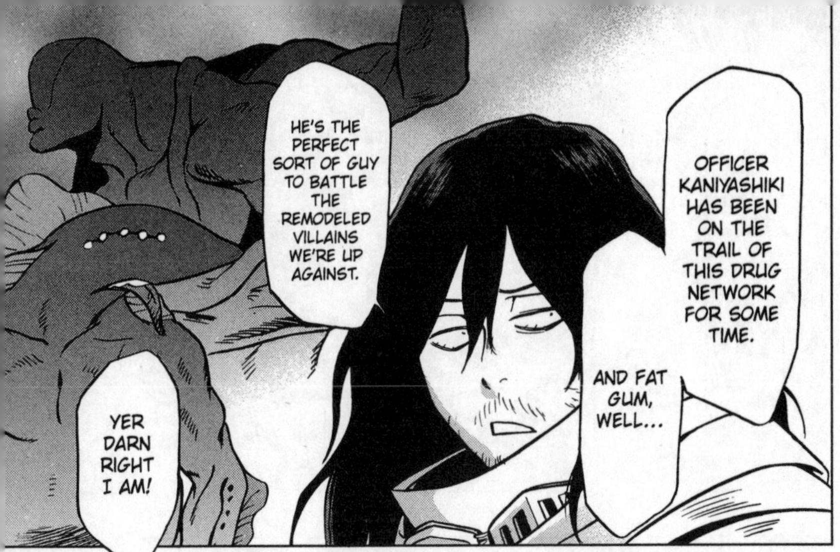
OFFICER KANIYASHIKI HAS BEEN ON THE TRAIL OF THIS DRUG NETWORK FOR SOME TIME.
AND FAT GUM, WELL...
HE'S THE PERFECT SORT OF GUY TO BATTLE THE REMODELED VILLAINS WE'RE UP AGAINST.
YER DARN RIGHT I AM!
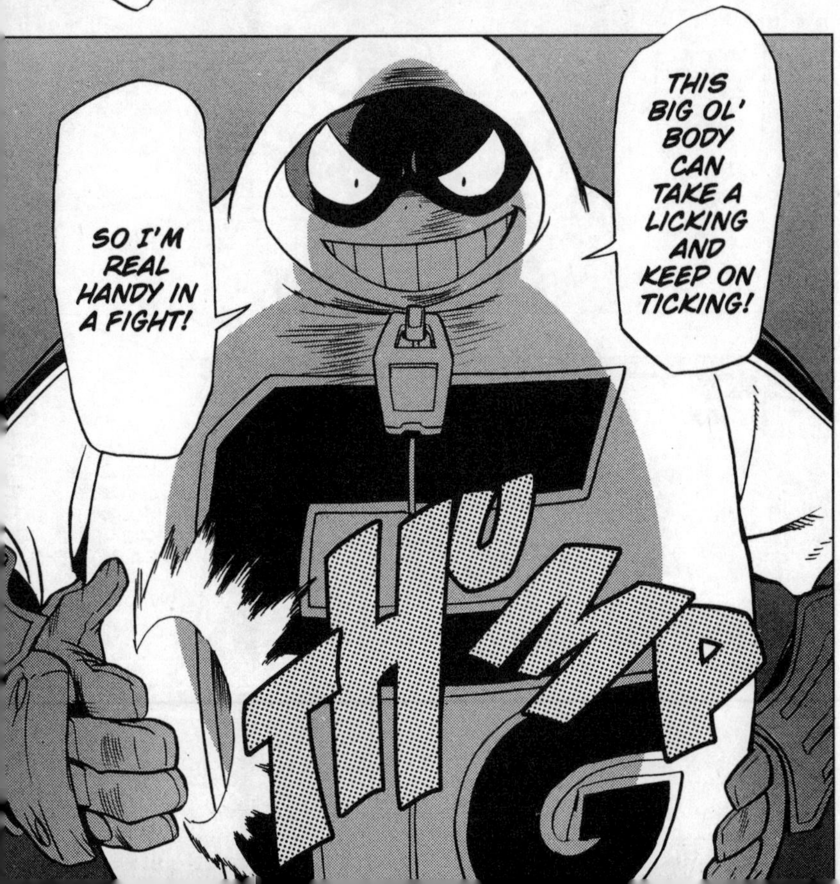
THIS BIG OL' BODY CAN TAKE A LICKING AND KEEP ON TICKING!
SO I'M REAL HANDY IN A FIGHT!
THUMP

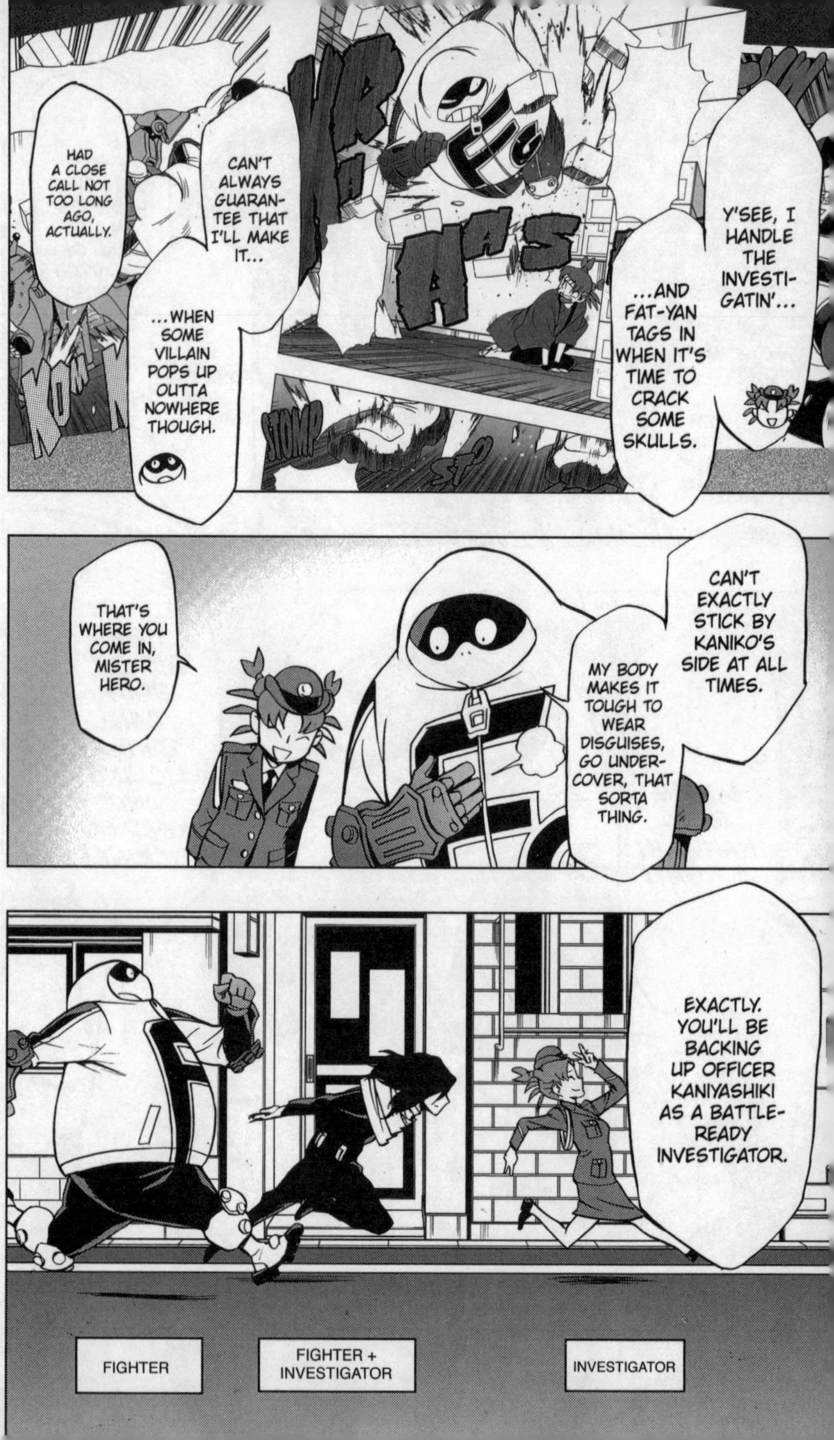
Y'SEE, I HANDLE THE INVESTI-GATIN'...
...AND FAT-YAN TAGS IN WHEN IT'S TIME TO CRACK SOME SKULLS.
STOMP
CAN'T ALWAYS GUARAN-TEE THAT I'LL MAKE IT...
...WHEN SOME VILLAIN POPS UP OUTTA NOWHERE THOUGH.
HAD A CLOSE CALL NOT TOO LONG AGO, ACTUALLY.
CAN'T EXACTLY STICK BY KANIKO'S SIDE AT ALL TIMES.
MY BODY MAKES IT TOUGH TO WEAR DISGUISES, GO UNDER-COVER, THAT SORTA THING.
THAT'S WHERE YOU COME IN, MISTER HERO.
EXACTLY. YOU'LL BE BACKING UP OFFICER KANIYASHIKI AS A BATTLE-READY INVESTIGATOR.
INVESTIGATOR
FIGHTER + INVESTIGATOR
FIGHTER

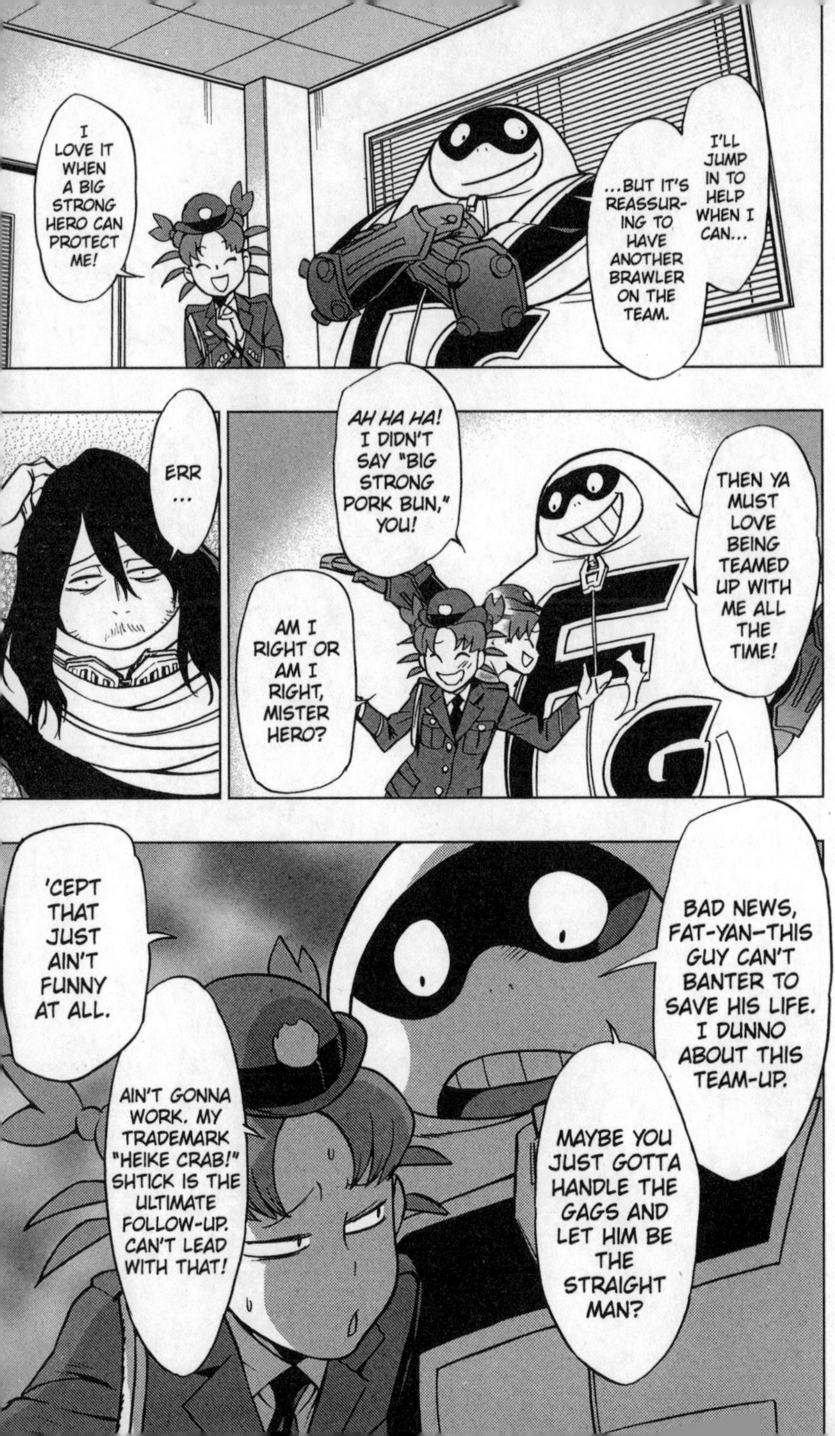
I'LL JUMP IN TO HELP WHEN I CAN...
...BUT IT'S REASSURING TO HAVE ANOTHER BRAWLER ON THE TEAM.
I LOVE IT WHEN A BIG STRONG HERO CAN PROTECT ME!
THEN YA MUST LOVE BEING TEAMED UP WITH ME ALL THE TIME!
AH HA HA! I DIDN'T SAY "BIG STRONG PORK BUN," YOU!
AM I RIGHT OR AM I RIGHT, MISTER HERO?
ERR ...
BAD NEWS, FAT-YAN—THIS GUY CAN'T BANTER TO SAVE HIS LIFE. I DUNNO ABOUT THIS TEAM-UP.
'CEPT THAT JUST AIN'T FUNNY AT ALL.
MAYBE YOU JUST GOTTA HANDLE THE GAGS AND LET HIM BE THE STRAIGHT MAN?
AIN'T GONNA WORK. MY TRADEMARK "HEIKE CRAB!" SHTICK IS THE ULTIMATE FOLLOW-UP. CAN'T LEAD WITH THAT!

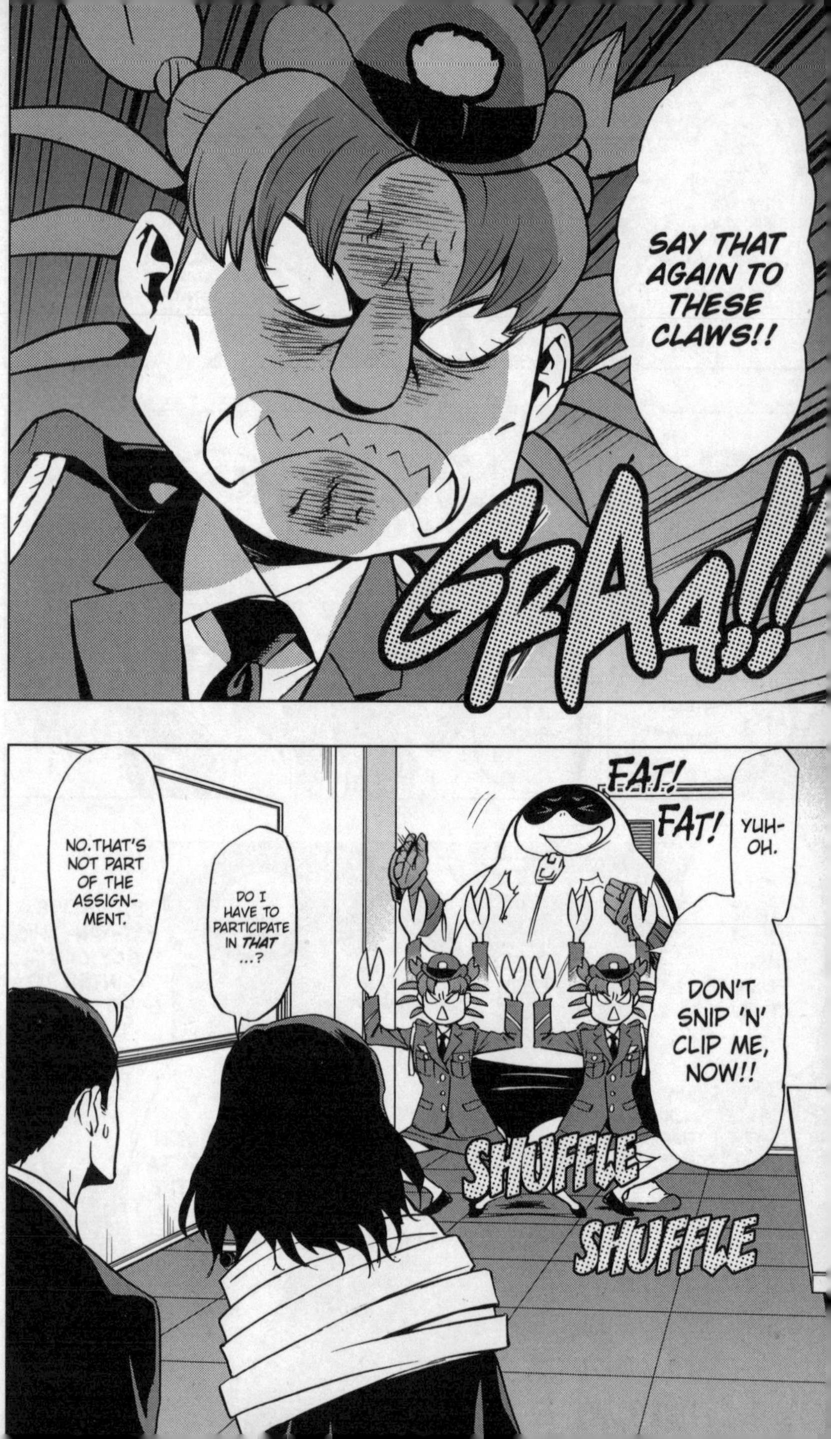
SAY THAT AGAIN TO THESE CLAWS!!
GRAA!!
FAT!
FAT!
YUH-OH.
DON'T SNIP 'N' CLIP ME, NOW!!
SHUFFLE
SHUFFLE
DO I HAVE TO PARTICIPATE IN *THAT* ...?
NO. THAT'S NOT PART OF THE ASSIGNMENT.

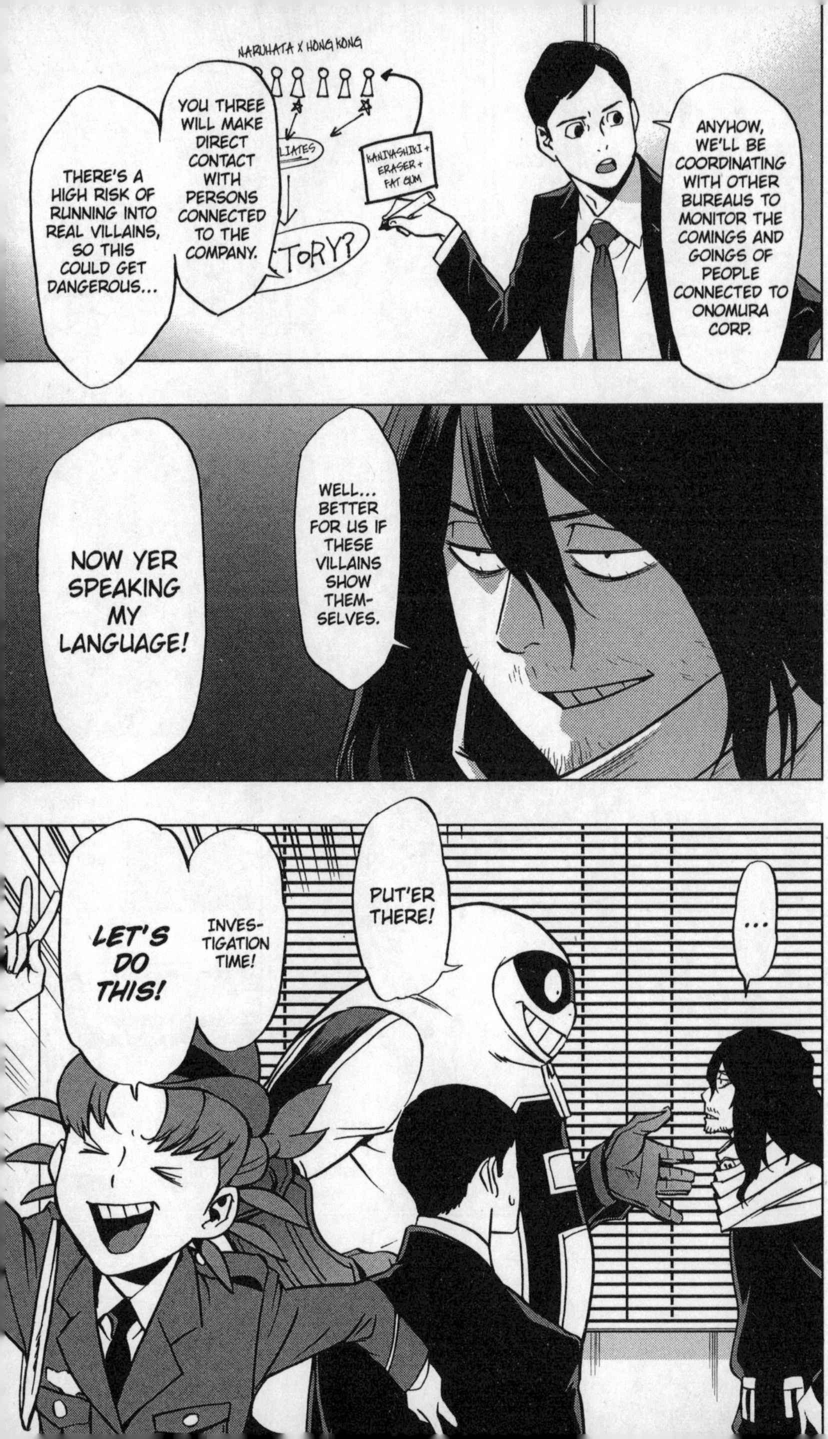
NARUHATA X HONG KONG
KANIYASHIKI + ERASER + FAT GUM
ANYHOW, WE'LL BE COORDINATING WITH OTHER BUREAUS TO MONITOR THE COMINGS AND GOINGS OF PEOPLE CONNECTED TO ONOMURA CORP.
YOU THREE WILL MAKE DIRECT CONTACT WITH PERSONS CONNECTED TO THE COMPANY.
THERE'S A HIGH RISK OF RUNNING INTO REAL VILLAINS, SO THIS COULD GET DANGEROUS...
WELL... BETTER FOR US IF THESE VILLAINS SHOW THEM-SELVES.
NOW YER SPEAKING MY LANGUAGE!
...
PUT'ER THERE!
INVES-TIGATION TIME!
LET'S DO THIS!

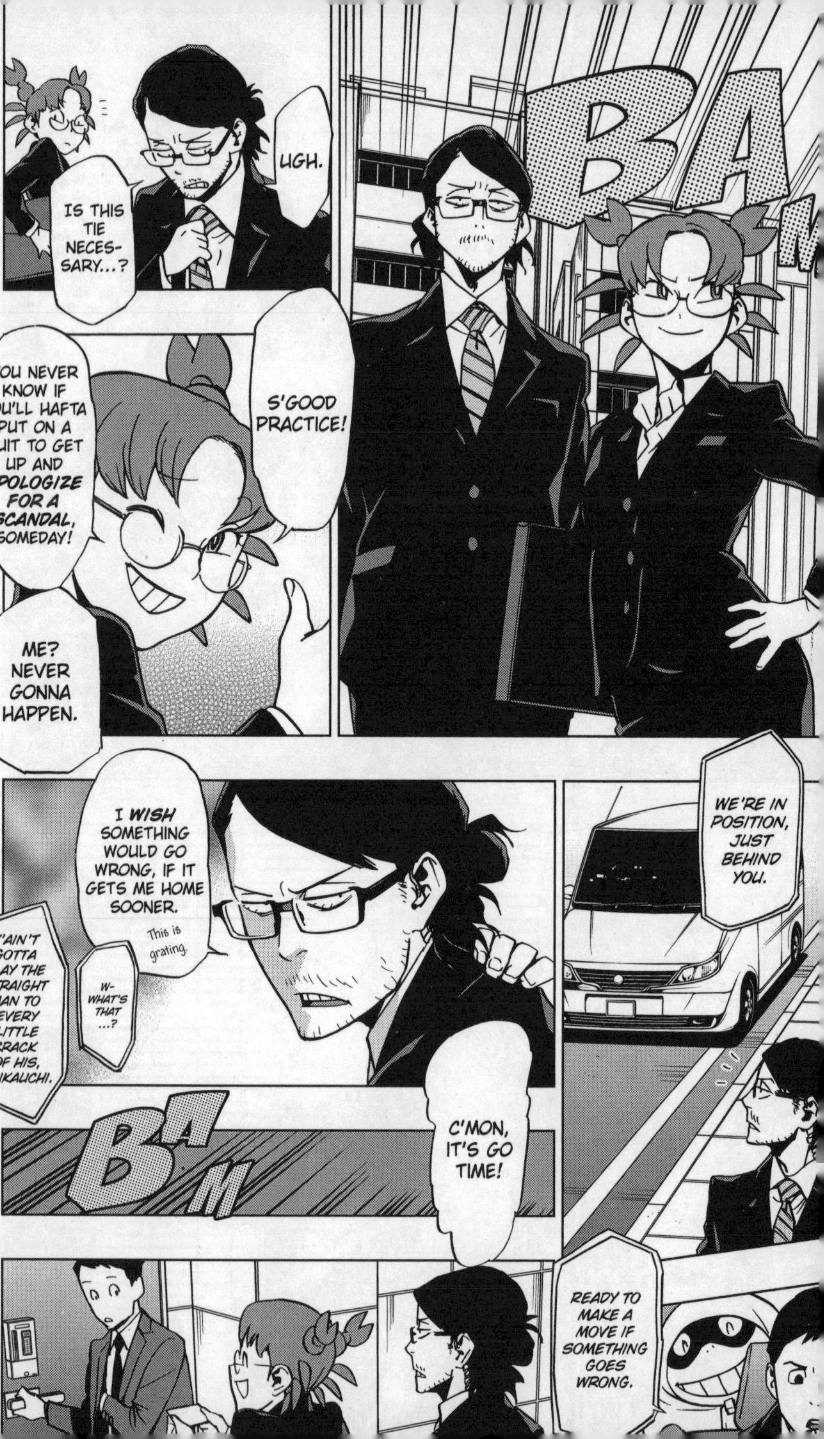
BAM
UGH.
IS THIS TIE NECES-SARY...?
S'GOOD PRACTICE!
YOU NEVER KNOW IF YOU'LL HAFTA PUT ON A SUIT TO GET UP AND APOLOGIZE FOR A SCANDAL, SOMEDAY!
ME? NEVER GONNA HAPPEN.
WE'RE IN POSITION, JUST BEHIND YOU.
I WISH SOMETHING WOULD GO WRONG, IF IT GETS ME HOME SOONER.
This is grating.
W-WHAT'S THAT...?
Y'AIN'T GOTTA PLAY THE STRAIGHT MAN TO EVERY LITTLE CRACK OF HIS, TSUKAUCHI.
BAM
C'MON, IT'S GO TIME!
READY TO MAKE A MOVE IF SOMETHING GOES WRONG.

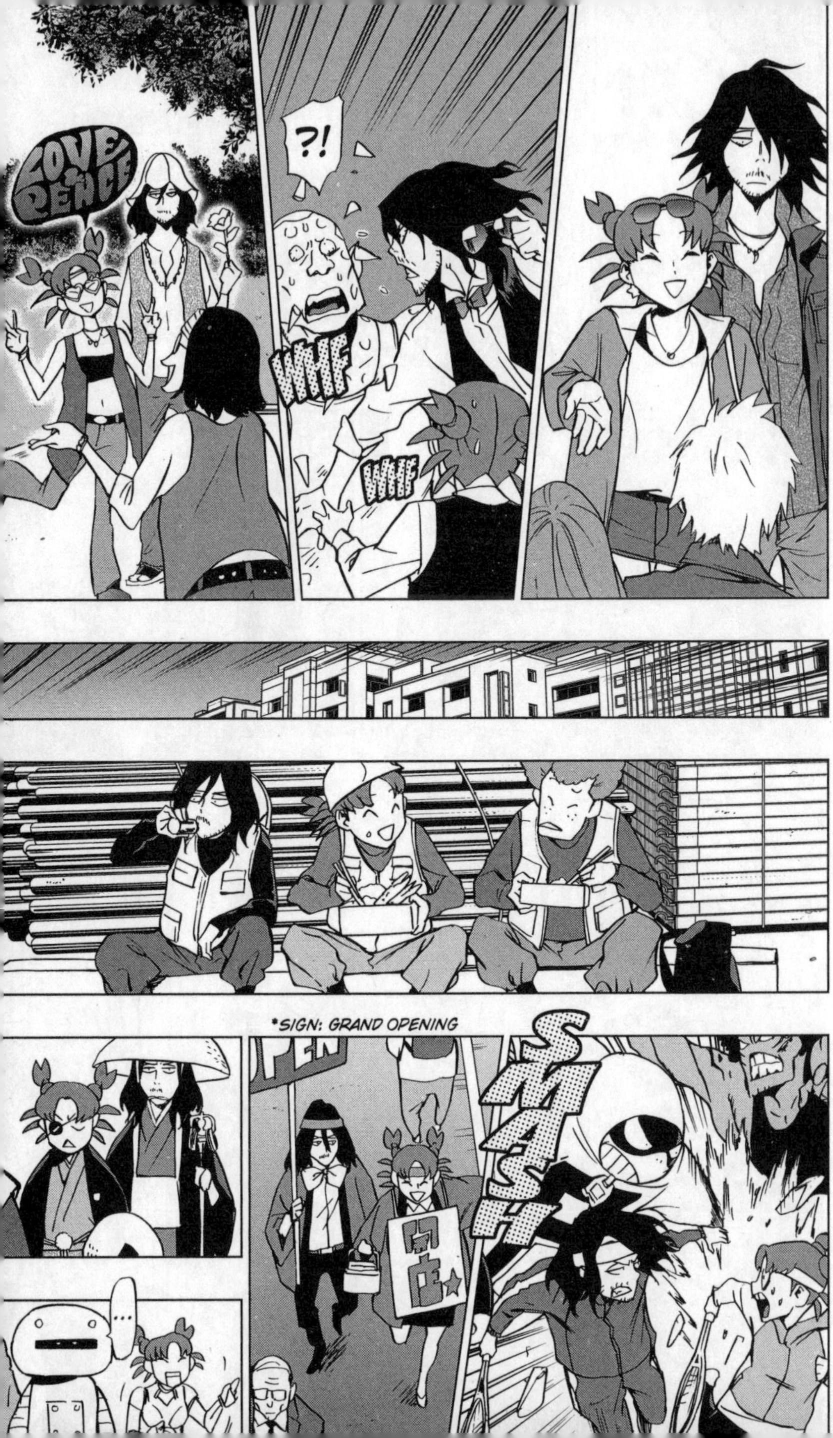

?!
WHF
WHF
LOVE & PEACE
*SIGN: GRAND OPENING
SMASH
...

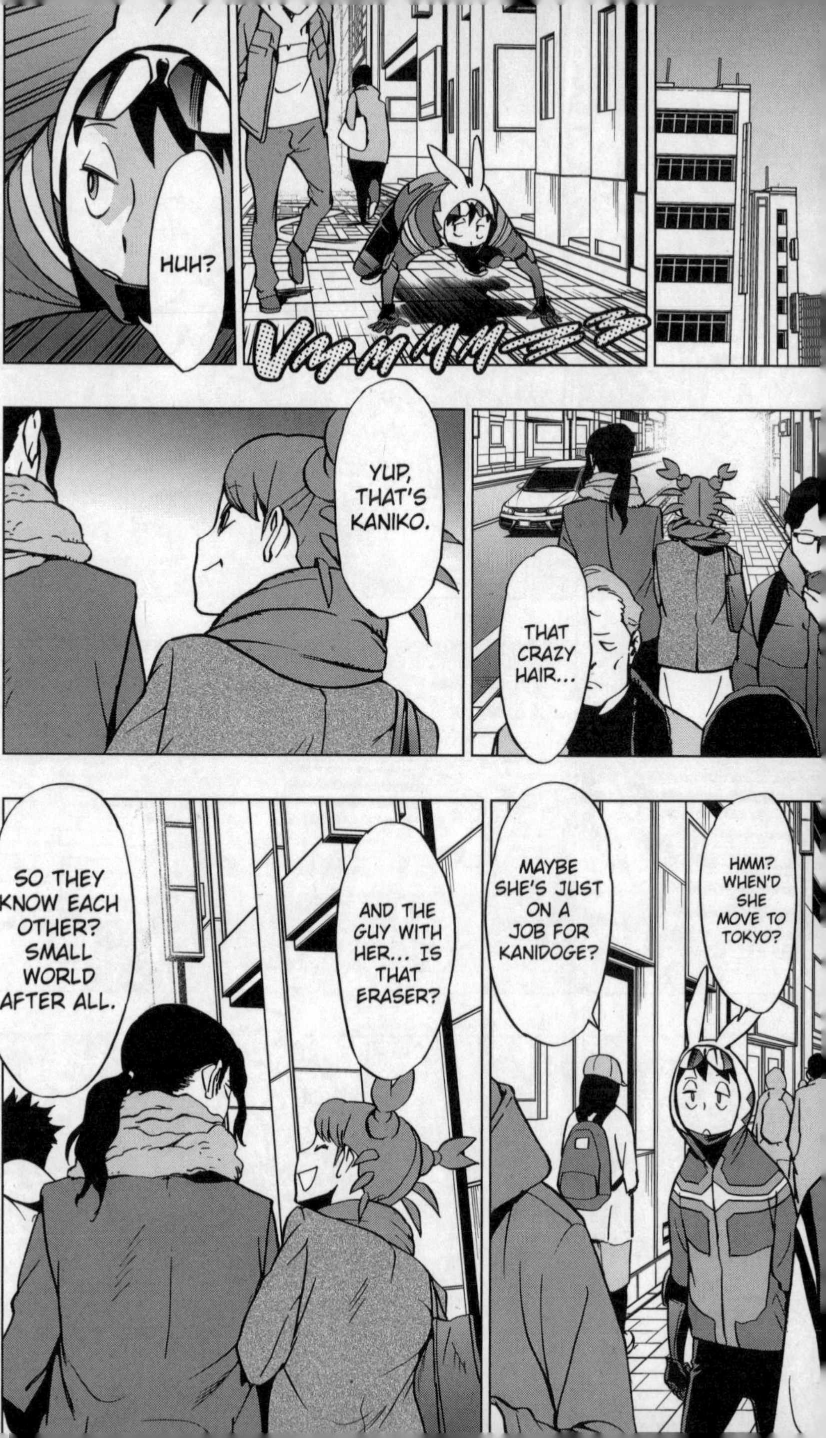
VMMMMM-ZZZ
HUH?
THAT CRAZY HAIR...
YUP, THAT'S KANIKO.
HMM? WHEN'D SHE MOVE TO TOKYO?
MAYBE SHE'S JUST ON A JOB FOR KANIDOGE?
AND THE GUY WITH HER... IS THAT ERASER?
SO THEY KNOW EACH OTHER? SMALL WORLD AFTER ALL.

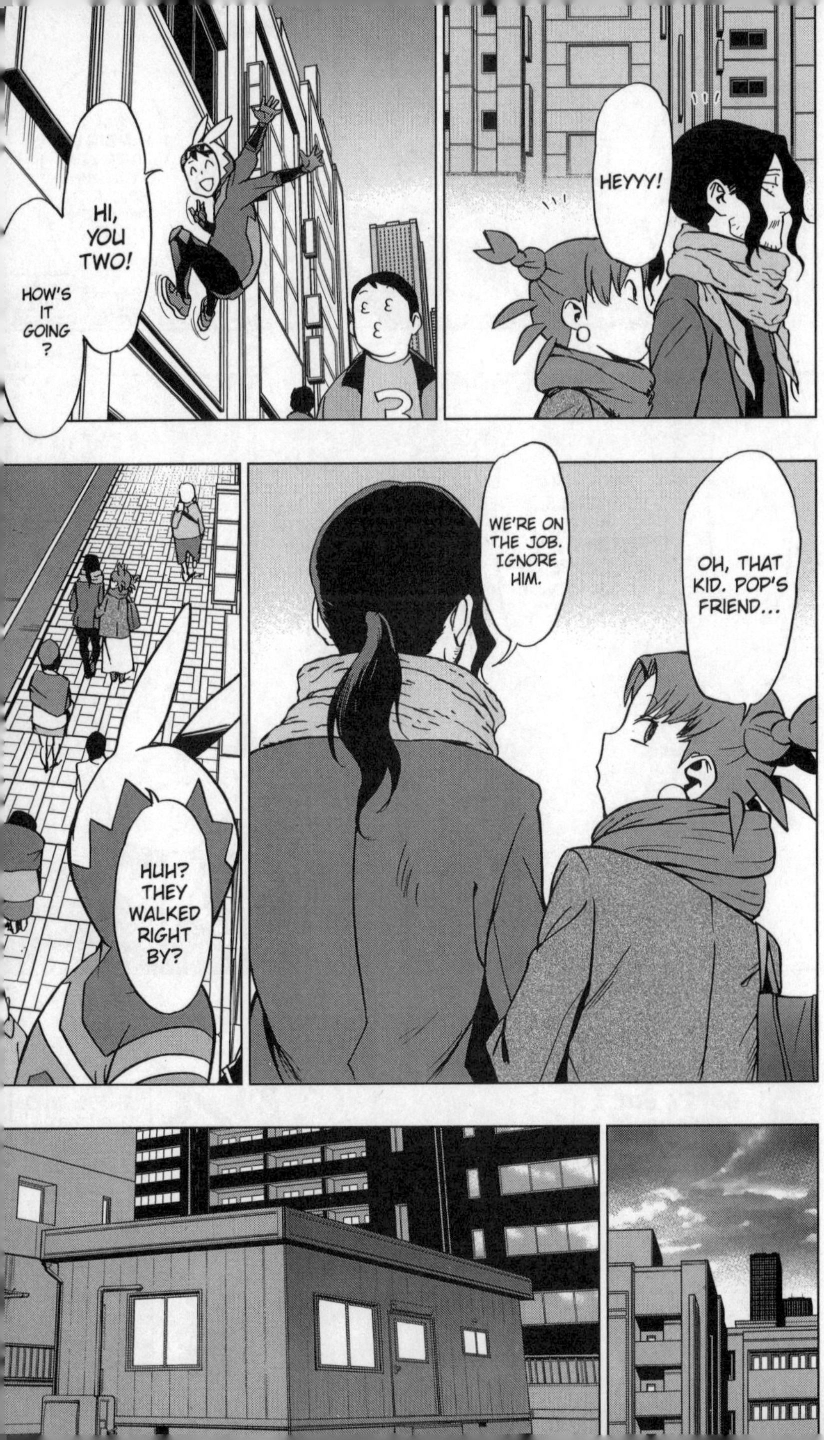
HEYYY!
HI, YOU TWO!
HOW'S IT GOING?
OH, THAT KID. POP'S FRIEND...
WE'RE ON THE JOB. IGNORE HIM.
HUH? THEY WALKED RIGHT BY?

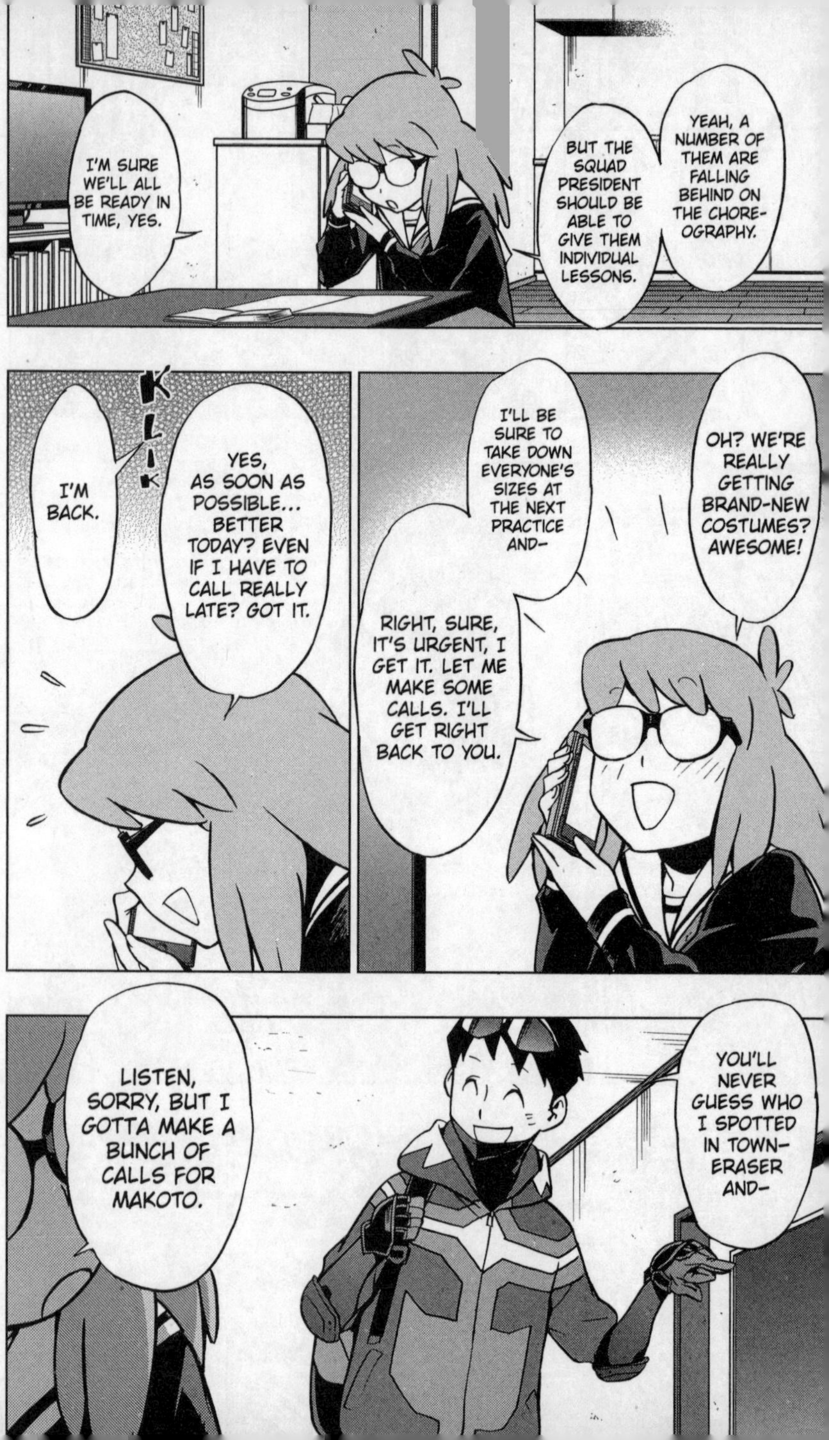
YEAH, A NUMBER OF THEM ARE FALLING BEHIND ON THE CHOREOGRAPHY.
BUT THE SQUAD PRESIDENT SHOULD BE ABLE TO GIVE THEM INDIVIDUAL LESSONS.
I'M SURE WE'LL ALL BE READY IN TIME, YES.
OH? WE'RE REALLY GETTING BRAND-NEW COSTUMES? AWESOME!
I'LL BE SURE TO TAKE DOWN EVERYONE'S SIZES AT THE NEXT PRACTICE AND–
RIGHT, SURE, IT'S URGENT, I GET IT. LET ME MAKE SOME CALLS. I'LL GET RIGHT BACK TO YOU.
YES, AS SOON AS POSSIBLE... BETTER TODAY? EVEN IF I HAVE TO CALL REALLY LATE? GOT IT.
KLIK
I'M BACK.
YOU'LL NEVER GUESS WHO I SPOTTED IN TOWN–ERASER AND–
LISTEN, SORRY, BUT I GOTTA MAKE A BUNCH OF CALLS FOR MAKOTO.

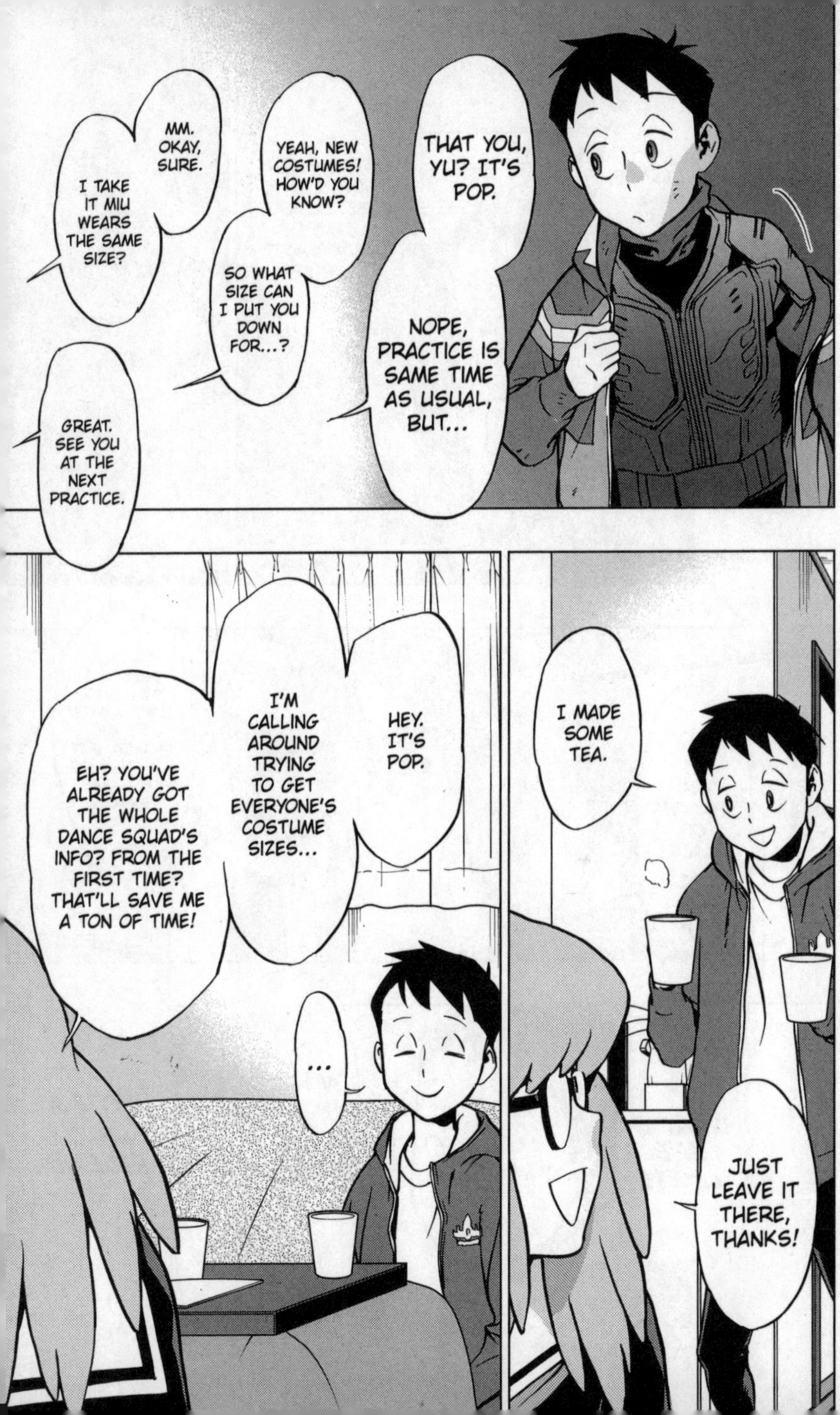
THAT YOU, YU? IT'S POP.
NOPE, PRACTICE IS SAME TIME AS USUAL, BUT...
YEAH, NEW COSTUMES! HOW'D YOU KNOW?
SO WHAT SIZE CAN I PUT YOU DOWN FOR...?
MM. OKAY, SURE.
I TAKE IT MIU WEARS THE SAME SIZE?
GREAT. SEE YOU AT THE NEXT PRACTICE.
I MADE SOME TEA.
JUST LEAVE IT THERE, THANKS!
HEY. IT'S POP.
I'M CALLING AROUND TRYING TO GET EVERYONE'S COSTUME SIZES...
EH? YOU'VE ALREADY GOT THE WHOLE DANCE SQUAD'S INFO? FROM THE FIRST TIME? THAT'LL SAVE ME A TON OF TIME!
...

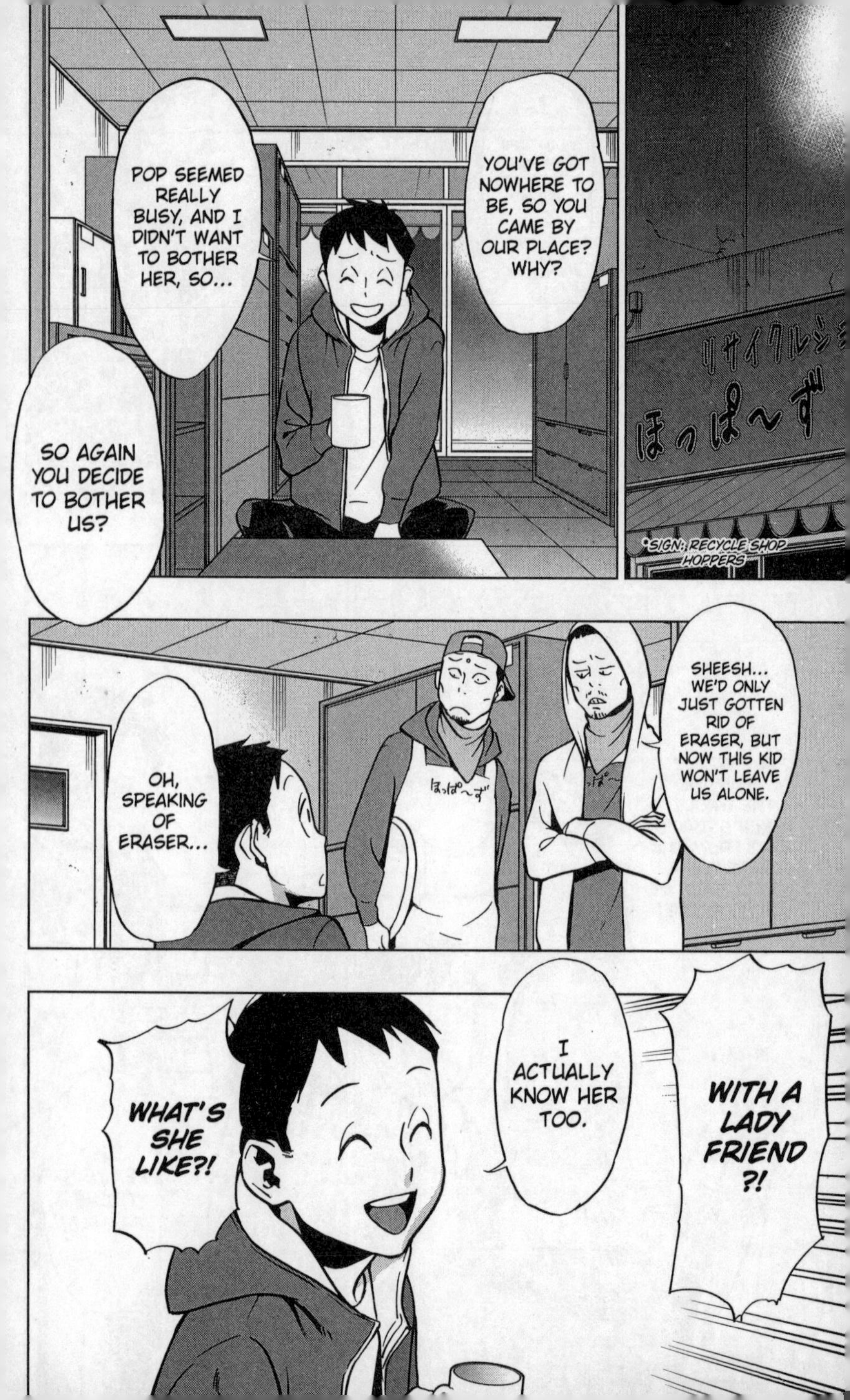
ほっぱ〜ず
*SIGN: RECYCLE SHOP HOPPERS
YOU'VE GOT NOWHERE TO BE, SO YOU CAME BY OUR PLACE? WHY?
POP SEEMED REALLY BUSY, AND I DIDN'T WANT TO BOTHER HER, SO...
SO AGAIN YOU DECIDE TO BOTHER US?
SHEESH... WE'D ONLY JUST GOTTEN RID OF ERASER, BUT NOW THIS KID WON'T LEAVE US ALONE.
ほっぱ〜ず
OH, SPEAKING OF ERASER...
WITH A LADY FRIEND?!
I ACTUALLY KNOW HER TOO.
WHAT'S SHE LIKE?!

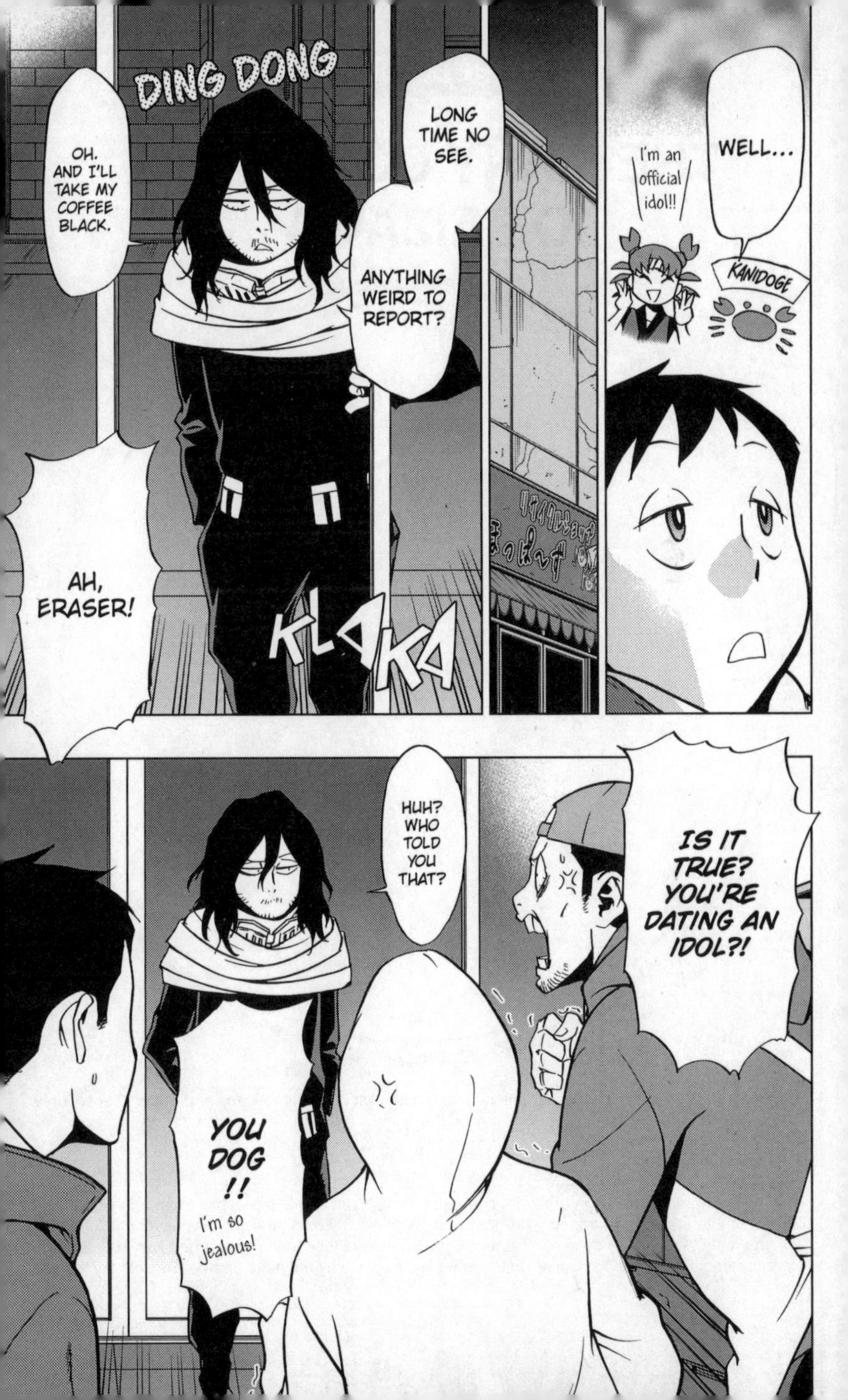
WELL...
I'm an official idol!!
KANIDOGE
LONG TIME NO SEE.
ANYTHING WEIRD TO REPORT?
DING DONG
OH. AND I'LL TAKE MY COFFEE BLACK.
KLAKA
AH, ERASER!
IS IT TRUE? YOU'RE DATING AN IDOL?!
HUH? WHO TOLD YOU THAT?
YOU DOG!!
I'm so jealous!

THE COLUMN

THE MANY COSTUMES OF AIZAWA

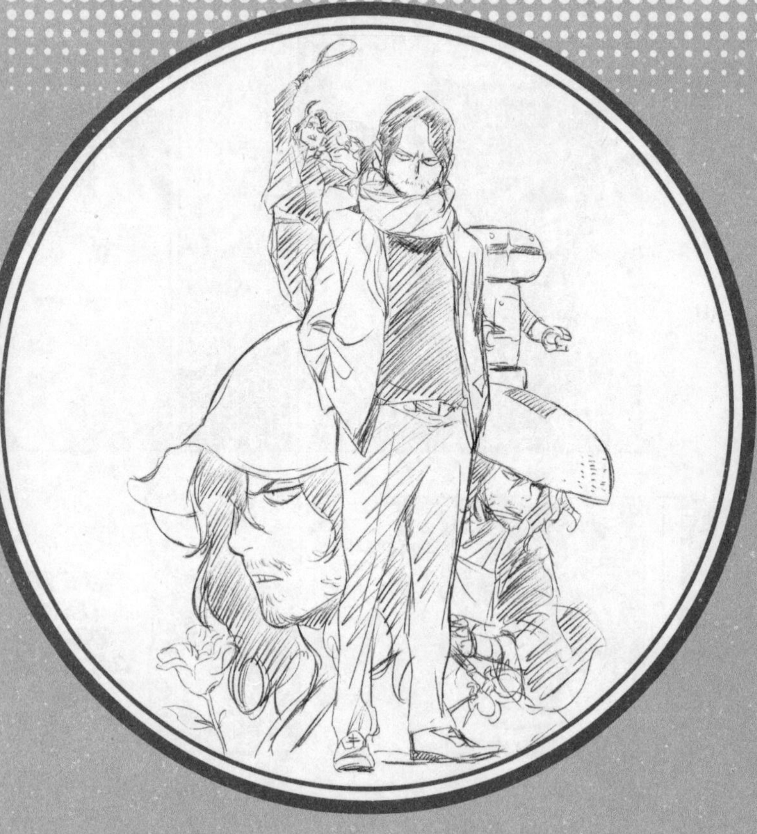

For the so-called Aizawa cosplay chapter, I submitted a list of costume ideas and Betten Sensei drew the best ones. Aizawa's such a serious guy so pretty much any costume looks funny on him.

—Furuhashi

Often when reading the rough draft of a chapter, I think, "Wah ha ha, this is hilarious!" But when it comes time to draw, I'm stumped. This time was no different. I didn't want to piss anyone off! That was the main thing on my mind while drawing. (LOL) A Japanese tennis player had just won some big tournament, so when I saw that on the news, I thought, why not have Aizawa Sensei play tennis too?

—Betten

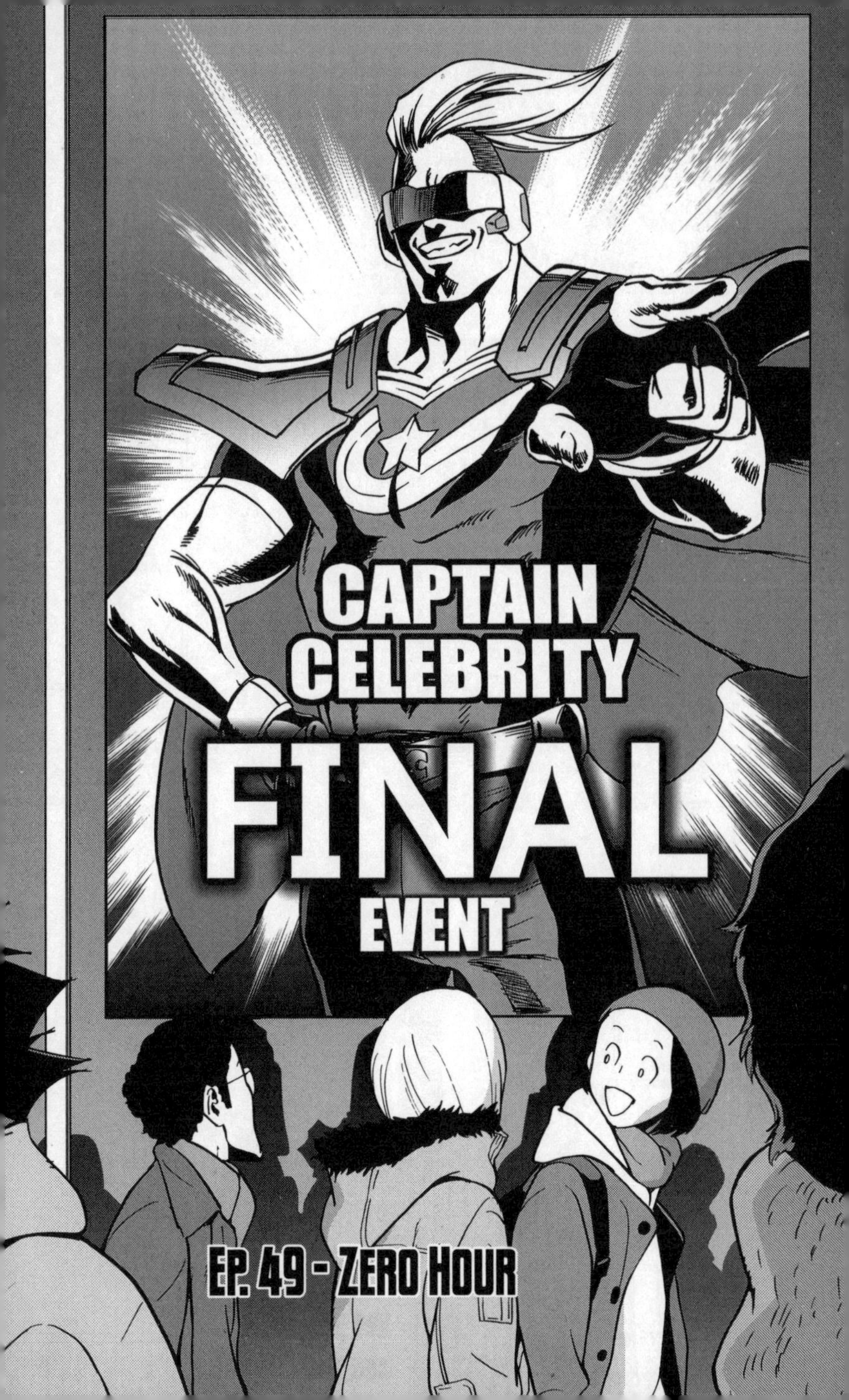
CAPTAIN
CELEBRITY
FINAL
EVENT
EP. 49 - ZERO HOUR

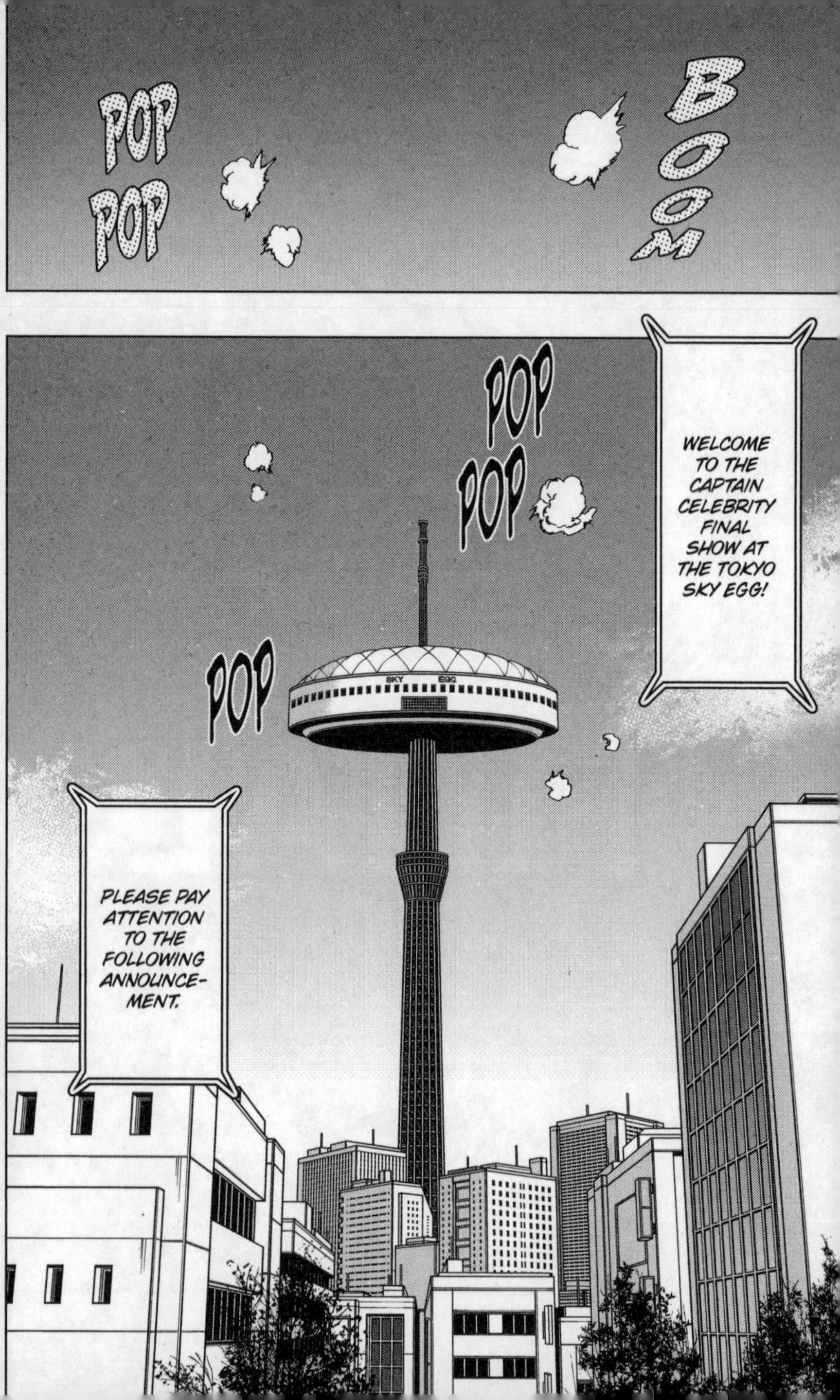
BOOM
POP POP
WELCOME TO THE CAPTAIN CELEBRITY FINAL SHOW AT THE TOKYO SKY EGG!
POP POP
SKY EGG
POP
PLEASE PAY ATTENTION TO THE FOLLOWING ANNOUNCE-MENT.

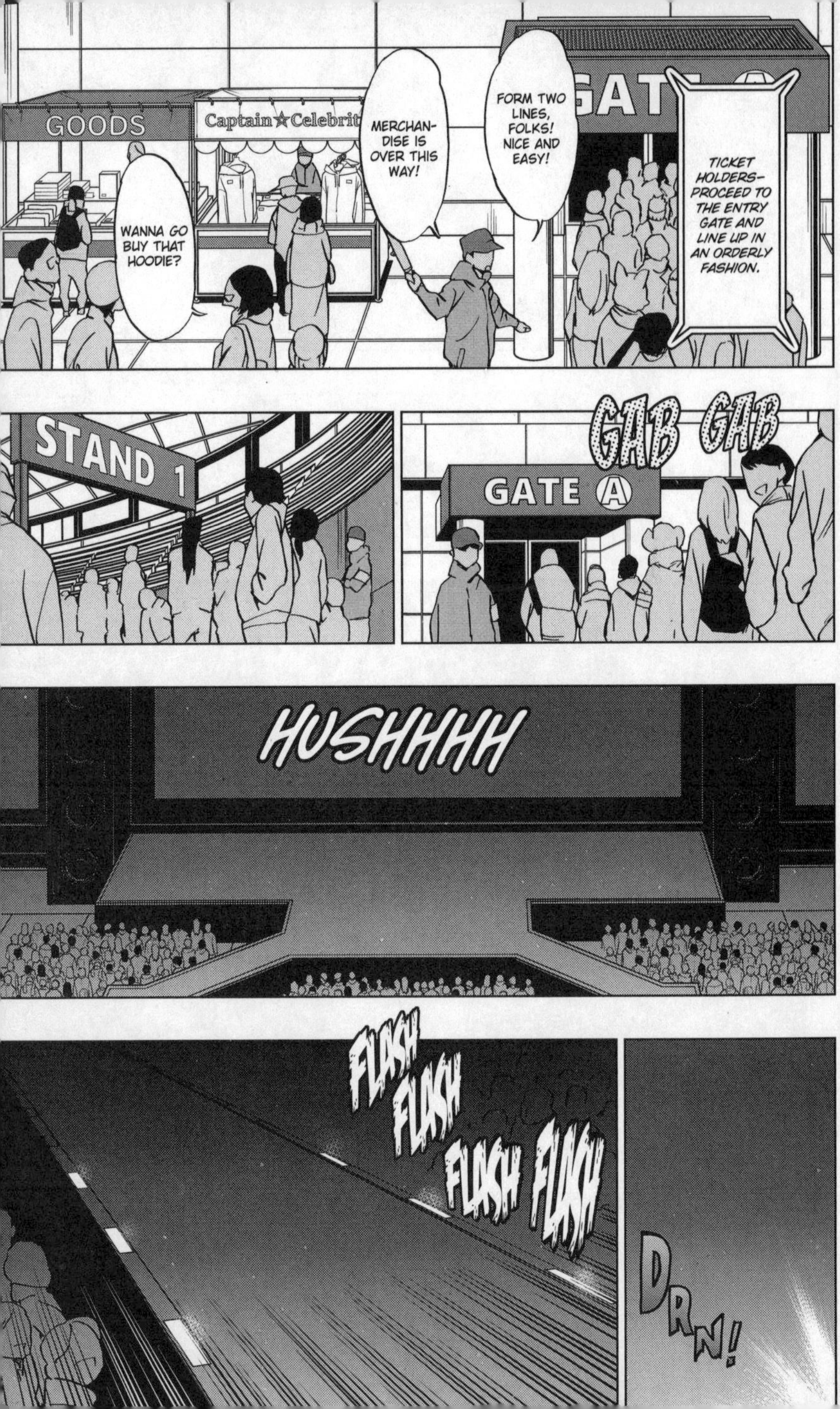
TICKET HOLDERS—PROCEED TO THE ENTRY GATE AND LINE UP IN AN ORDERLY FASHION.
FORM TWO LINES, FOLKS! NICE AND EASY!
MERCHANDISE IS OVER THIS WAY!
GOODS
WANNA GO BUY THAT HOODIE?
GAB GAB
GATE A
STAND 1
HUSHHHH
DRN!
FLASH FLASH FLASH FLASH

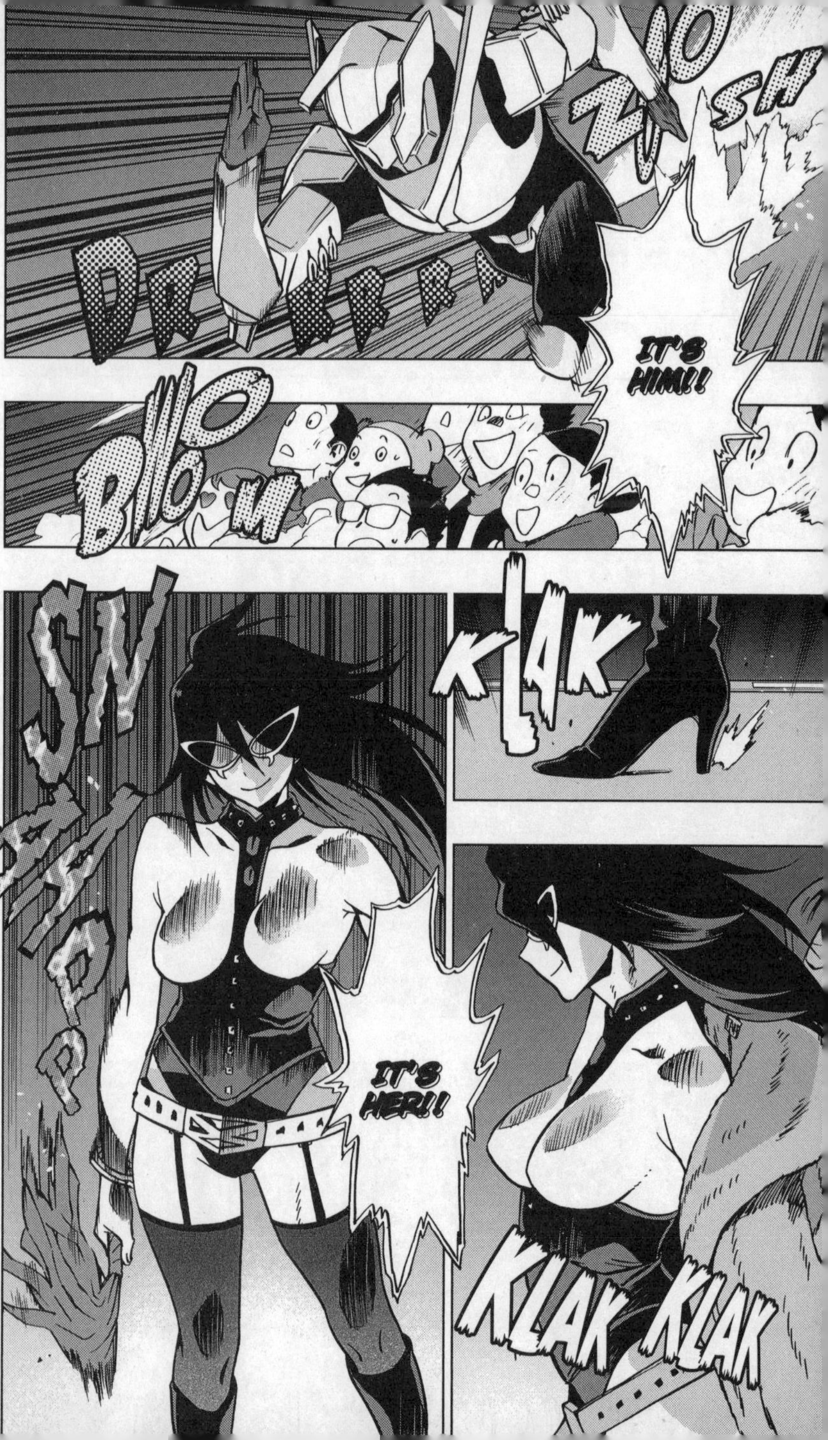
ZOOSH
DRRRRM
IT'S HIM!!
BOOM
KLAK
KLAK KLAK
SWAPP
IT'S HER!!

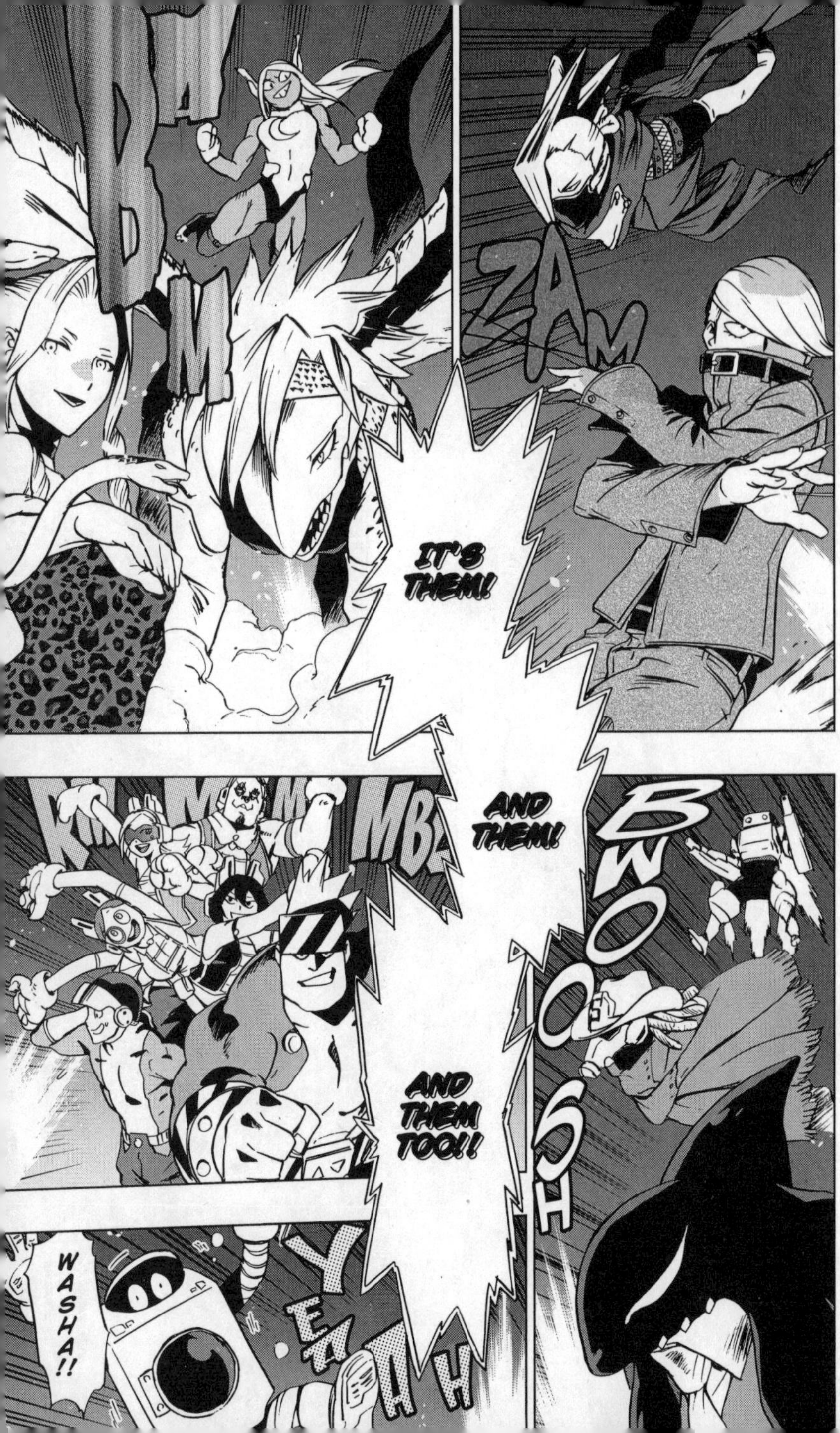
ZAM
BAM
IT'S THEM!
AND THEM!
AND THEM TOO!!
BWOOOSH
WASHA!!
YEAHH

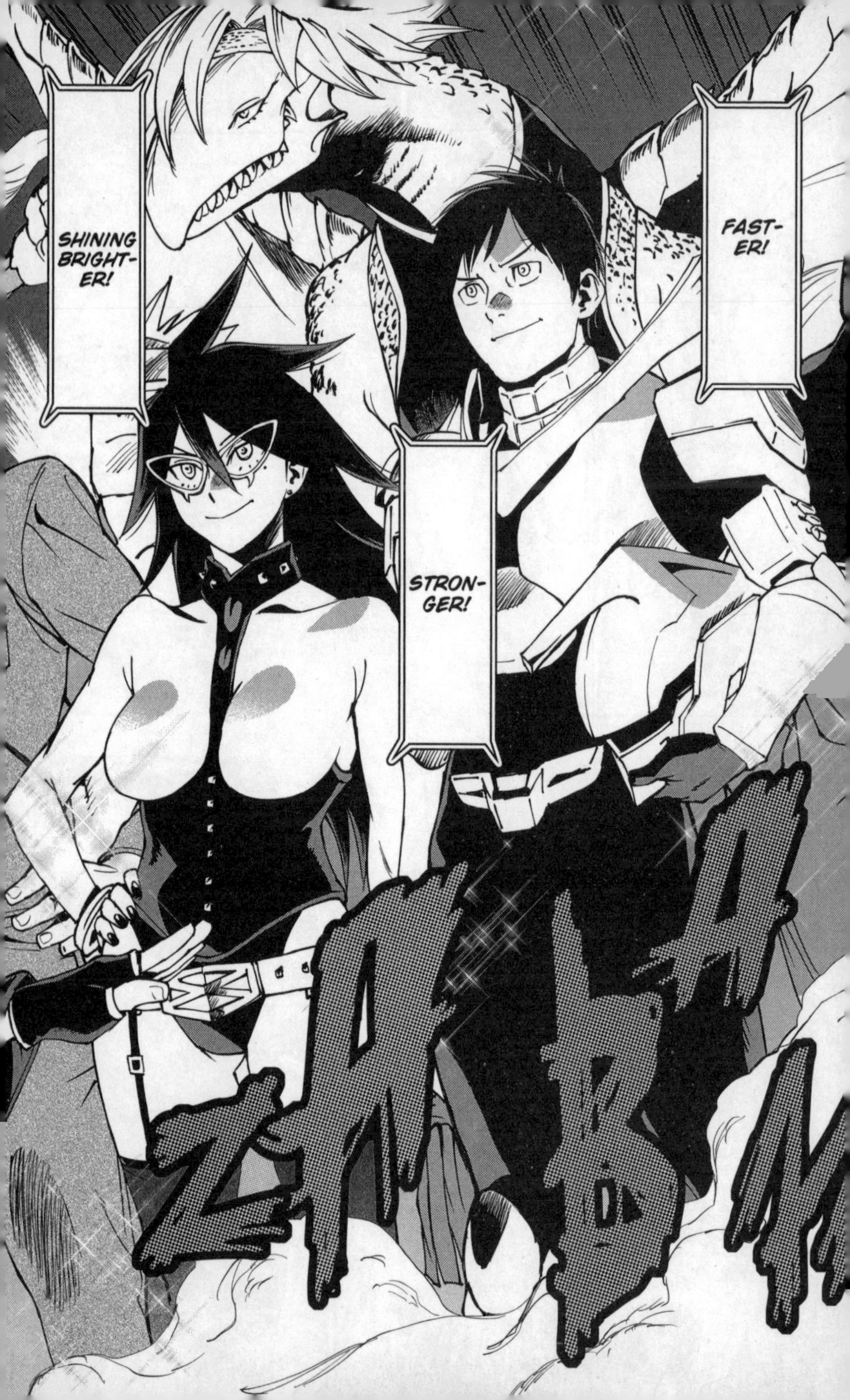
FAST-ER!
SHINING BRIGHT-ER!
STRON-GER!

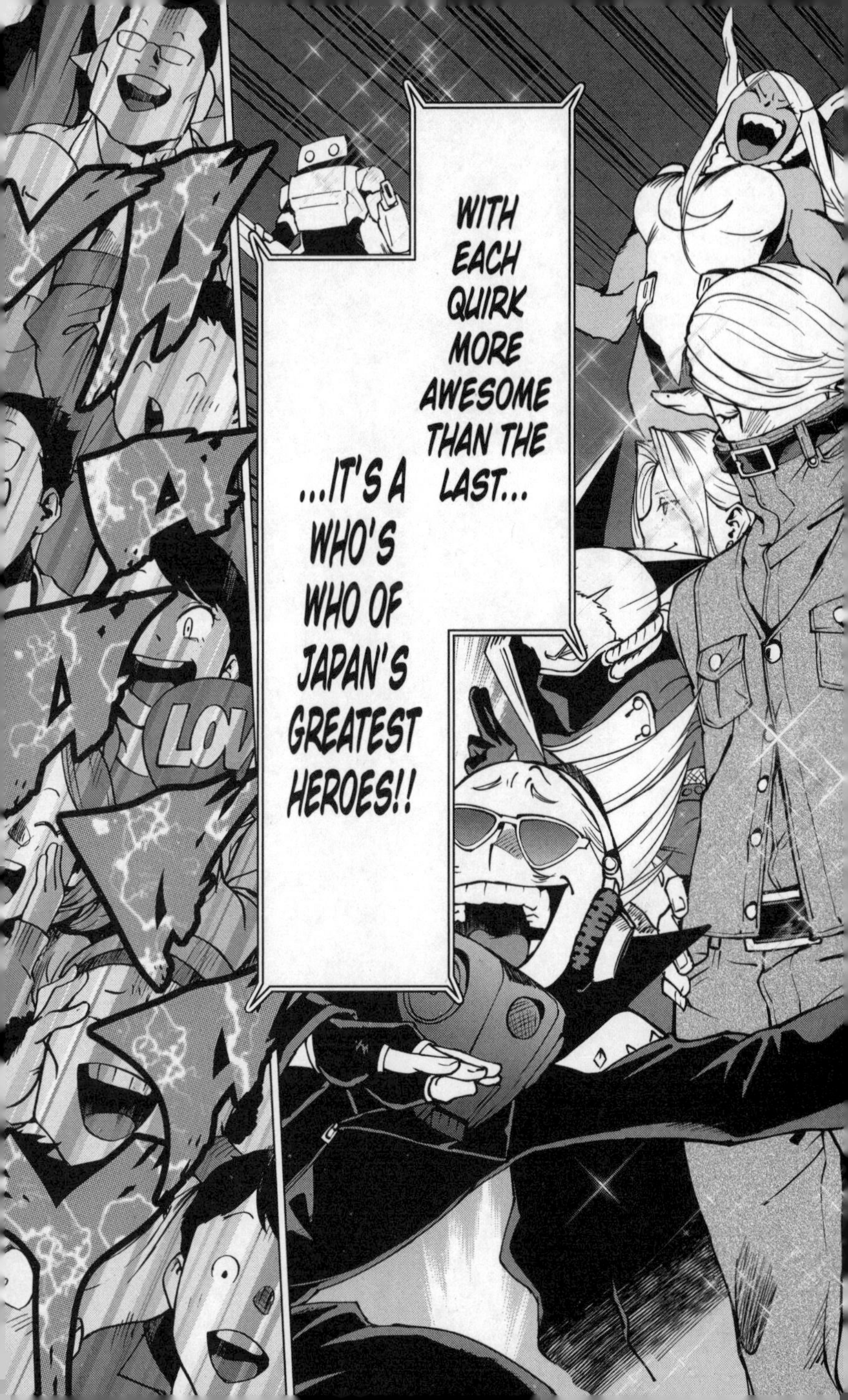
WITH EACH QUIRK MORE AWESOME THAN THE LAST...
...IT'S A WHO'S WHO OF JAPAN'S GREATEST HEROES!!

BUT HOLD ON TO YOUR SEATS!

CUZ WE'VE GOT ONE MIGHTY INVASIVE SPECIES BUSTING IN!

THAT'S RIGHT— THE MAN WHO CAME SOARING IN FROM THE U.S. OF A.!

HE'S BEEN TOP-TEN MATERIAL FOR TEN YEARS RUNNING, EVER SINCE HIS DEBUT!

GIVE IT UP FOR ...

THE MAN WHOSE FLIGHT QUIRK SENT HIM ZOOMING UP THE AMERICAN RANKINGS.

CAPTAIN CELEBRITY!

OOOOH

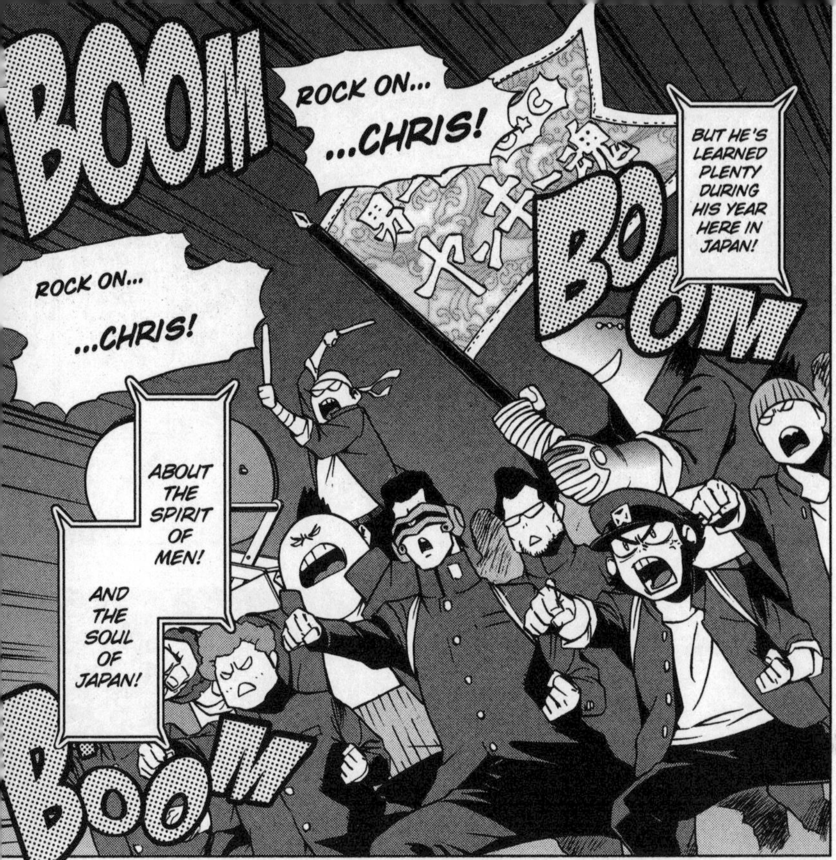
BOOM
BUT HE'S LEARNED PLENTY DURING HIS YEAR HERE IN JAPAN!
ROCK ON...
...CHRIS!
BOOM
ROCK ON...
...CHRIS!
ABOUT THE SPIRIT OF MEN!
AND THE SOUL OF JAPAN!
BOOM

*FLAG: A MAN'S MAN YANKEE SPIRIT

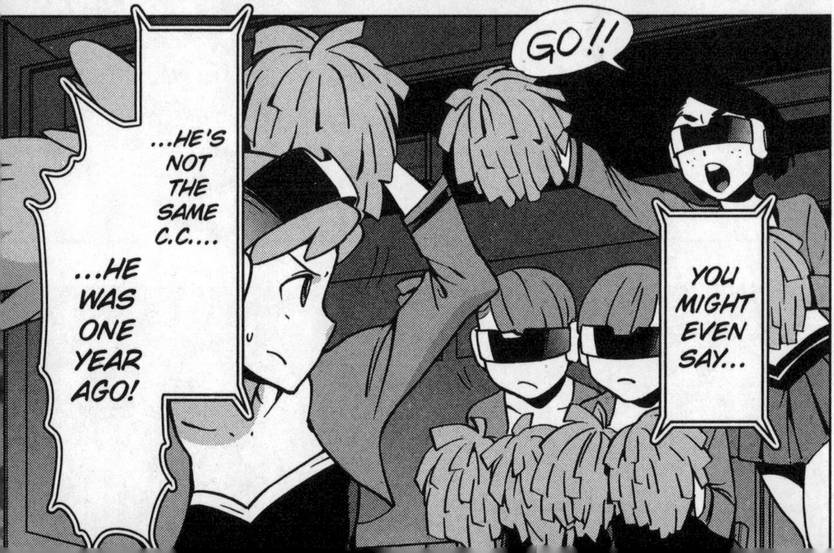
GO!!
YOU MIGHT EVEN SAY...
...HE'S NOT THE SAME C.C....
...HE WAS ONE YEAR AGO!

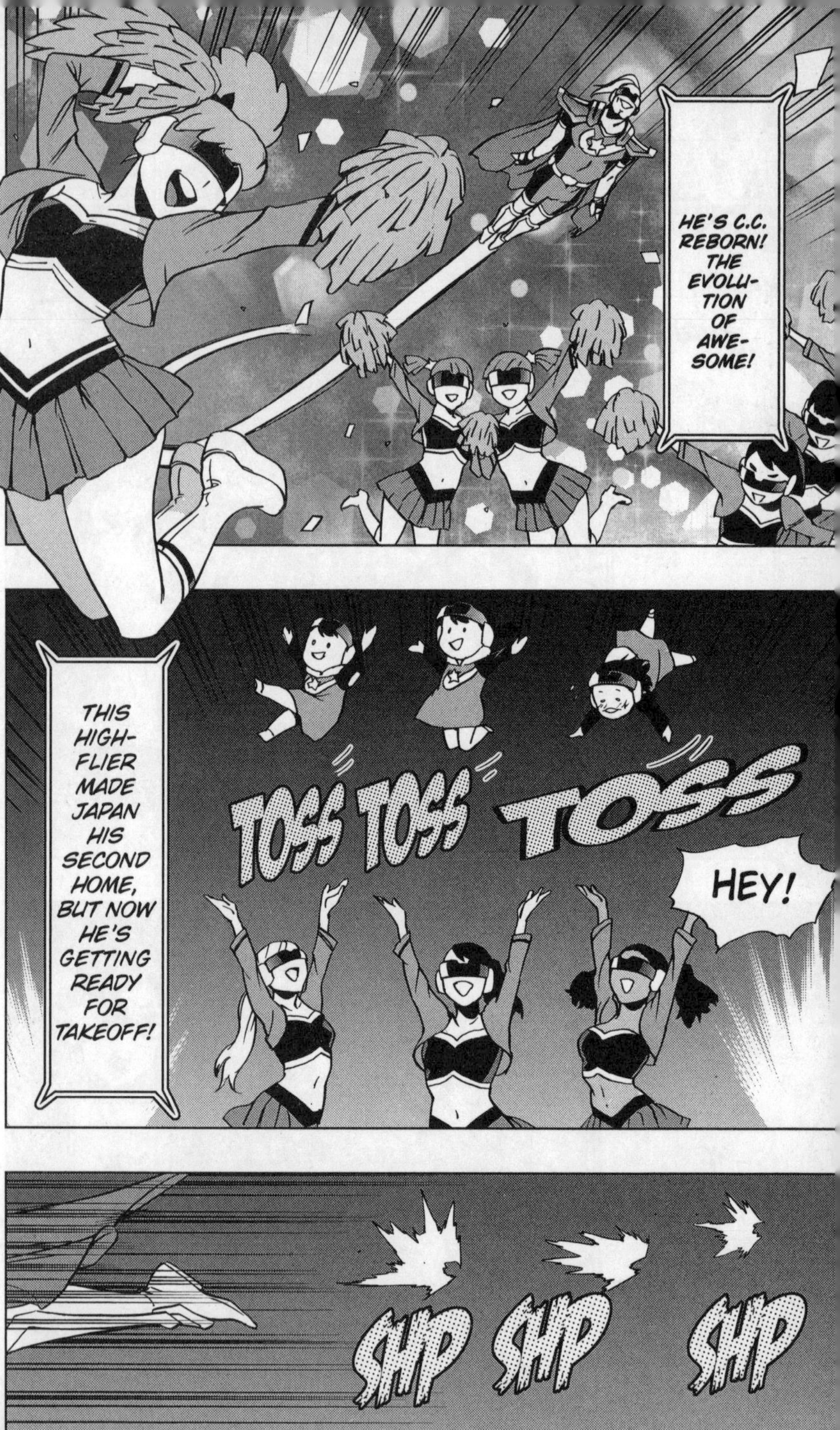
HE'S C.C. REBORN! THE EVOLUTION OF AWESOME!
HEY!
THIS HIGH-FLIER MADE JAPAN HIS SECOND HOME, BUT NOW HE'S GETTING READY FOR TAKEOFF!
TOSS TOSS TOSS
SHP SHP SHP

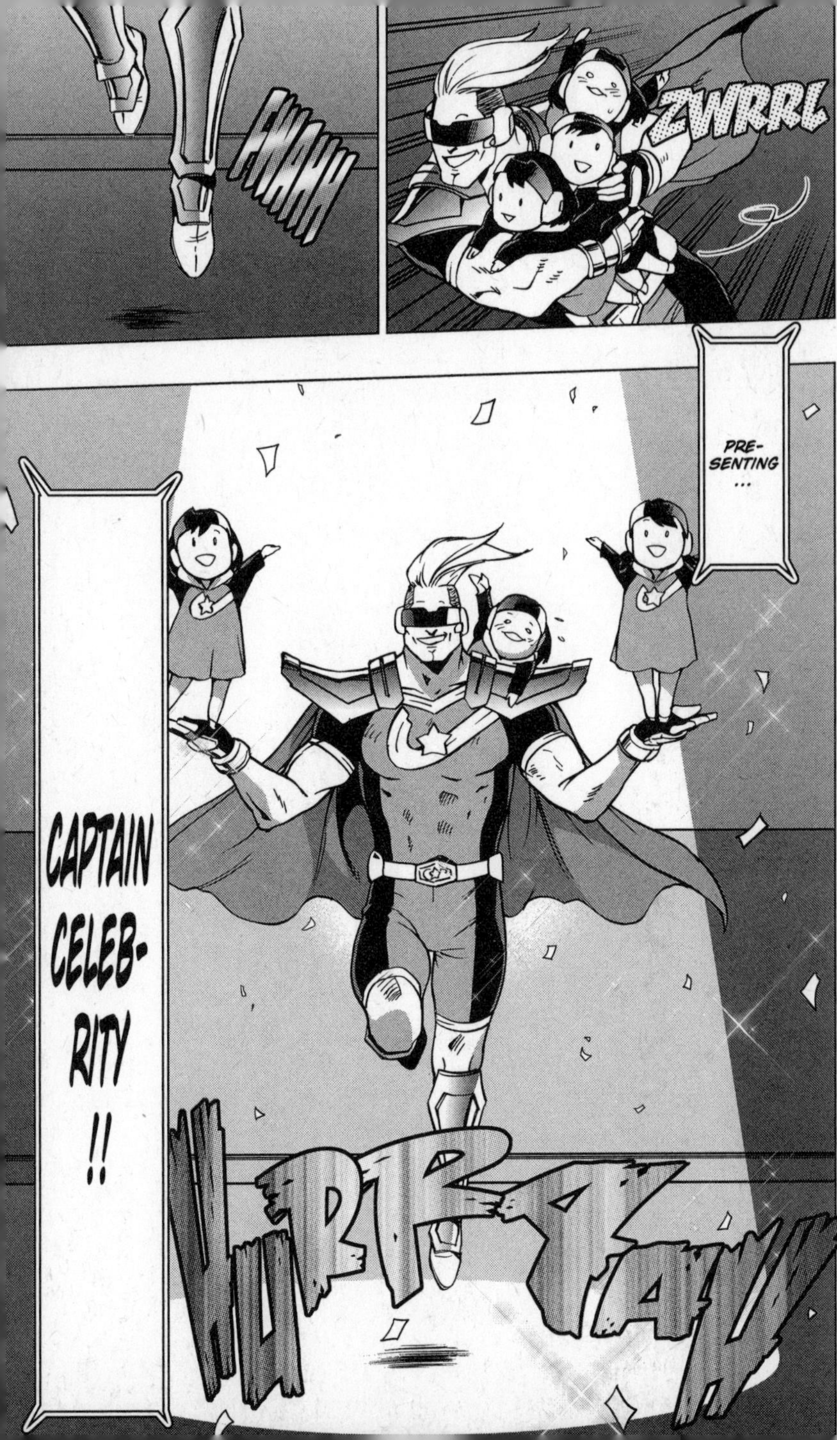
ZWRRL
PRE-
SENTING
...
CAPTAIN
CELEB-
RITY
!!

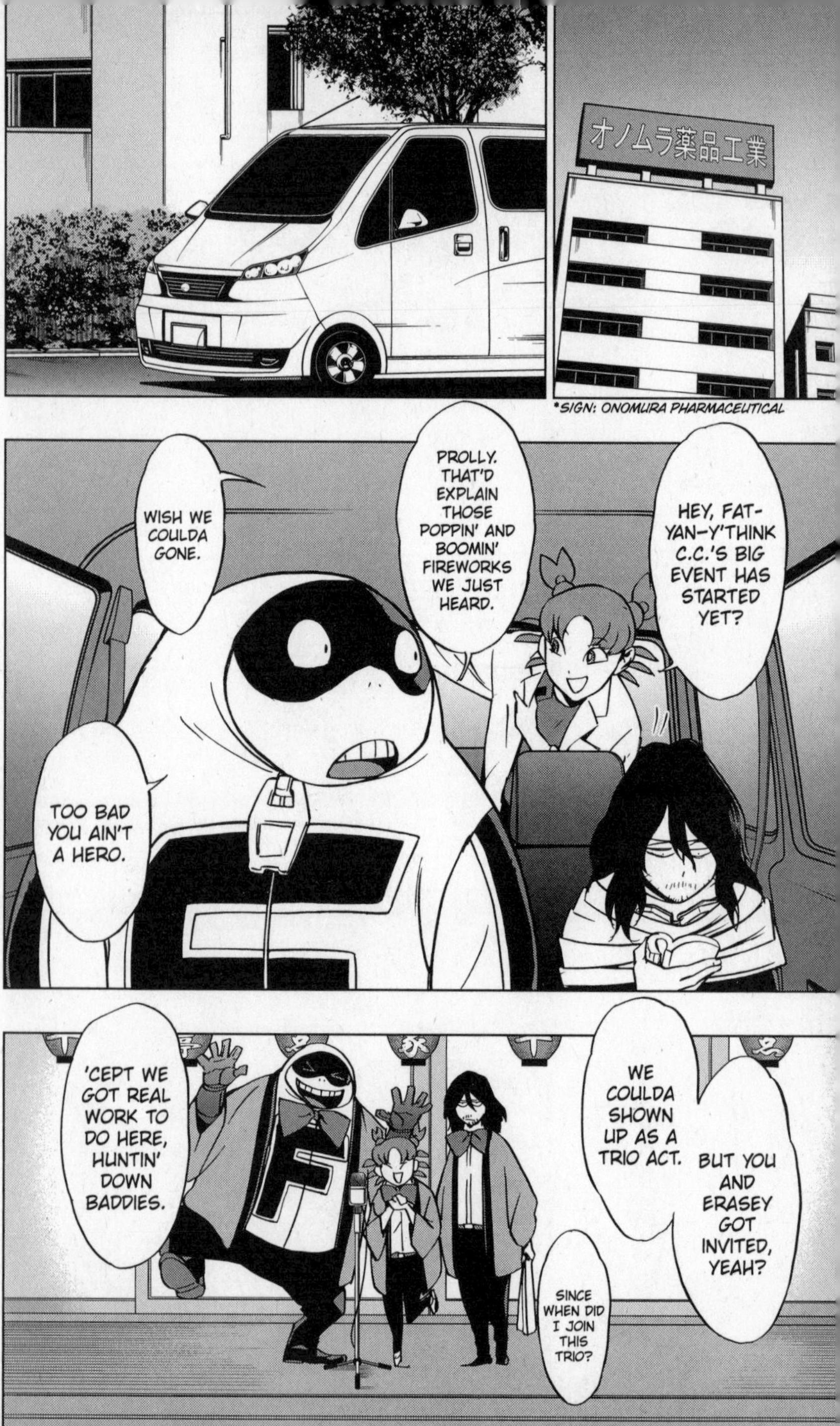
オノムラ薬品工業
*SIGN: ONOMURA PHARMACEUTICAL
HEY, FAT-YAN—Y'THINK C.C.'S BIG EVENT HAS STARTED YET?
PROLLY. THAT'D EXPLAIN THOSE POPPIN' AND BOOMIN' FIREWORKS WE JUST HEARD.
WISH WE COULDA GONE.
TOO BAD YOU AIN'T A HERO.
WE COULDA SHOWN UP AS A TRIO ACT.
BUT YOU AND ERASEY GOT INVITED, YEAH?
'CEPT WE GOT REAL WORK TO DO HERE, HUNTIN' DOWN BADDIES.
SINCE WHEN DID I JOIN THIS TRIO?

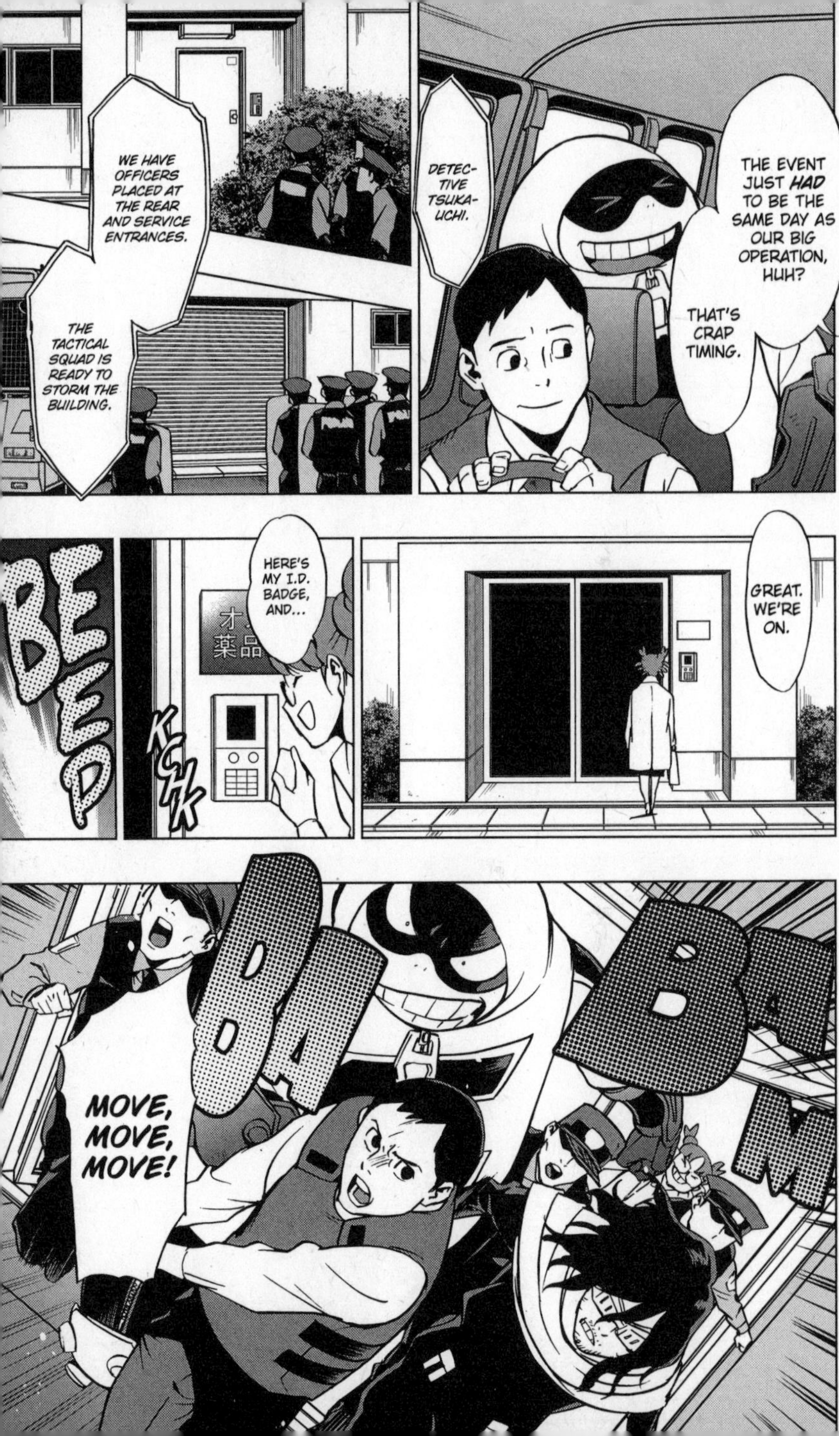
THE EVENT JUST HAD TO BE THE SAME DAY AS OUR BIG OPERATION, HUH?
THAT'S CRAP TIMING.
DETECTIVE TSUKAUCHI.
WE HAVE OFFICERS PLACED AT THE REAR AND SERVICE ENTRANCES.
THE TACTICAL SQUAD IS READY TO STORM THE BUILDING.
GREAT. WE'RE ON.
HERE'S MY I.D. BADGE, AND...
薬品
KCHK
BEEP
BAM
MOVE, MOVE, MOVE!

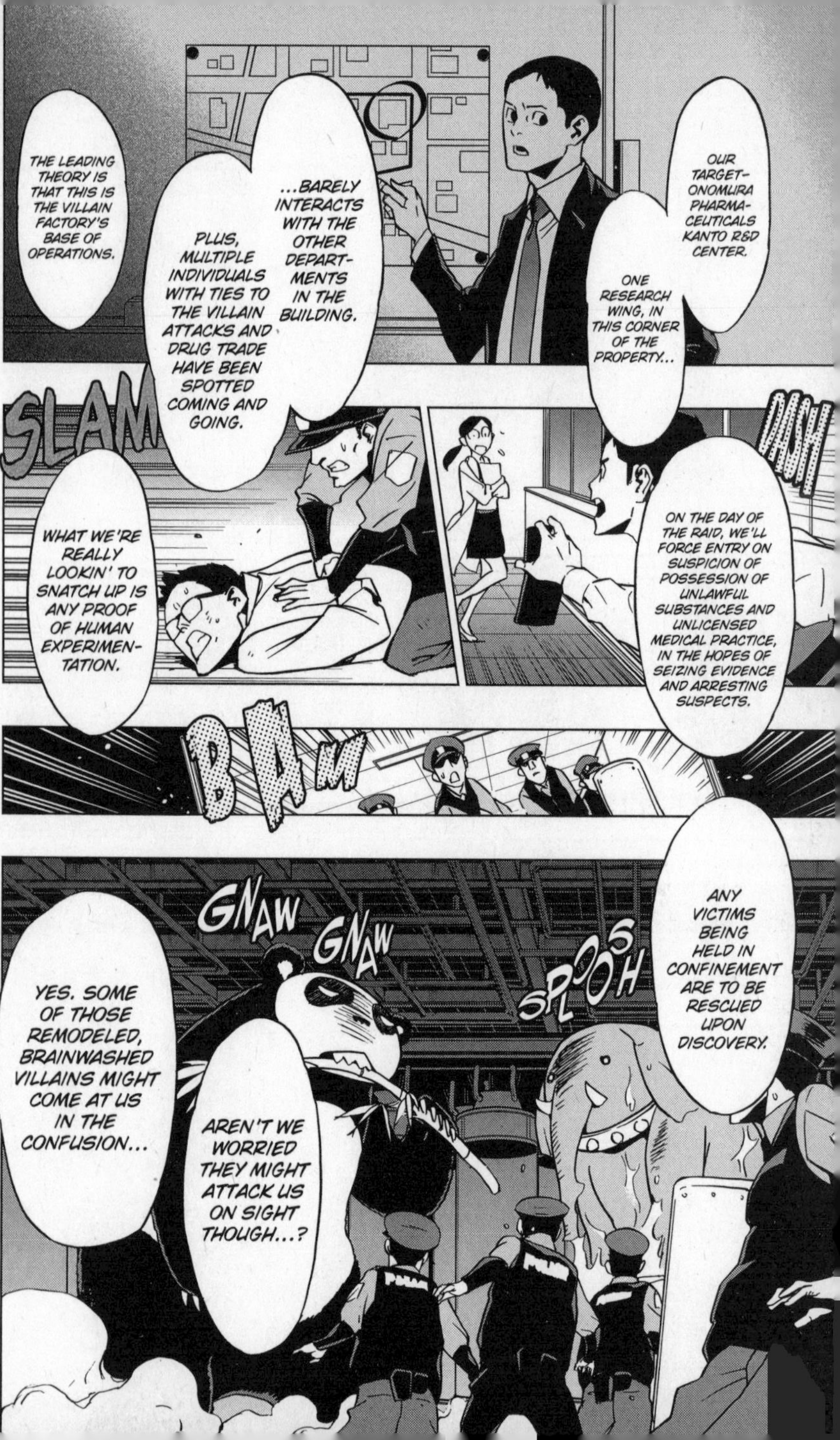

OUR TARGET- ONOMURA PHARMACEUTICALS KANTO R&D CENTER.
ONE RESEARCH WING, IN THIS CORNER OF THE PROPERTY...
...BARELY INTERACTS WITH THE OTHER DEPARTMENTS IN THE BUILDING.
PLUS, MULTIPLE INDIVIDUALS WITH TIES TO THE VILLAIN ATTACKS AND DRUG TRADE HAVE BEEN SPOTTED COMING AND GOING.
THE LEADING THEORY IS THAT THIS IS THE VILLAIN FACTORY'S BASE OF OPERATIONS.
DASH
ON THE DAY OF THE RAID, WE'LL FORCE ENTRY ON SUSPICION OF POSSESSION OF UNLAWFUL SUBSTANCES AND UNLICENSED MEDICAL PRACTICE, IN THE HOPES OF SEIZING EVIDENCE AND ARRESTING SUSPECTS.
SLAM
WHAT WE'RE REALLY LOOKIN' TO SNATCH UP IS ANY PROOF OF HUMAN EXPERIMENTATION.
BAM
ANY VICTIMS BEING HELD IN CONFINEMENT ARE TO BE RESCUED UPON DISCOVERY.
SPLOOSH
GNAW GNAW
YES. SOME OF THOSE REMODELED, BRAINWASHED VILLAINS MIGHT COME AT US IN THE CONFUSION...
AREN'T WE WORRIED THEY MIGHT ATTACK US ON SIGHT THOUGH...?

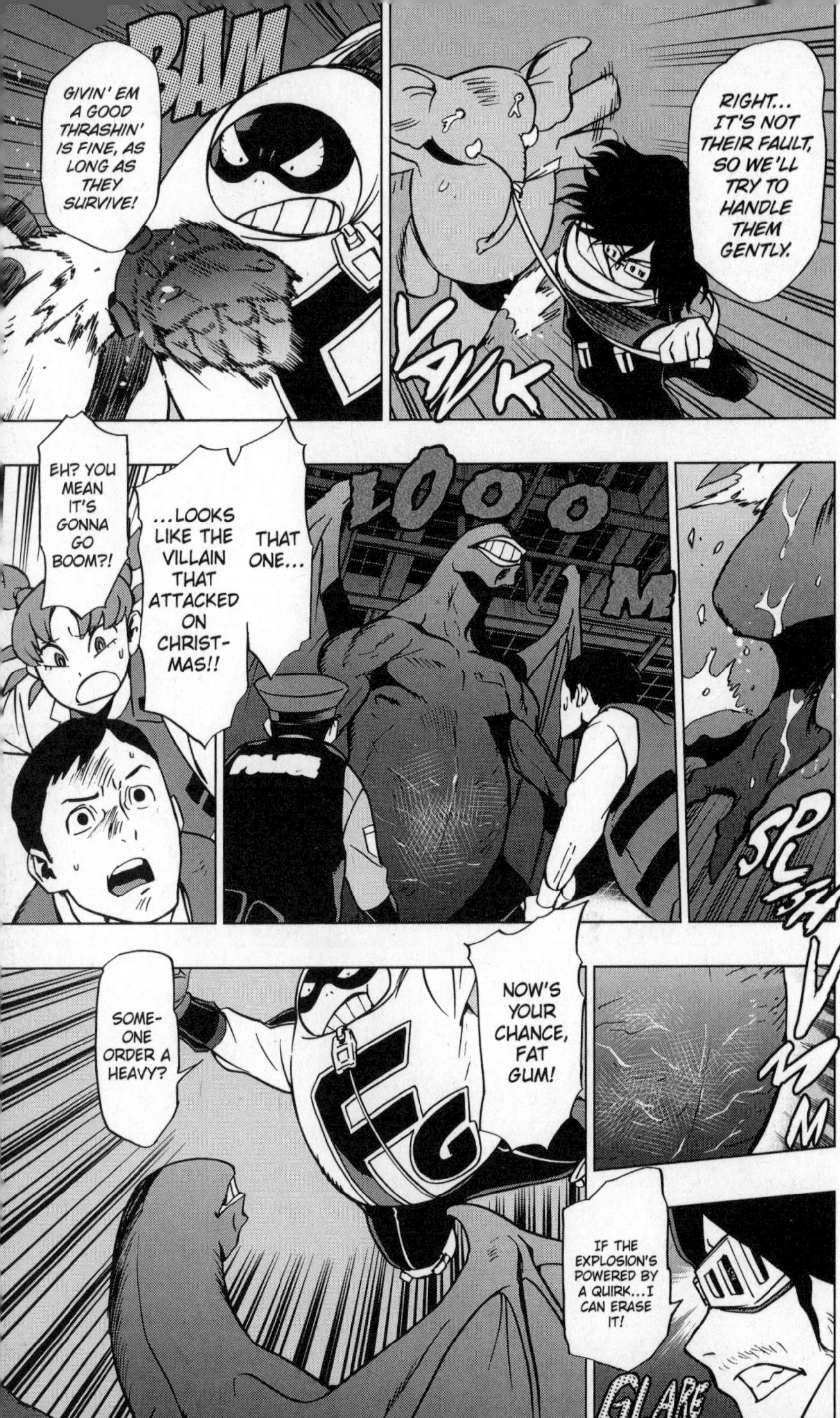
RIGHT... IT'S NOT THEIR FAULT, SO WE'LL TRY TO HANDLE THEM GENTLY.
YANK
BAM
GIVIN' EM A GOOD THRASHIN' IS FINE, AS LONG AS THEY SURVIVE!
SPLSH
LOOOOM
THAT ONE...
...LOOKS LIKE THE VILLAIN THAT ATTACKED ON CHRIST-MAS!!
EH? YOU MEAN IT'S GONNA GO BOOM?!
VMMM
IF THE EXPLOSION'S POWERED BY A QUIRK...I CAN ERASE IT!
GLARE
NOW'S YOUR CHANCE, FAT GUM!
SOME-ONE ORDER A HEAVY?

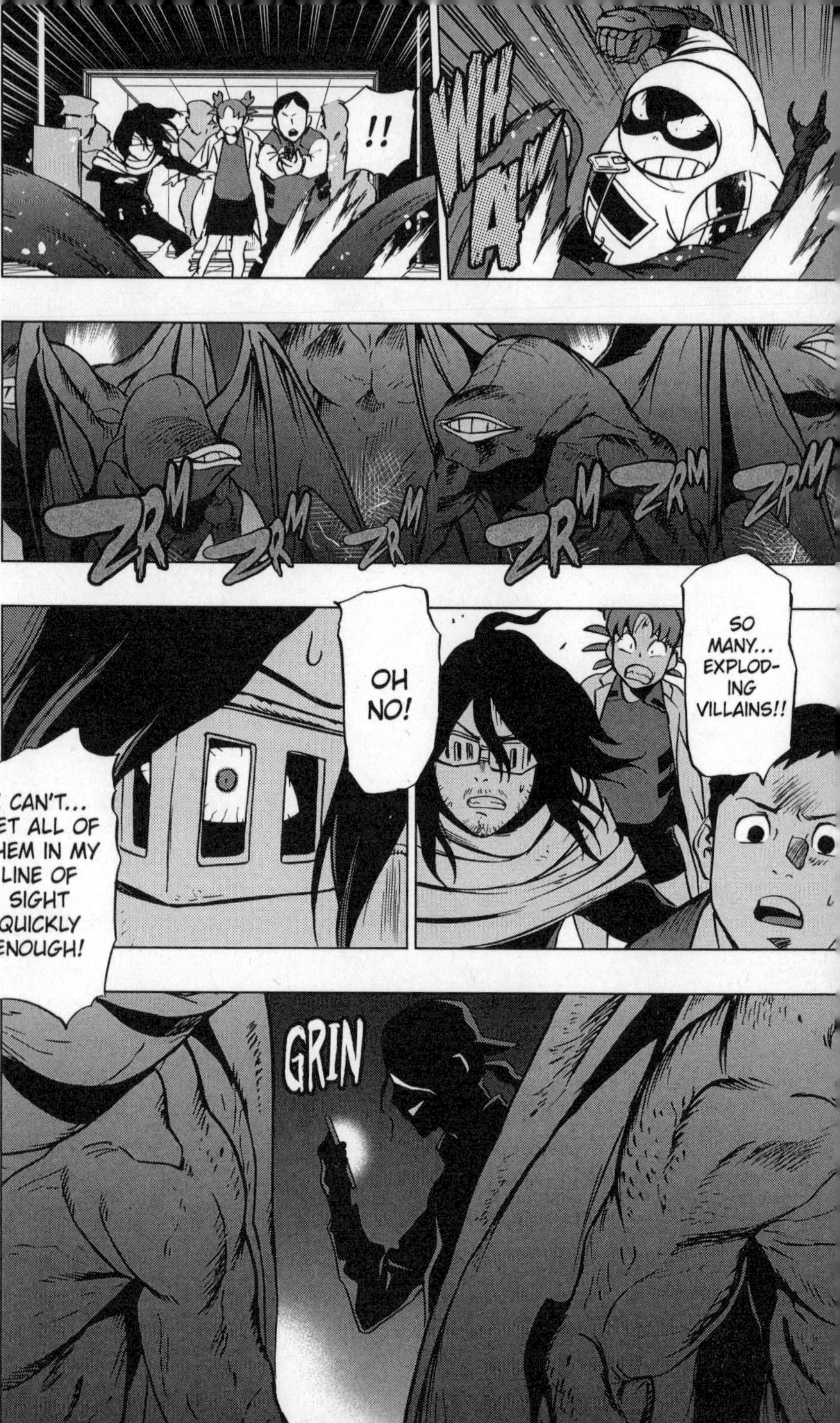
WHA
!!
ZRM ZRM ZRM ZRM ZRM ZRM ZRM
SO MANY... EXPLOD-ING VILLAINS!!
OH NO!
I CAN'T... GET ALL OF THEM IN MY LINE OF SIGHT QUICKLY ENOUGH!
GRIN

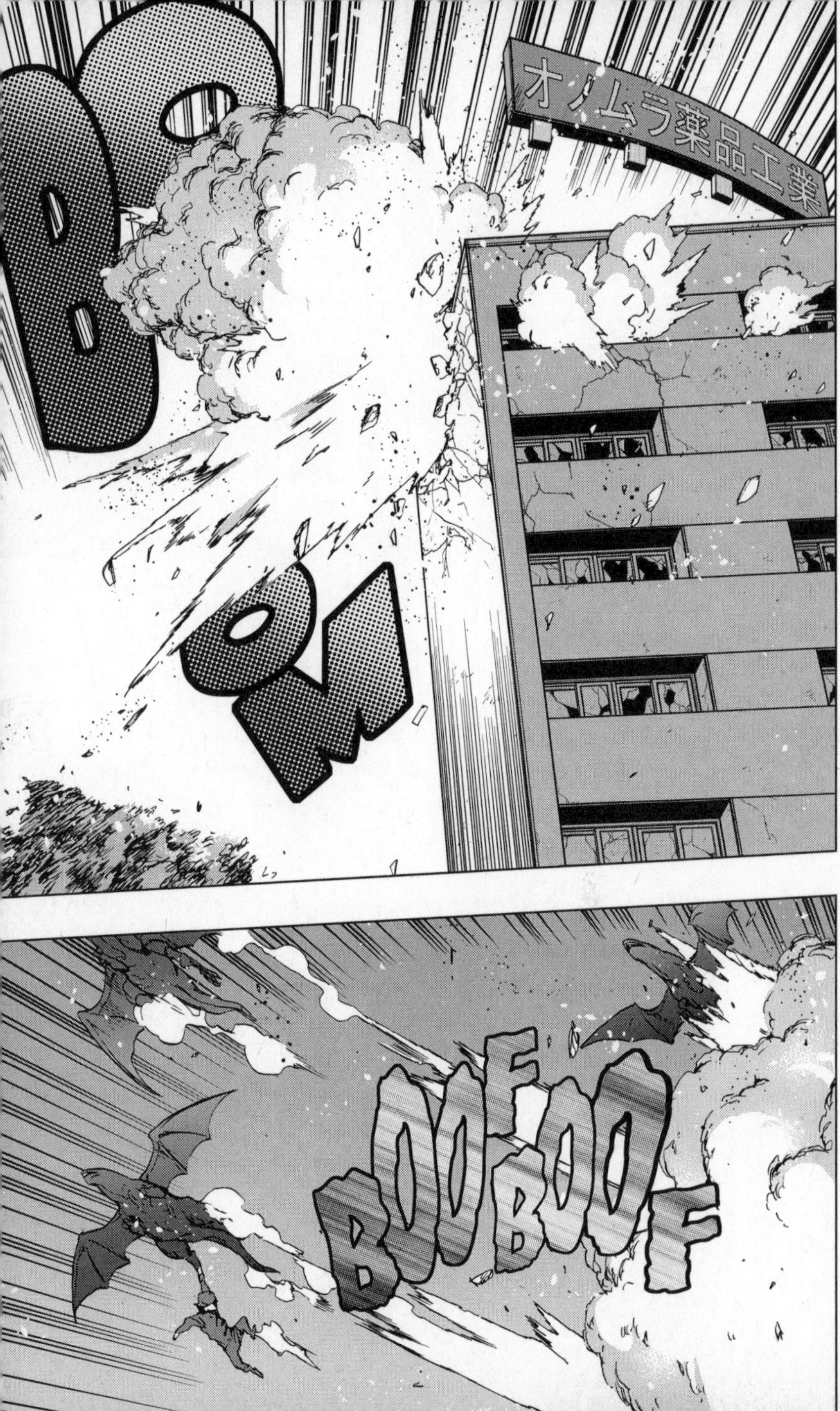
オノムラ薬品工業
BOOM
BOOF
BOOF

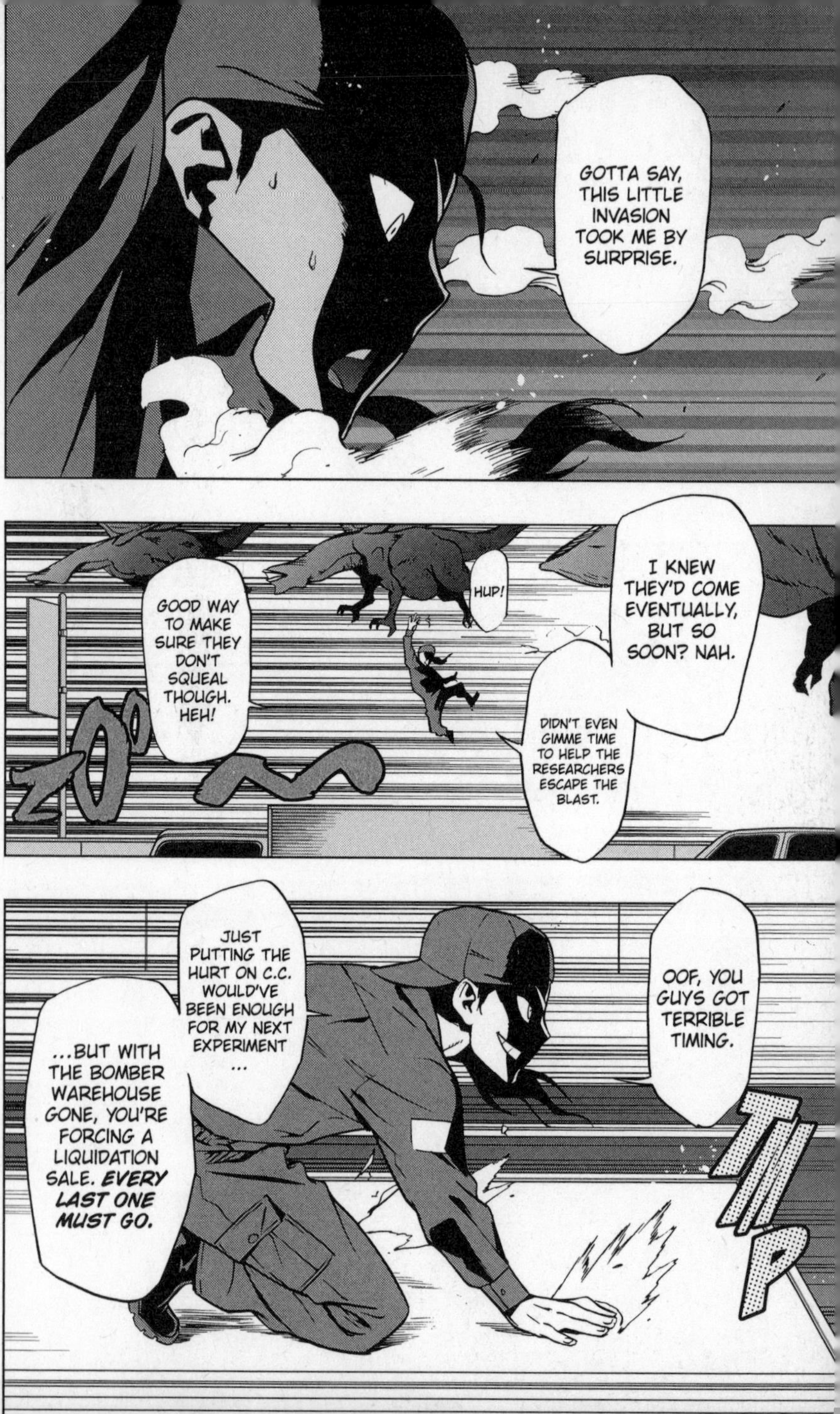
GOTTA SAY, THIS LITTLE INVASION TOOK ME BY SURPRISE.
I KNEW THEY'D COME EVENTUALLY, BUT SO SOON? NAH.
DIDN'T EVEN GIMME TIME TO HELP THE RESEARCHERS ESCAPE THE BLAST.
HUP!
GOOD WAY TO MAKE SURE THEY DON'T SQUEAL THOUGH. HEH!
OOF, YOU GUYS GOT TERRIBLE TIMING.
JUST PUTTING THE HURT ON C.C. WOULD'VE BEEN ENOUGH FOR MY NEXT EXPERIMENT...
...BUT WITH THE BOMBER WAREHOUSE GONE, YOU'RE FORCING A LIQUIDATION SALE. ***EVERY LAST ONE MUST GO.***

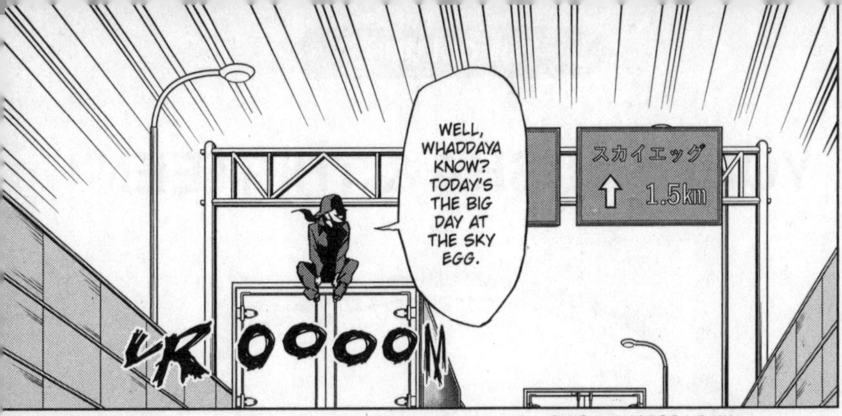
スカイエッグ
1.5km
WELL, WHADDAYA KNOW? TODAY'S THE BIG DAY AT THE SKY EGG.
VROOOOM

*SIGN: SKY EGG 1.5 KM

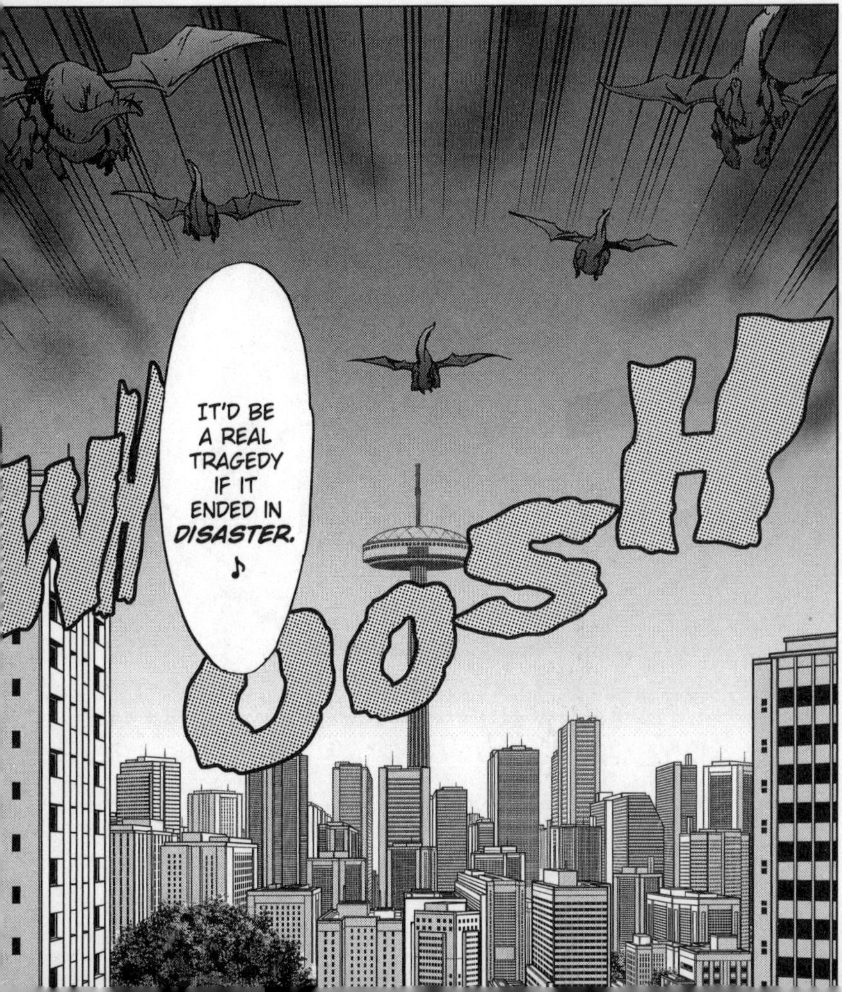
IT'D BE A REAL TRAGEDY IF IT ENDED IN DISASTER. ♪
WHOOSH

THE COLUMN

YOROI MUSHA & THIRTEEN

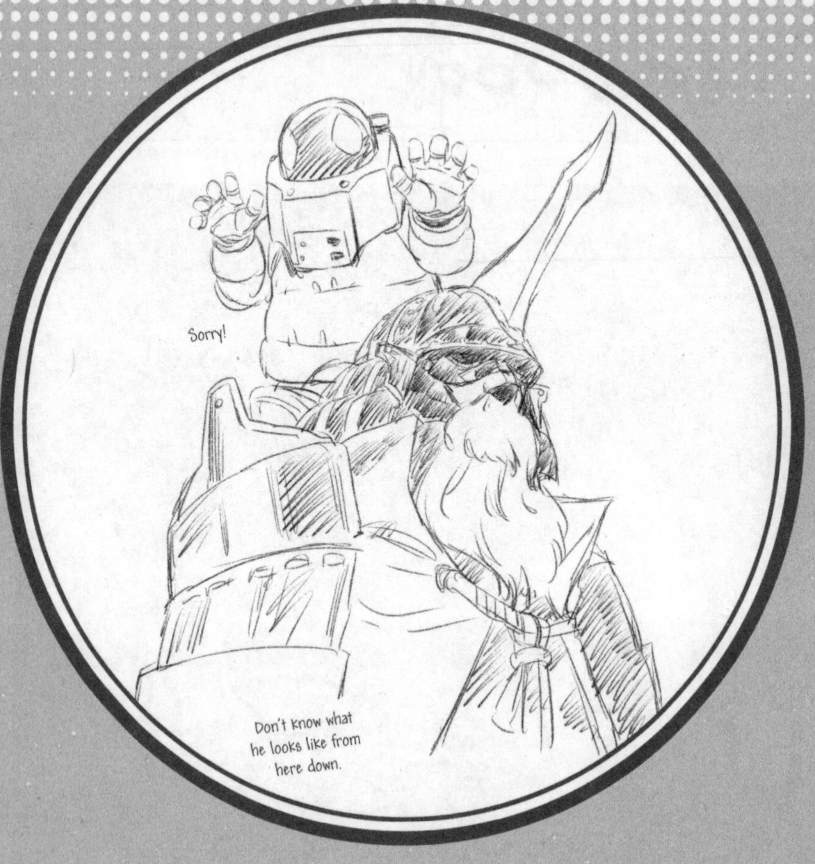
Sorry!
Don't know what he looks like from here down.

These two didn't appear at the big hero event. If they had, I'm sure they would've made a splash with their abilities. I love coming up with action scenes based around a character's personality and gimmicks.

—Furuhashi

Yoroi Musha and Thirteen were included in the rough draft of chapter 47 I got from Furuhashi Sensei, but due to time constraints (mostly my own), they didn't make it into the final version. I'm sorry... m(_ _)m

—Betten

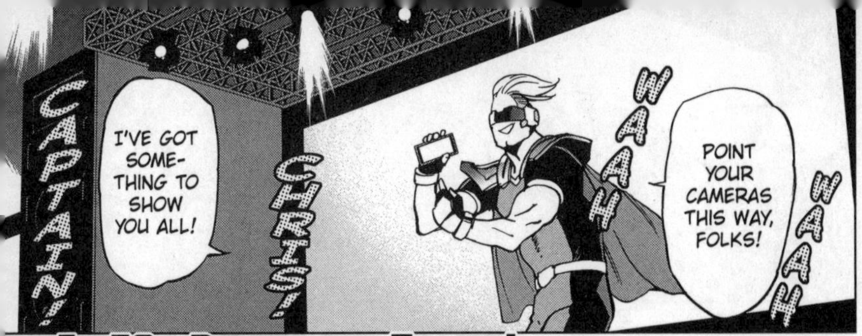
WAAAH
POINT YOUR CAMERAS THIS WAY, FOLKS!
WAAAH
CHRIS!
I'VE GOT SOME-THING TO SHOW YOU ALL!
CAPTAIN!

EP. 50 - DEFEND THE TOWER!

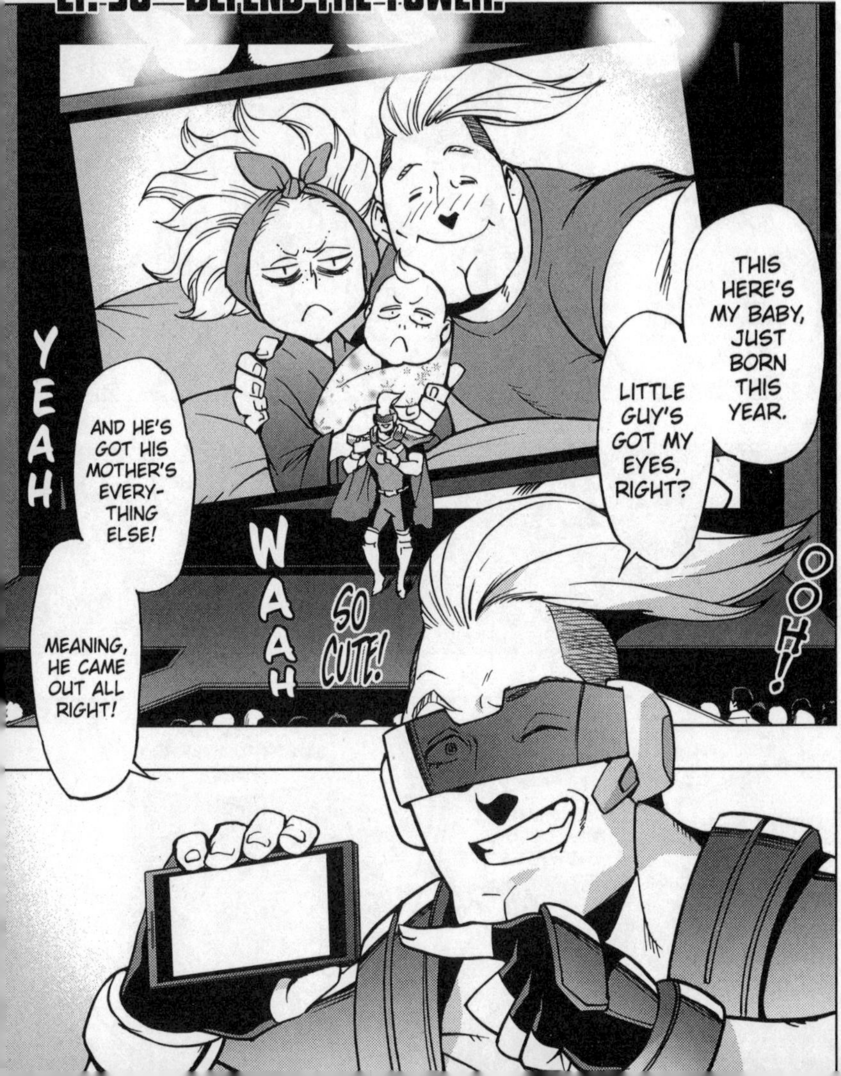
THIS HERE'S MY BABY, JUST BORN THIS YEAR.
LITTLE GUY'S GOT MY EYES, RIGHT?
OOOH!
AND HE'S GOT HIS MOTHER'S EVERY-THING ELSE!
YEAH
WAAAH
SO CUTE!
MEANING, HE CAME OUT ALL RIGHT!

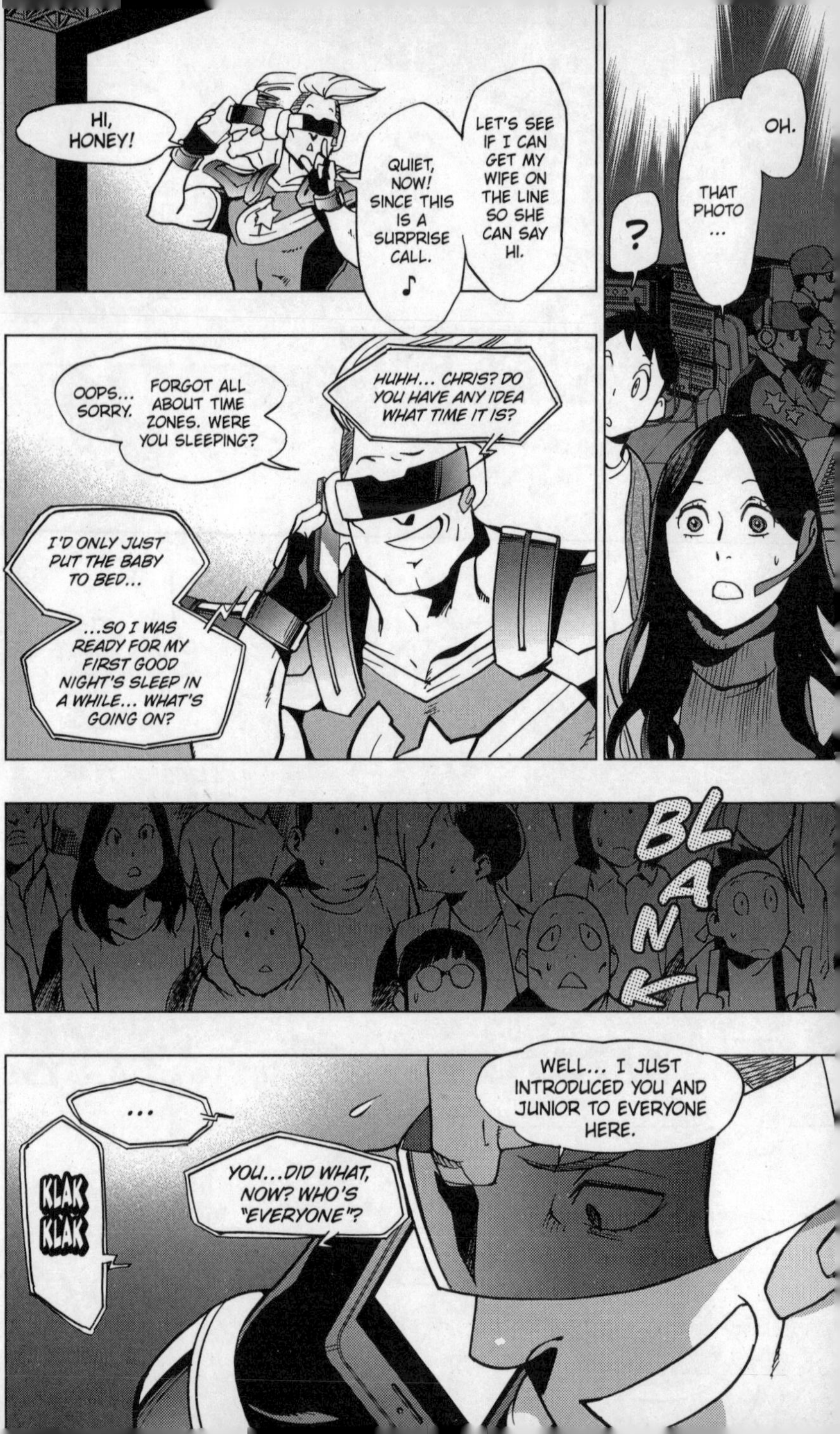
OH.
THAT PHOTO ...
?
LET'S SEE IF I CAN GET MY WIFE ON THE LINE SO SHE CAN SAY HI.
QUIET, NOW! SINCE THIS IS A SURPRISE CALL. ♪
HI, HONEY!
HUHH... CHRIS? DO YOU HAVE ANY IDEA WHAT TIME IT IS?
OOPS... SORRY.
FORGOT ALL ABOUT TIME ZONES. WERE YOU SLEEPING?
I'D ONLY JUST PUT THE BABY TO BED...
...SO I WAS READY FOR MY FIRST GOOD NIGHT'S SLEEP IN A WHILE... WHAT'S GOING ON?
BLANK
WELL... I JUST INTRODUCED YOU AND JUNIOR TO EVERYONE HERE.
...
YOU...DID WHAT, NOW? WHO'S "EVERYONE"?
KLAK KLAK

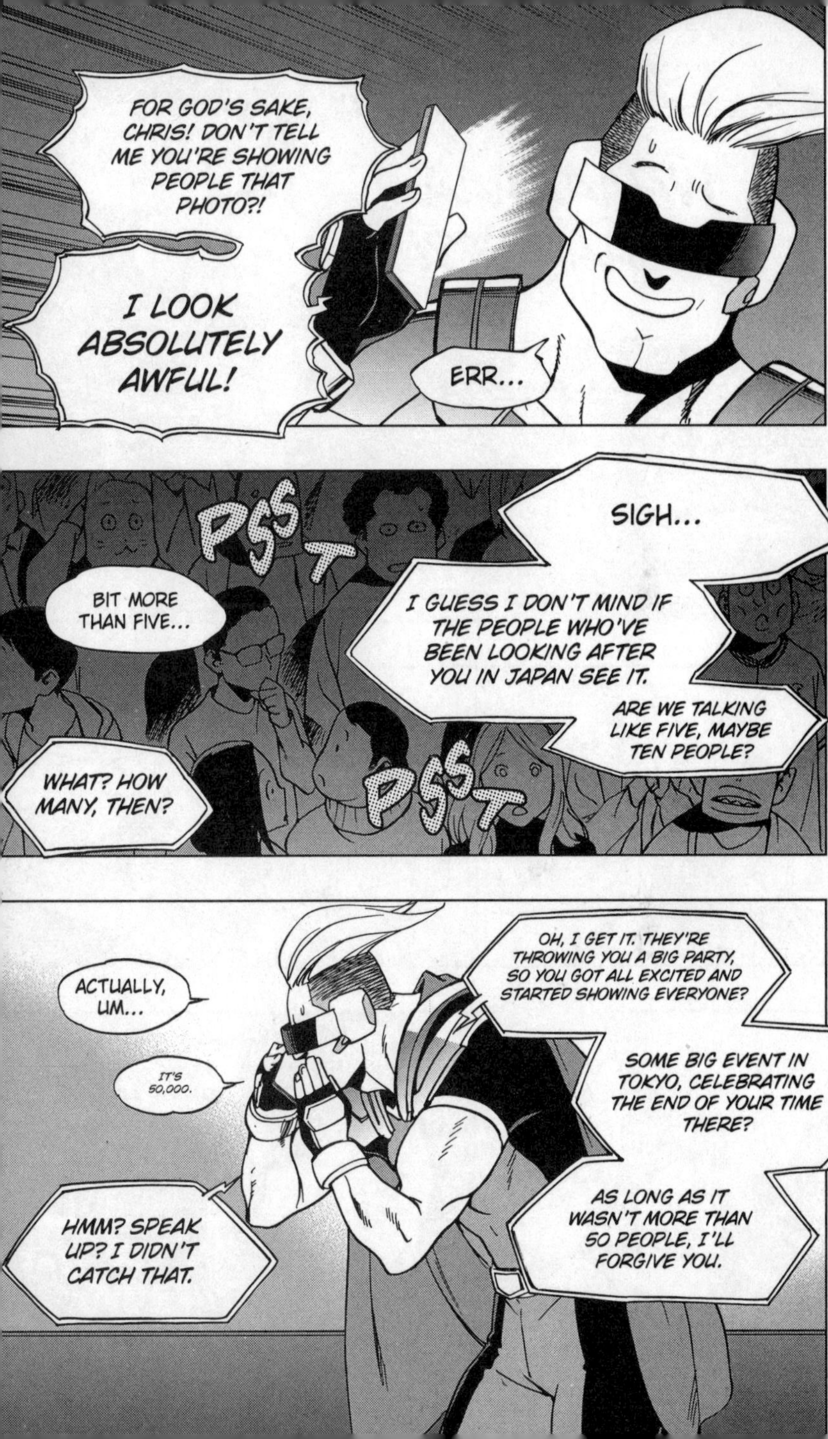
FOR GOD'S SAKE, CHRIS! DON'T TELL ME YOU'RE SHOWING PEOPLE THAT PHOTO?!
I LOOK ABSOLUTELY AWFUL!
ERR...
SIGH...
I GUESS I DON'T MIND IF THE PEOPLE WHO'VE BEEN LOOKING AFTER YOU IN JAPAN SEE IT.
ARE WE TALKING LIKE FIVE, MAYBE TEN PEOPLE?
PSST
BIT MORE THAN FIVE...
PSST
WHAT? HOW MANY, THEN?
OH, I GET IT. THEY'RE THROWING YOU A BIG PARTY, SO YOU GOT ALL EXCITED AND STARTED SHOWING EVERYONE?
SOME BIG EVENT IN TOKYO, CELEBRATING THE END OF YOUR TIME THERE?
AS LONG AS IT WASN'T MORE THAN 50 PEOPLE, I'LL FORGIVE YOU.
ACTUALLY, UM...
IT'S 50,000.
HMM? SPEAK UP? I DIDN'T CATCH THAT.

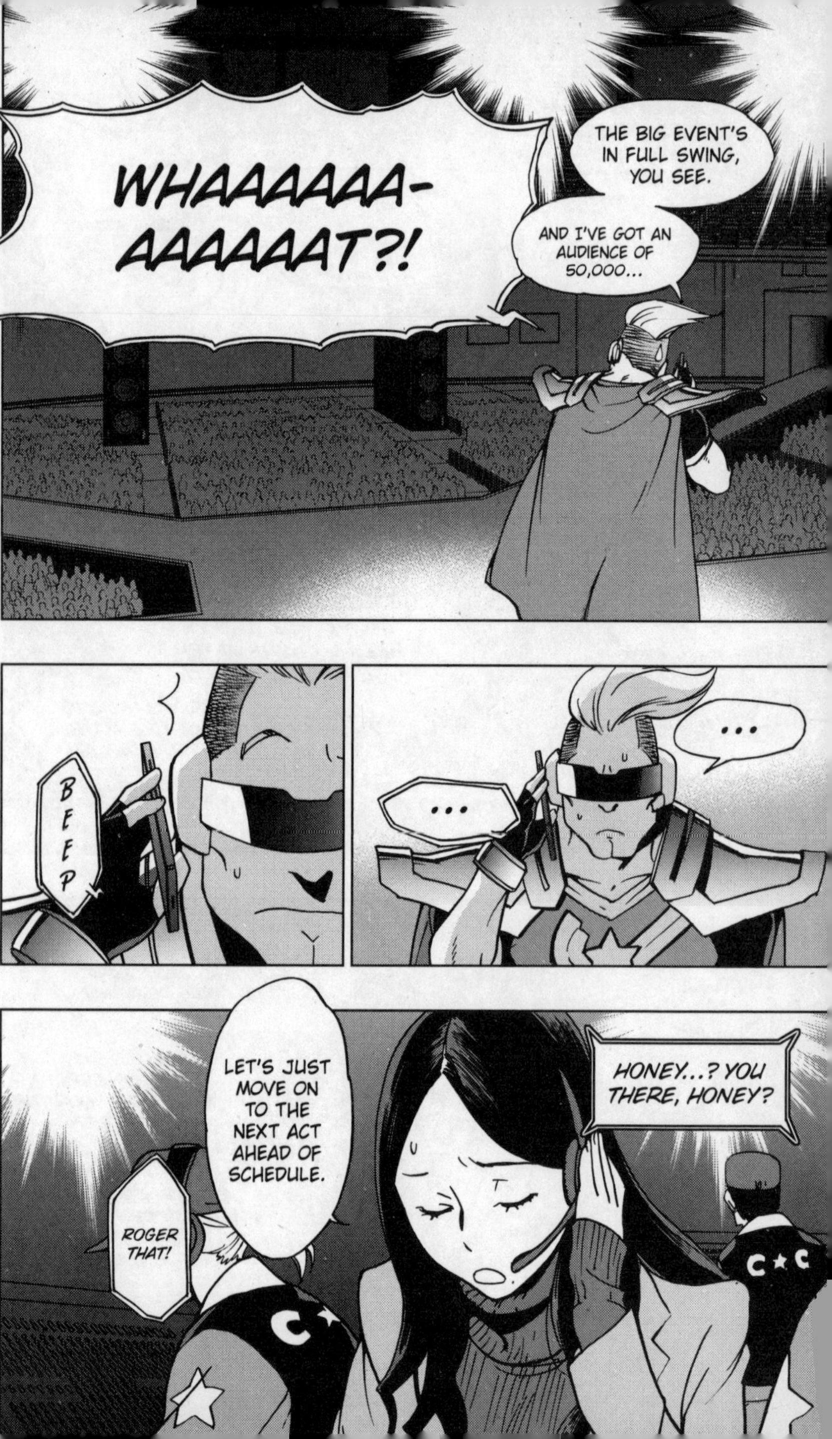
THE BIG EVENT'S IN FULL SWING, YOU SEE.
AND I'VE GOT AN AUDIENCE OF 50,000...
WHAAAAAAA-AAAAAAT?!
...
...
BEEP
HONEY...? YOU THERE, HONEY?
LET'S JUST MOVE ON TO THE NEXT ACT AHEAD OF SCHEDULE.
ROGER THAT!

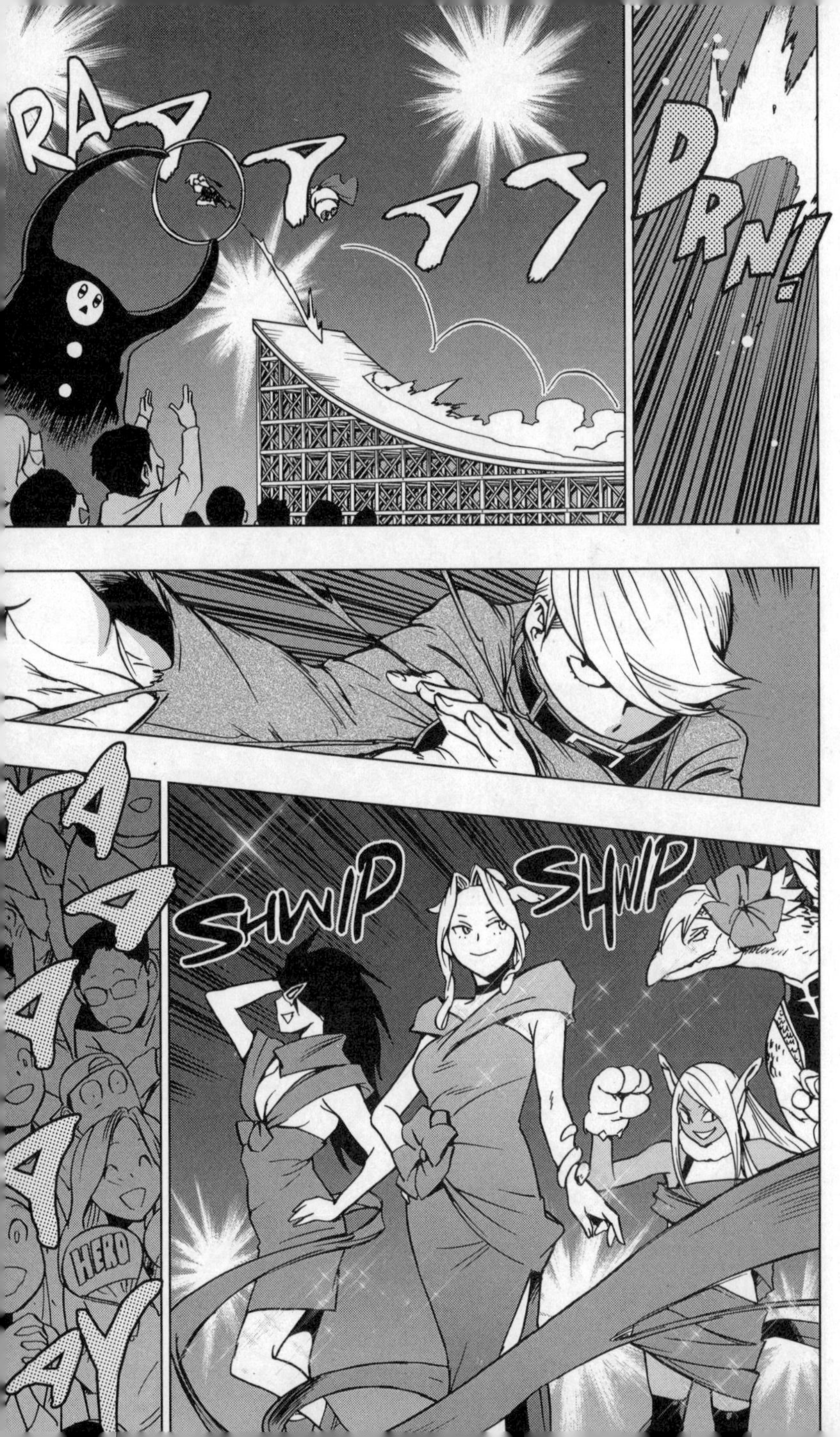
DRN!
RAAAAY
SHWIP
SHWIP
YAAAAY
HERO

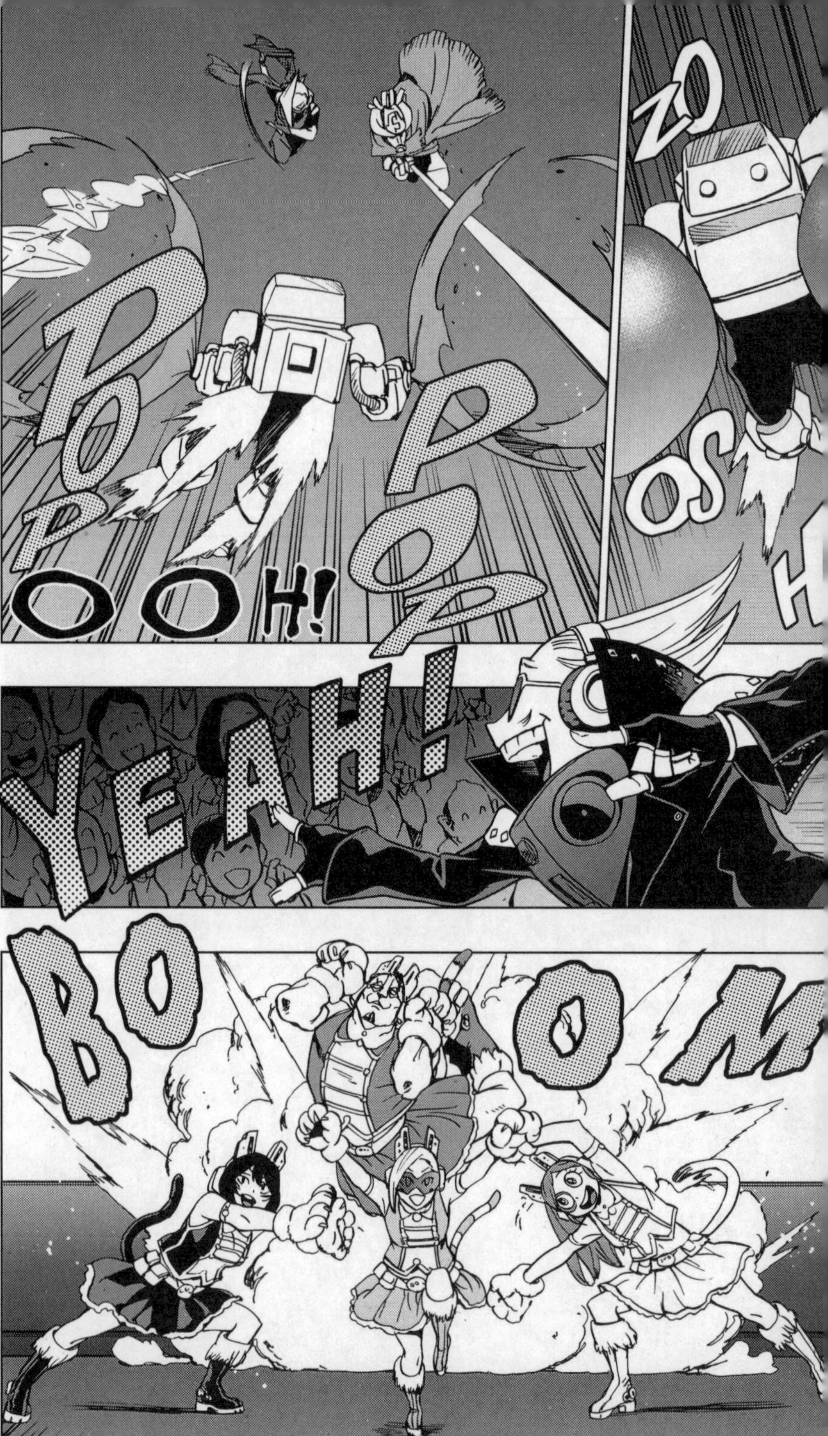

ZO
OS
H
OOH!
YEAH!
BOOM

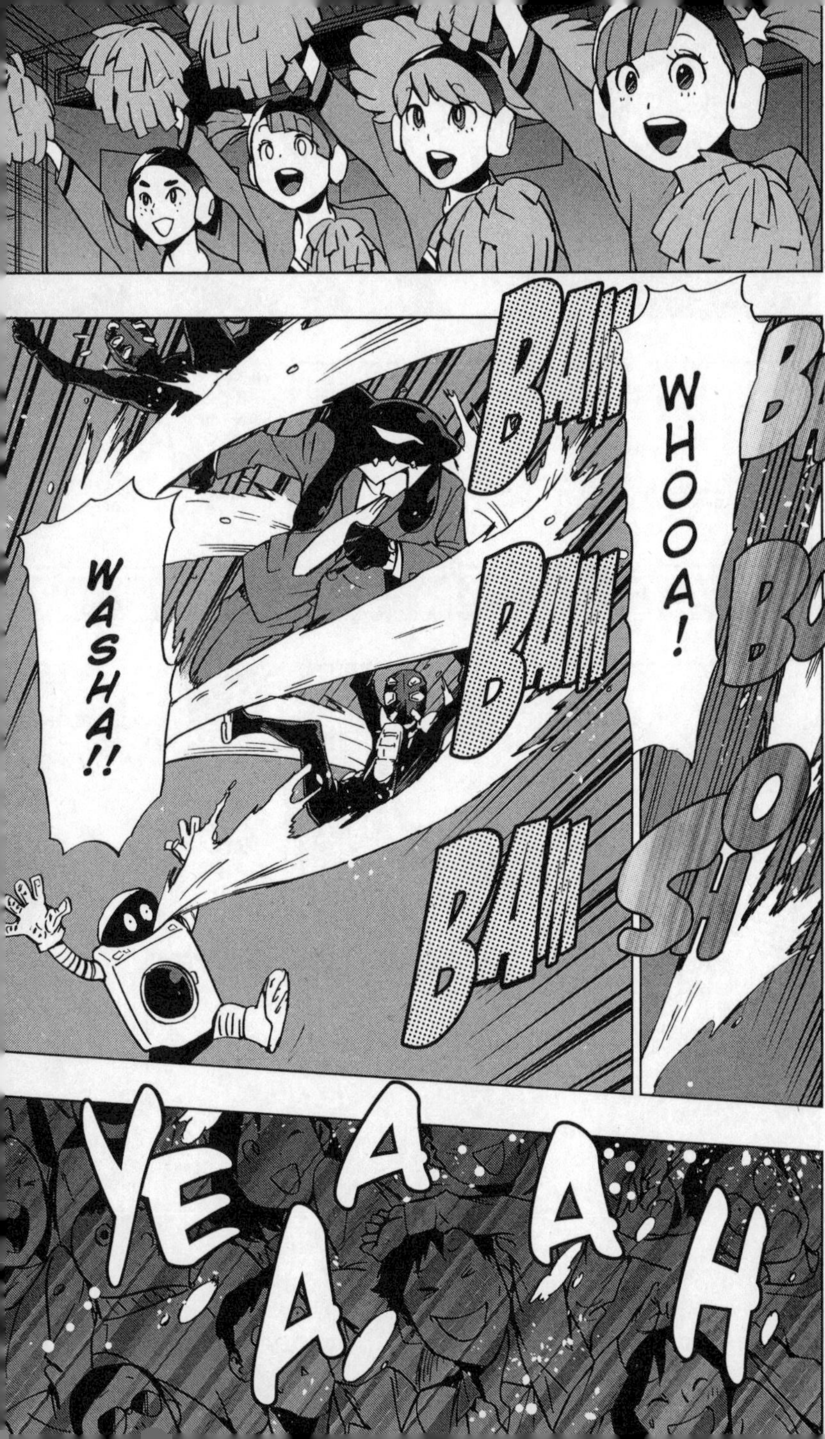

BABOOSH
WHOOA!
BAM
BAM
BAM
WASHA!!
YEAAAAH

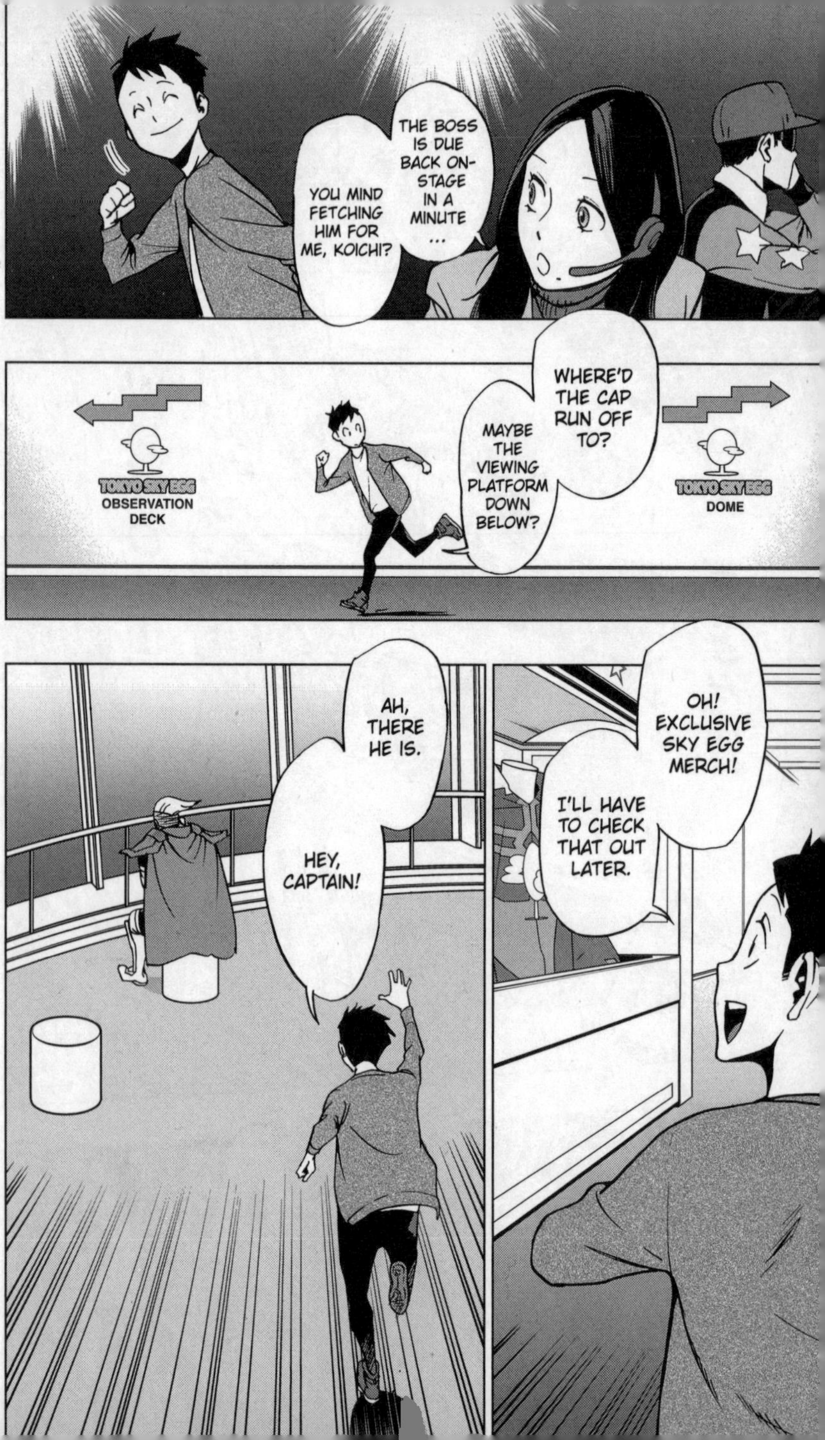
THE BOSS IS DUE BACK ON-STAGE IN A MINUTE ...
YOU MIND FETCHING HIM FOR ME, KOICHI?
WHERE'D THE CAP RUN OFF TO?
TOKYO SKY EGG DOME
MAYBE THE VIEWING PLATFORM DOWN BELOW?
TOKYO SKY EGG OBSERVATION DECK
OH! EXCLUSIVE SKY EGG MERCH!
I'LL HAVE TO CHECK THAT OUT LATER.
AH, THERE HE IS.
HEY, CAPTAIN!

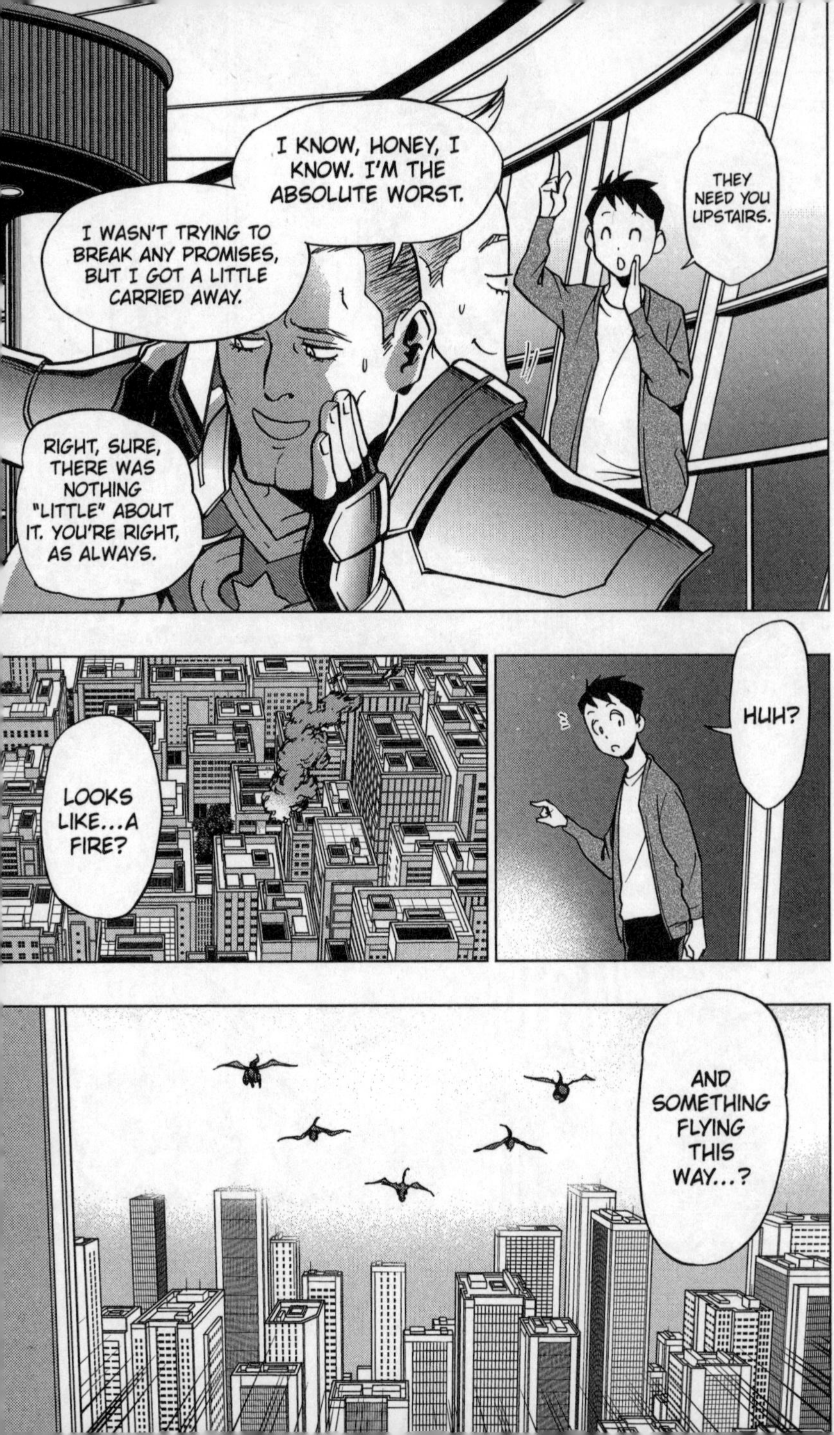

THEY NEED YOU UPSTAIRS.
I KNOW, HONEY, I KNOW. I'M THE ABSOLUTE WORST.
I WASN'T TRYING TO BREAK ANY PROMISES, BUT I GOT A LITTLE CARRIED AWAY.
RIGHT, SURE, THERE WAS NOTHING "LITTLE" ABOUT IT. YOU'RE RIGHT, AS ALWAYS.
HUH?
LOOKS LIKE...A FIRE?
AND SOMETHING FLYING THIS WAY...?

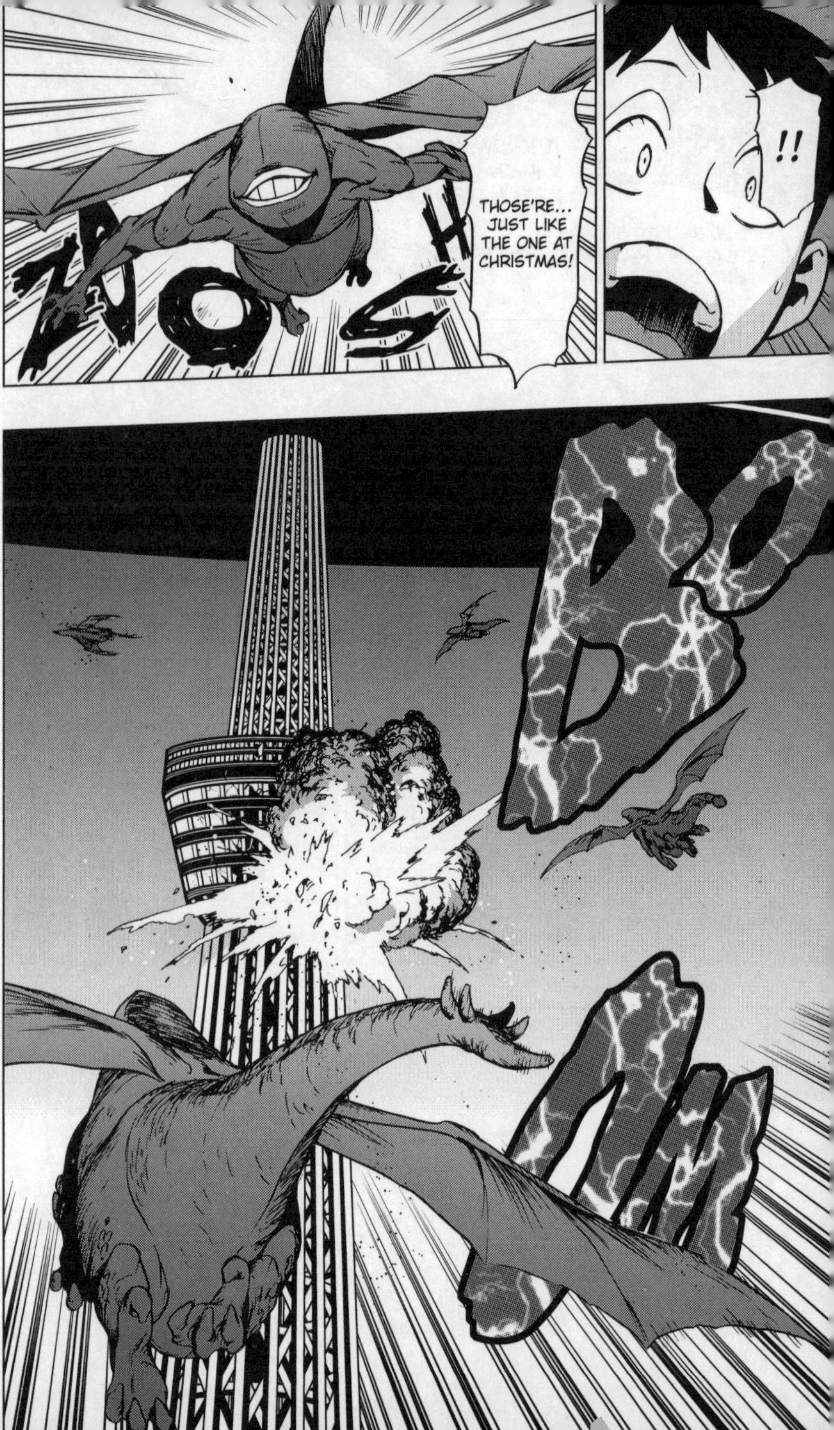
!!
THOSE'RE... JUST LIKE THE ONE AT CHRISTMAS!
ZWOOSH
BOOM

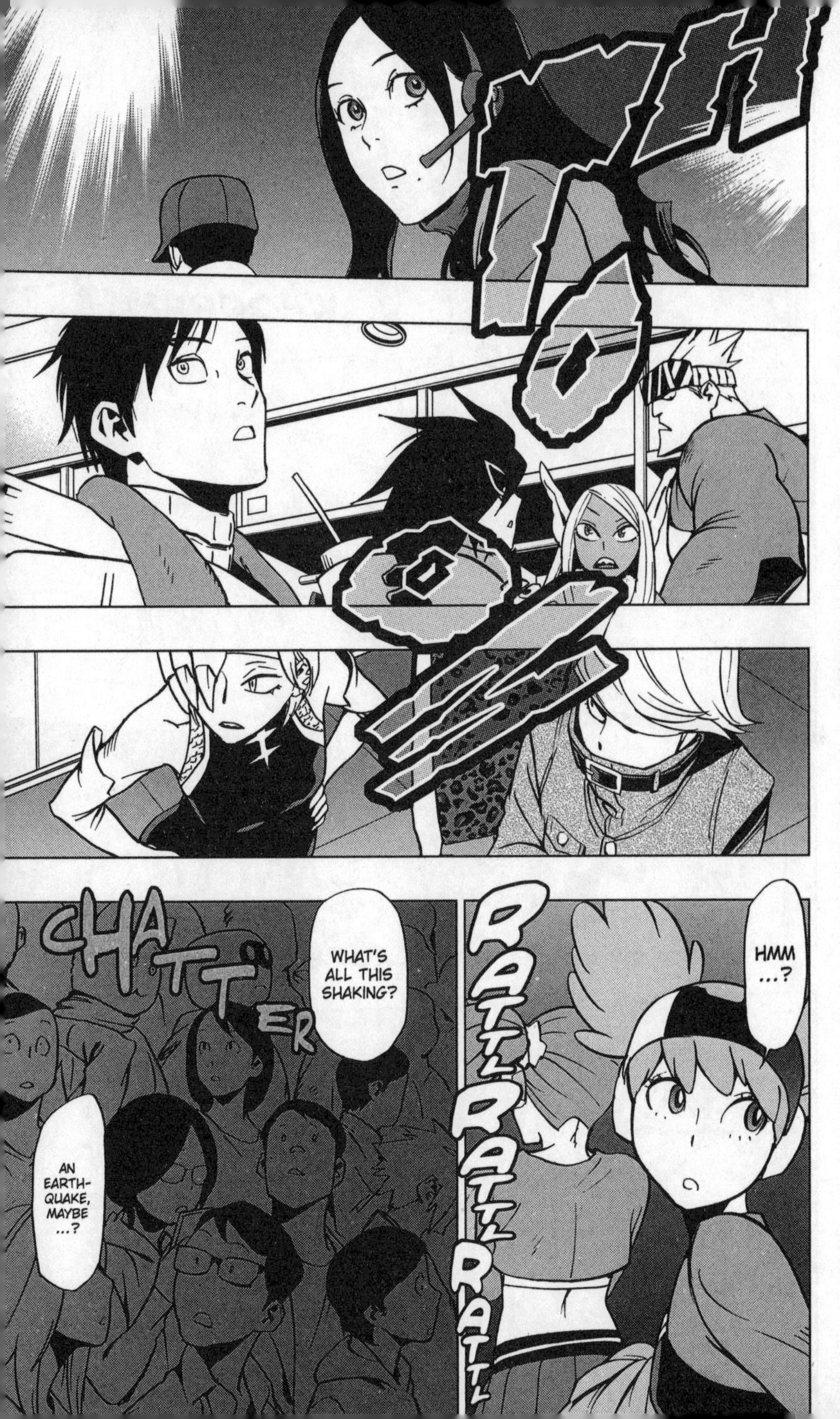
RATTL RATTL RATTL
HMM ...?
CHATTER
WHAT'S ALL THIS SHAKING?
AN EARTH-QUAKE, MAYBE ...?

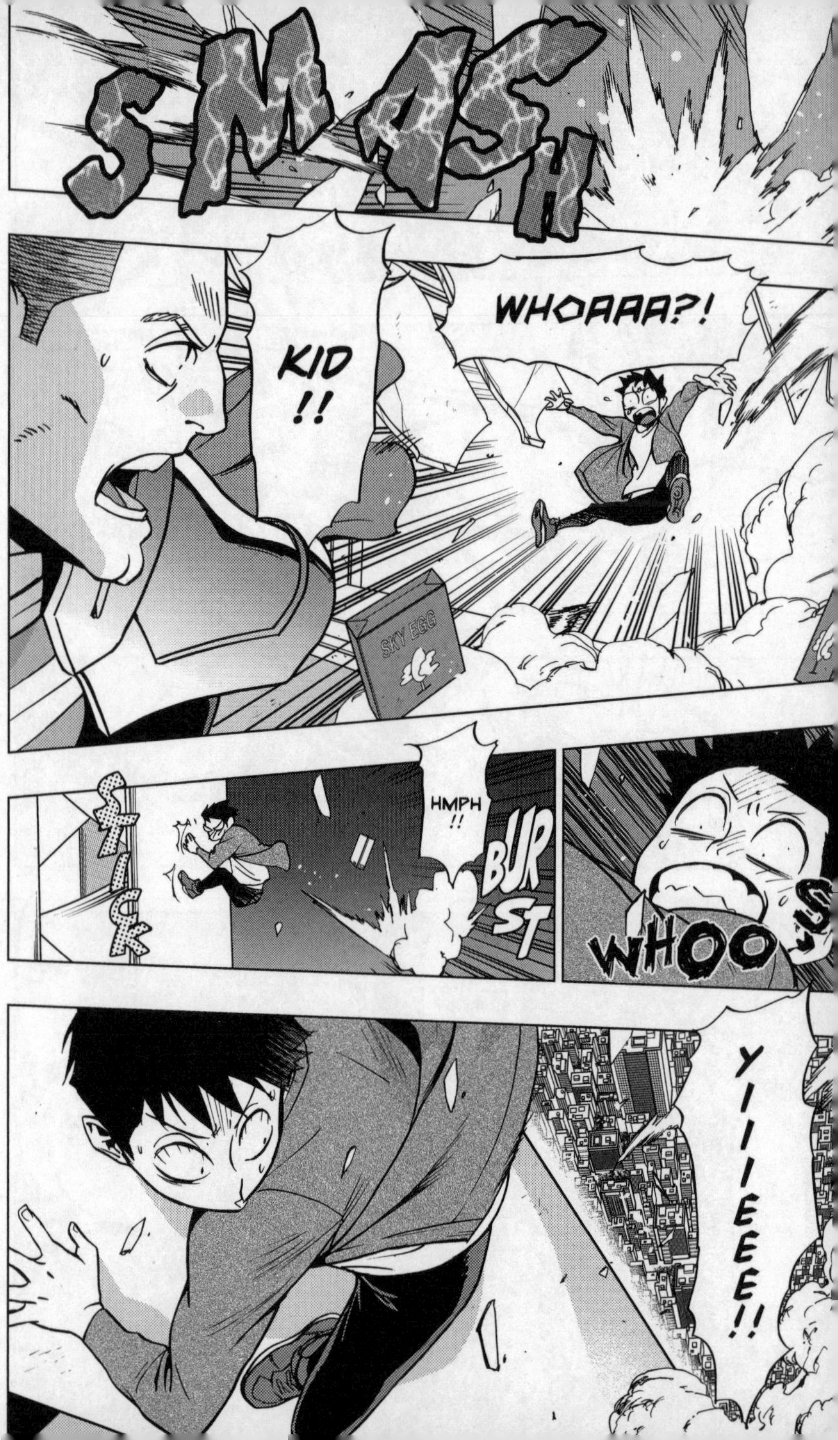
SMASH
WHOAAA?!
KID!!
SKY EGG
WHOOSH
HMPH!!
BURST
STICK
YIIIEEE!!

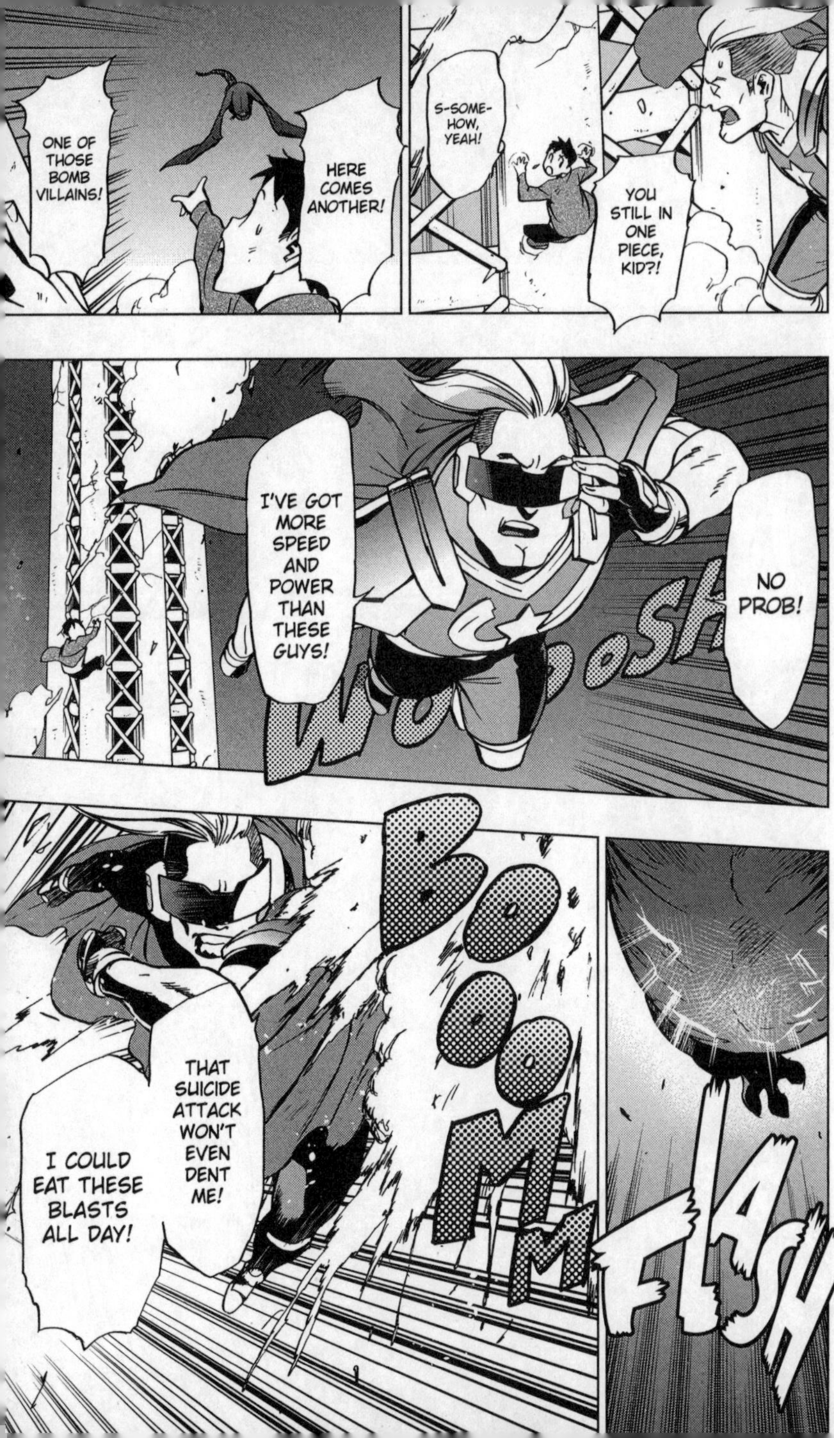
YOU STILL IN ONE PIECE, KID?!
S-SOME-HOW, YEAH!
HERE COMES ANOTHER!
ONE OF THOSE BOMB VILLAINS!
NO PROB!
I'VE GOT MORE SPEED AND POWER THAN THESE GUYS!
FLASH
BOOOM
THAT SUICIDE ATTACK WON'T EVEN DENT ME!
I COULD EAT THESE BLASTS ALL DAY!

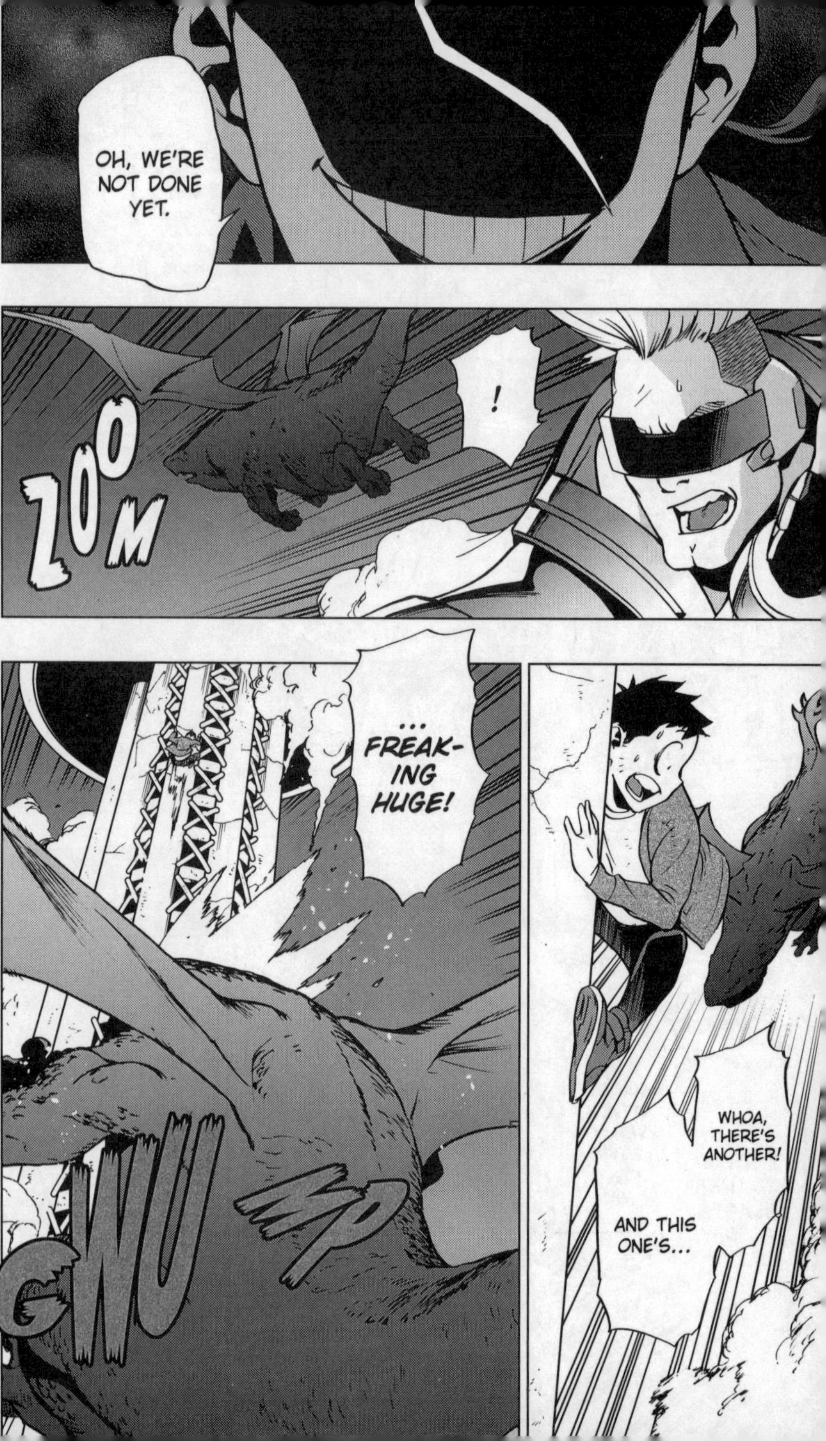
OH, WE'RE NOT DONE YET.
!
ZOOM
WHOA, THERE'S ANOTHER!
AND THIS ONE'S...
...FREAKING HUGE!
GWUMP

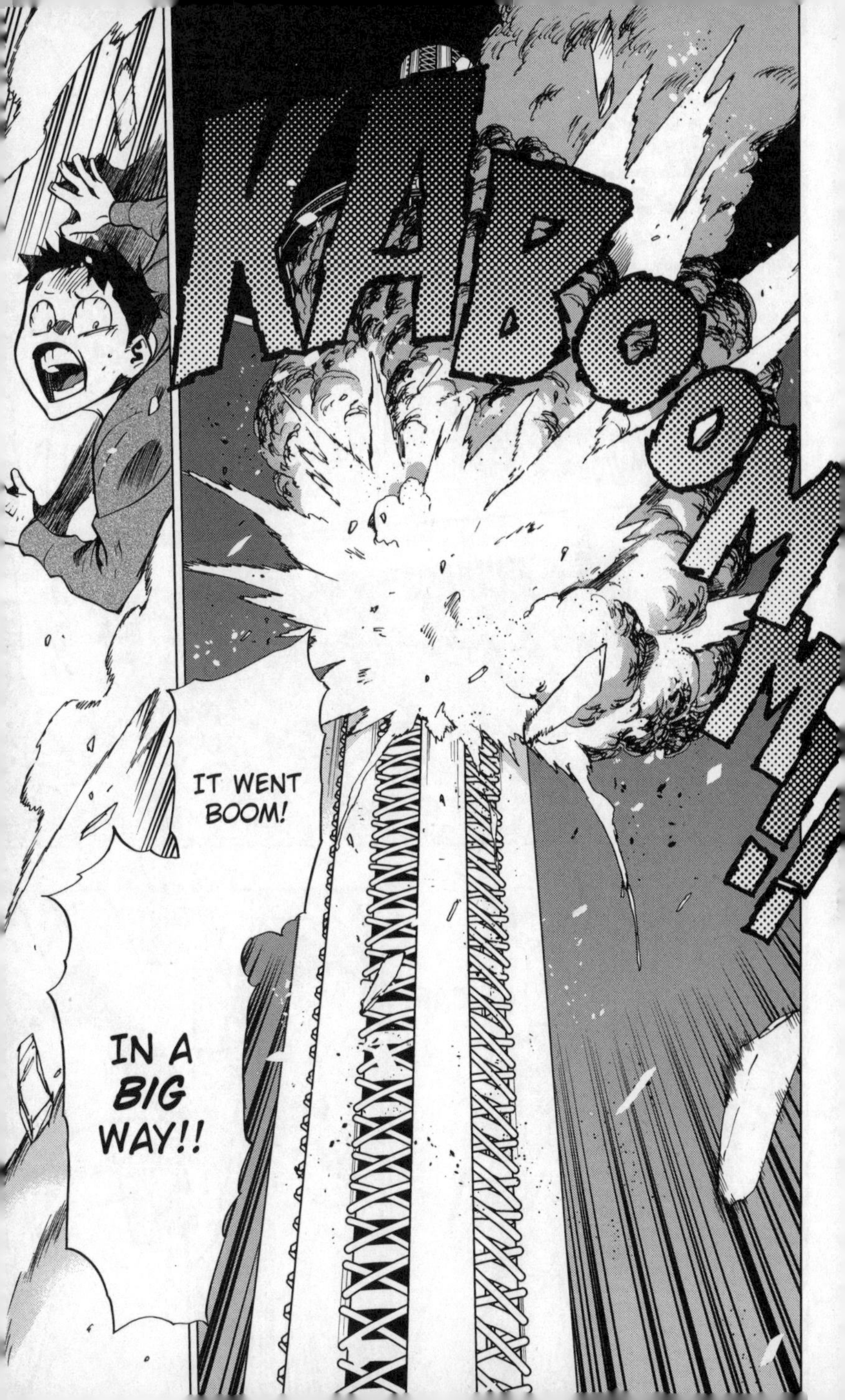
KABOOM!!!
IT WENT BOOM!
IN A BIG WAY!!

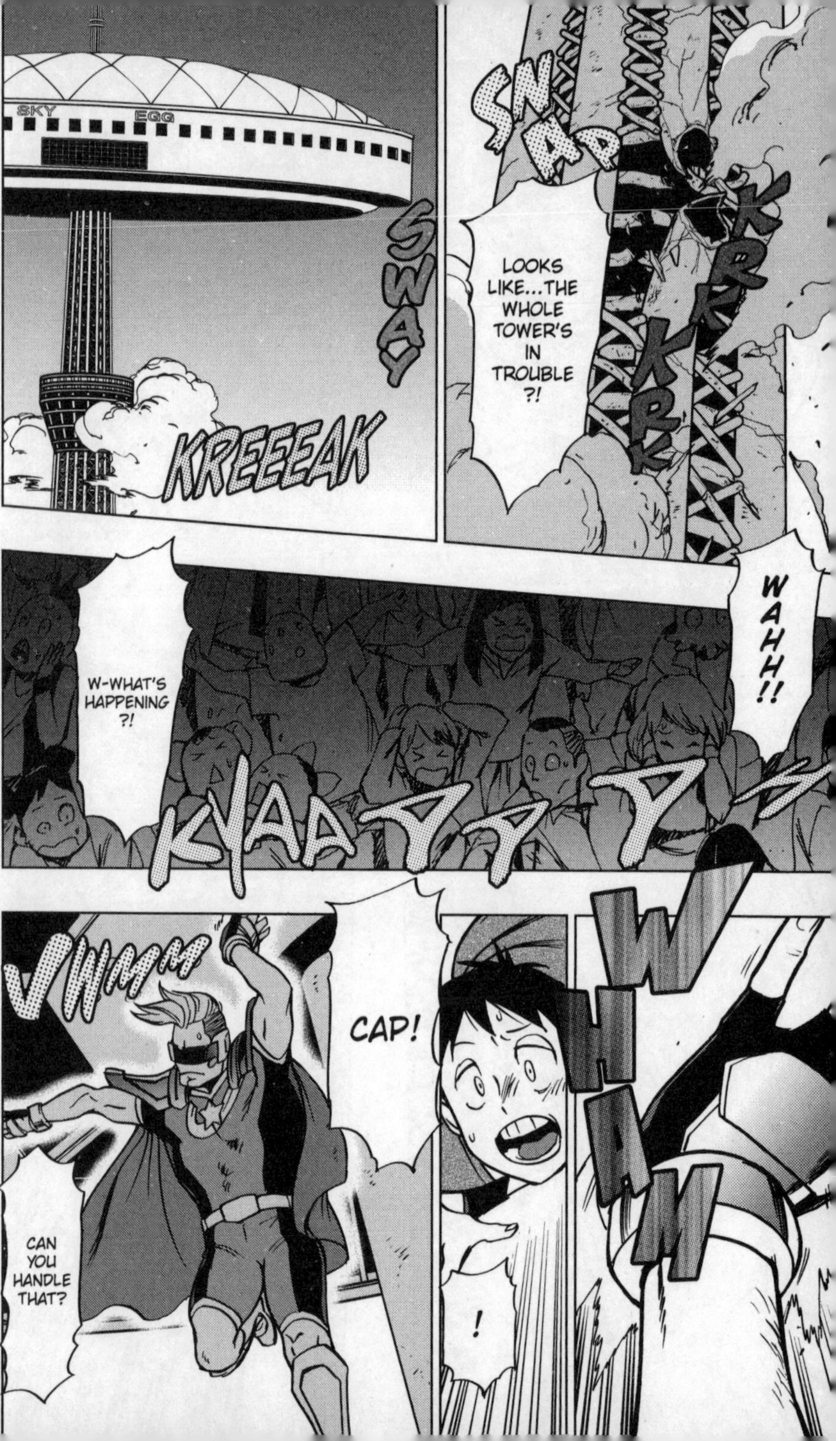
SNAP
KRRKKRK
LOOKS LIKE...THE WHOLE TOWER'S IN TROUBLE ?!
SKY EGG
SWAY
KREEEAK
WAHH!!
KYAAAA
W-WHAT'S HAPPENING ?!
WHAM
!
CAP!
VWMMM
CAN YOU HANDLE THAT?

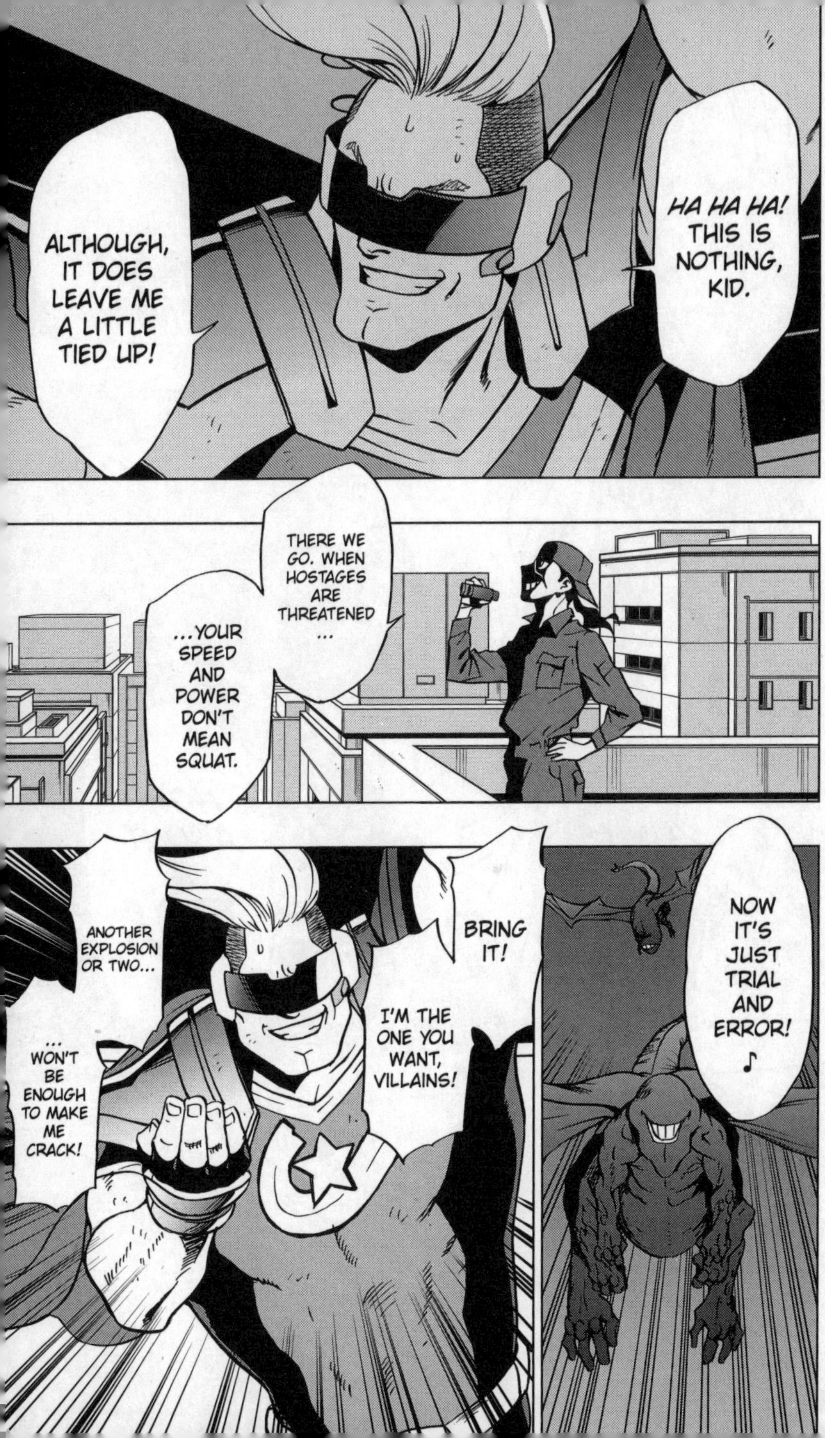
HA HA HA! THIS IS NOTHING, KID.
ALTHOUGH, IT DOES LEAVE ME A LITTLE TIED UP!
THERE WE GO. WHEN HOSTAGES ARE THREATENED...
...YOUR SPEED AND POWER DON'T MEAN SQUAT.
NOW IT'S JUST TRIAL AND ERROR! ♪
BRING IT!
I'M THE ONE YOU WANT, VILLAINS!
ANOTHER EXPLOSION OR TWO...
...WON'T BE ENOUGH TO MAKE ME CRACK!

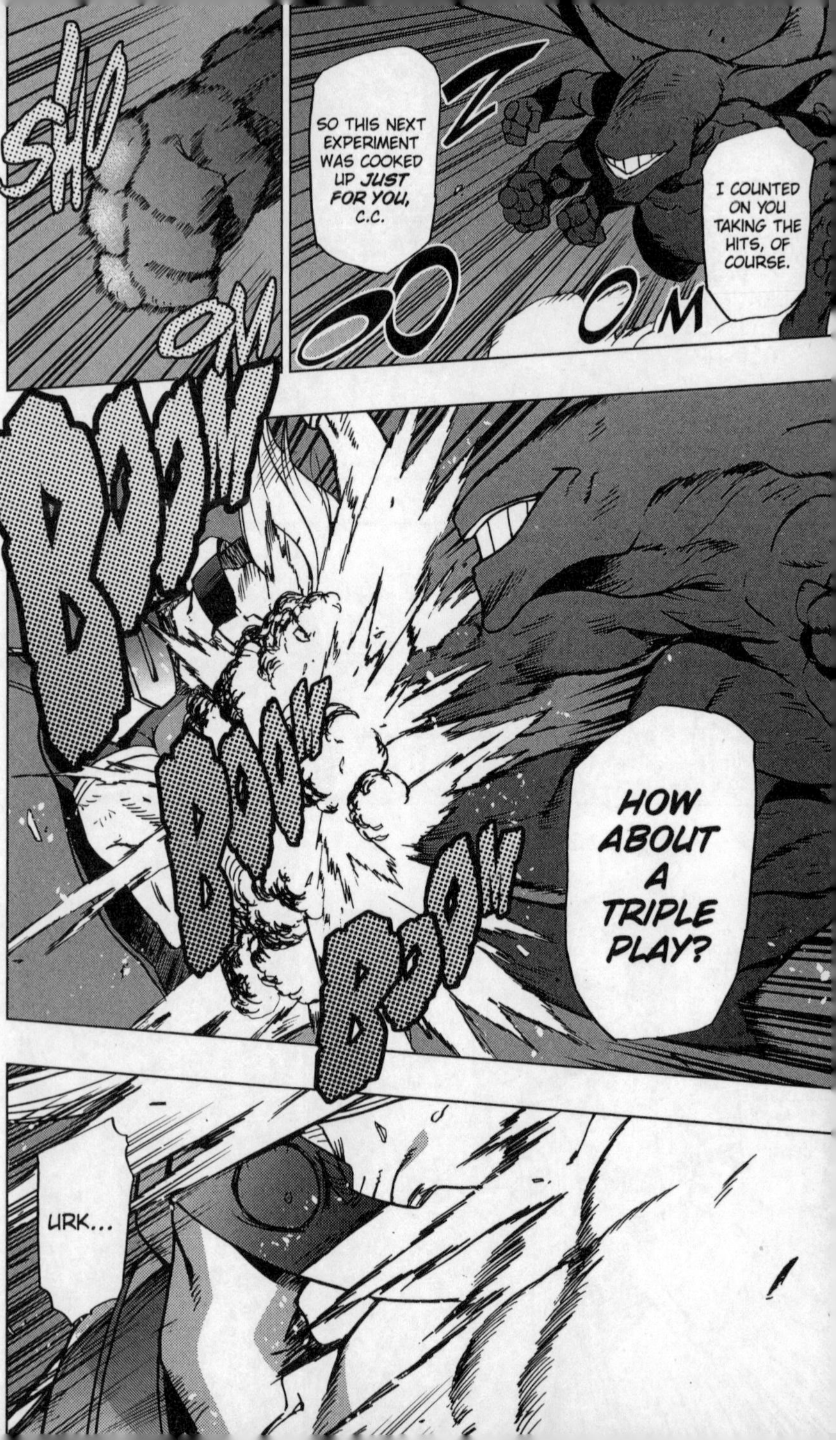
I COUNTED ON YOU TAKING THE HITS, OF COURSE.
SO THIS NEXT EXPERIMENT WAS COOKED UP *JUST FOR YOU,* C.C.
ZOOOM
SHOOM
HOW ABOUT A TRIPLE PLAY?
BOOM
BOOM
BOOM
URK...

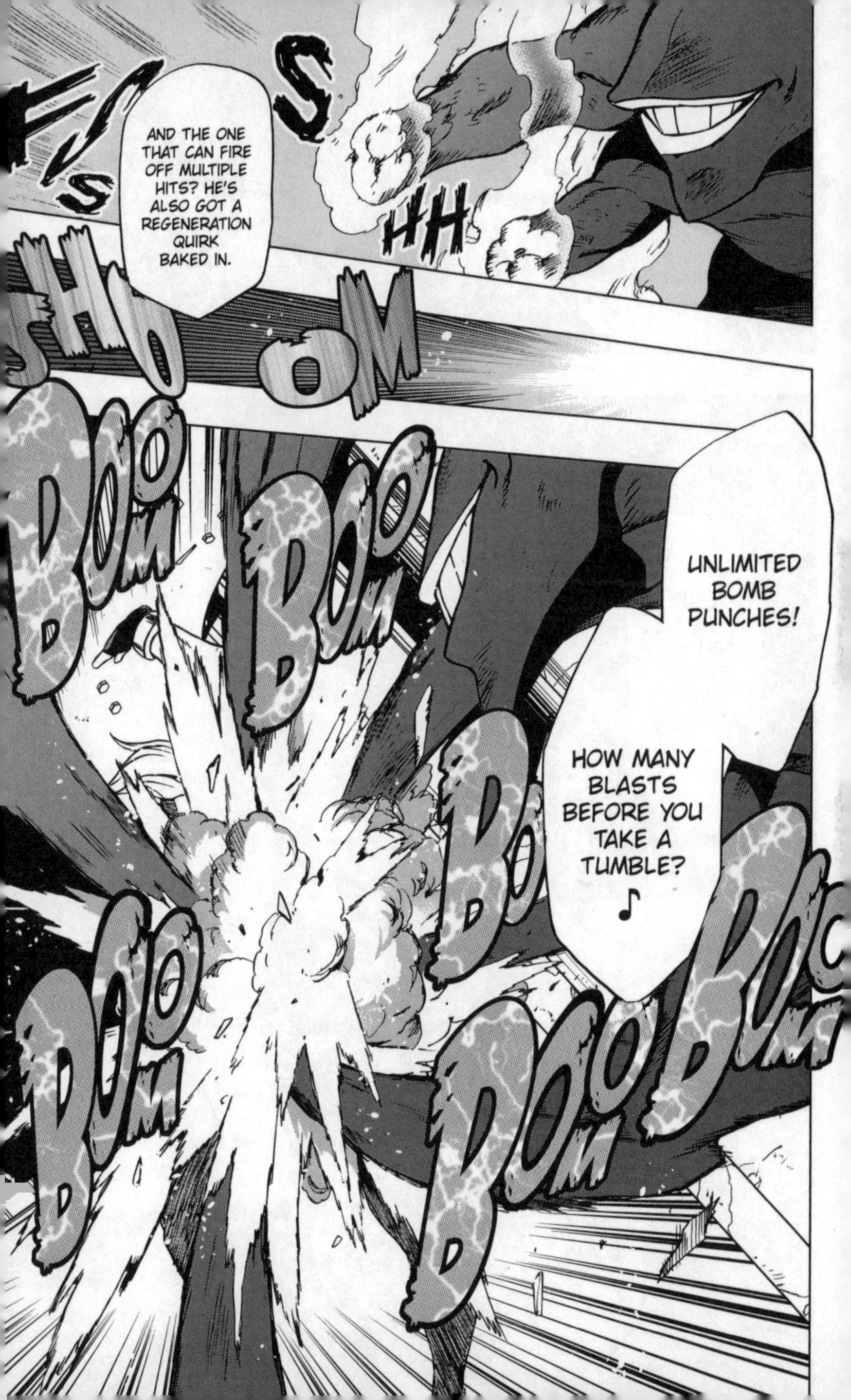
AND THE ONE THAT CAN FIRE OFF MULTIPLE HITS? HE'S ALSO GOT A REGENERATION QUIRK BAKED IN.
UNLIMITED BOMB PUNCHES!
HOW MANY BLASTS BEFORE YOU TAKE A TUMBLE? ♪

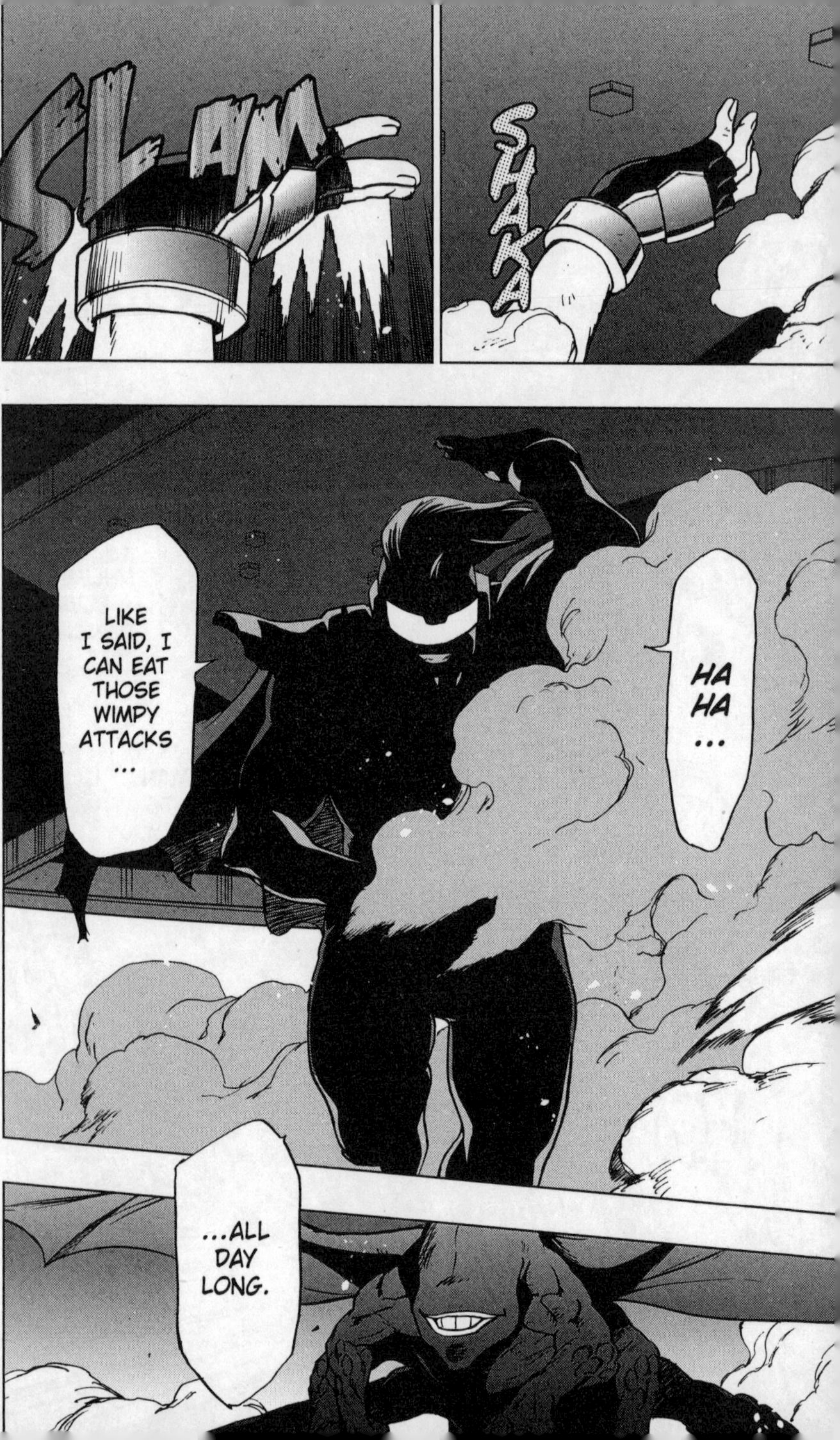
SHAKA
SLAM
HA HA ...
LIKE I SAID, I CAN EAT THOSE WIMPY ATTACKS ...
...ALL DAY LONG.

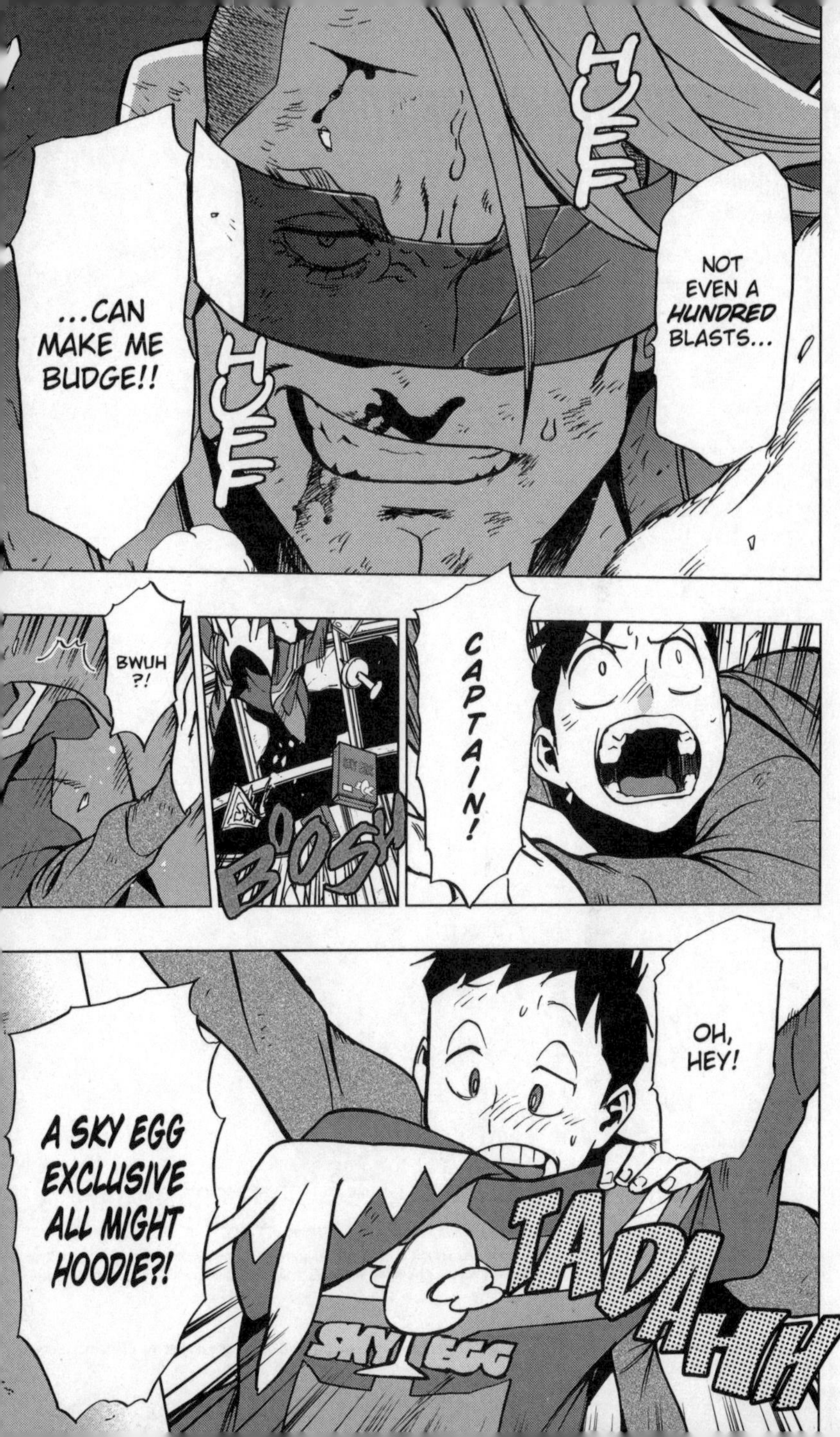
HUFF
NOT EVEN A HUNDRED BLASTS...
HUFF
...CAN MAKE ME BUDGE!!
CAPTAIN!
BOSH
BWUH?!
OH, HEY!
TADAHHH
A SKY EGG EXCLUSIVE ALL MIGHT HOODIE?!
SKY EGG

BOMBER VILLAINS: VARIATIONS

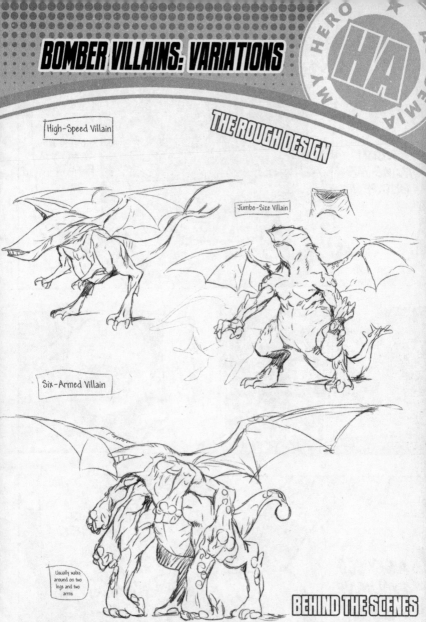

THE ROUGH DESIGN

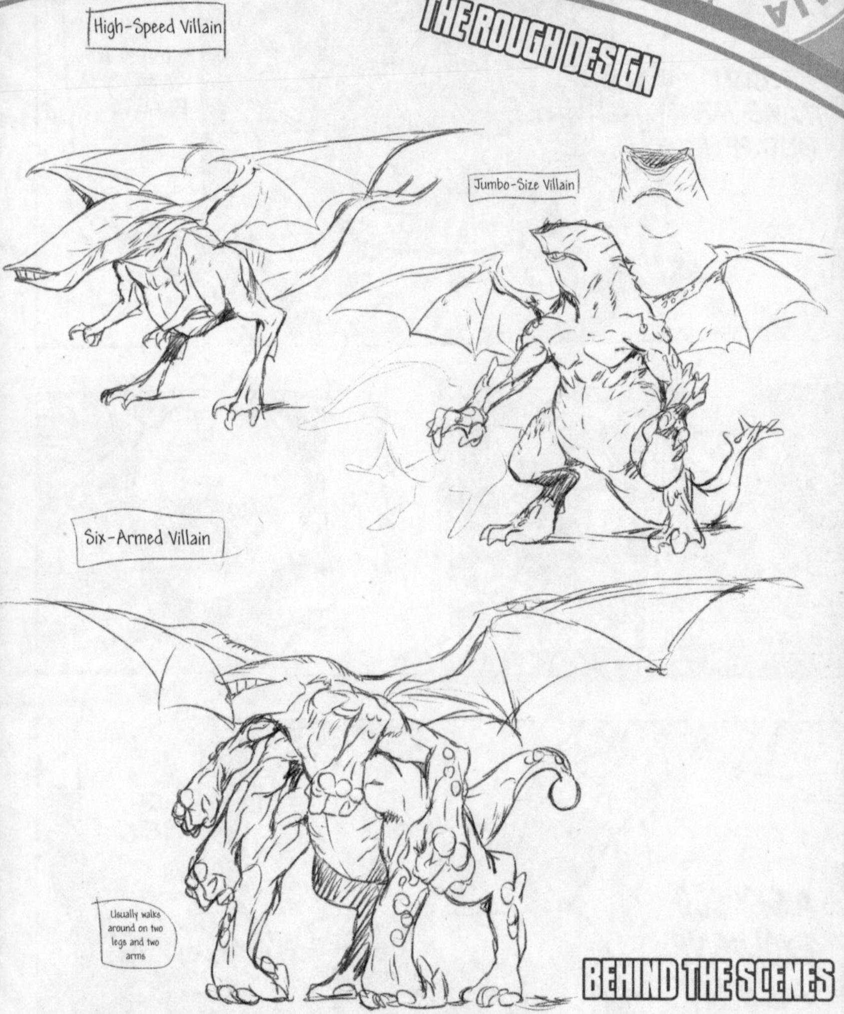
High-Speed Villain
Jumbo-Size Villain
Six-Armed Villain
Usually walks around on two legs and two arms

BEHIND THE SCENES

I thought it'd get boring if every member of the bomber squad was identical, so I requested two or three variations. The one with multiple arms really ended up pulling his own weight, story wise. Multiplication plus bombs is a nasty combo.

—Furuhashi

Think they're all the same? Think again! …Is what I'd like to say, but I messed up when drawing some of them, so don't inspect the images too closely!

—Betten

Ep. 51 - I Do What I Can

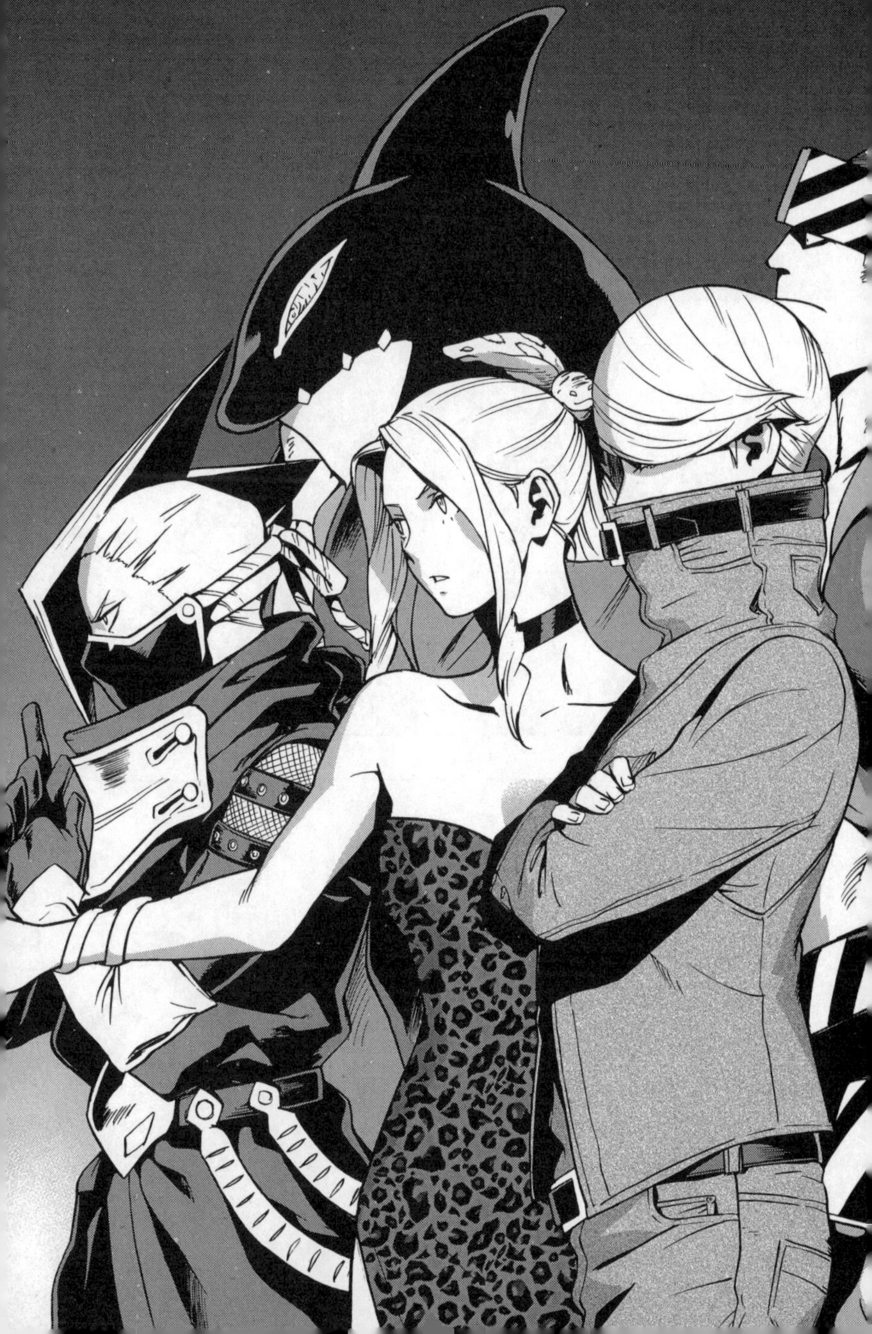

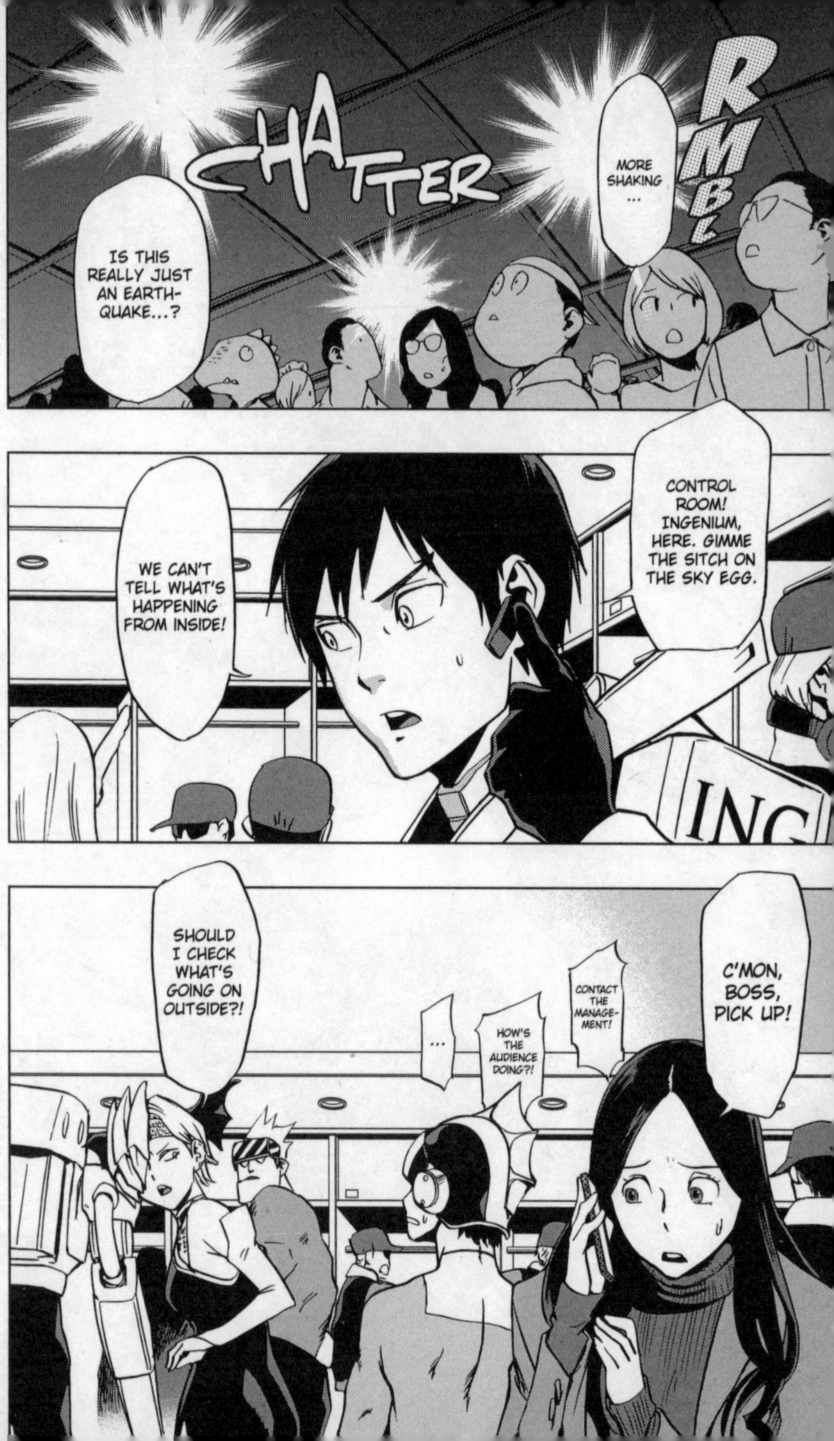
RMBL
MORE SHAKING ...
CHATTER
IS THIS REALLY JUST AN EARTH-QUAKE...?
CONTROL ROOM! INGENIUM, HERE. GIMME THE SITCH ON THE SKY EGG.
WE CAN'T TELL WHAT'S HAPPENING FROM INSIDE!
ING
C'MON, BOSS, PICK UP!
CONTACT THE MANAGE-MENT!
HOW'S THE AUDIENCE DOING?!
...
SHOULD I CHECK WHAT'S GOING ON OUTSIDE?!

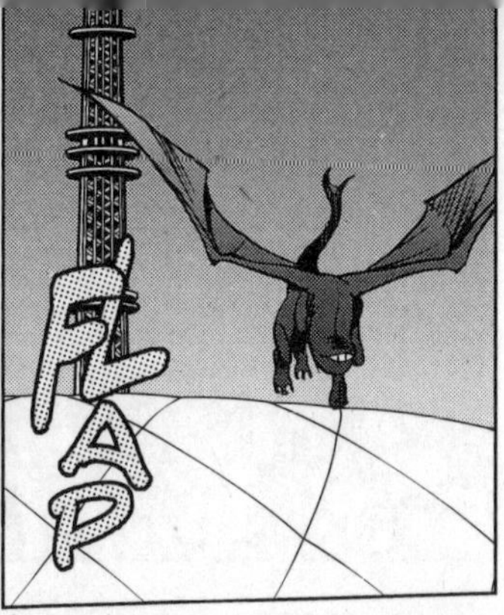
FLAP
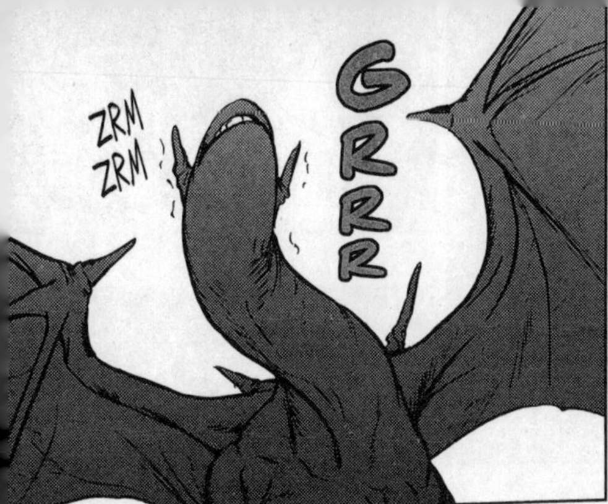
GRRR
ZRM
ZRM
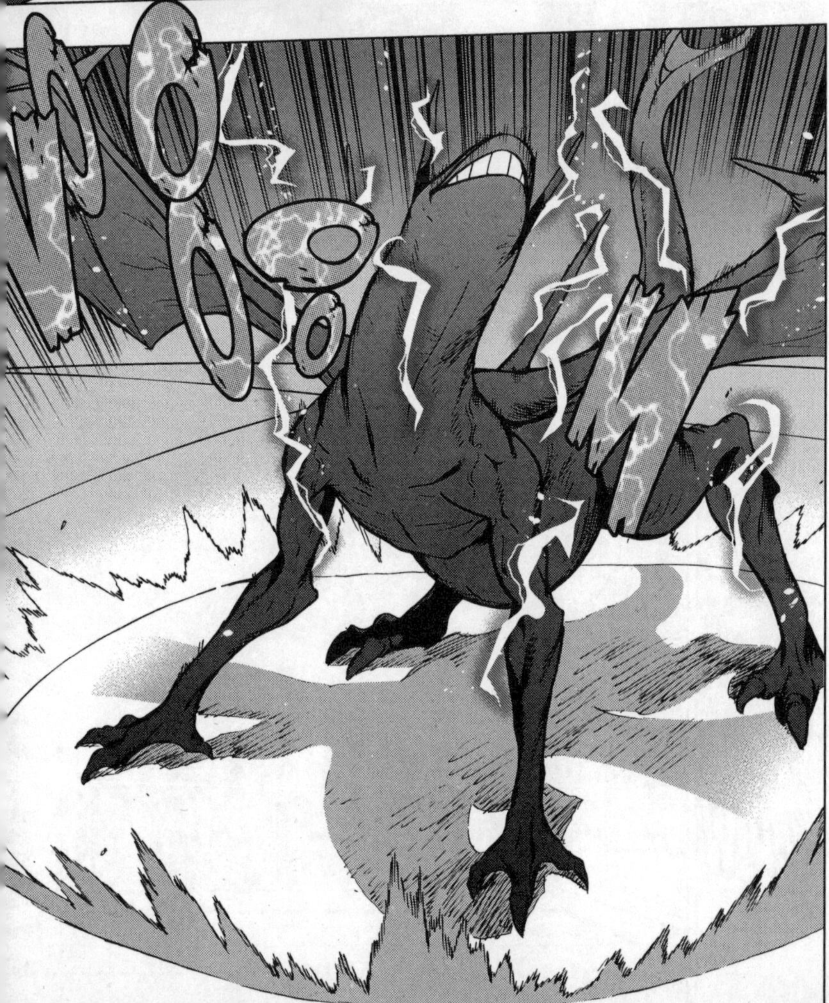

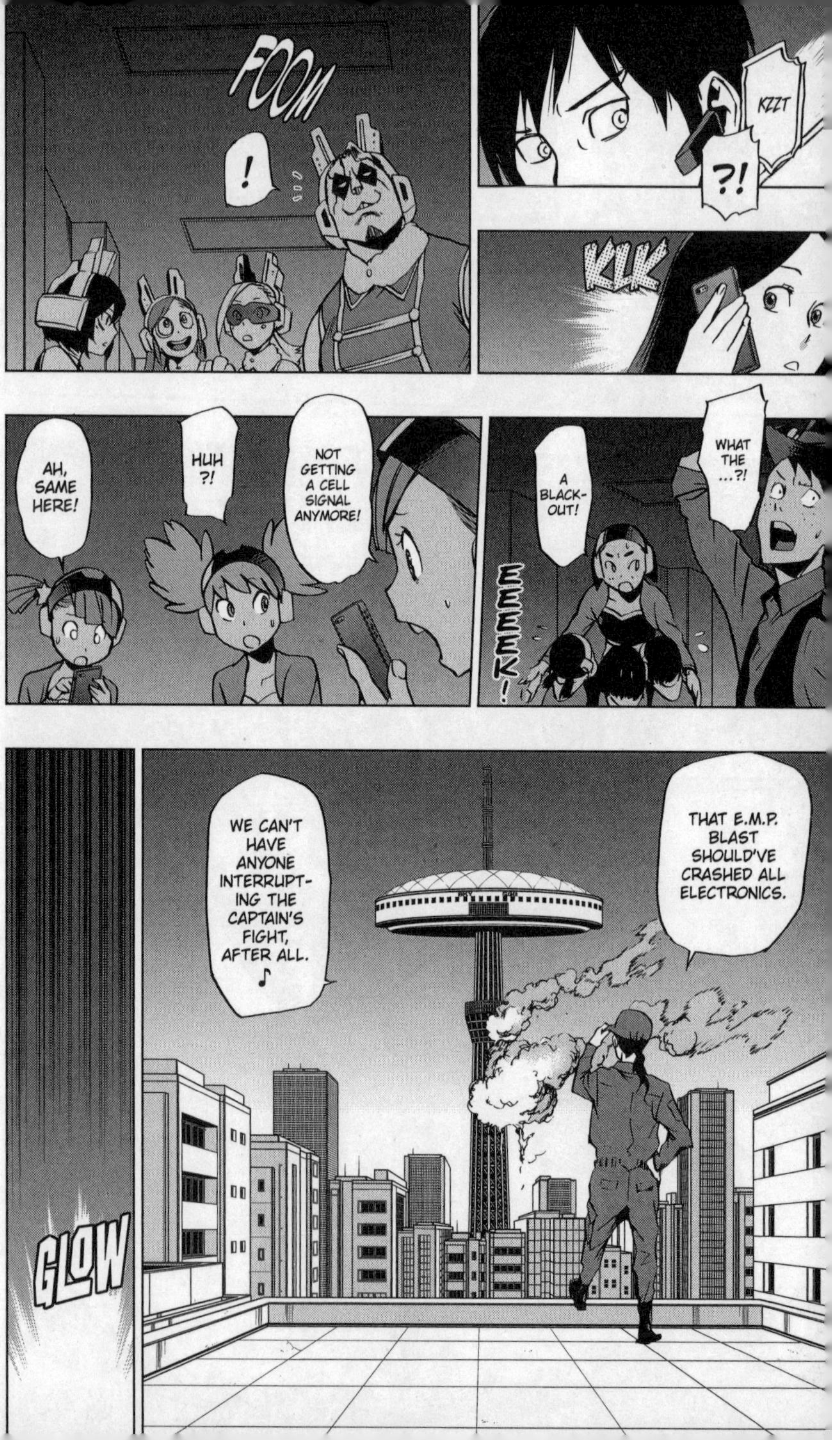
KZZT
?!
KLK
FOOM
!
WHAT THE ...?!
A BLACK-OUT!
EEEEEK!
NOT GETTING A CELL SIGNAL ANYMORE!
HUH ?!
AH, SAME HERE!
THAT E.M.P. BLAST SHOULD'VE CRASHED ALL ELECTRONICS.
WE CAN'T HAVE ANYONE INTERRUPT-ING THE CAPTAIN'S FIGHT, AFTER ALL. ♪
GLOW

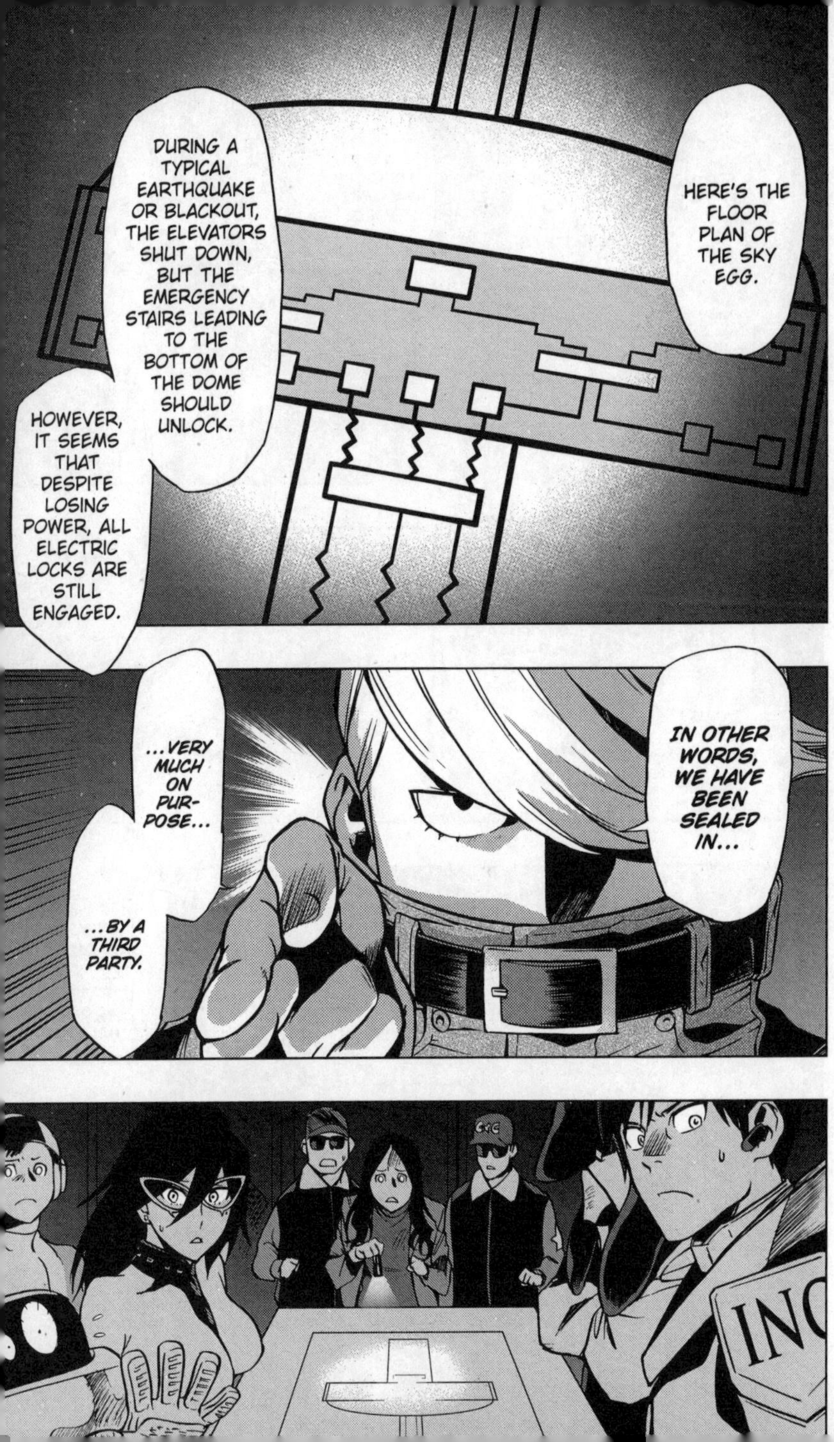
HERE'S THE FLOOR PLAN OF THE SKY EGG.
DURING A TYPICAL EARTHQUAKE OR BLACKOUT, THE ELEVATORS SHUT DOWN, BUT THE EMERGENCY STAIRS LEADING TO THE BOTTOM OF THE DOME SHOULD UNLOCK.
HOWEVER, IT SEEMS THAT DESPITE LOSING POWER, ALL ELECTRIC LOCKS ARE STILL ENGAGED.
IN OTHER WORDS, WE HAVE BEEN SEALED IN...
...VERY MUCH ON PURPOSE...
...BY A THIRD PARTY.

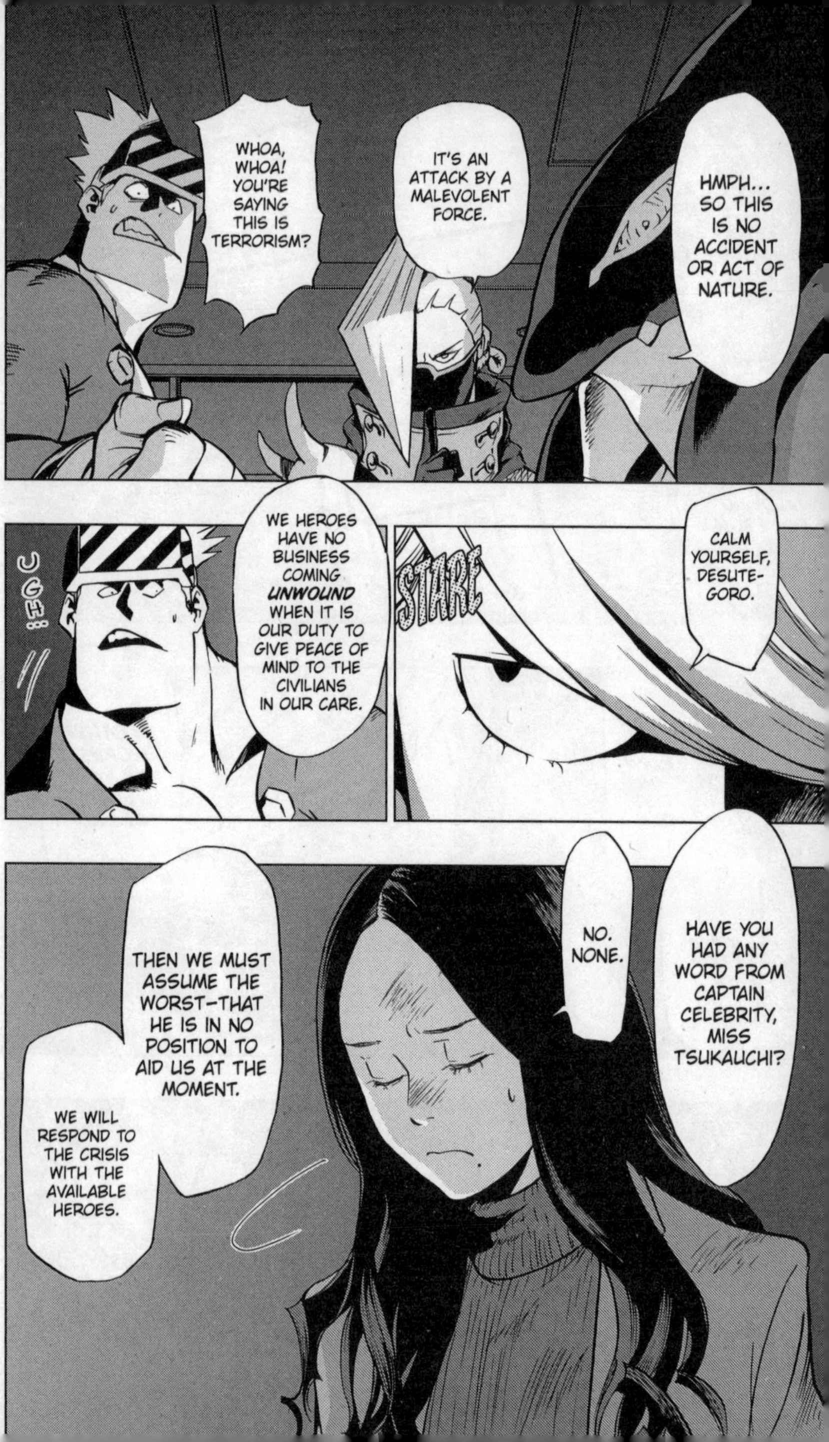
HMPH... SO THIS IS NO ACCIDENT OR ACT OF NATURE.
IT'S AN ATTACK BY A MALEVOLENT FORCE.
WHOA, WHOA! YOU'RE SAYING THIS IS TERRORISM?
CALM YOURSELF, DESUTE-GORO.
STARE
WE HEROES HAVE NO BUSINESS COMING ***UNWOUND*** WHEN IT IS OUR DUTY TO GIVE PEACE OF MIND TO THE CIVILIANS IN OUR CARE.
UGH!!
HAVE YOU HAD ANY WORD FROM CAPTAIN CELEBRITY, MISS TSUKAUCHI?
NO. NONE.
THEN WE MUST ASSUME THE WORST—THAT HE IS IN NO POSITION TO AID US AT THE MOMENT.
WE WILL RESPOND TO THE CRISIS WITH THE AVAILABLE HEROES.

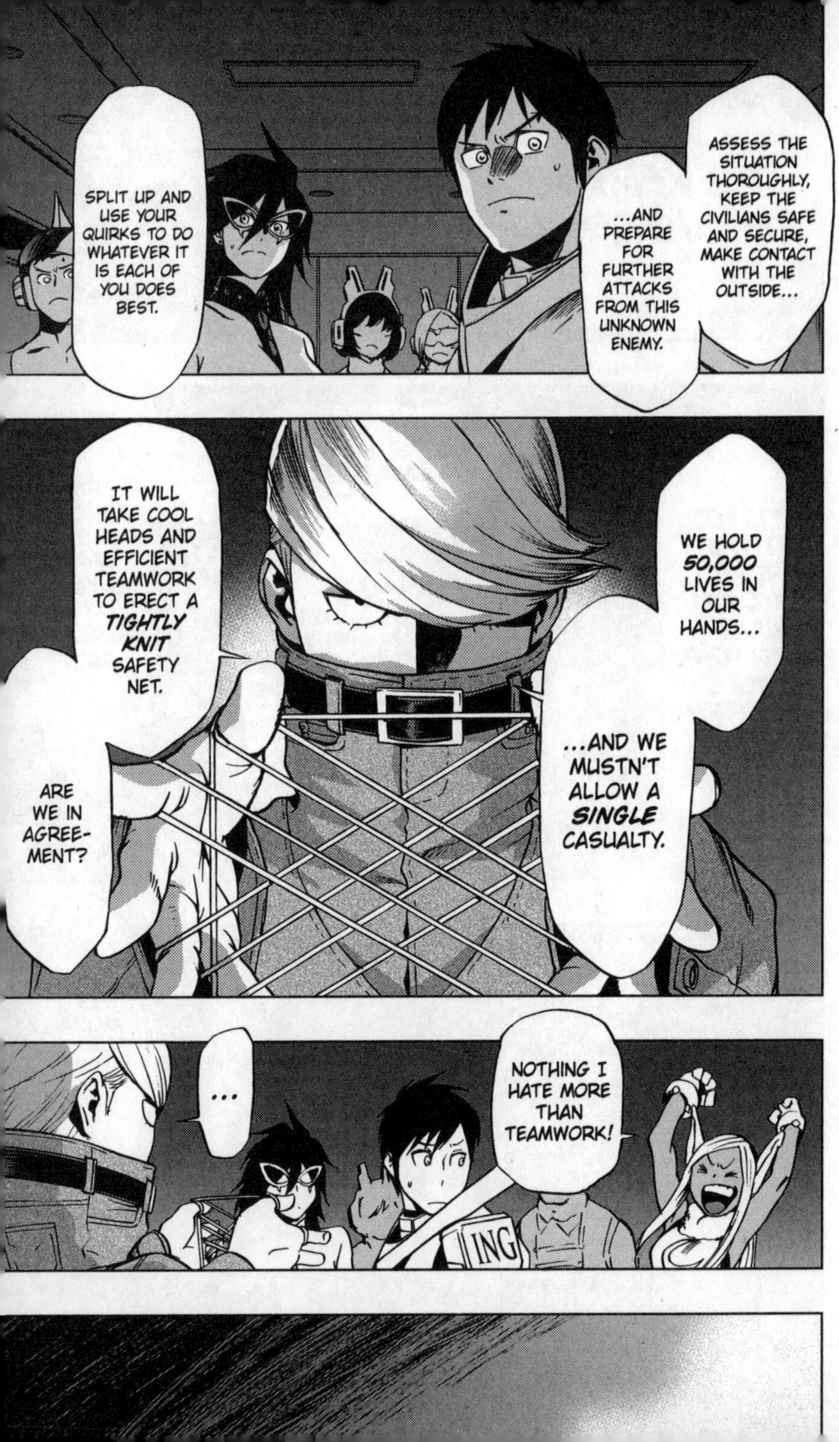
ASSESS THE SITUATION THOROUGHLY, KEEP THE CIVILIANS SAFE AND SECURE, MAKE CONTACT WITH THE OUTSIDE...
...AND PREPARE FOR FURTHER ATTACKS FROM THIS UNKNOWN ENEMY.
SPLIT UP AND USE YOUR QUIRKS TO DO WHATEVER IT IS EACH OF YOU DOES BEST.
WE HOLD **50,000** LIVES IN OUR HANDS...
...AND WE MUSTN'T ALLOW A ***SINGLE*** CASUALTY.
IT WILL TAKE COOL HEADS AND EFFICIENT TEAMWORK TO ERECT A ***TIGHTLY KNIT*** SAFETY NET.
ARE WE IN AGREEMENT?
NOTHING I HATE MORE THAN TEAMWORK!
...
ING

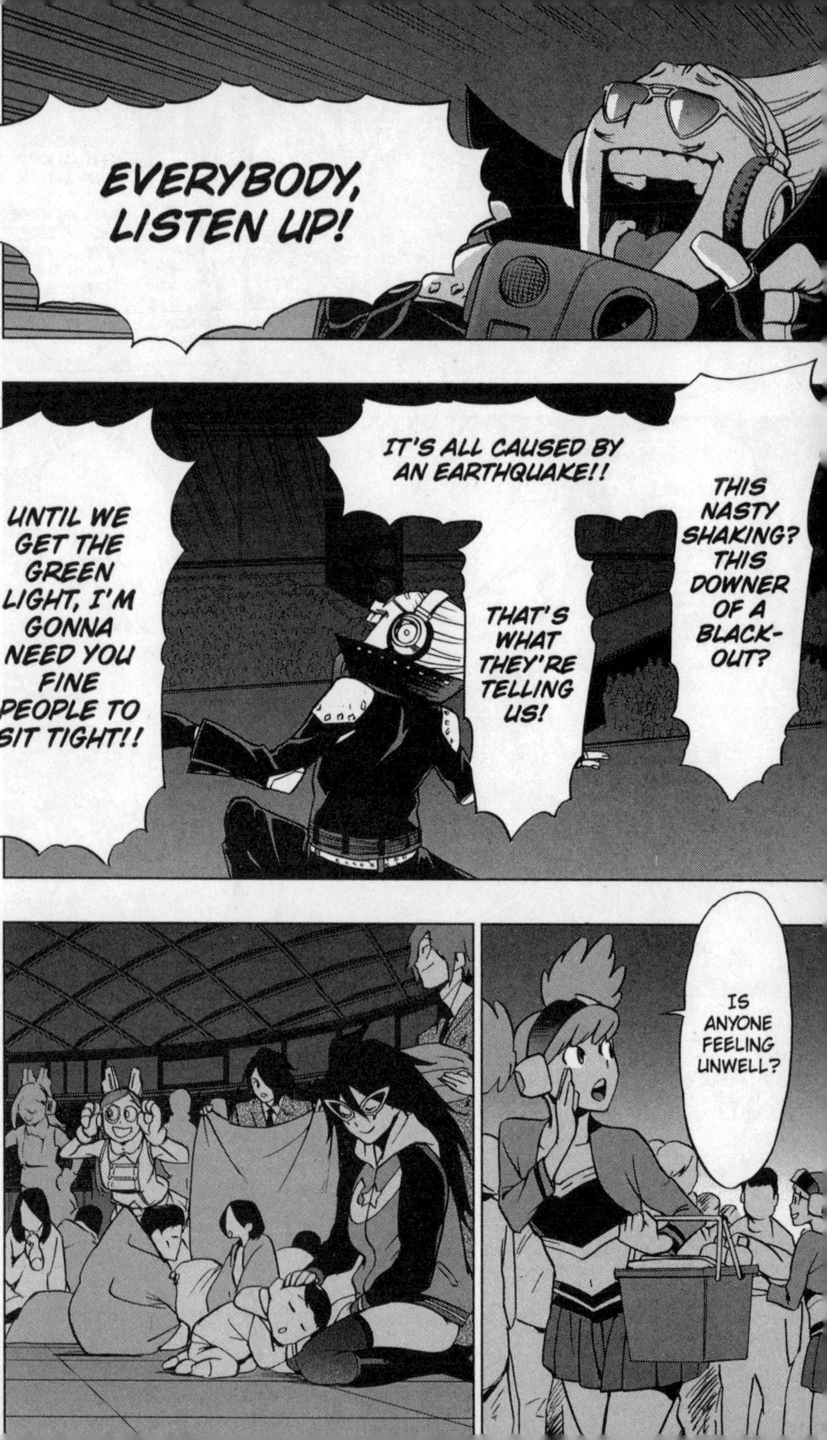
EVERYBODY, LISTEN UP!
THIS NASTY SHAKING? THIS DOWNER OF A BLACK-OUT?
IT'S ALL CAUSED BY AN EARTHQUAKE!!
THAT'S WHAT THEY'RE TELLING US!
UNTIL WE GET THE GREEN LIGHT, I'M GONNA NEED YOU FINE PEOPLE TO SIT TIGHT!!
IS ANYONE FEELING UNWELL?

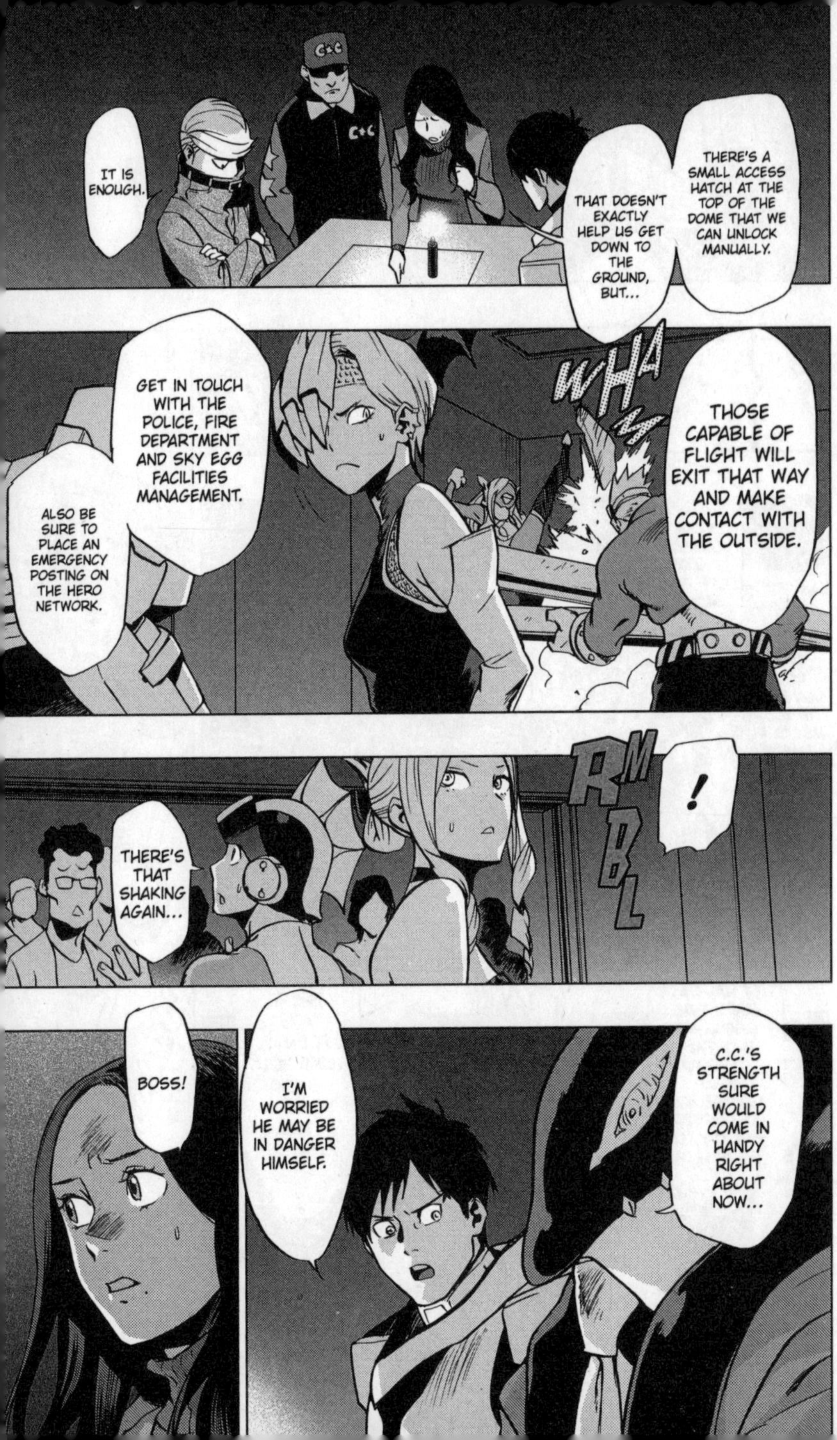
THERE'S A SMALL ACCESS HATCH AT THE TOP OF THE DOME THAT WE CAN UNLOCK MANUALLY.
THAT DOESN'T EXACTLY HELP US GET DOWN TO THE GROUND, BUT...
IT IS ENOUGH.
THOSE CAPABLE OF FLIGHT WILL EXIT THAT WAY AND MAKE CONTACT WITH THE OUTSIDE.
WHAM
GET IN TOUCH WITH THE POLICE, FIRE DEPARTMENT AND SKY EGG FACILITIES MANAGEMENT.
ALSO BE SURE TO PLACE AN EMERGENCY POSTING ON THE HERO NETWORK.
!
RMBL
THERE'S THAT SHAKING AGAIN...
C.C.'S STRENGTH SURE WOULD COME IN HANDY RIGHT ABOUT NOW...
I'M WORRIED HE MAY BE IN DANGER HIMSELF.
BOSS!

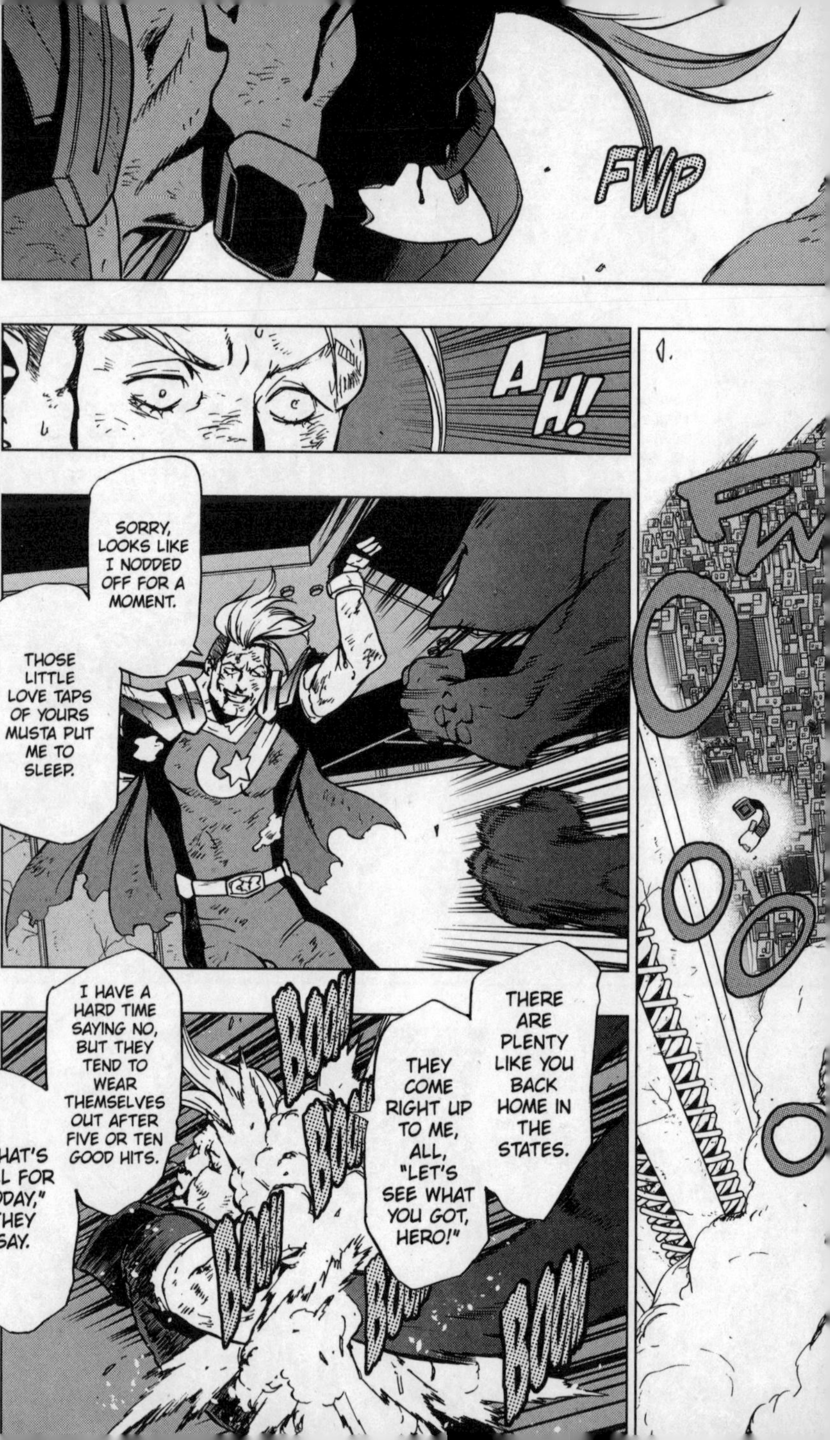
FWP
FWOOOO
AH!
SORRY, LOOKS LIKE I NODDED OFF FOR A MOMENT.
THOSE LITTLE LOVE TAPS OF YOURS MUSTA PUT ME TO SLEEP.
THERE ARE PLENTY LIKE YOU BACK HOME IN THE STATES.
THEY COME RIGHT UP TO ME, ALL, "LET'S SEE WHAT YOU GOT, HERO!"
I HAVE A HARD TIME SAYING NO, BUT THEY TEND TO WEAR THEMSELVES OUT AFTER FIVE OR TEN GOOD HITS.
"THAT'S ALL FOR TODAY," THEY SAY.
BOOM
BOOM
BOOM

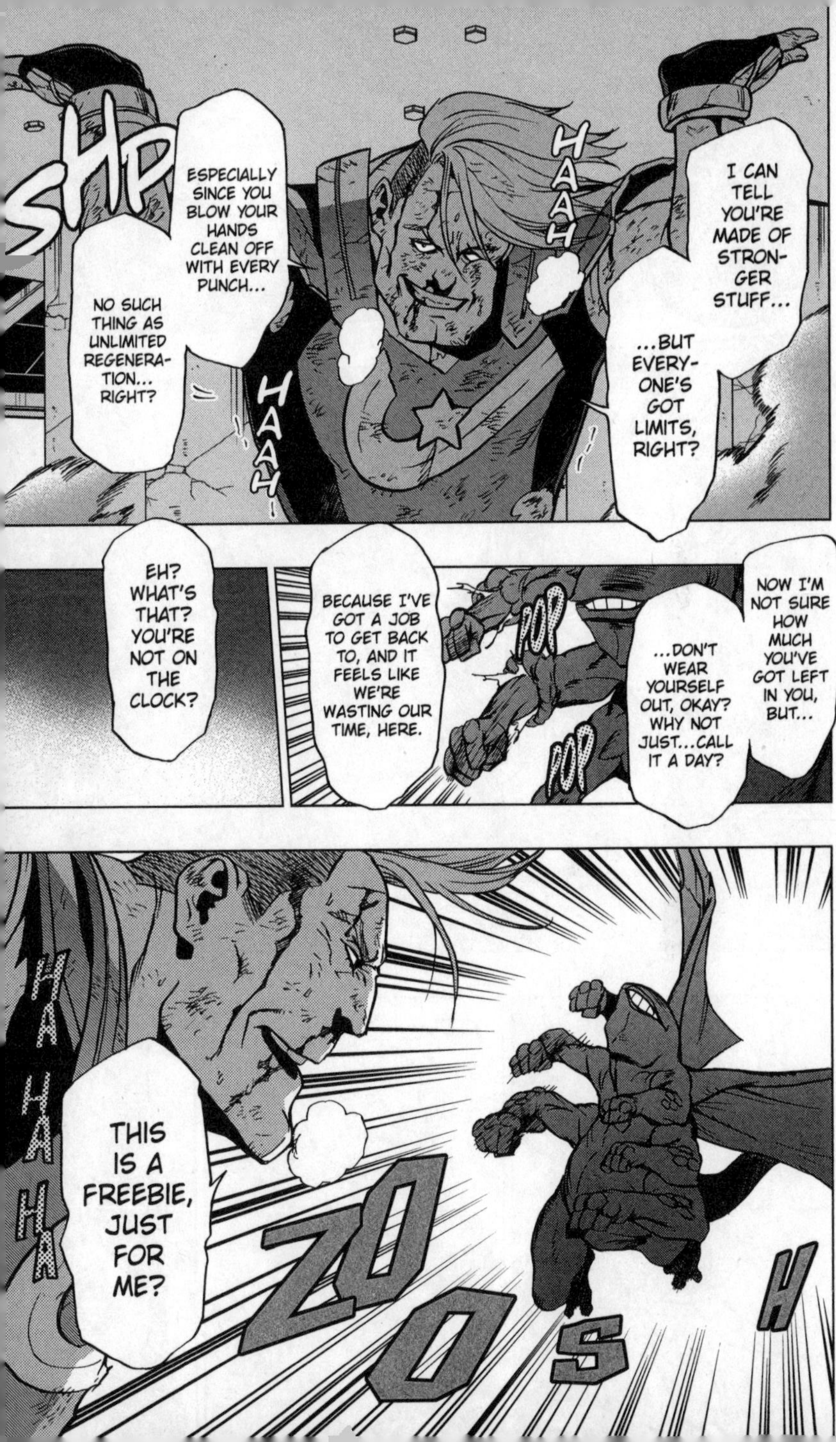
I CAN TELL YOU'RE MADE OF STRONGER STUFF...
...BUT EVERYONE'S GOT LIMITS, RIGHT?
HAAAH
ESPECIALLY SINCE YOU BLOW YOUR HANDS CLEAN OFF WITH EVERY PUNCH...
NO SUCH THING AS UNLIMITED REGENERATION... RIGHT?
SHP
HAAAH
NOW I'M NOT SURE HOW MUCH YOU'VE GOT LEFT IN YOU, BUT...
...DON'T WEAR YOURSELF OUT, OKAY? WHY NOT JUST...CALL IT A DAY?
POP
POP
BECAUSE I'VE GOT A JOB TO GET BACK TO, AND IT FEELS LIKE WE'RE WASTING OUR TIME, HERE.
EH? WHAT'S THAT? YOU'RE NOT ON THE CLOCK?
ZOOSH
THIS IS A FREEBIE, JUST FOR ME?
HAHAHAHA

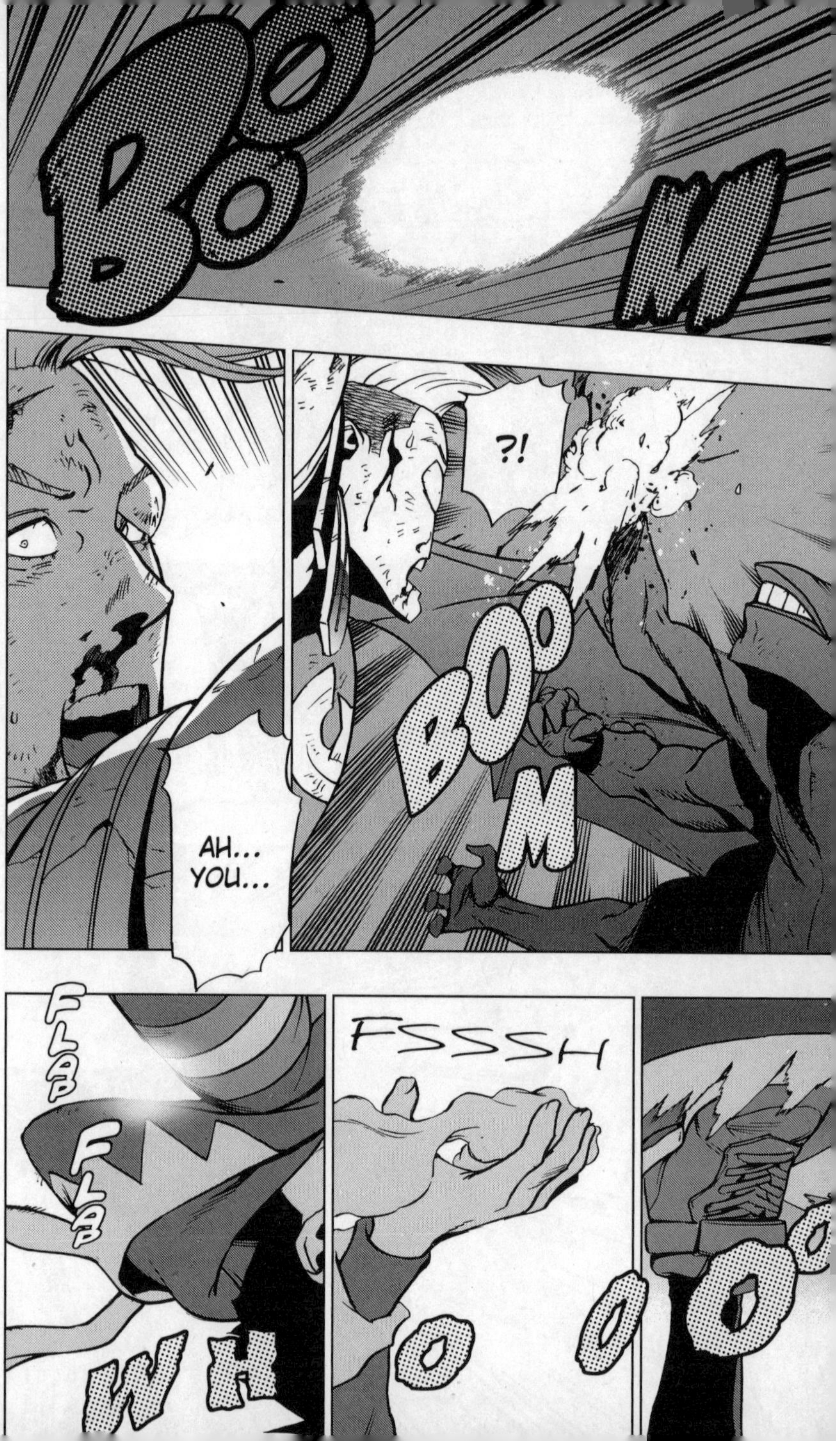
BOOOM
?!
BOOOM
AH... YOU...
FSSSH
FLAP FLAP
WHOOOOO

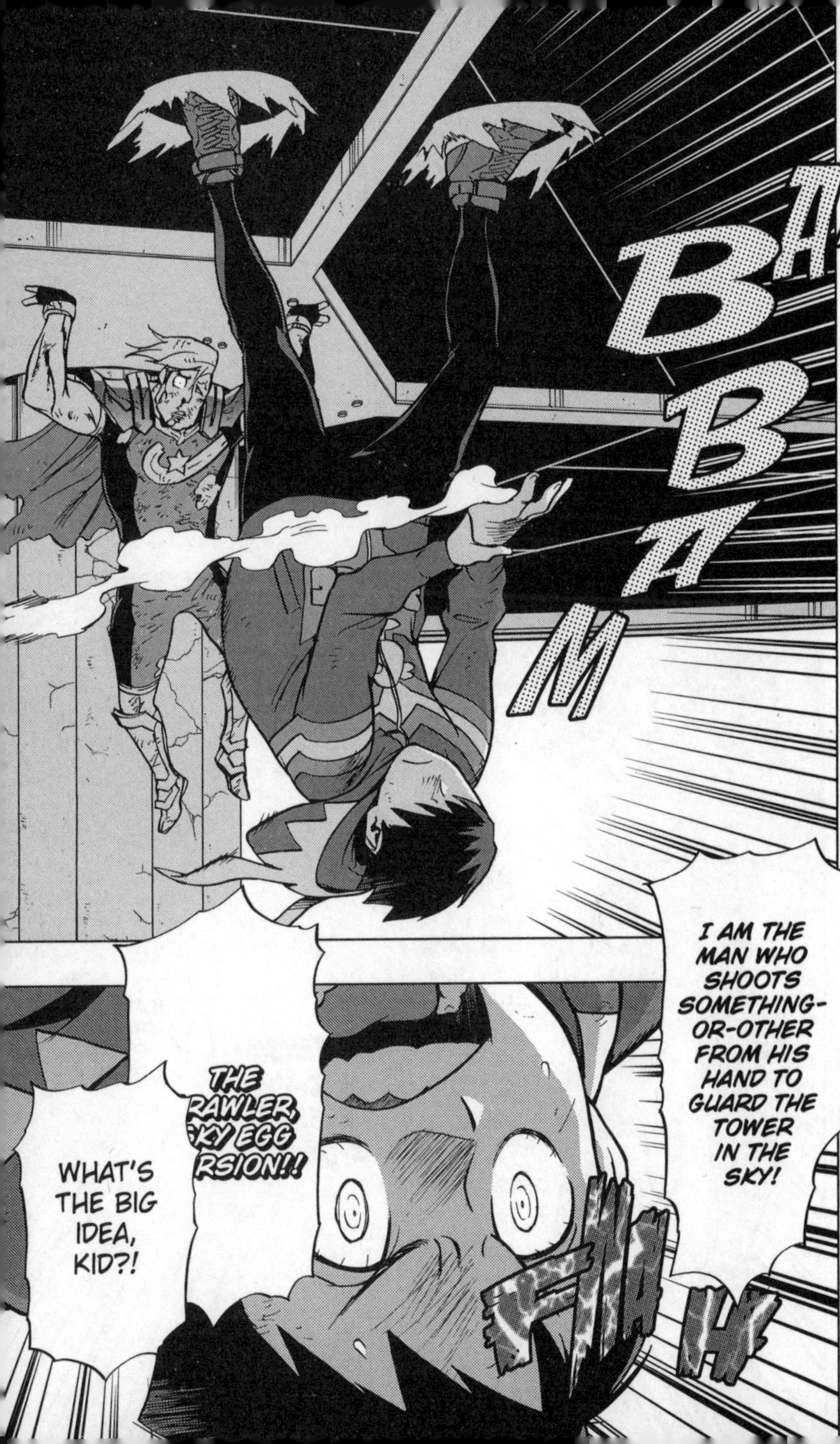
BA-BA-BAM
I AM THE MAN WHO SHOOTS SOMETHING-OR-OTHER FROM HIS HAND TO GUARD THE TOWER IN THE SKY!
THE RAWLER, KY EGG RSION!!
FWAH
WHAT'S THE BIG IDEA, KID?!

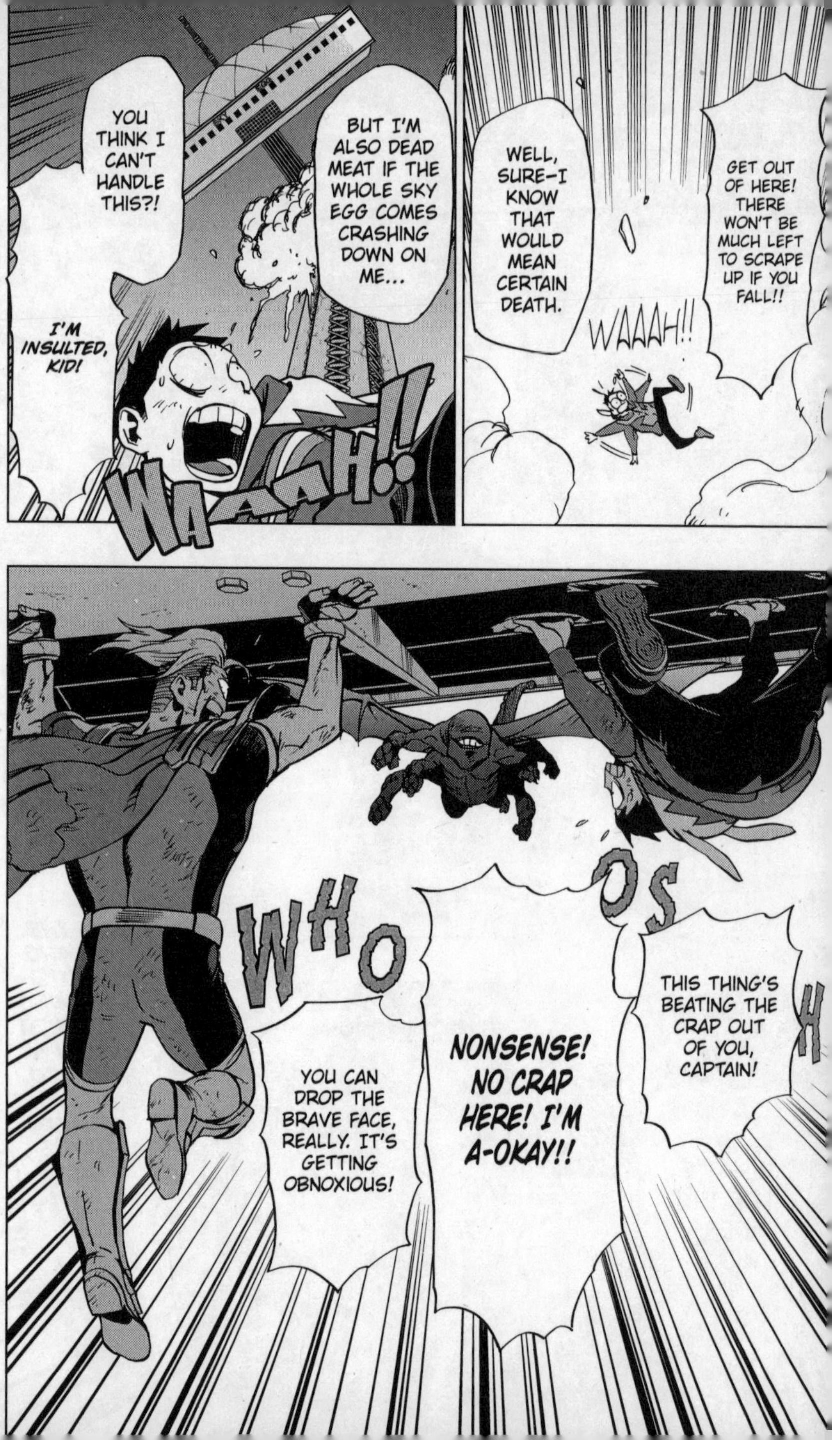
GET OUT OF HERE! THERE WON'T BE MUCH LEFT TO SCRAPE UP IF YOU FALL!!
WELL, SURE—I KNOW THAT WOULD MEAN CERTAIN DEATH.
WAAAH!!
BUT I'M ALSO DEAD MEAT IF THE WHOLE SKY EGG COMES CRASHING DOWN ON ME...
YOU THINK I CAN'T HANDLE THIS?!
I'M INSULTED, KID!
WAAAH!!
WHOOSH
THIS THING'S BEATING THE CRAP OUT OF YOU, CAPTAIN!
NONSENSE! NO CRAP HERE! I'M A-OKAY!!
YOU CAN DROP THE BRAVE FACE, REALLY. IT'S GETTING OBNOXIOUS!

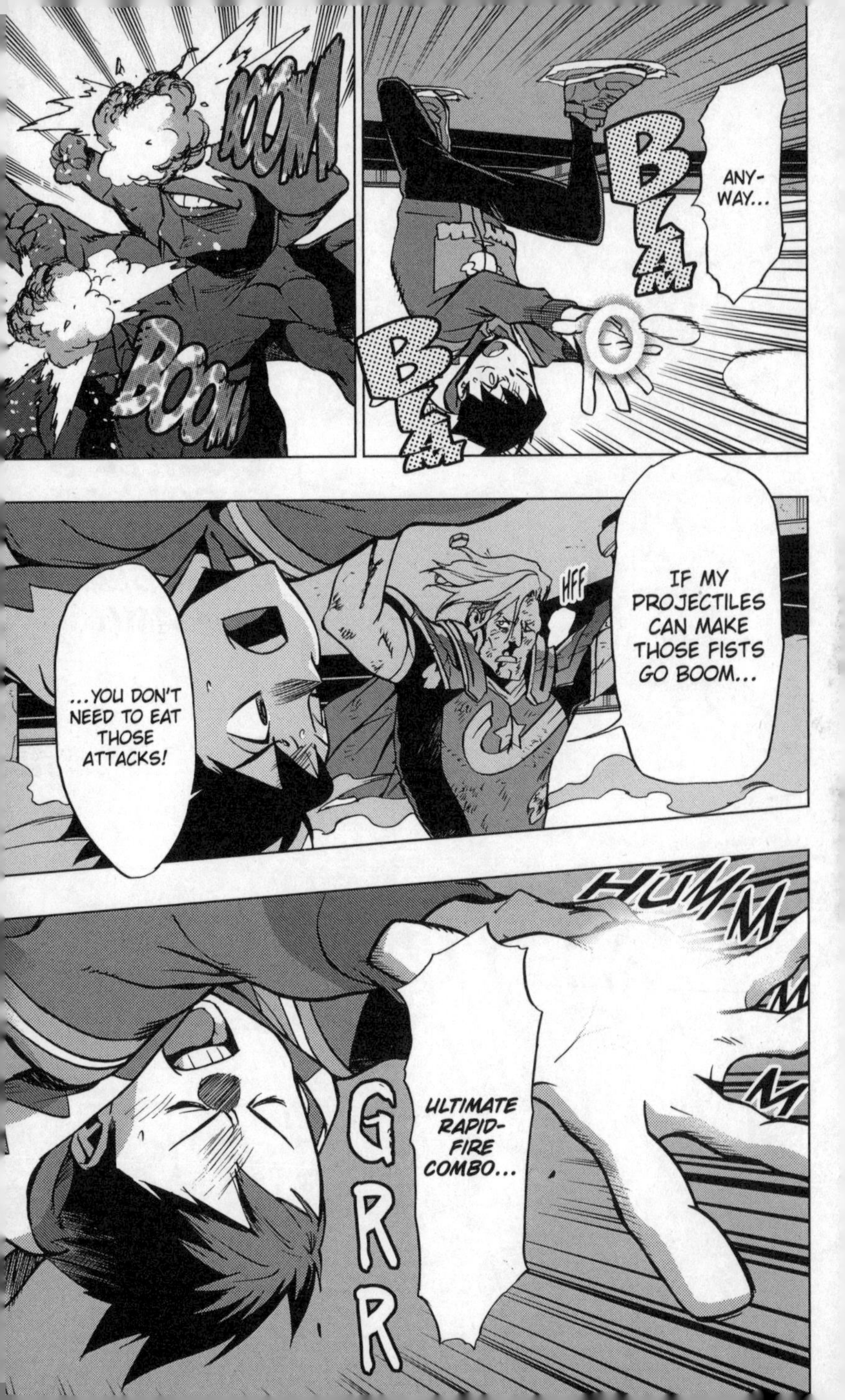
BOOM
BOOM
ANY-WAY...
BLAM
BLAM
IF MY PROJECTILES CAN MAKE THOSE FISTS GO BOOM...
HFF
...YOU DON'T NEED TO EAT THOSE ATTACKS!
HUMMM
ULTIMATE RAPID-FIRE COMBO...
GRR

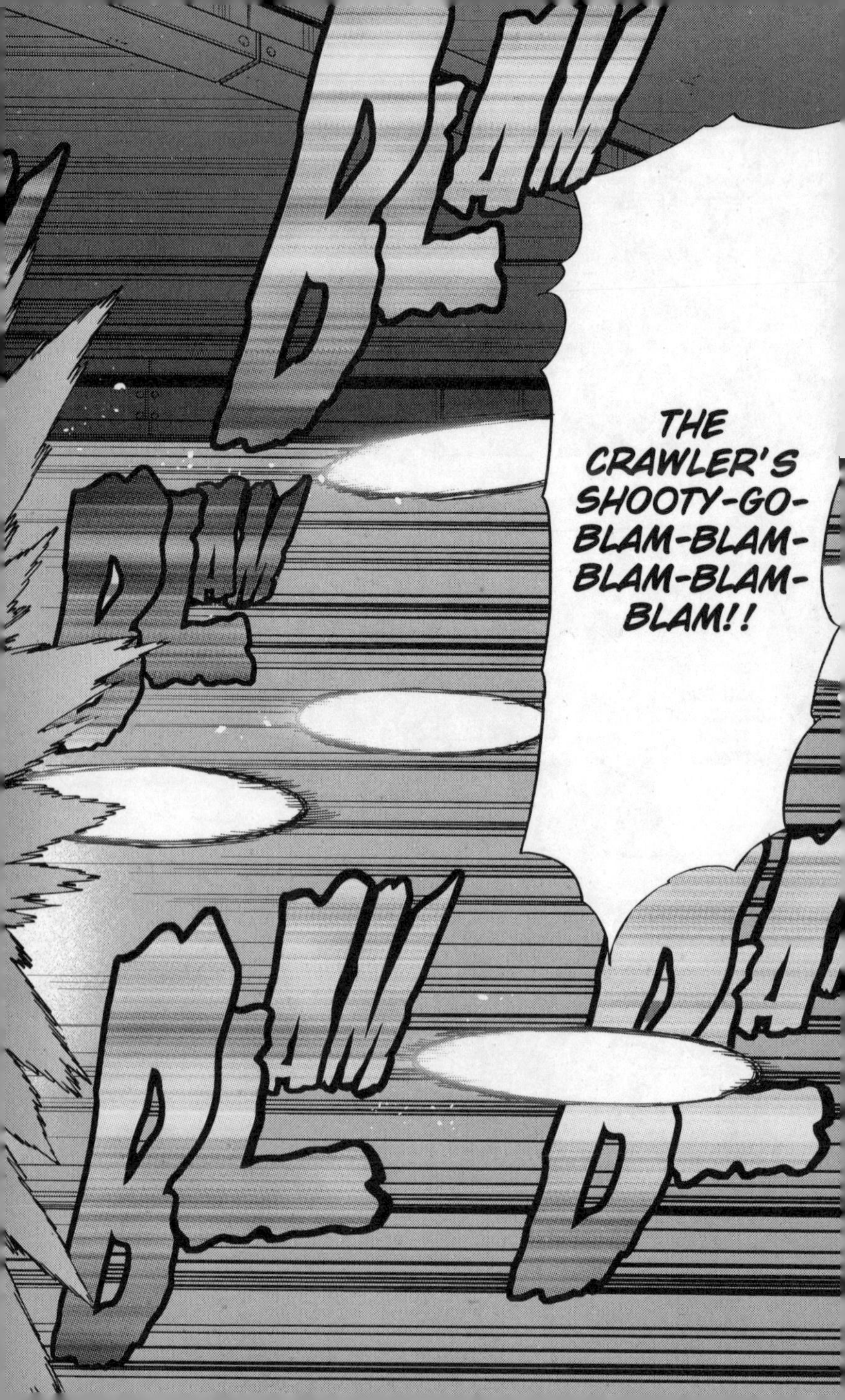
THE CRAWLER'S SHOOTY-GO-BLAM-BLAM-BLAM-BLAM-BLAM!!

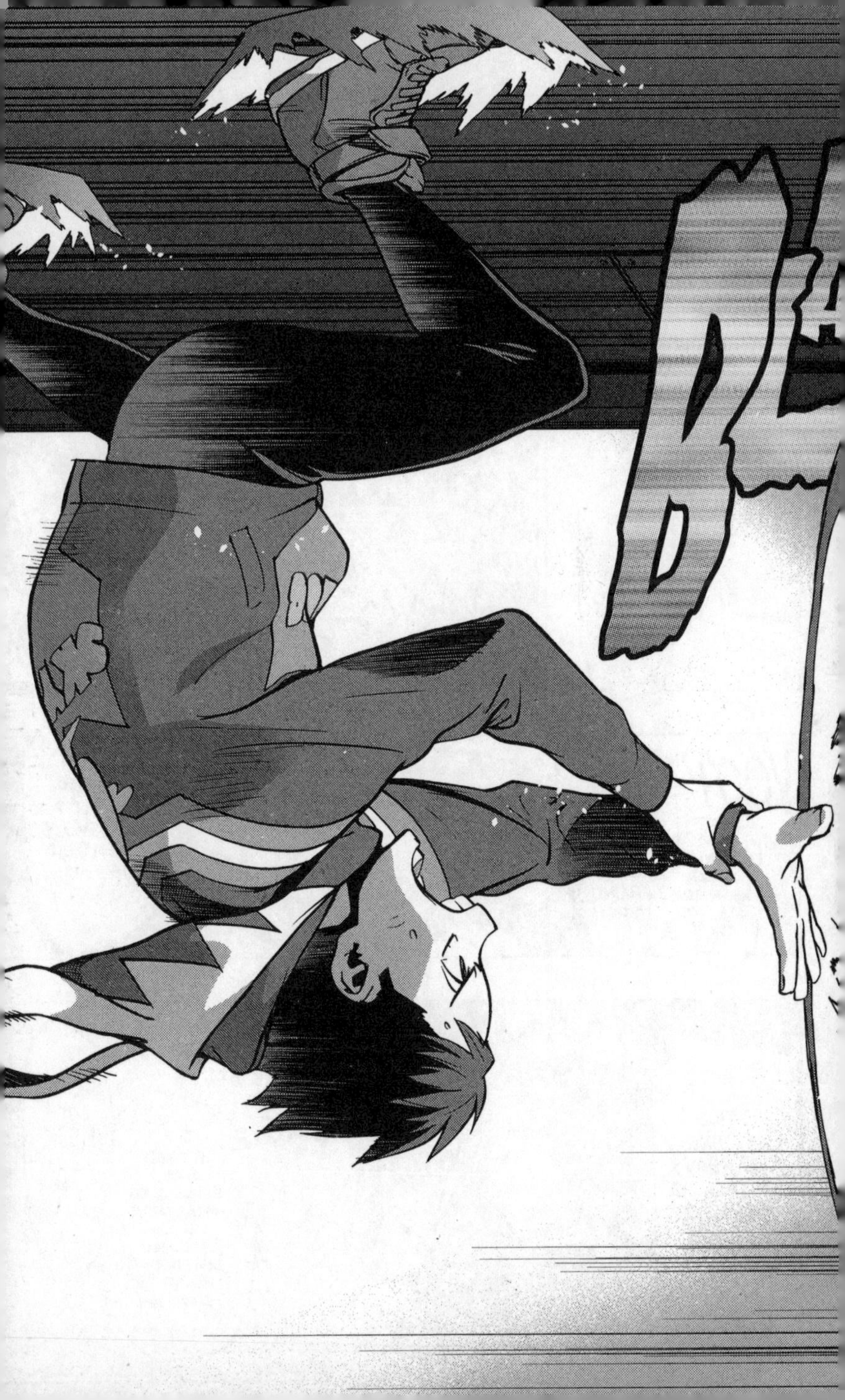

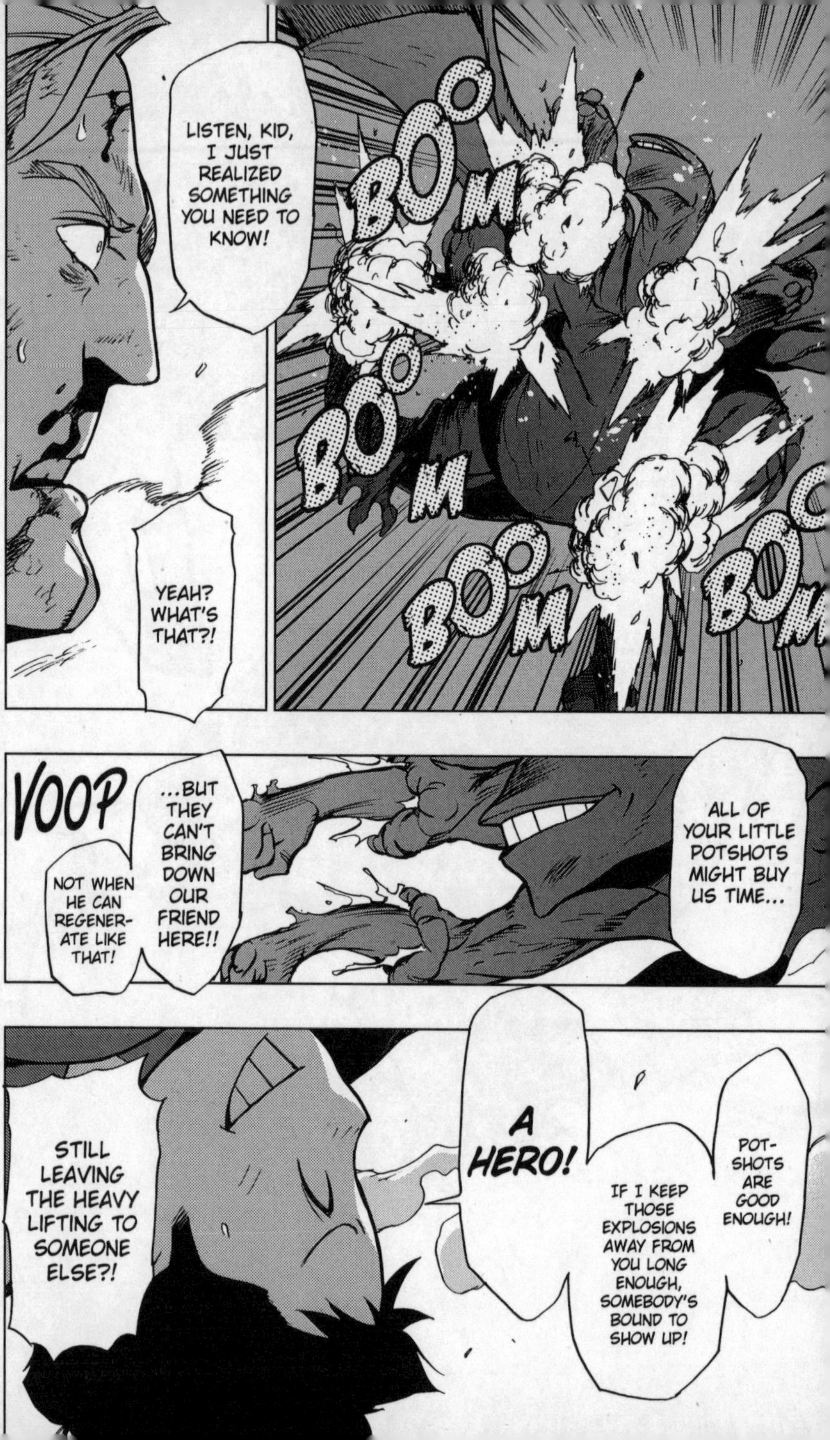
BOOOM
BOOOM
BOOOM
BOOOM
LISTEN, KID, I JUST REALIZED SOMETHING YOU NEED TO KNOW!
YEAH? WHAT'S THAT?!
ALL OF YOUR LITTLE POTSHOTS MIGHT BUY US TIME...
...BUT THEY CAN'T BRING DOWN OUR FRIEND HERE!!
NOT WHEN HE CAN REGENER-ATE LIKE THAT!
VOOP
POT-SHOTS ARE GOOD ENOUGH!
IF I KEEP THOSE EXPLOSIONS AWAY FROM YOU LONG ENOUGH, SOMEBODY'S BOUND TO SHOW UP!
A HERO!
STILL LEAVING THE HEAVY LIFTING TO SOMEONE ELSE?!

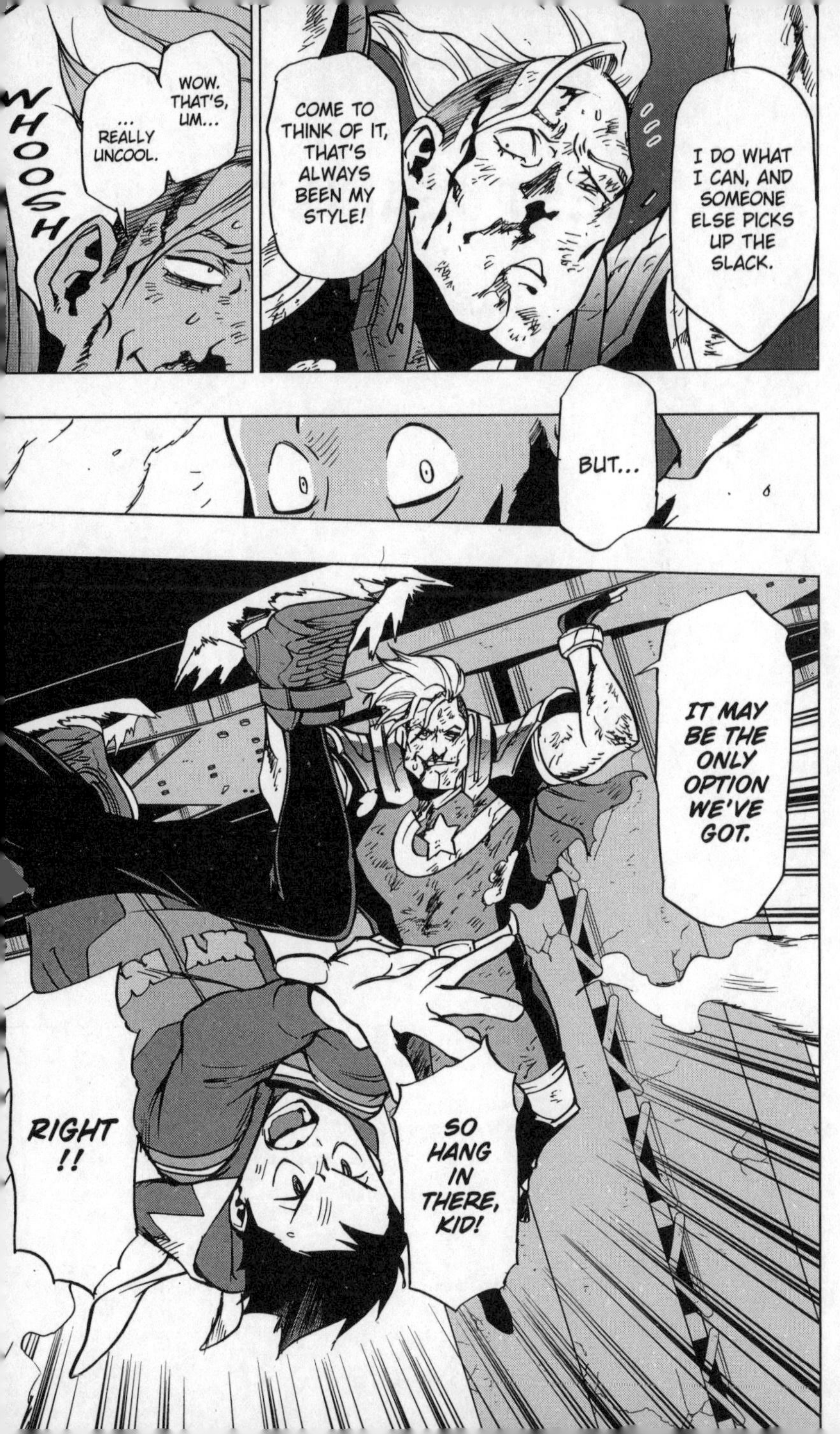
I DO WHAT I CAN, AND SOMEONE ELSE PICKS UP THE SLACK.
COME TO THINK OF IT, THAT'S ALWAYS BEEN MY STYLE!
WOW. THAT'S, UM...
... REALLY UNCOOL.
WHOOSH
BUT...
IT MAY BE THE ONLY OPTION WE'VE GOT.
SO HANG IN THERE, KID!
RIGHT!!

THE COLUMN

BEST JEANIST

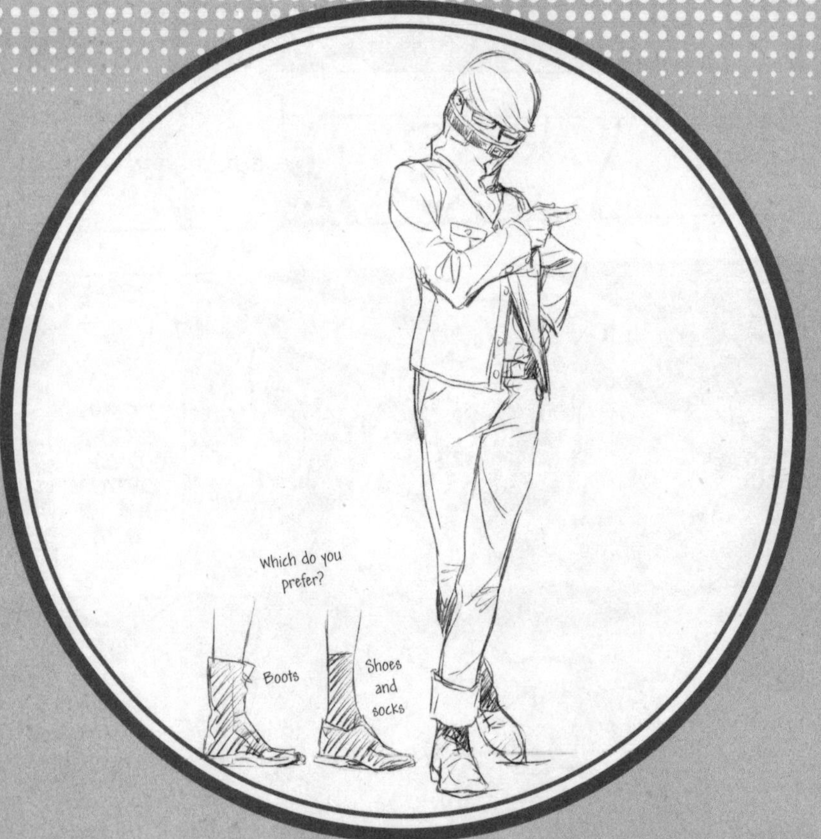
Which do you prefer?
Boots
Shoes and socks

As one of Japan's top-class heroes, Jeanist has to come off as a big shot with flashy moves. I like his whole sleeve gimmick.

—Furuhashi

Drawing Jeanist is tons of fun. In this case, I wasn't sure whether to give him shoes or boots, so I just kind of swept the issue under the rug by drawing his footwear ambiguously. (Ha!) But which version do you prefer?

—Betten

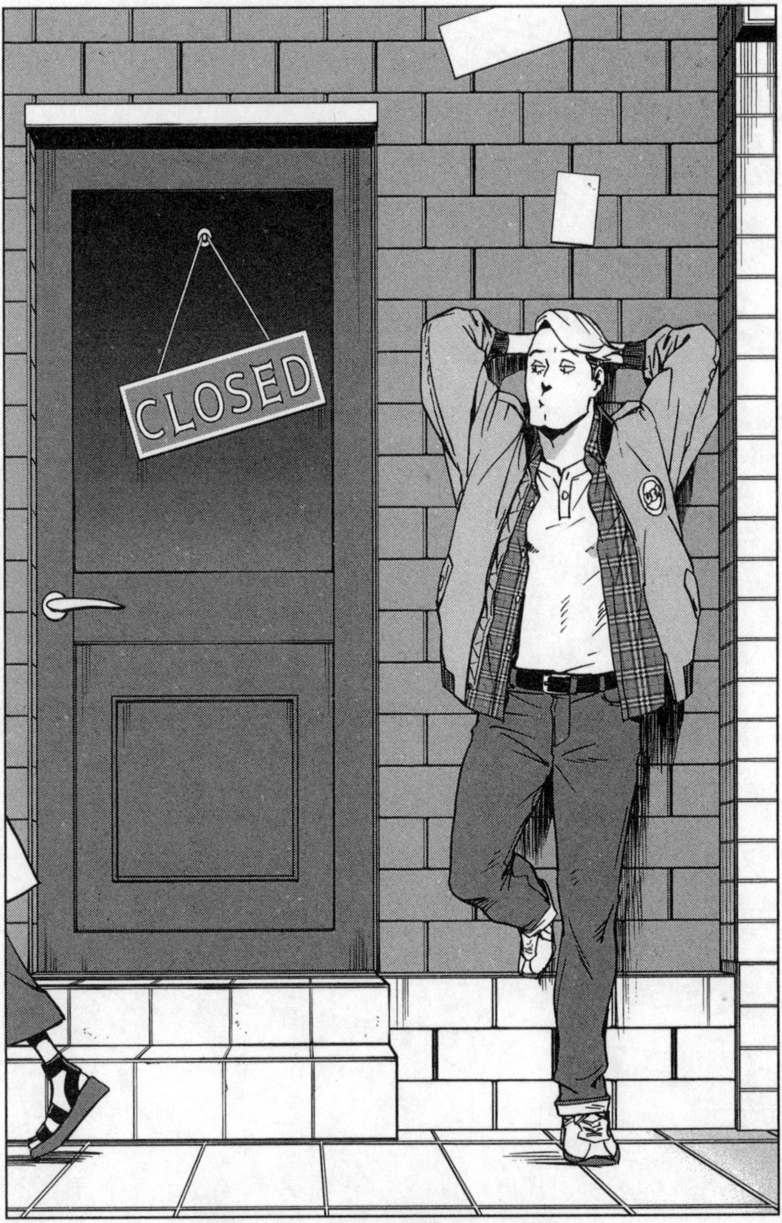
CLOSED

Ep. 52 - Balloon Soul

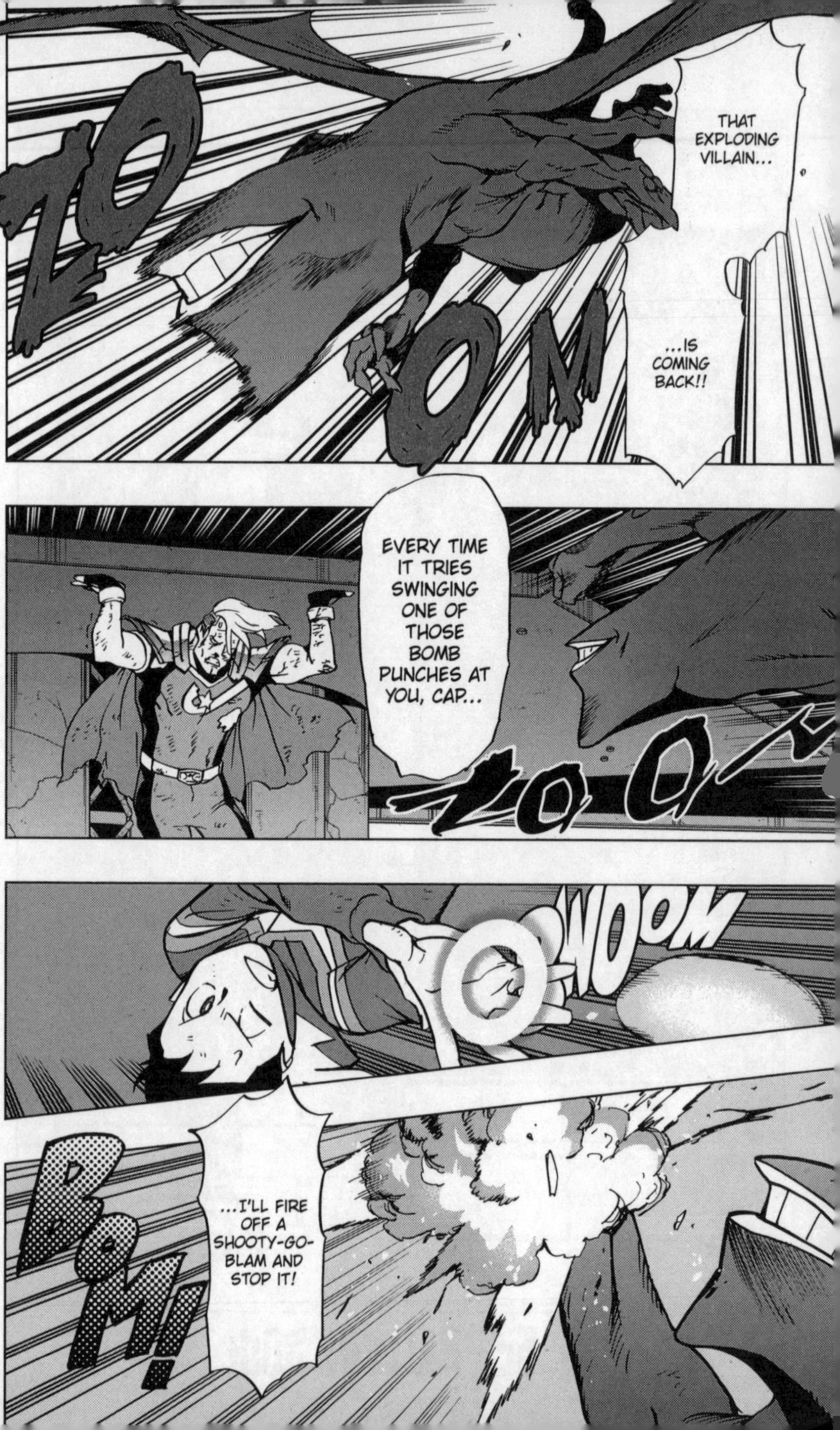
THAT EXPLODING VILLAIN...
...IS COMING BACK!!
ZOOM
EVERY TIME IT TRIES SWINGING ONE OF THOSE BOMB PUNCHES AT YOU, CAP...
...I'LL FIRE OFF A SHOOTY-GO-BLAM AND STOP IT!

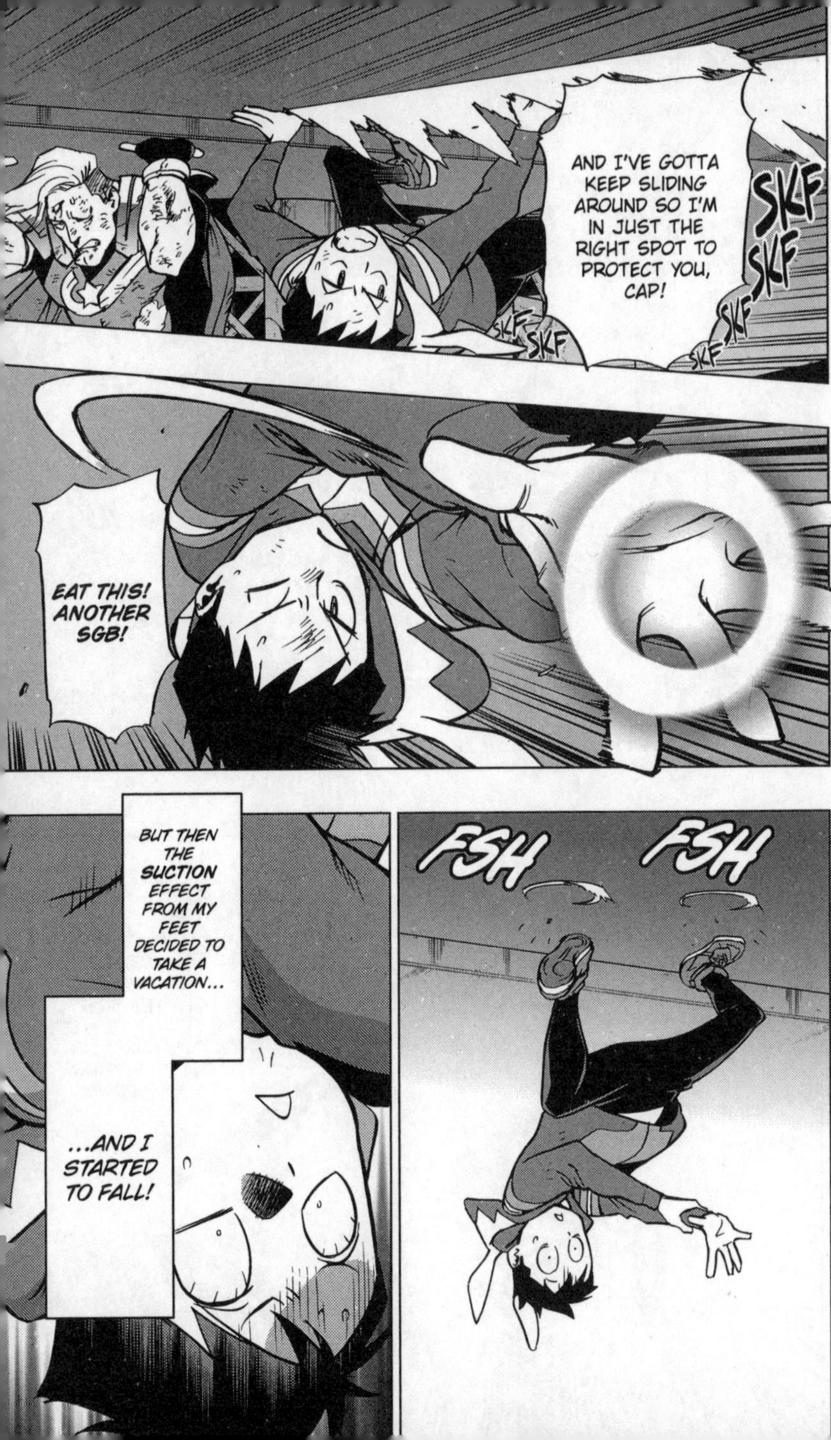
AND I'VE GOTTA KEEP SLIDING AROUND SO I'M IN JUST THE RIGHT SPOT TO PROTECT YOU, CAP!
SKF SKF
SKF SKF
SKF SKF SKF
EAT THIS! ANOTHER SGB!
FSH FSH
BUT THEN THE SUCTION EFFECT FROM MY FEET DECIDED TO TAKE A VACATION...
...AND I STARTED TO FALL!

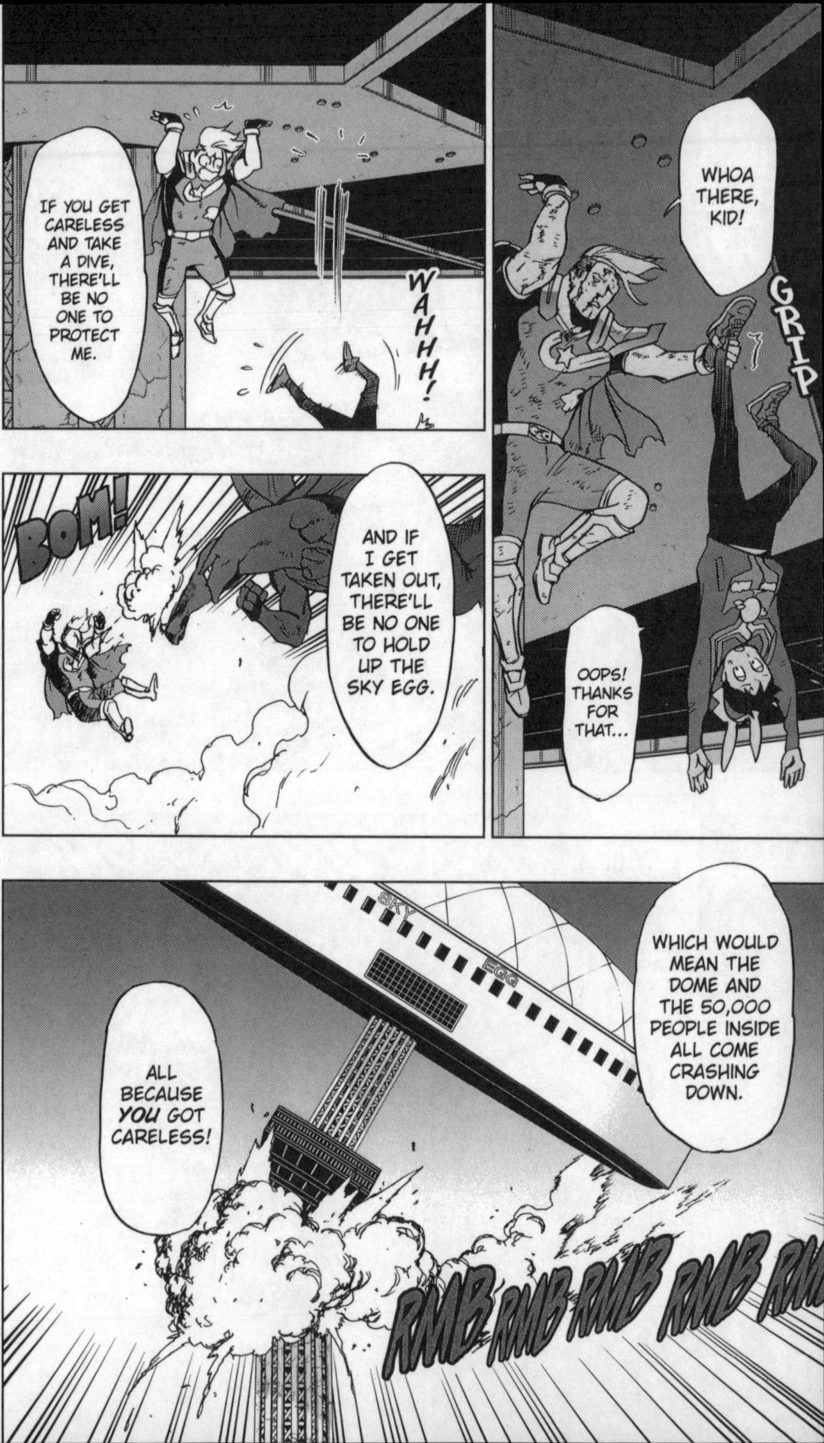
WHOA THERE, KID!
GRIP
OOPS! THANKS FOR THAT...
IF YOU GET CARELESS AND TAKE A DIVE, THERE'LL BE NO ONE TO PROTECT ME.
WAHHHH!
AND IF I GET TAKEN OUT, THERE'LL BE NO ONE TO HOLD UP THE SKY EGG.
BOM!
WHICH WOULD MEAN THE DOME AND THE 50,000 PEOPLE INSIDE ALL COME CRASHING DOWN.
SKY EGG
ALL BECAUSE YOU GOT CARELESS!
RMB RMB RMB RMB

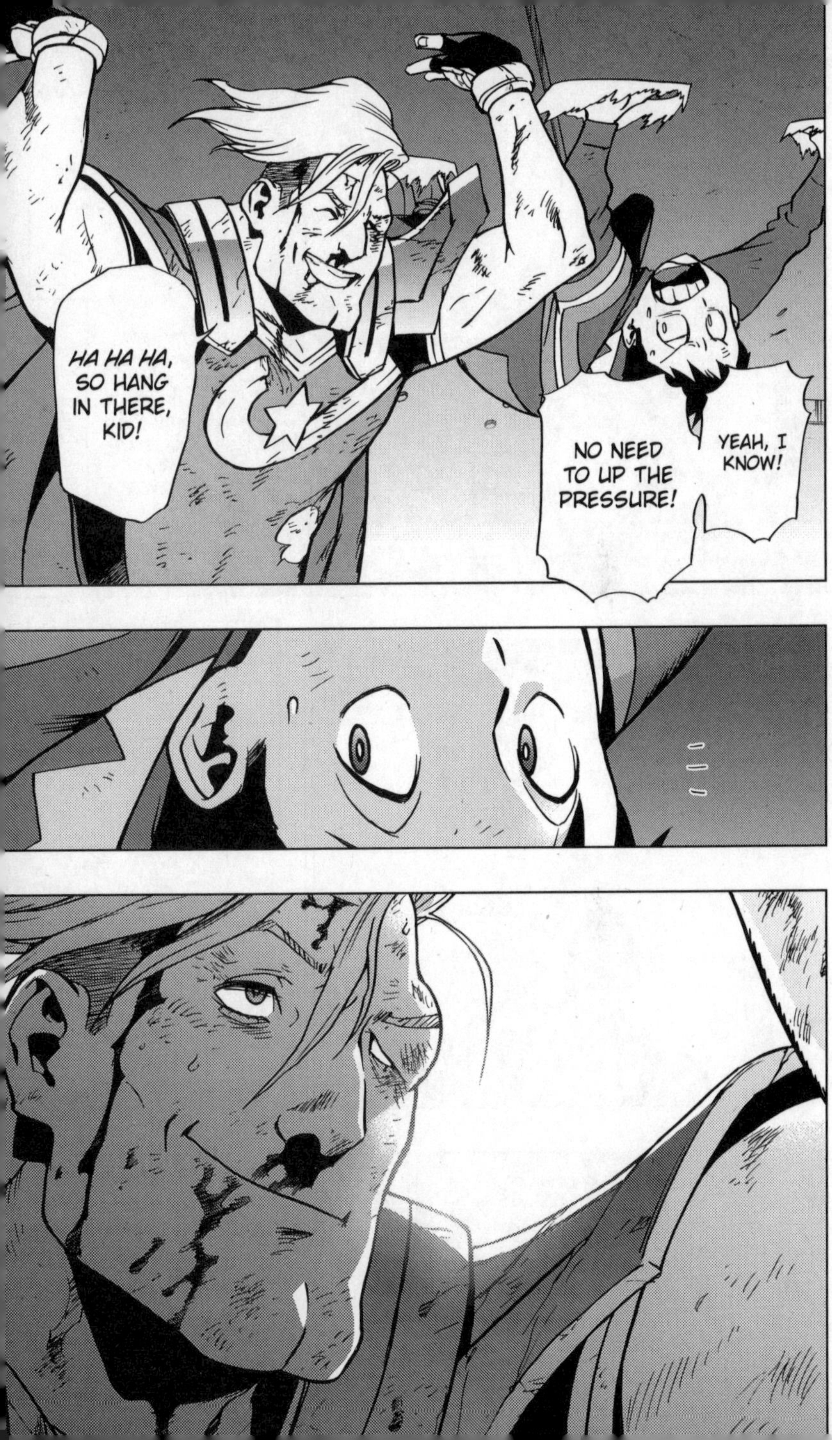
HA HA HA, SO HANG IN THERE, KID!
YEAH, I KNOW!
NO NEED TO UP THE PRESSURE!

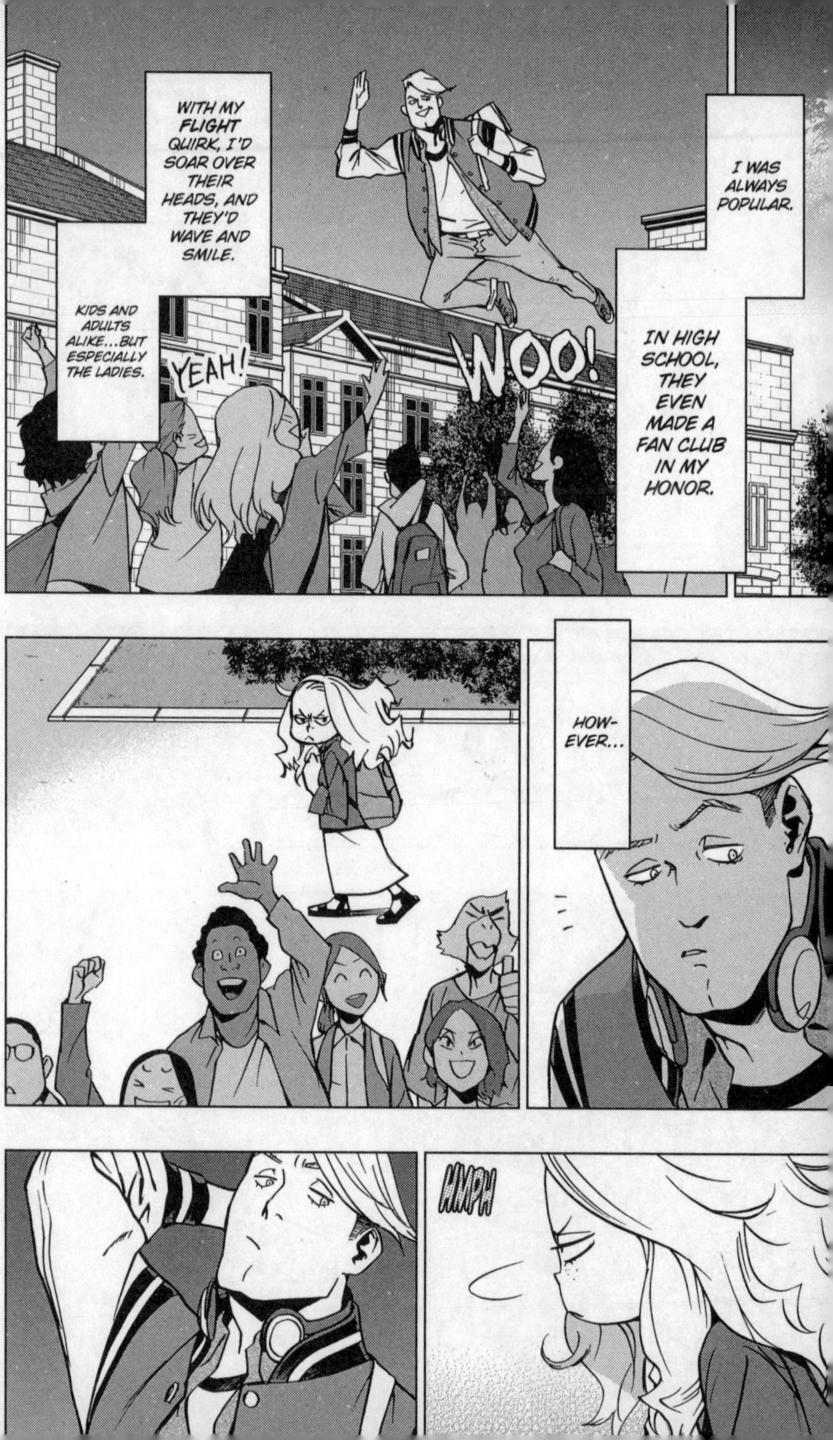
I WAS ALWAYS POPULAR.
WITH MY FLIGHT QUIRK, I'D SOAR OVER THEIR HEADS, AND THEY'D WAVE AND SMILE.
WOO!
IN HIGH SCHOOL, THEY EVEN MADE A FAN CLUB IN MY HONOR.
KIDS AND ADULTS ALIKE...BUT ESPECIALLY THE LADIES.
YEAH!
HOW-EVER...
HMPH

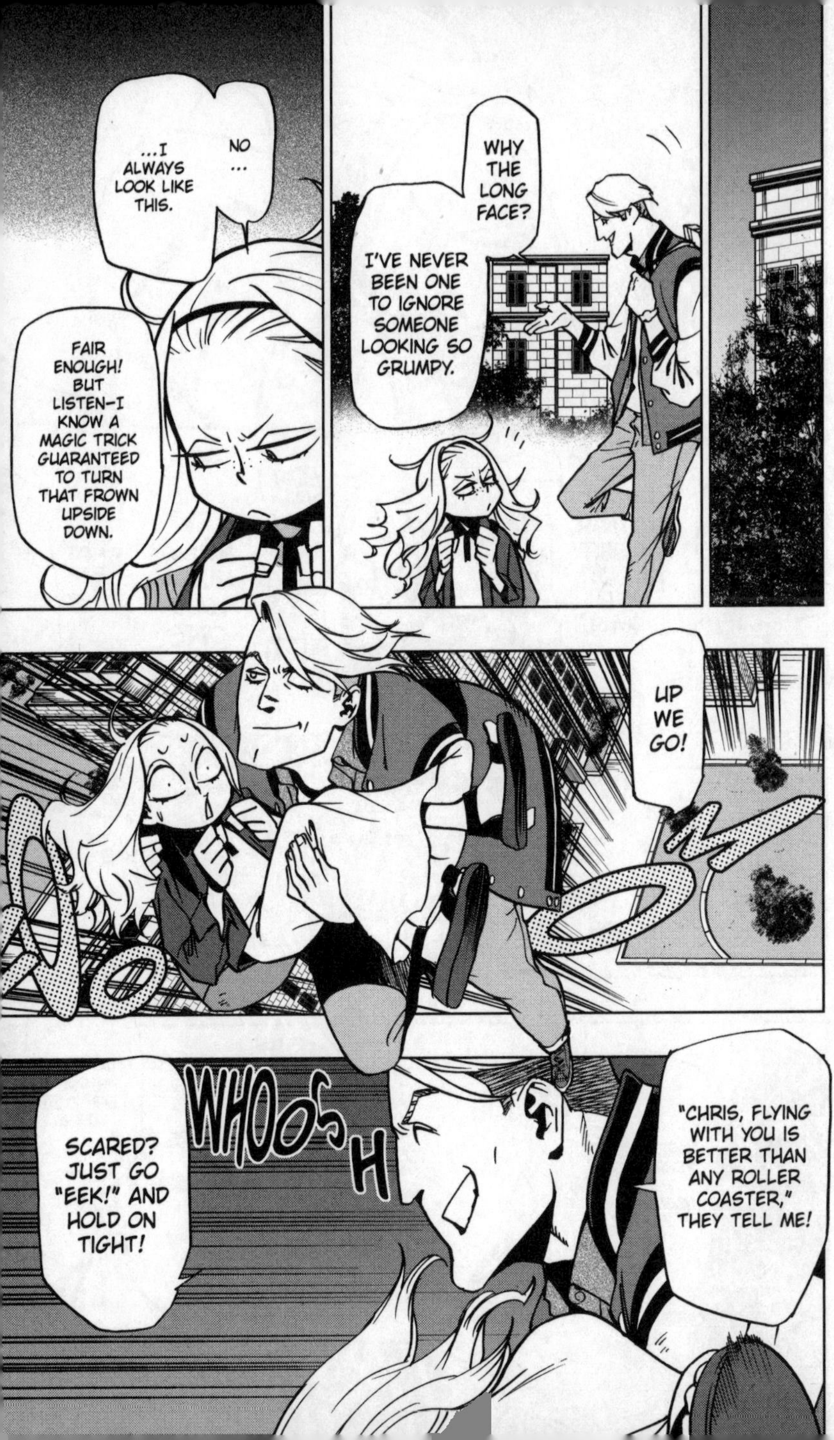
WHY THE LONG FACE?
I'VE NEVER BEEN ONE TO IGNORE SOMEONE LOOKING SO GRUMPY.
NO...
...I ALWAYS LOOK LIKE THIS.
FAIR ENOUGH! BUT LISTEN—I KNOW A MAGIC TRICK GUARANTEED TO TURN THAT FROWN UPSIDE DOWN.
UP WE GO!
"CHRIS, FLYING WITH YOU IS BETTER THAN ANY ROLLER COASTER," THEY TELL ME!
WHOOSH
SCARED? JUST GO "EEK!" AND HOLD ON TIGHT!

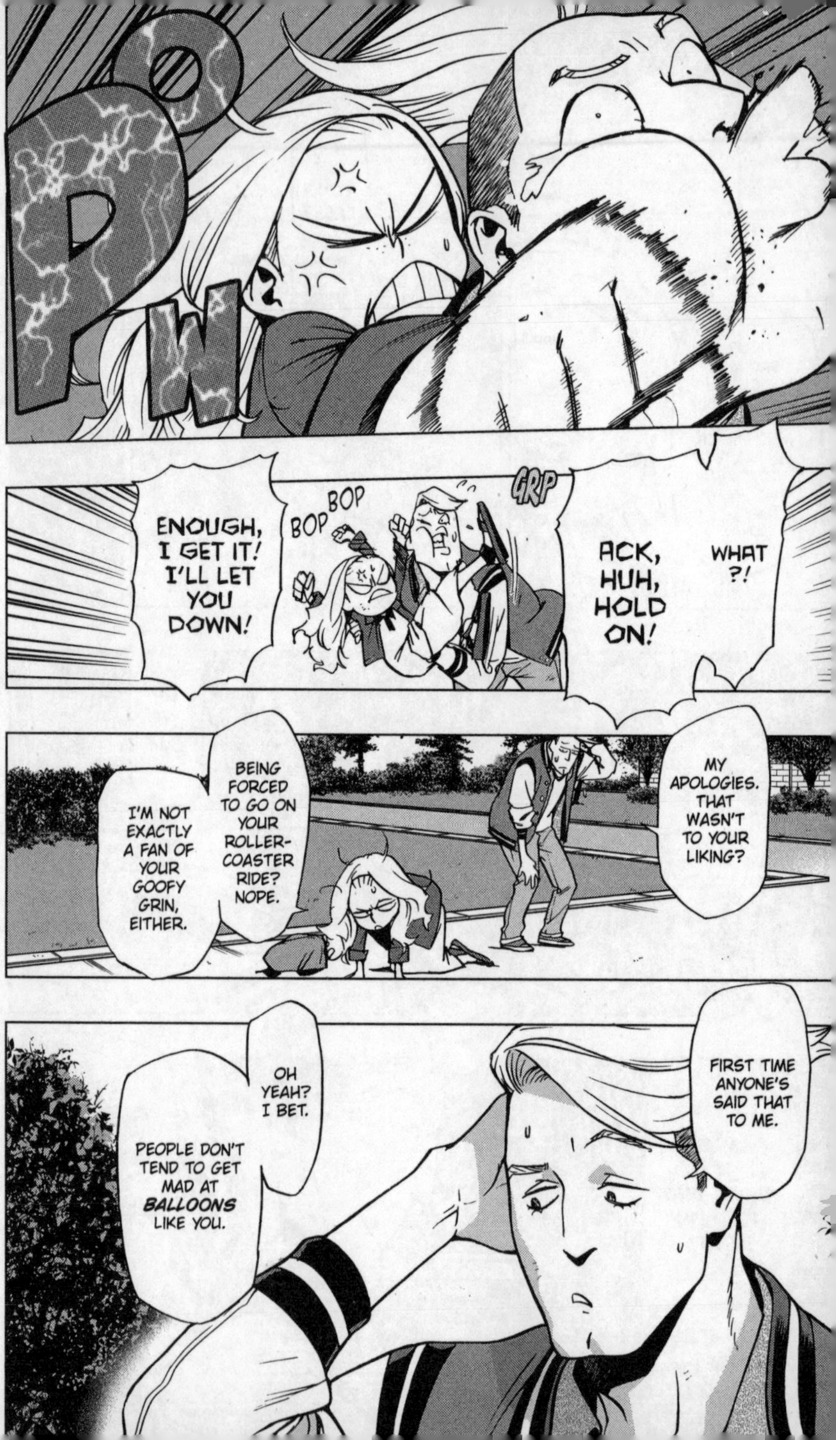
POW
WHAT ?!
ACK, HUH, HOLD ON!
GRIP
BOP BOP
ENOUGH, I GET IT! I'LL LET YOU DOWN!
MY APOLOGIES. THAT WASN'T TO YOUR LIKING?
BEING FORCED TO GO ON YOUR ROLLER-COASTER RIDE? NOPE.
I'M NOT EXACTLY A FAN OF YOUR GOOFY GRIN, EITHER.
FIRST TIME ANYONE'S SAID THAT TO ME.
OH YEAH? I BET.
PEOPLE DON'T TEND TO GET MAD AT *BALLOONS* LIKE YOU.

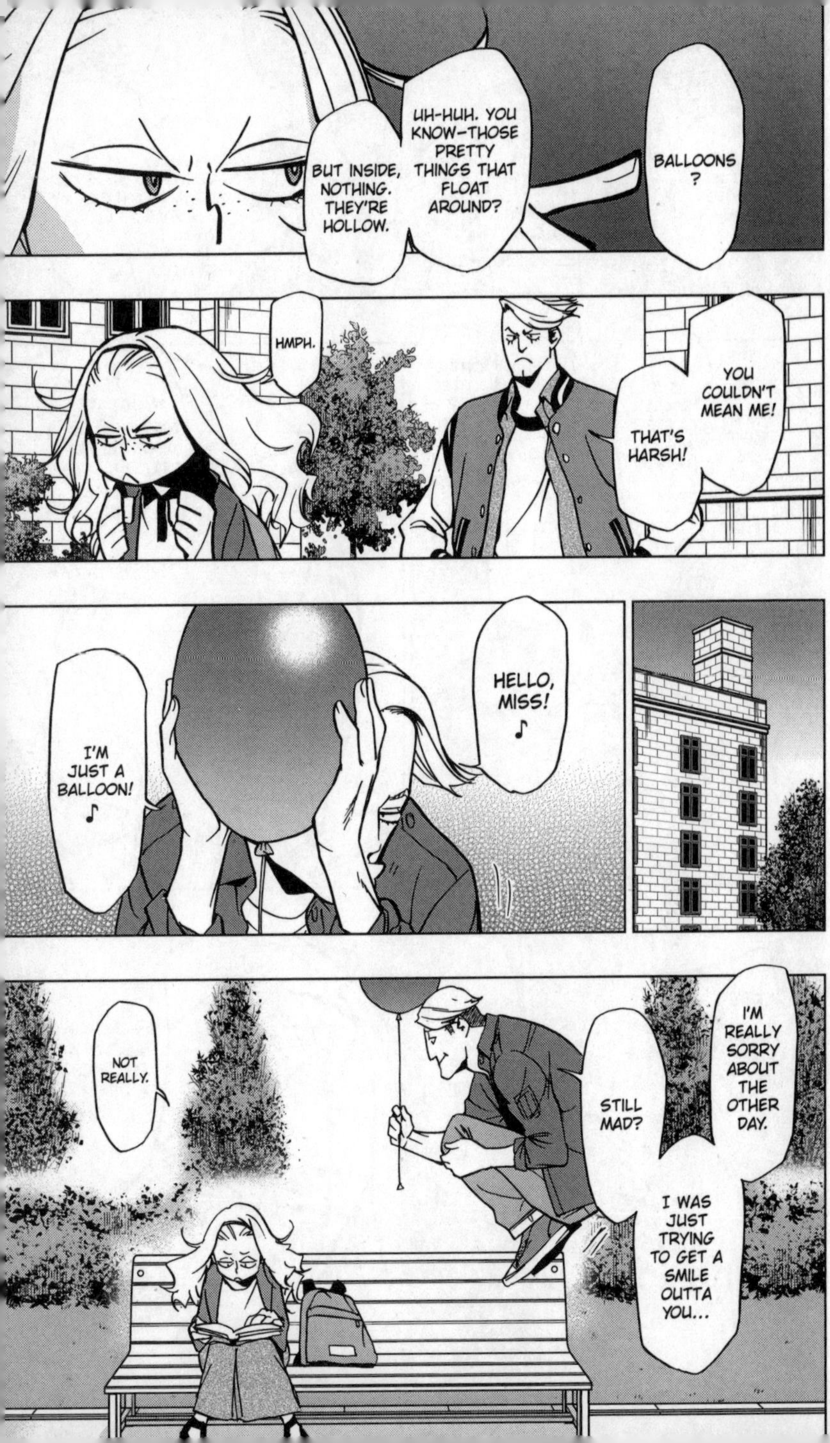
BALLOONS?
UH-HUH. YOU KNOW—THOSE PRETTY THINGS THAT FLOAT AROUND?
BUT INSIDE, NOTHING. THEY'RE HOLLOW.
YOU COULDN'T MEAN ME!
THAT'S HARSH!
HMPH.
HELLO, MISS! ♪
I'M JUST A BALLOON! ♪
I'M REALLY SORRY ABOUT THE OTHER DAY.
I WAS JUST TRYING TO GET A SMILE OUTTA YOU...
STILL MAD?
NOT REALLY.

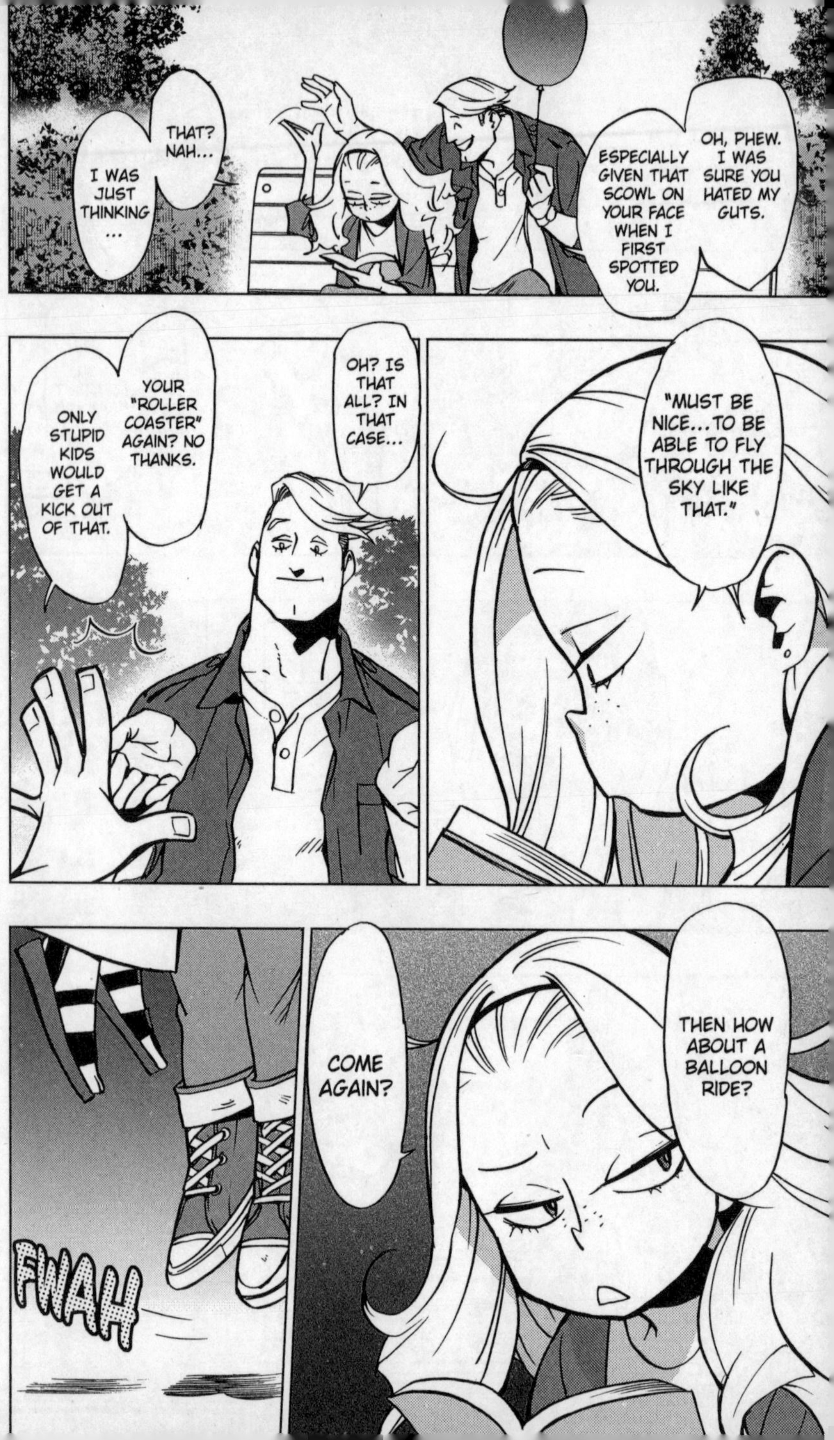
OH, PHEW. I WAS SURE YOU HATED MY GUTS.
ESPECIALLY GIVEN THAT SCOWL ON YOUR FACE WHEN I FIRST SPOTTED YOU.
THAT? NAH...
I WAS JUST THINKING...
"MUST BE NICE...TO BE ABLE TO FLY THROUGH THE SKY LIKE THAT."
OH? IS THAT ALL? IN THAT CASE...
YOUR "ROLLER COASTER" AGAIN? NO THANKS.
ONLY STUPID KIDS WOULD GET A KICK OUT OF THAT.
THEN HOW ABOUT A BALLOON RIDE?
COME AGAIN?
FWAH

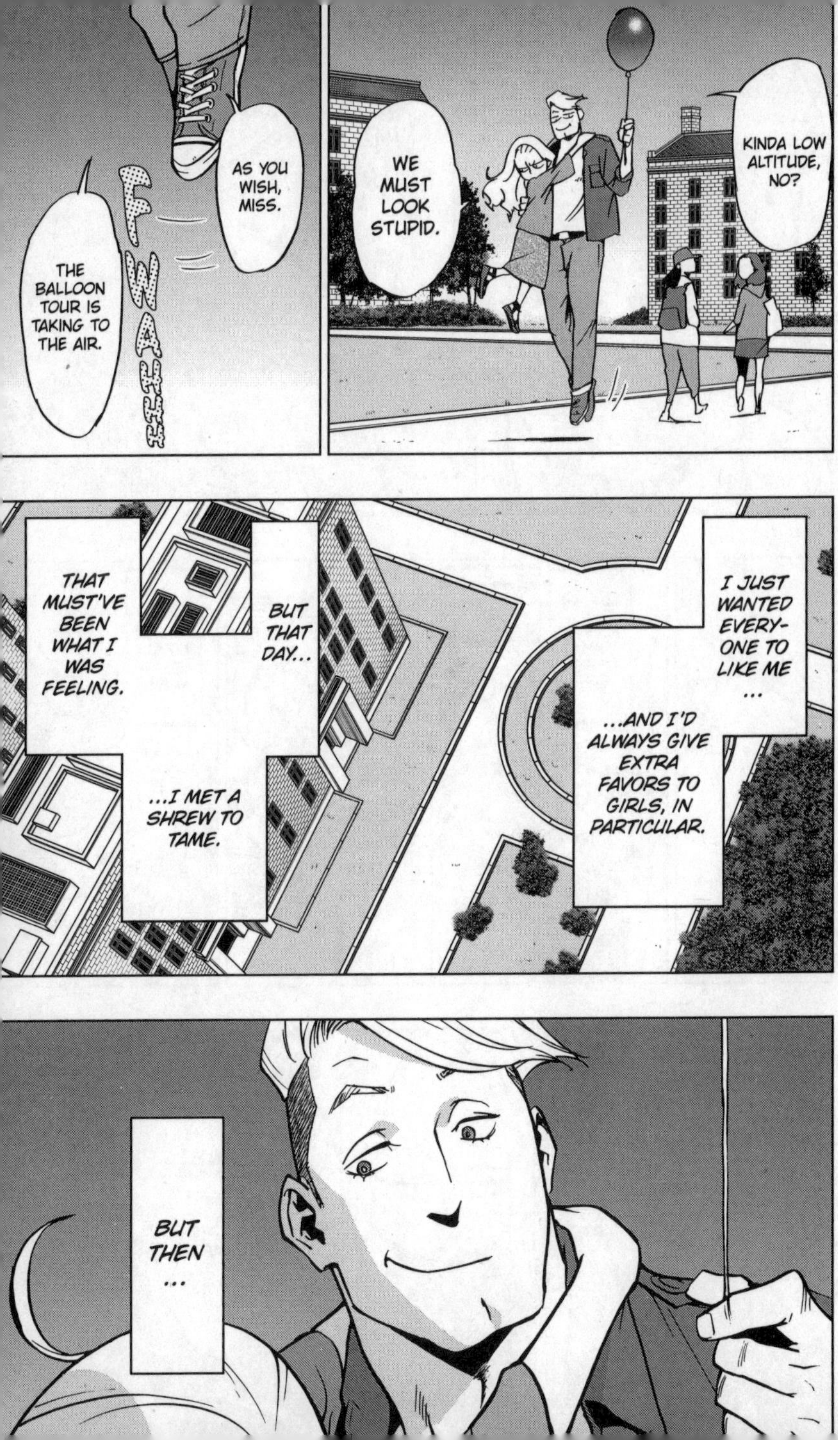
KINDA LOW ALTITUDE, NO?
WE MUST LOOK STUPID.
AS YOU WISH, MISS.
THE BALLOON TOUR IS TAKING TO THE AIR.
I JUST WANTED EVERY-ONE TO LIKE ME...
...AND I'D ALWAYS GIVE EXTRA FAVORS TO GIRLS, IN PARTICULAR.
THAT MUST'VE BEEN WHAT I WAS FEELING.
BUT THAT DAY...
...I MET A SHREW TO TAME.
BUT THEN...

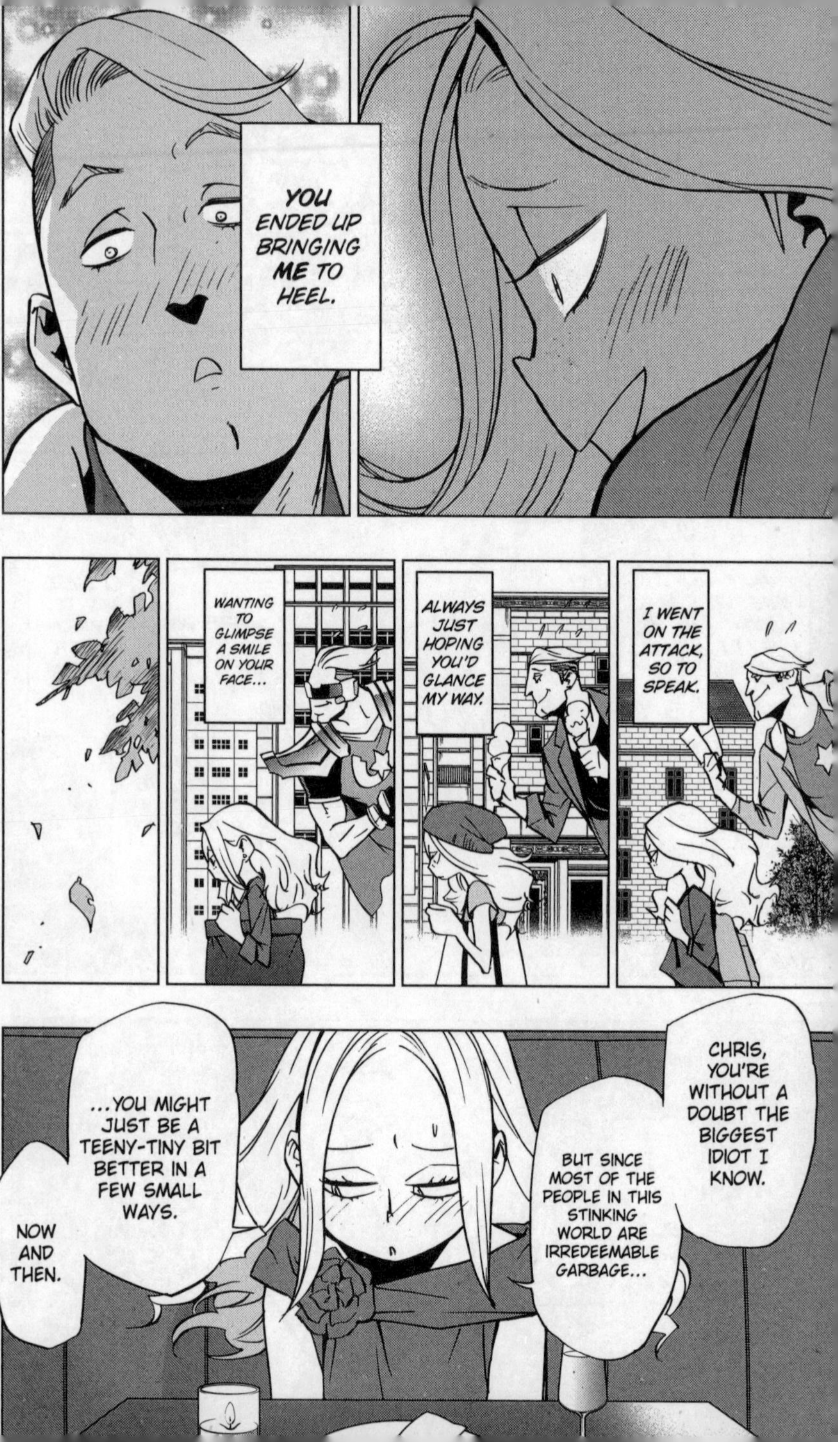
YOU ENDED UP BRINGING ME TO HEEL.
I WENT ON THE ATTACK, SO TO SPEAK.
ALWAYS JUST HOPING YOU'D GLANCE MY WAY.
WANTING TO GLIMPSE A SMILE ON YOUR FACE...
CHRIS, YOU'RE WITHOUT A DOUBT THE BIGGEST IDIOT I KNOW.
BUT SINCE MOST OF THE PEOPLE IN THIS STINKING WORLD ARE IRREDEEMABLE GARBAGE...
...YOU MIGHT JUST BE A TEENY-TINY BIT BETTER IN A FEW SMALL WAYS.
NOW AND THEN.

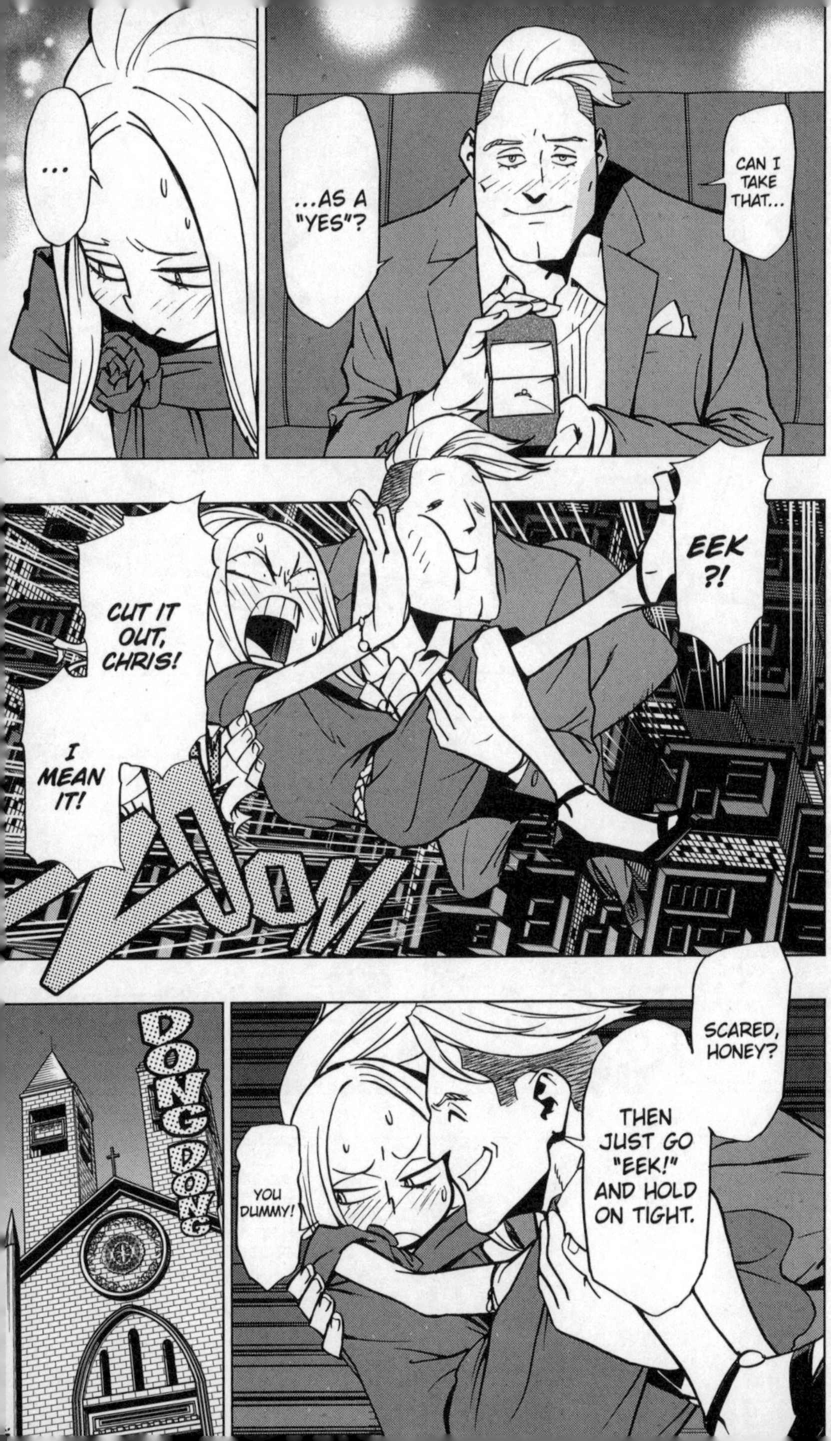
CAN I TAKE THAT...
...AS A "YES"?
...
EEK ?!
CUT IT OUT, CHRIS!
I MEAN IT!
SCARED, HONEY?
THEN JUST GO "EEK!" AND HOLD ON TIGHT.
YOU DUMMY!
DONG DONG

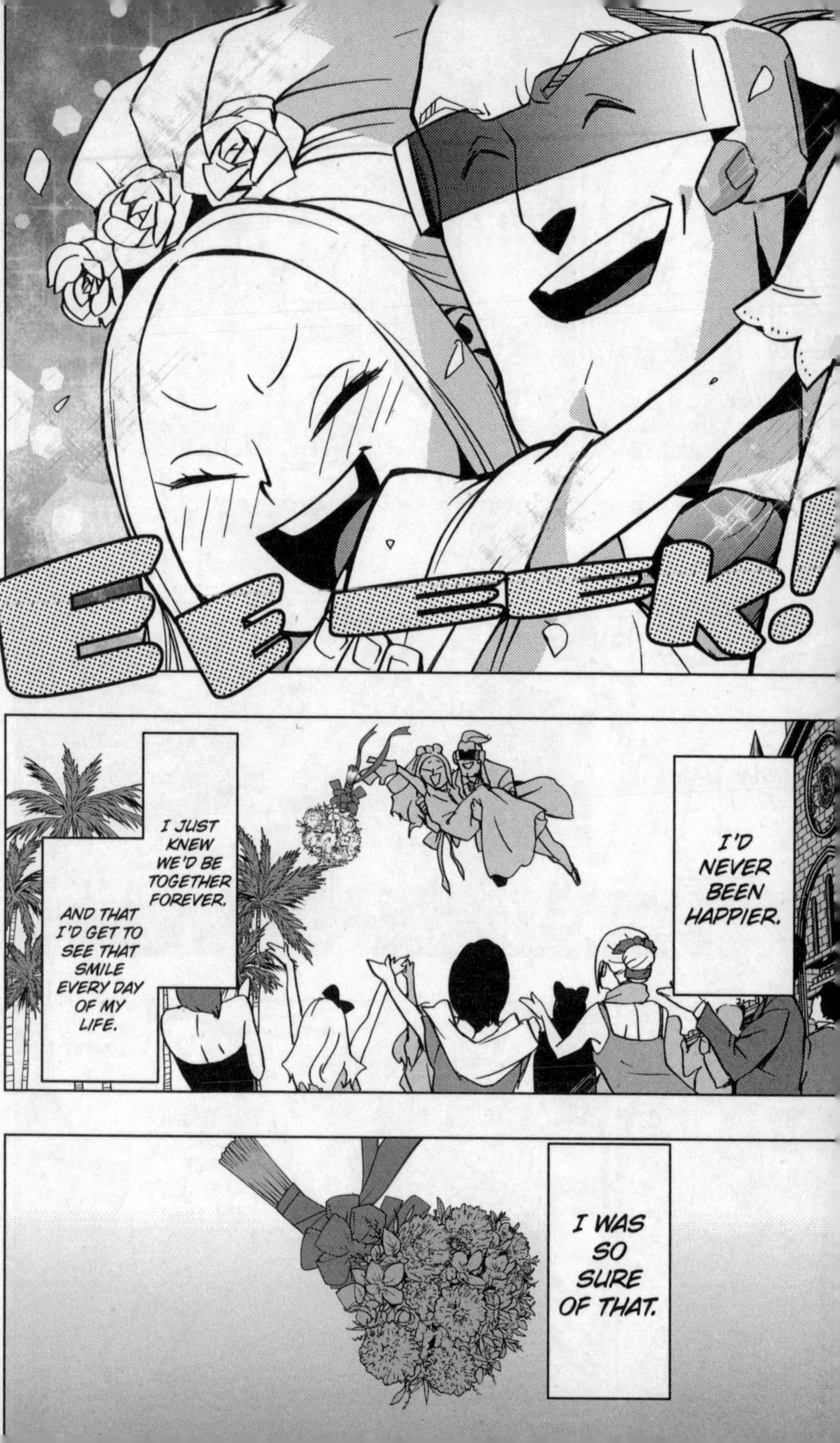
EEEEEK!
I'D NEVER BEEN HAPPIER.
I JUST KNEW WE'D BE TOGETHER FOREVER.
AND THAT I'D GET TO SEE THAT SMILE EVERY DAY OF MY LIFE.
I WAS SO SURE OF THAT.

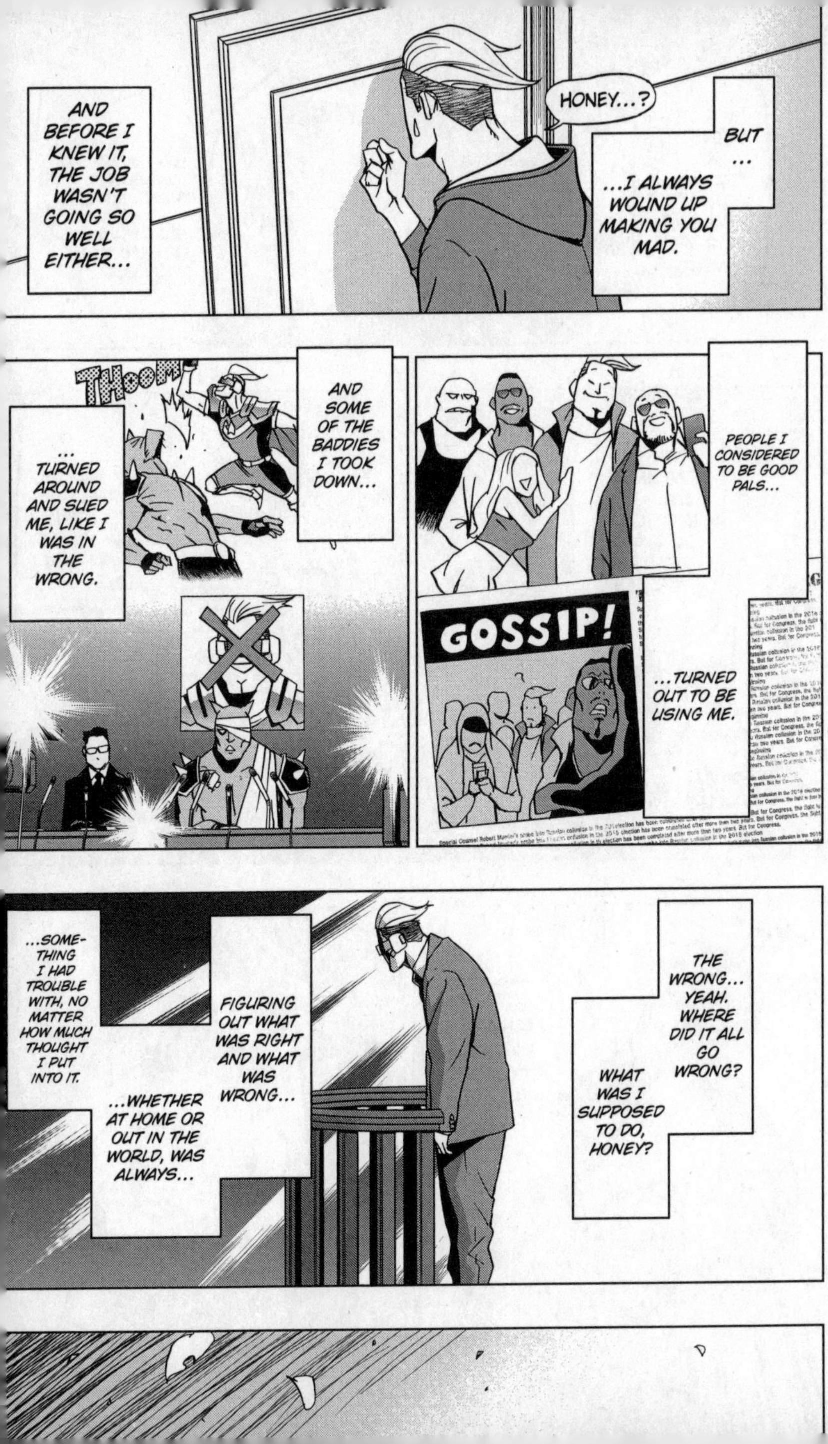
HONEY...?
BUT... ...I ALWAYS WOUND UP MAKING YOU MAD.
AND BEFORE I KNEW IT, THE JOB WASN'T GOING SO WELL EITHER...
PEOPLE I CONSIDERED TO BE GOOD PALS...
...TURNED OUT TO BE USING ME.
GOSSIP!
AND SOME OF THE BADDIES I TOOK DOWN...
THOOM
...TURNED AROUND AND SUED ME, LIKE I WAS IN THE WRONG.
THE WRONG... YEAH. WHERE DID IT ALL GO WRONG?
WHAT WAS I SUPPOSED TO DO, HONEY?
FIGURING OUT WHAT WAS RIGHT AND WHAT WAS WRONG...
...WHETHER AT HOME OR OUT IN THE WORLD, WAS ALWAYS...
...SOMETHING I HAD TROUBLE WITH, NO MATTER HOW MUCH THOUGHT I PUT INTO IT.

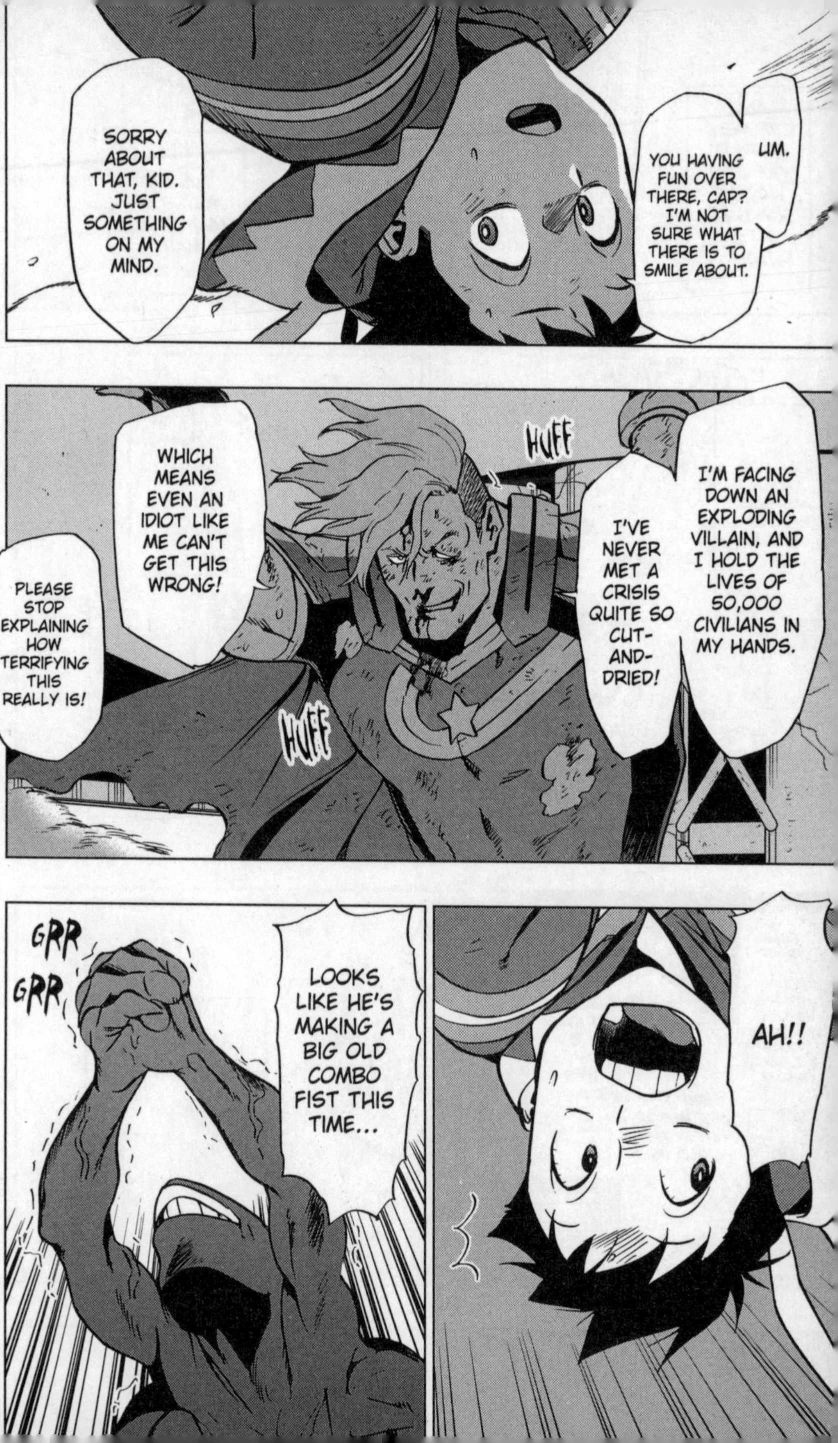
UM.
YOU HAVING FUN OVER THERE, CAP? I'M NOT SURE WHAT THERE IS TO SMILE ABOUT.
SORRY ABOUT THAT, KID. JUST SOMETHING ON MY MIND.
I'M FACING DOWN AN EXPLODING VILLAIN, AND I HOLD THE LIVES OF 50,000 CIVILIANS IN MY HANDS.
I'VE NEVER MET A CRISIS QUITE SO CUT-AND-DRIED!
HUFF
WHICH MEANS EVEN AN IDIOT LIKE ME CAN'T GET THIS WRONG!
HUFF
PLEASE STOP EXPLAINING HOW TERRIFYING THIS REALLY IS!
AH!!
LOOKS LIKE HE'S MAKING A BIG OLD COMBO FIST THIS TIME...
GRR
GRR

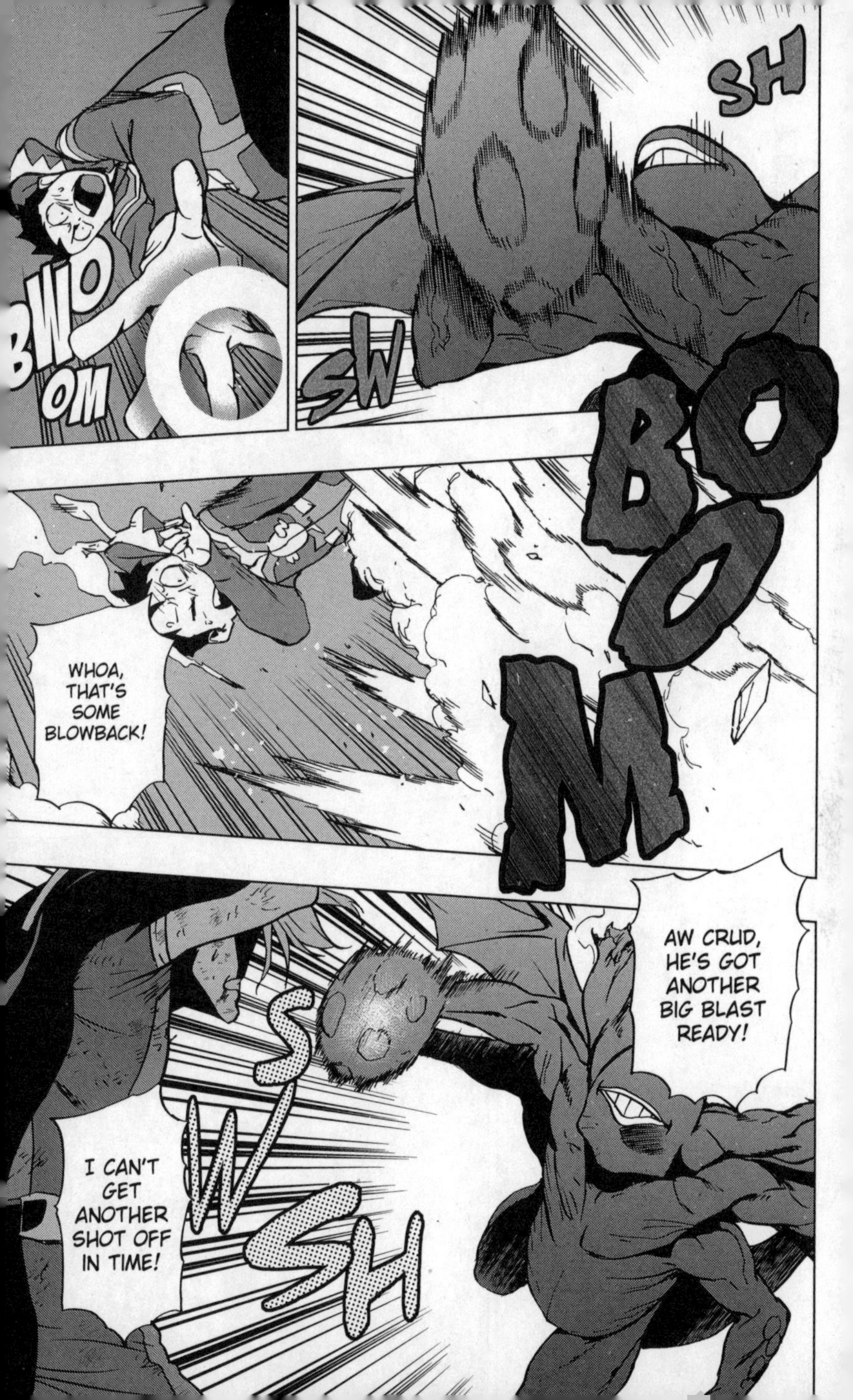
SH
SW
BWOOM
BOOM
WHOA, THAT'S SOME BLOWBACK!
AW CRUD, HE'S GOT ANOTHER BIG BLAST READY!
SWSH
I CAN'T GET ANOTHER SHOT OFF IN TIME!

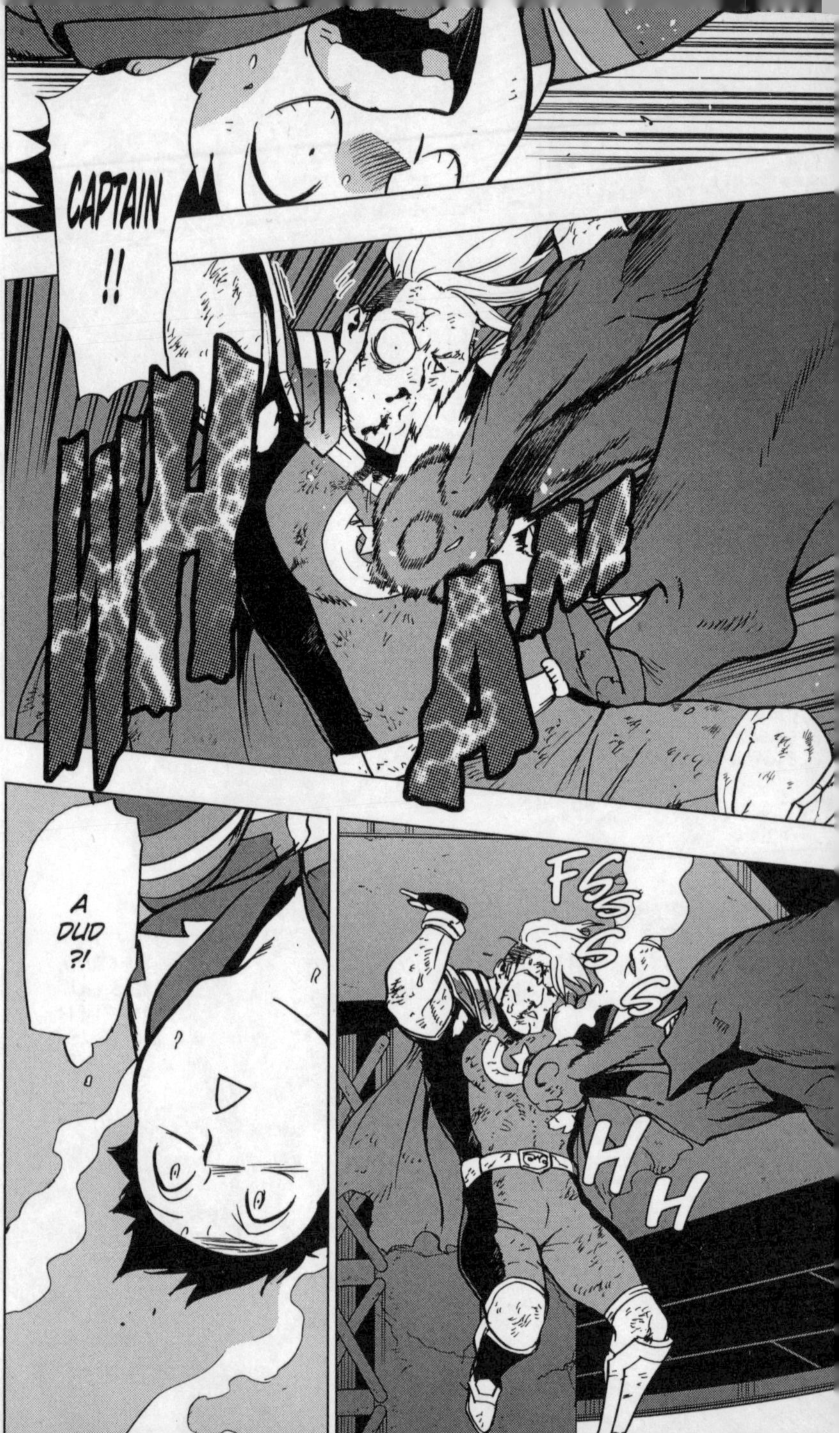

CAPTAIN!!
FSSSSSHHH
A DUD?!

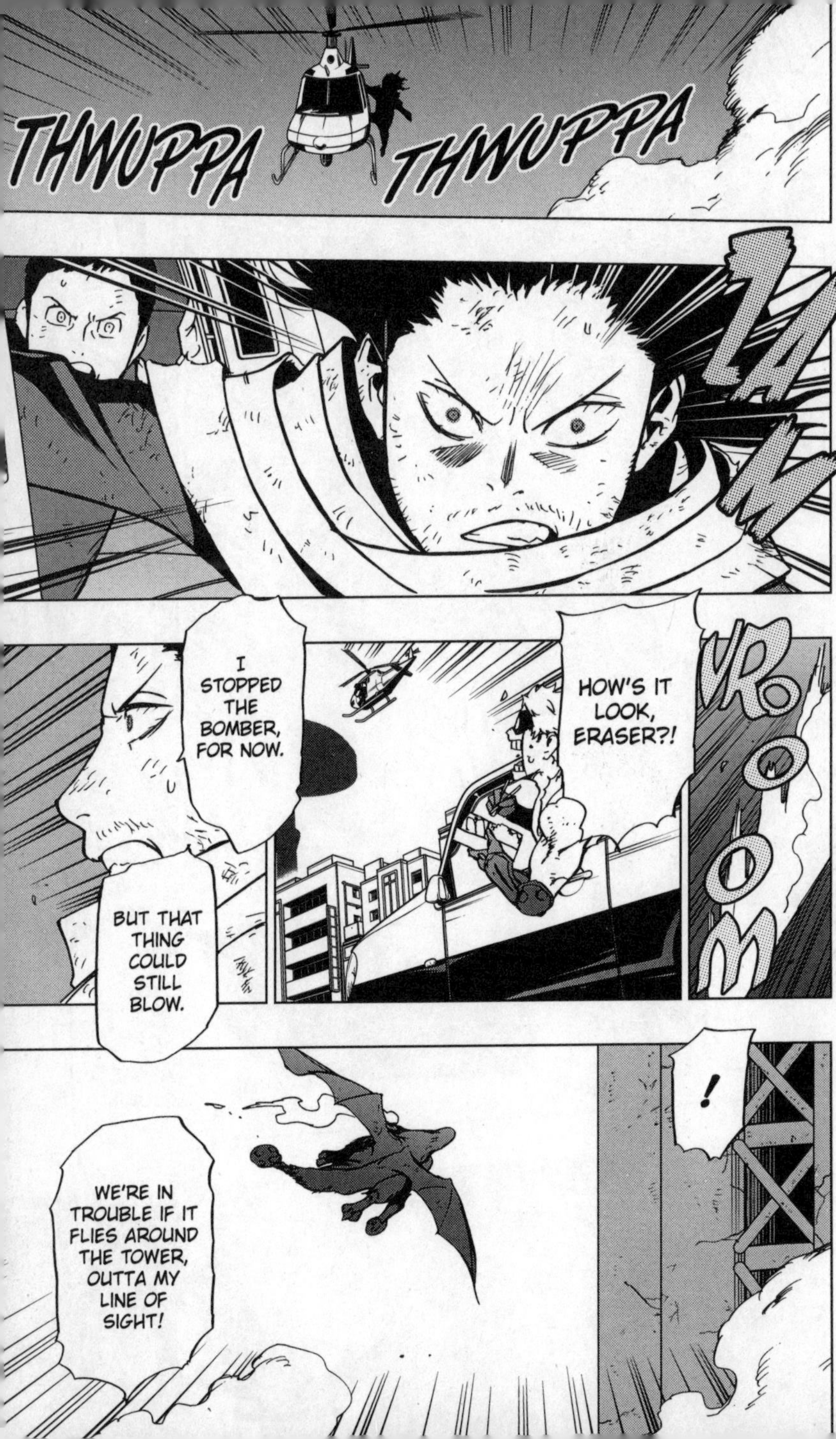
THWUPPA
THWUPPA
ZAWN
VROOOOM
HOW'S IT LOOK, ERASER?!
I STOPPED THE BOMBER, FOR NOW.
BUT THAT THING COULD STILL BLOW.
!
WE'RE IN TROUBLE IF IT FLIES AROUND THE TOWER, OUTTA MY LINE OF SIGHT!

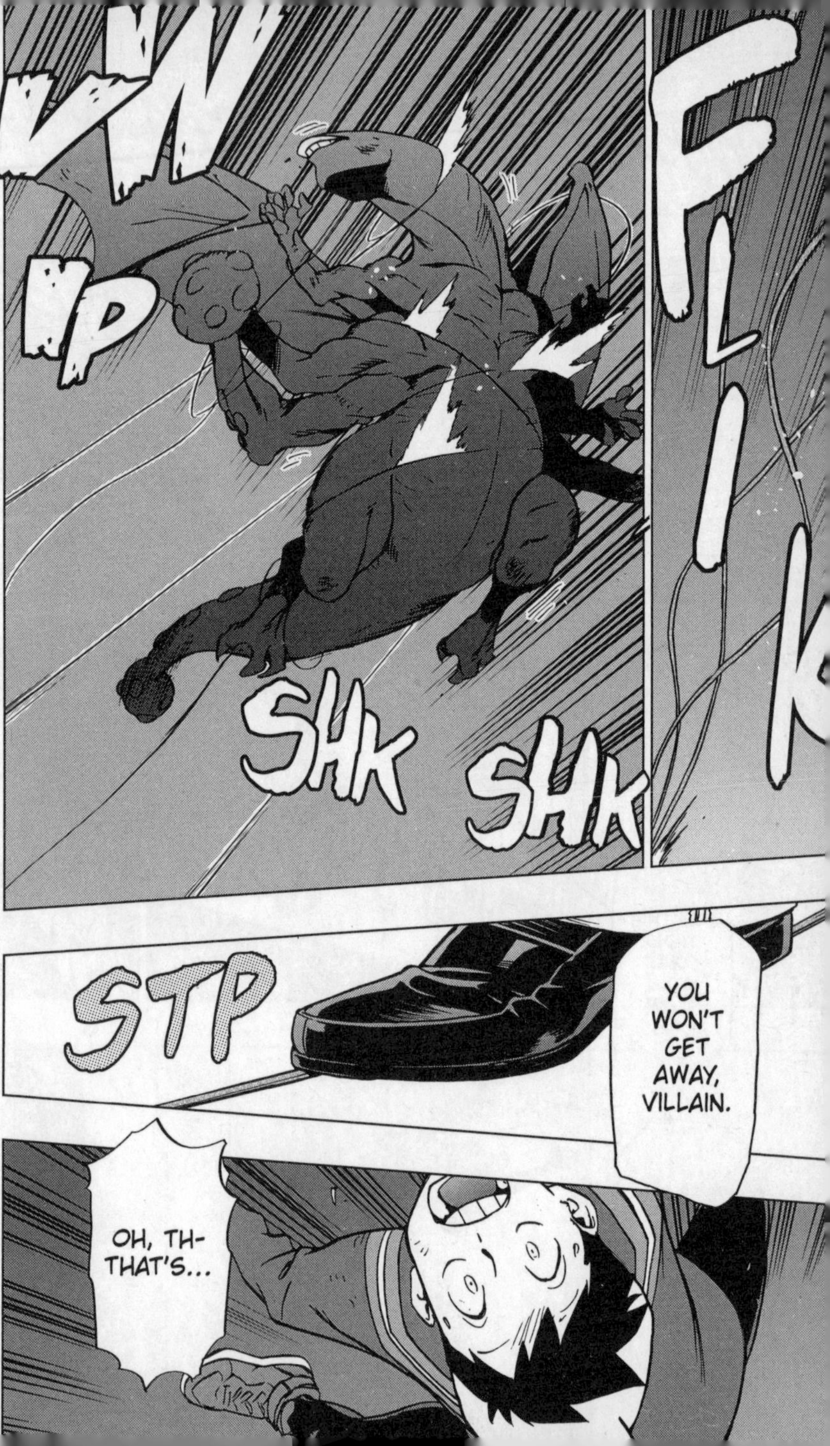
FLIK
VWIP
SHK SHK
YOU WON'T GET AWAY, VILLAIN.
STP
OH, TH-THAT'S...

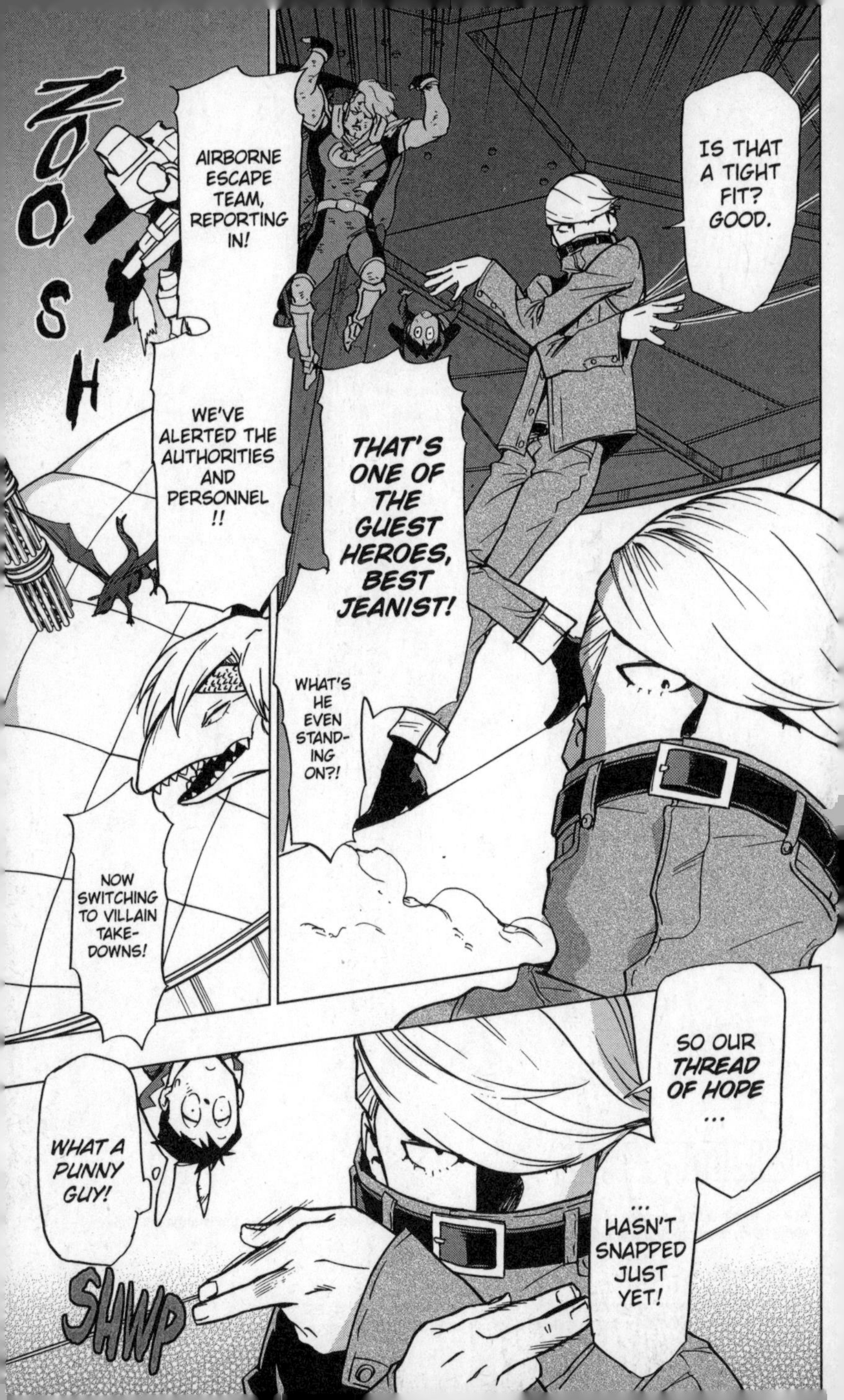
IS THAT A TIGHT FIT? GOOD.
THAT'S ONE OF THE GUEST HEROES, BEST JEANIST!
WHAT'S HE EVEN STANDING ON?!
ZOOOSH
AIRBORNE ESCAPE TEAM, REPORTING IN!
WE'VE ALERTED THE AUTHORITIES AND PERSONNEL!!
NOW SWITCHING TO VILLAIN TAKE-DOWNS!
SO OUR THREAD OF HOPE...
...HASN'T SNAPPED JUST YET!
WHAT A PUNNY GUY!
SHWP

CHRIS AND PAMELA

THE ROUGH DESIGN

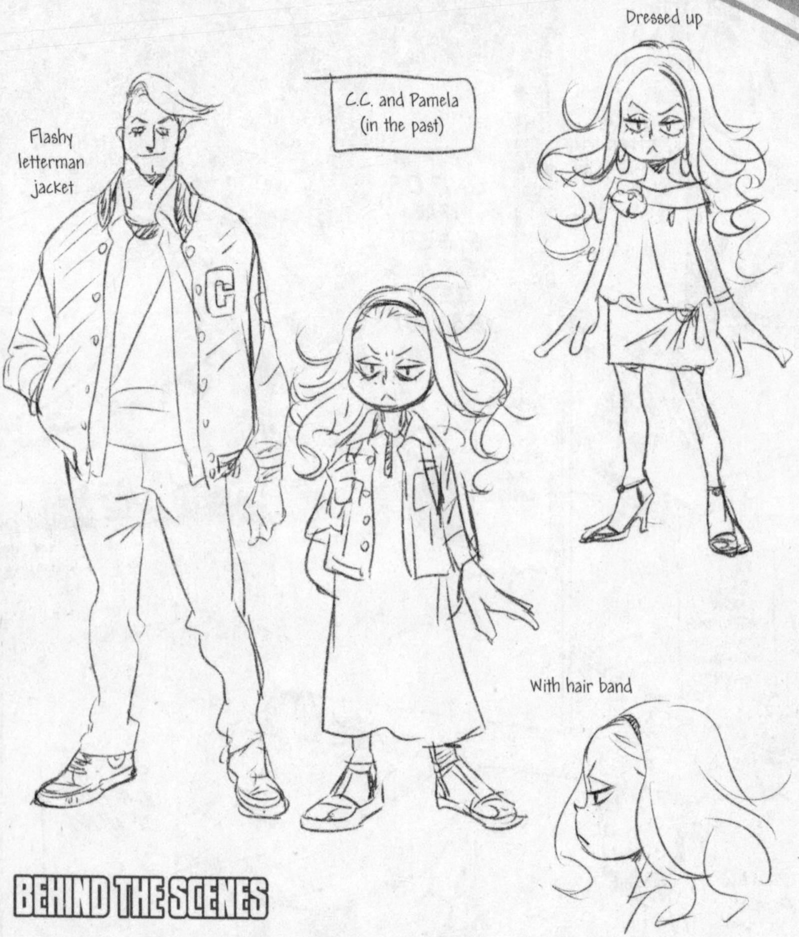

Dressed up
C.C. and Pamela
(in the past)
Flashy
letterman
jacket
With hair band

BEHIND THE SCENES

At first, Cap's wife was more of a vicious, henpecking harpy, but her image changed in the flashback chapter about them meeting. She's actually a cutie.

—Furuhashi

Cap's early look seems straight out of *Back to the Future* or *Beverly Hills, 90210*.
His wife is more on the cartoony side (like Mineta or La Brava), with a hint of Edmond Kiraz's style.

—Betten

Ep. 53 - Limits and Catastrophe

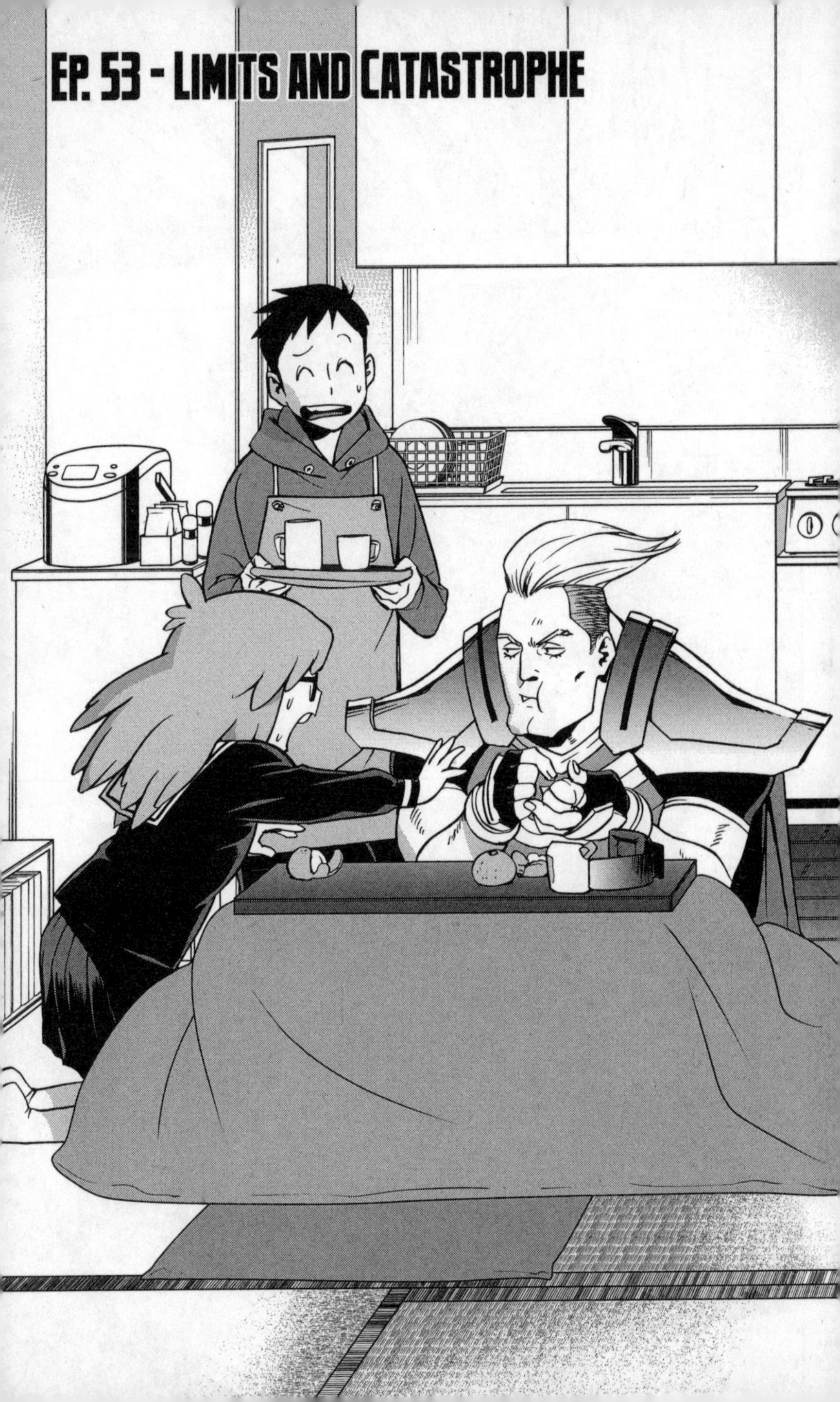

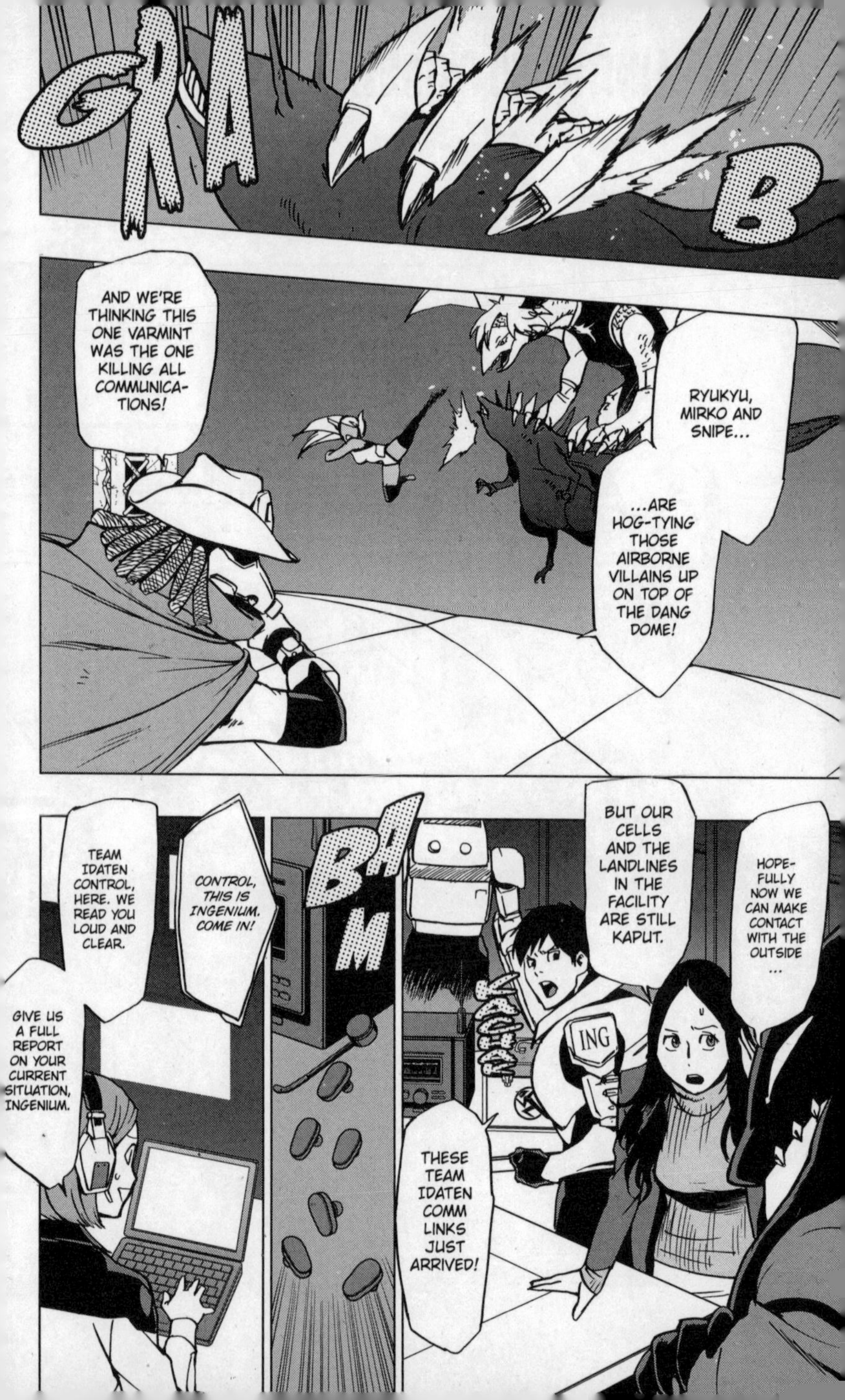
GRAB
RYUKYU, MIRKO AND SNIPE...
...ARE HOG-TYING THOSE AIRBORNE VILLAINS UP ON TOP OF THE DANG DOME!
AND WE'RE THINKING THIS ONE VARMINT WAS THE ONE KILLING ALL COMMUNICATIONS!
HOPEFULLY NOW WE CAN MAKE CONTACT WITH THE OUTSIDE ...
BUT OUR CELLS AND THE LANDLINES IN THE FACILITY ARE STILL KAPUT.
THESE TEAM IDATEN COMM LINKS JUST ARRIVED!
ING
BAM
CONTROL, THIS IS INGENIUM. COME IN!
TEAM IDATEN CONTROL, HERE. WE READ YOU LOUD AND CLEAR.
GIVE US A FULL REPORT ON YOUR CURRENT SITUATION, INGENIUM.

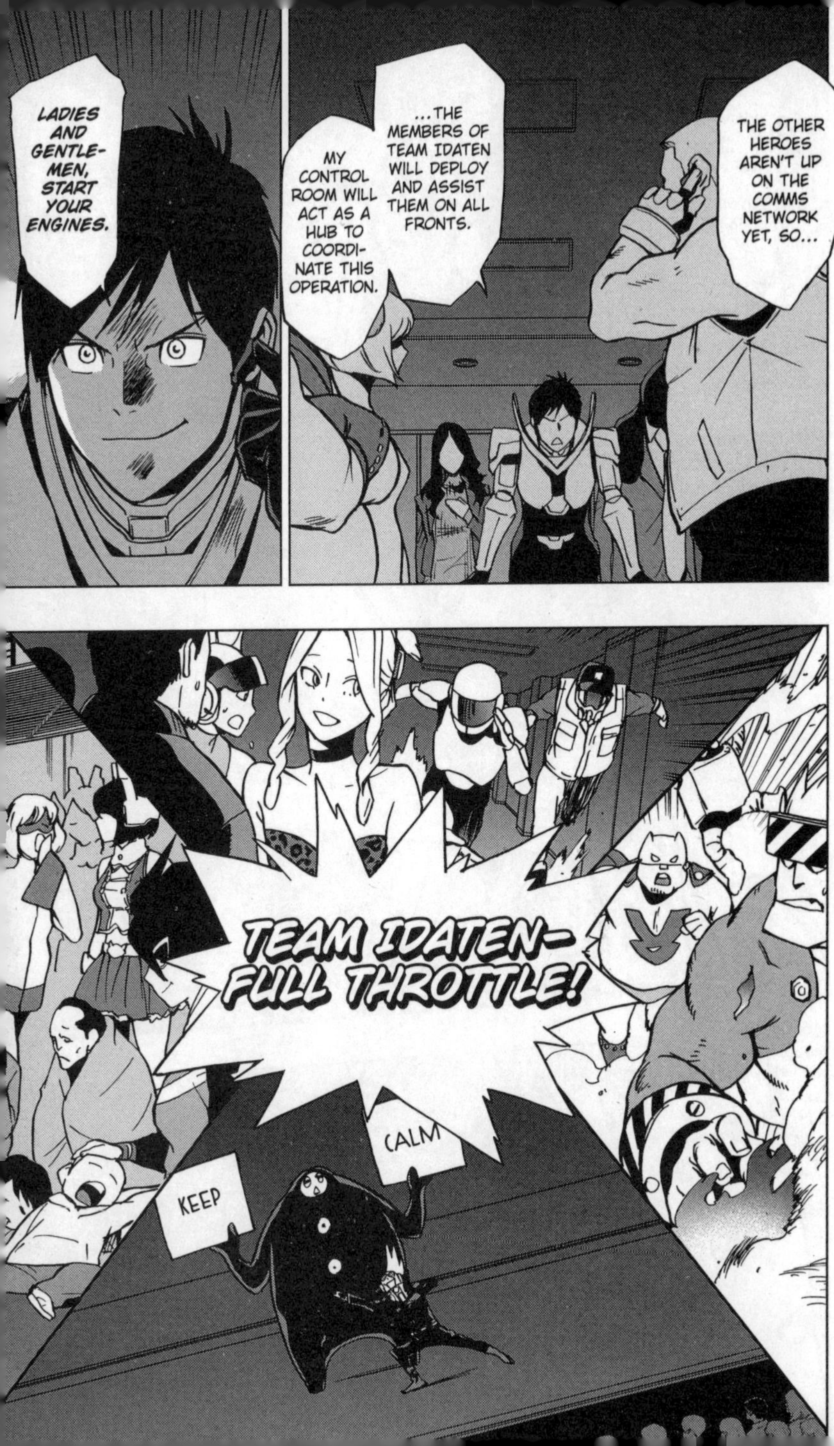
THE OTHER HEROES AREN'T UP ON THE COMMS NETWORK YET, SO...
...THE MEMBERS OF TEAM IDATEN WILL DEPLOY AND ASSIST THEM ON ALL FRONTS.
MY CONTROL ROOM WILL ACT AS A HUB TO COORDINATE THIS OPERATION.
LADIES AND GENTLEMEN, START YOUR ENGINES.
TEAM IDATEN—FULL THROTTLE!
CALM
KEEP

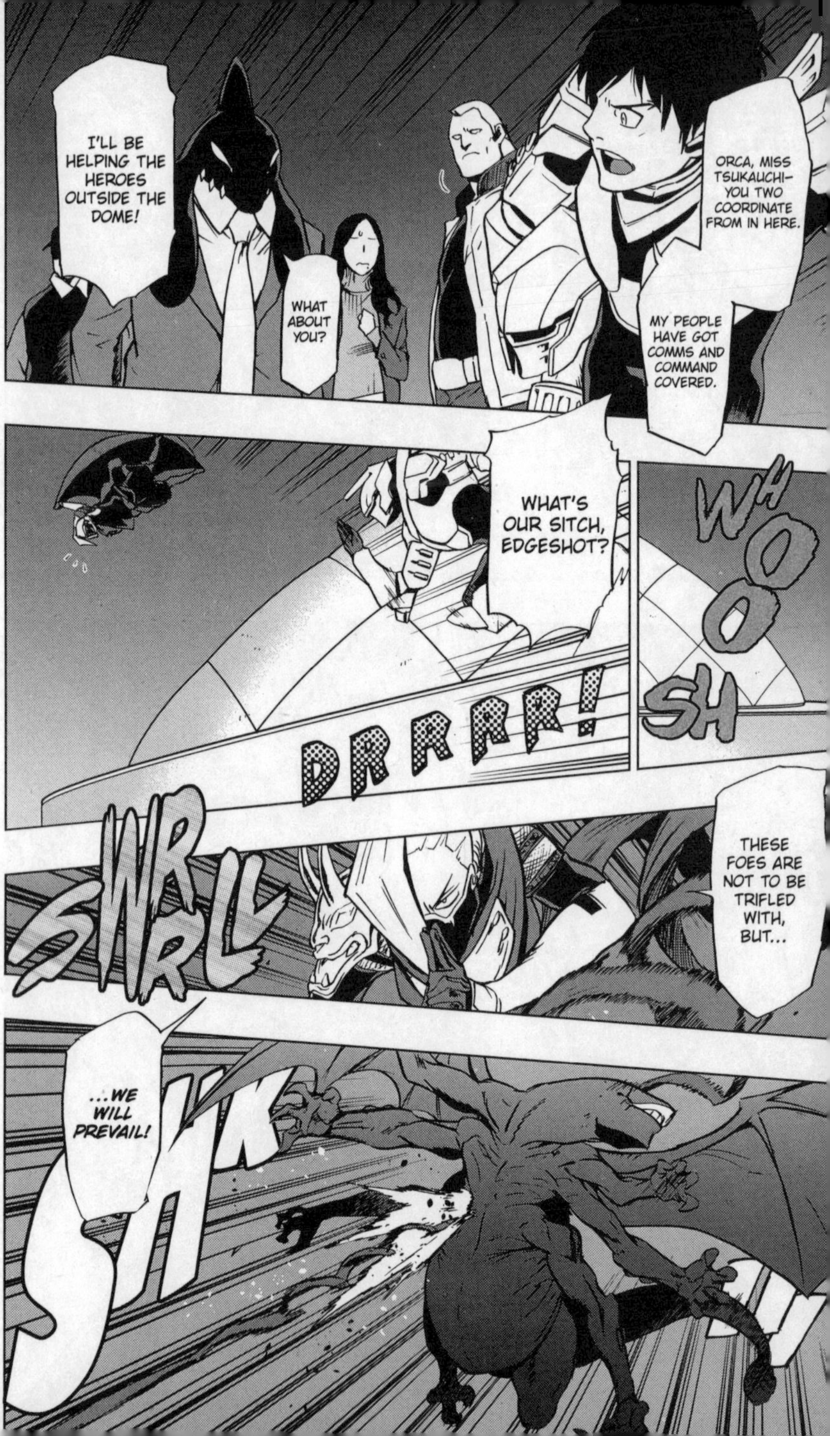
ORCA, MISS TSUKAUCHI— YOU TWO COORDINATE FROM IN HERE.
MY PEOPLE HAVE GOT COMMS AND COMMAND COVERED.
WHAT ABOUT YOU?
I'LL BE HELPING THE HEROES OUTSIDE THE DOME!
WHOOOSH
WHAT'S OUR SITCH, EDGESHOT?
DRRRR!
THESE FOES ARE NOT TO BE TRIFLED WITH, BUT...
SWRL SWRL
...WE WILL PREVAIL!
SHK

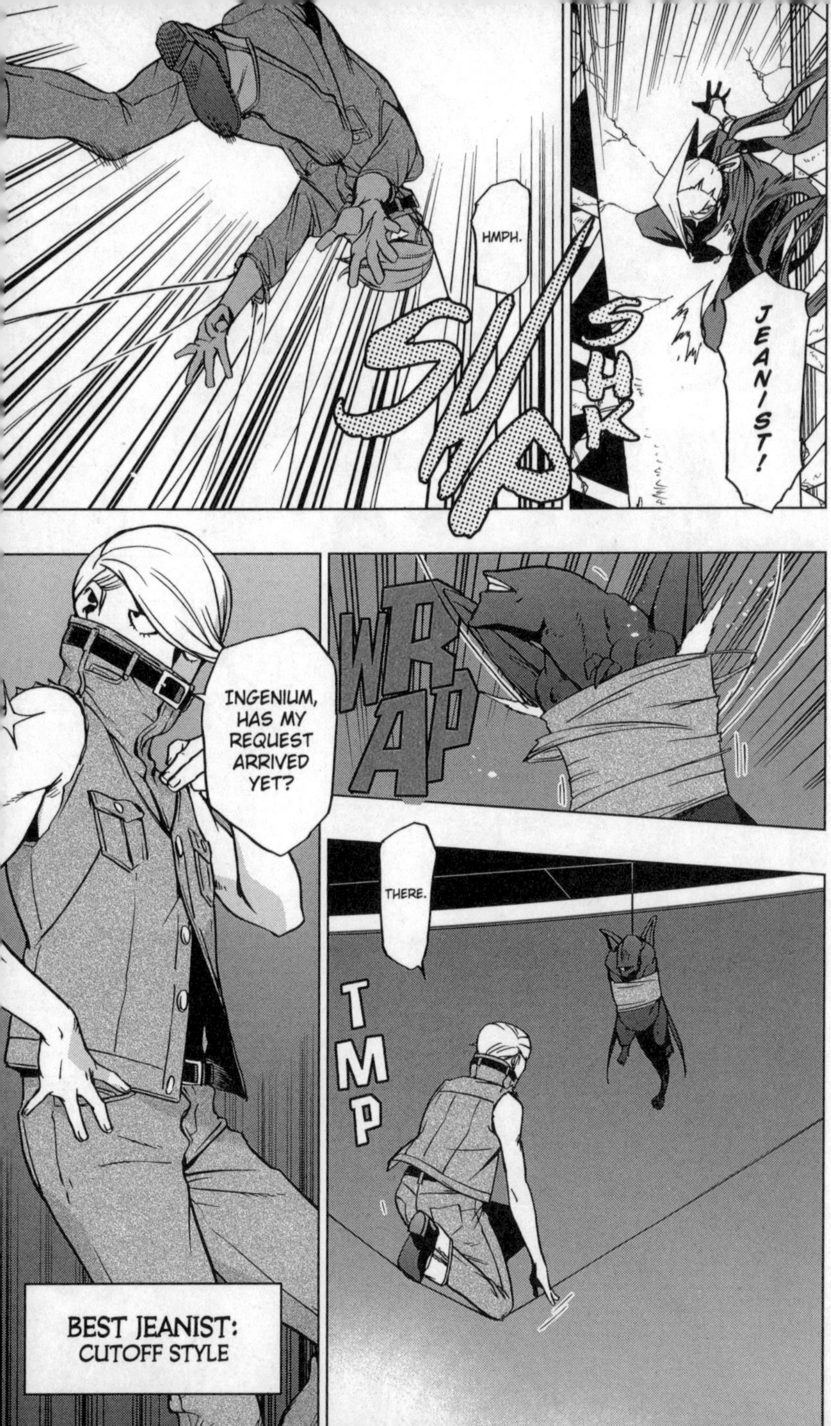
JEANIST!
SHK
HMPH.
SHA
WRAP
THERE.
TMP
INGENIUM, HAS MY REQUEST ARRIVED YET?
BEST JEANIST: CUTOFF STYLE

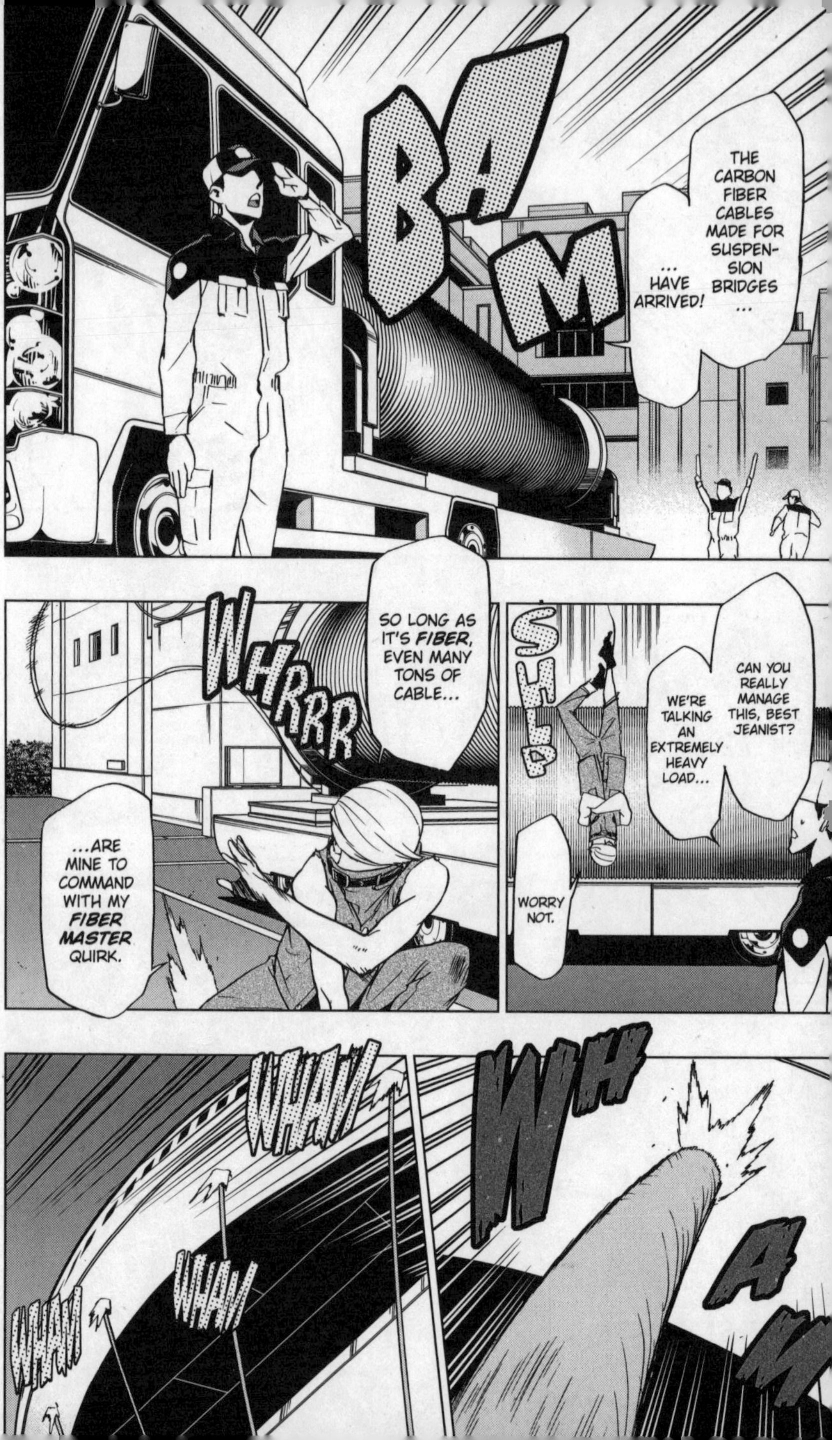
BAM
THE CARBON FIBER CABLES MADE FOR SUSPENSION BRIDGES...
...HAVE ARRIVED!
CAN YOU REALLY MANAGE THIS, BEST JEANIST?
WE'RE TALKING AN EXTREMELY HEAVY LOAD...
SHLP
WORRY NOT.
SO LONG AS IT'S *FIBER*, EVEN MANY TONS OF CABLE...
WHRRR
...ARE MINE TO COMMAND WITH MY *FIBER MASTER* QUIRK.
WHAA
WHAM
WHAM
WHAM

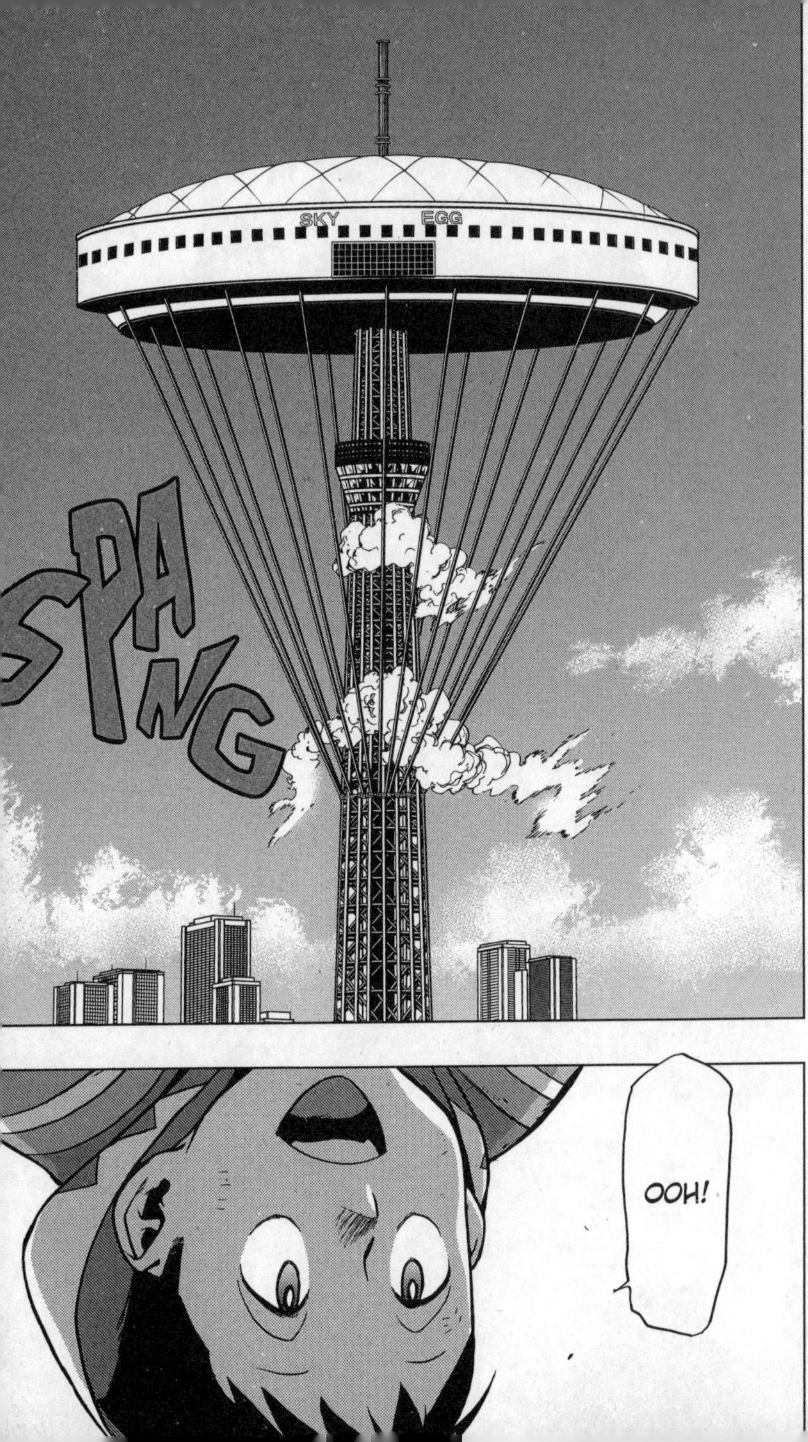
SKY EGG
SPANG
OOH!

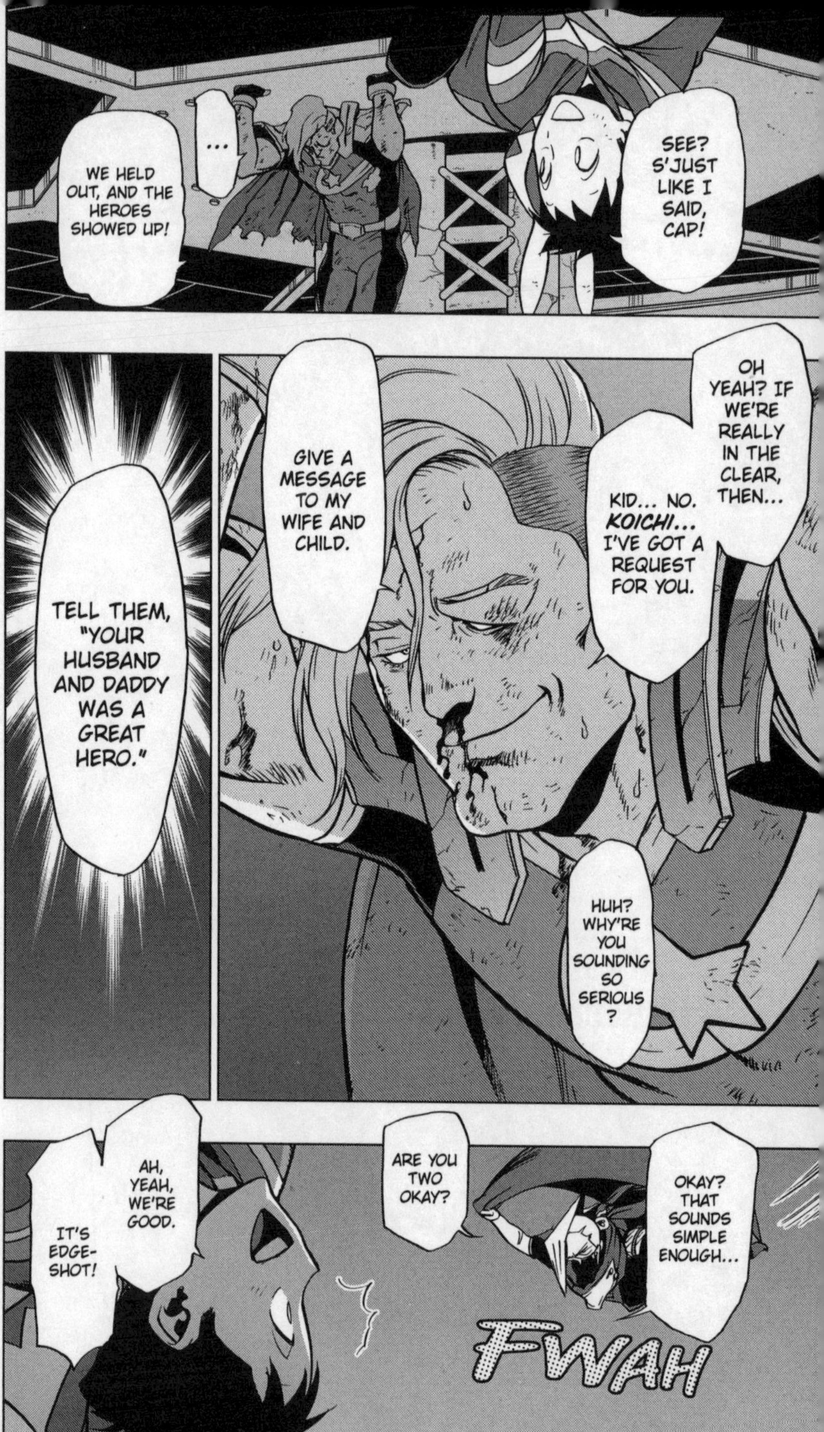
SEE? S'JUST LIKE I SAID, CAP!
...
WE HELD OUT, AND THE HEROES SHOWED UP!
OH YEAH? IF WE'RE REALLY IN THE CLEAR, THEN...
KID... NO. *KOICHI*... I'VE GOT A REQUEST FOR YOU.
GIVE A MESSAGE TO MY WIFE AND CHILD.
HUH? WHY'RE YOU SOUNDING SO SERIOUS?
TELL THEM, "YOUR HUSBAND AND DADDY WAS A GREAT HERO."
OKAY? THAT SOUNDS SIMPLE ENOUGH...
FWAH
ARE YOU TWO OKAY?
AH, YEAH, WE'RE GOOD.
IT'S EDGE-SHOT!

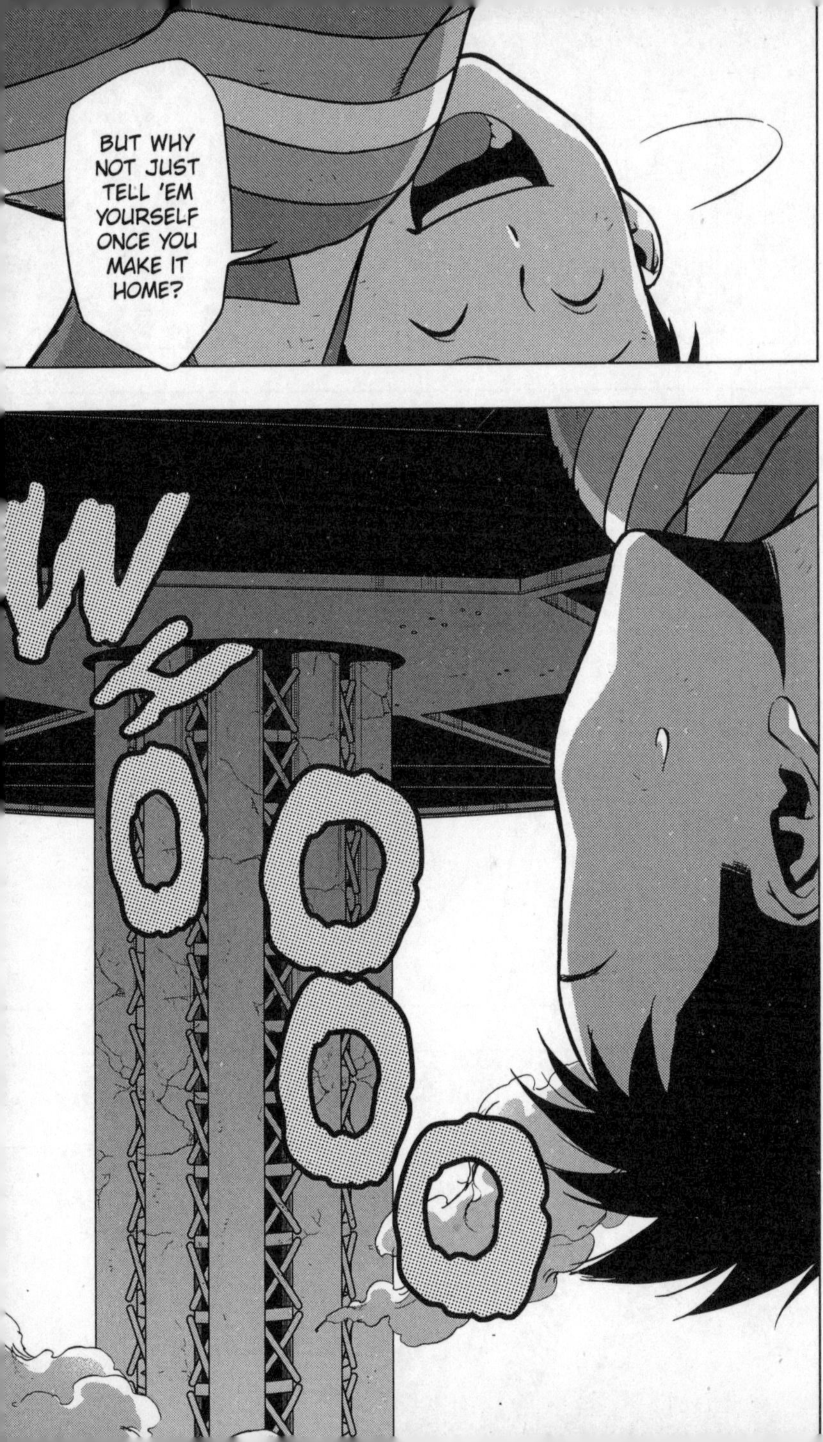
BUT WHY NOT JUST TELL 'EM YOURSELF ONCE YOU MAKE IT HOME?
WHOOOO

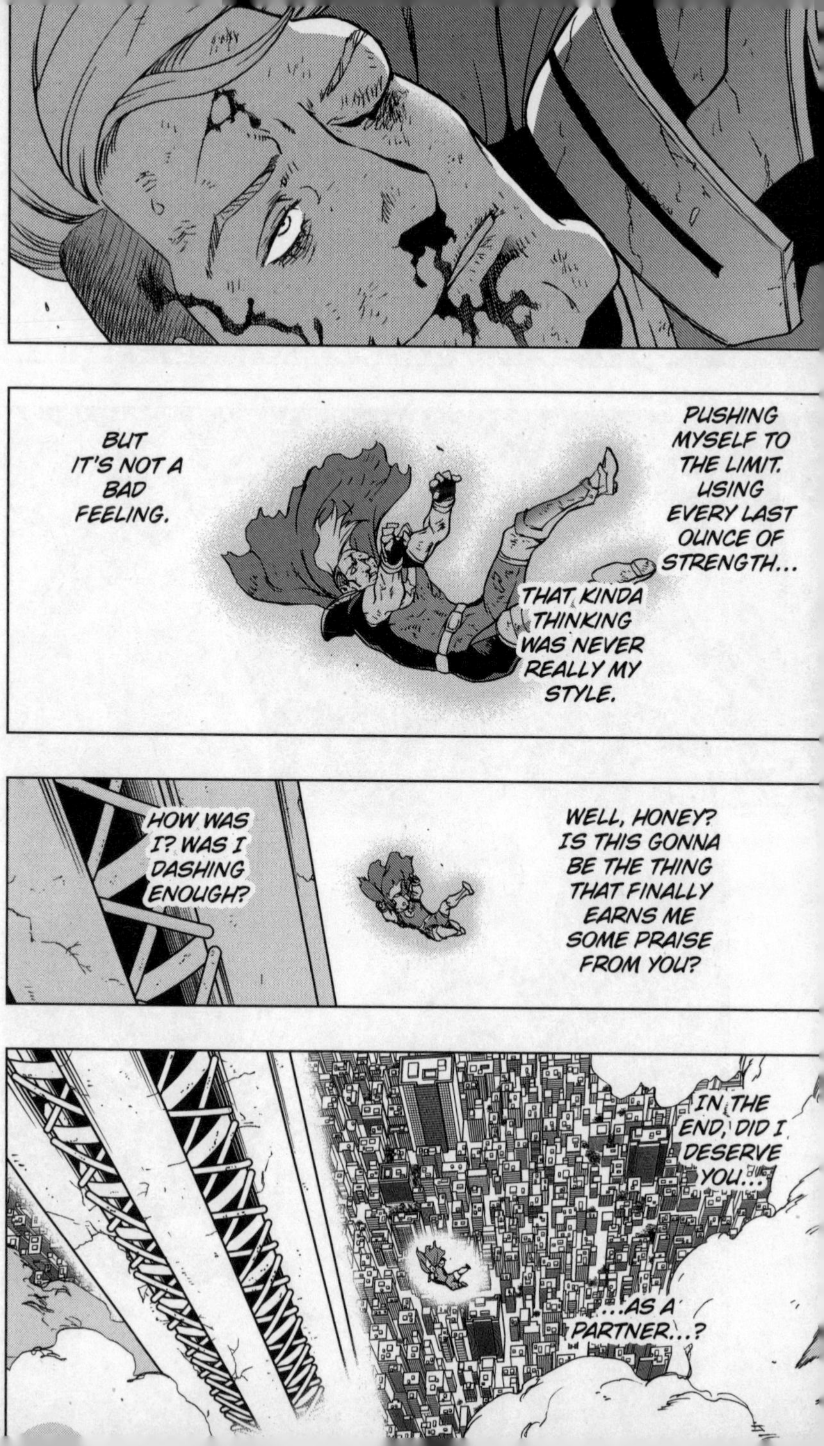
PUSHING MYSELF TO THE LIMIT. USING EVERY LAST OUNCE OF STRENGTH...
THAT KINDA THINKING WAS NEVER REALLY MY STYLE.
BUT IT'S NOT A BAD FEELING.
WELL, HONEY? IS THIS GONNA BE THE THING THAT FINALLY EARNS ME SOME PRAISE FROM YOU?
HOW WAS I? WAS I DASHING ENOUGH?
IN THE END, DID I DESERVE YOU...
...AS A PARTNER...?

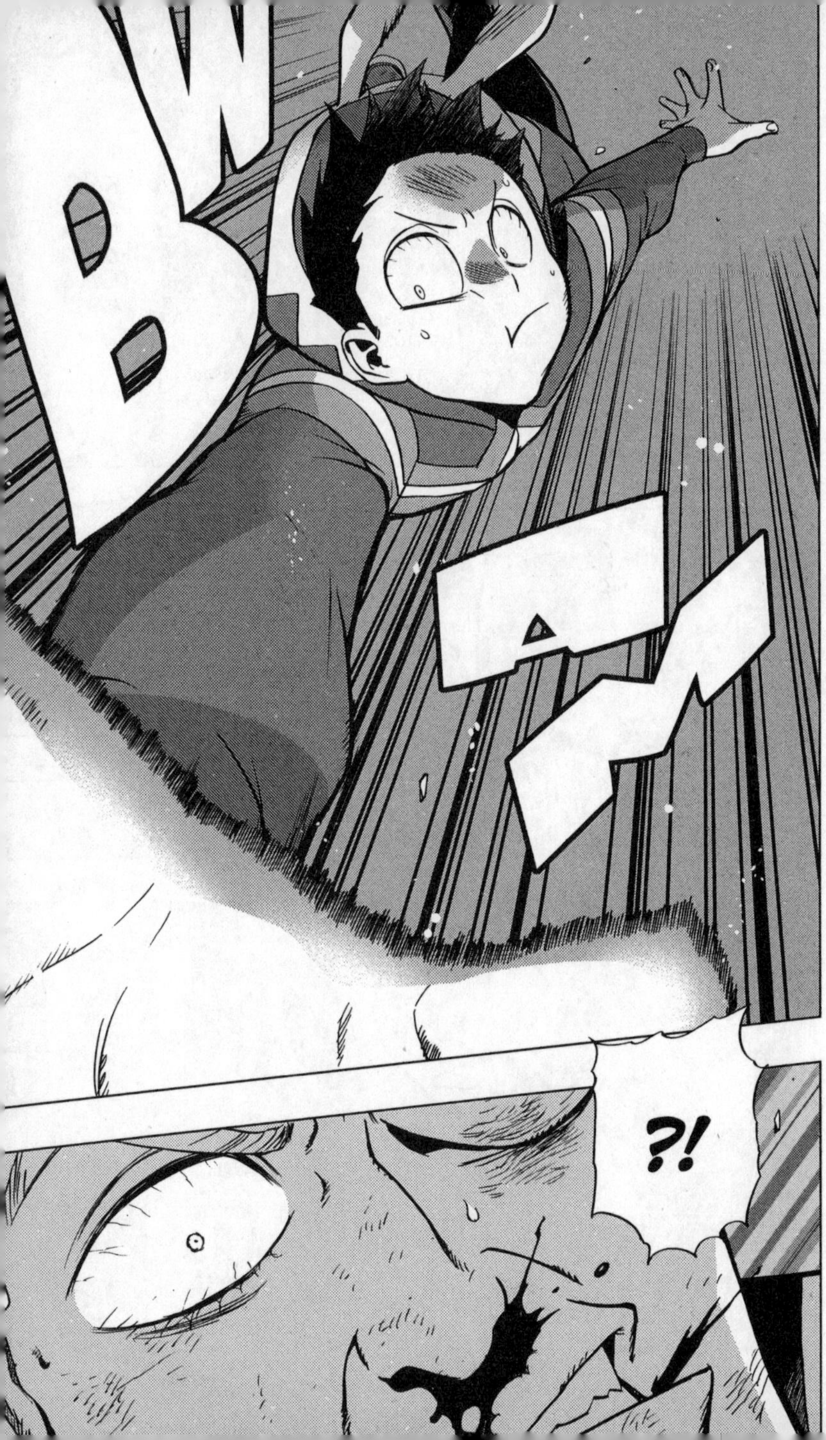
?!

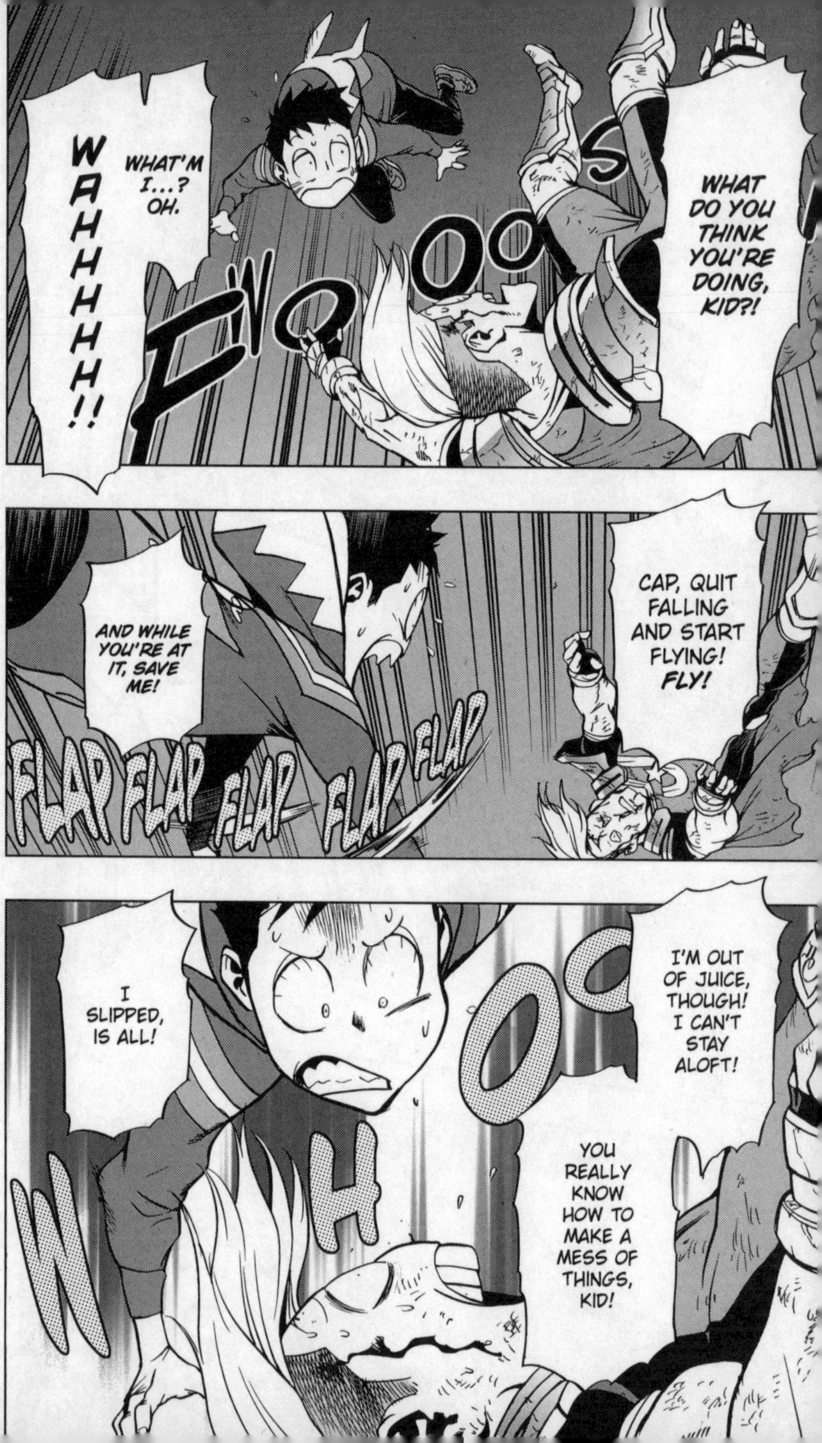
WHAT DO YOU THINK YOU'RE DOING, KID?!
WHAT'M I...? OH.
WAHHHHHH!!
FWOOOS
CAP, QUIT FALLING AND START FLYING! FLY!
AND WHILE YOU'RE AT IT, SAVE ME!
FLAP FLAP FLAP FLAP FLAP
I'M OUT OF JUICE, THOUGH! I CAN'T STAY ALOFT!
YOU REALLY KNOW HOW TO MAKE A MESS OF THINGS, KID!
I SLIPPED, IS ALL!
WHOO

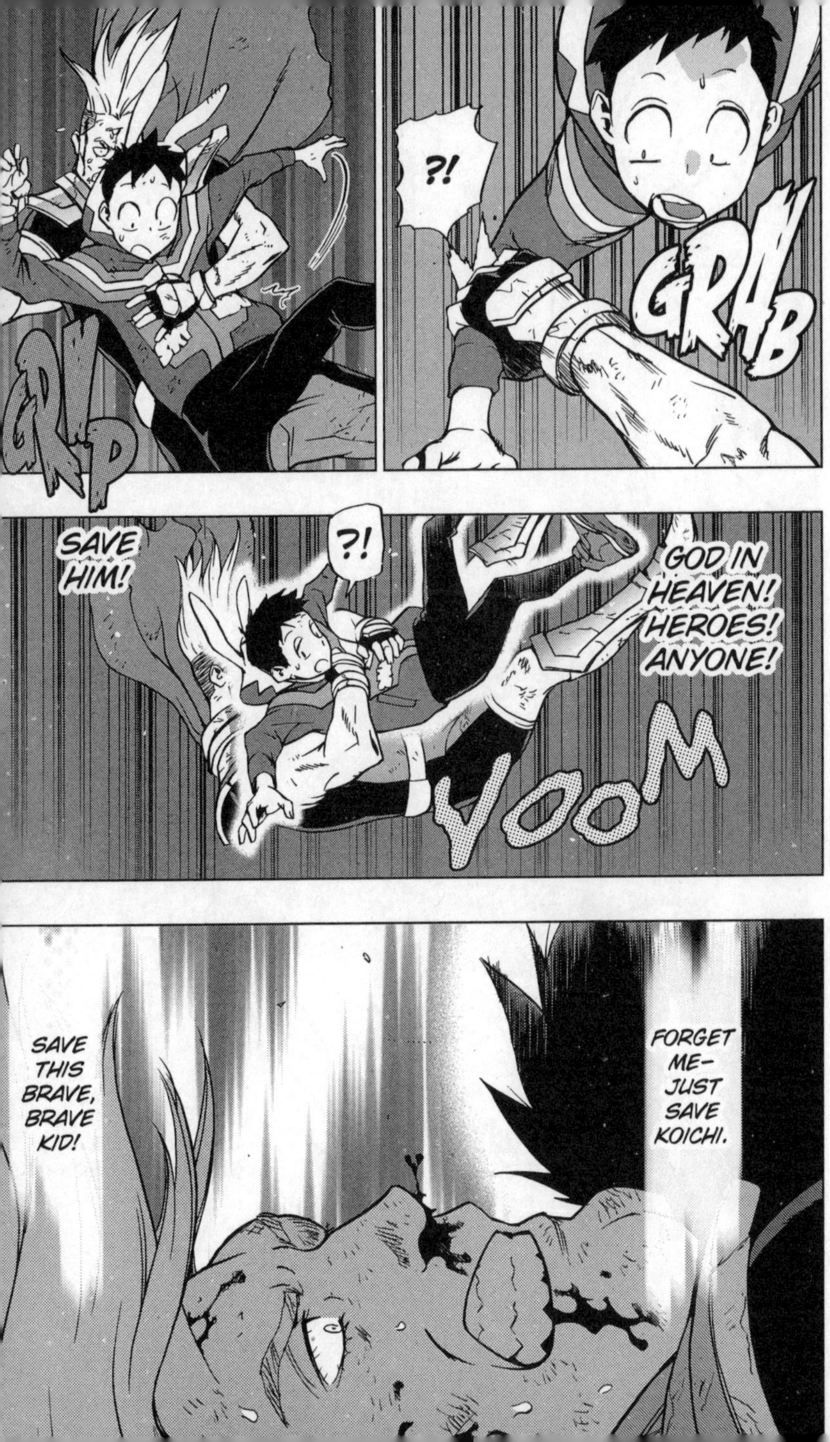
?!
GRAB
GRIP
GOD IN HEAVEN! HEROES! ANYONE!
?!
SAVE HIM!
VOOM
FORGET ME- JUST SAVE KOICHI.
SAVE THIS BRAVE, BRAVE KID!

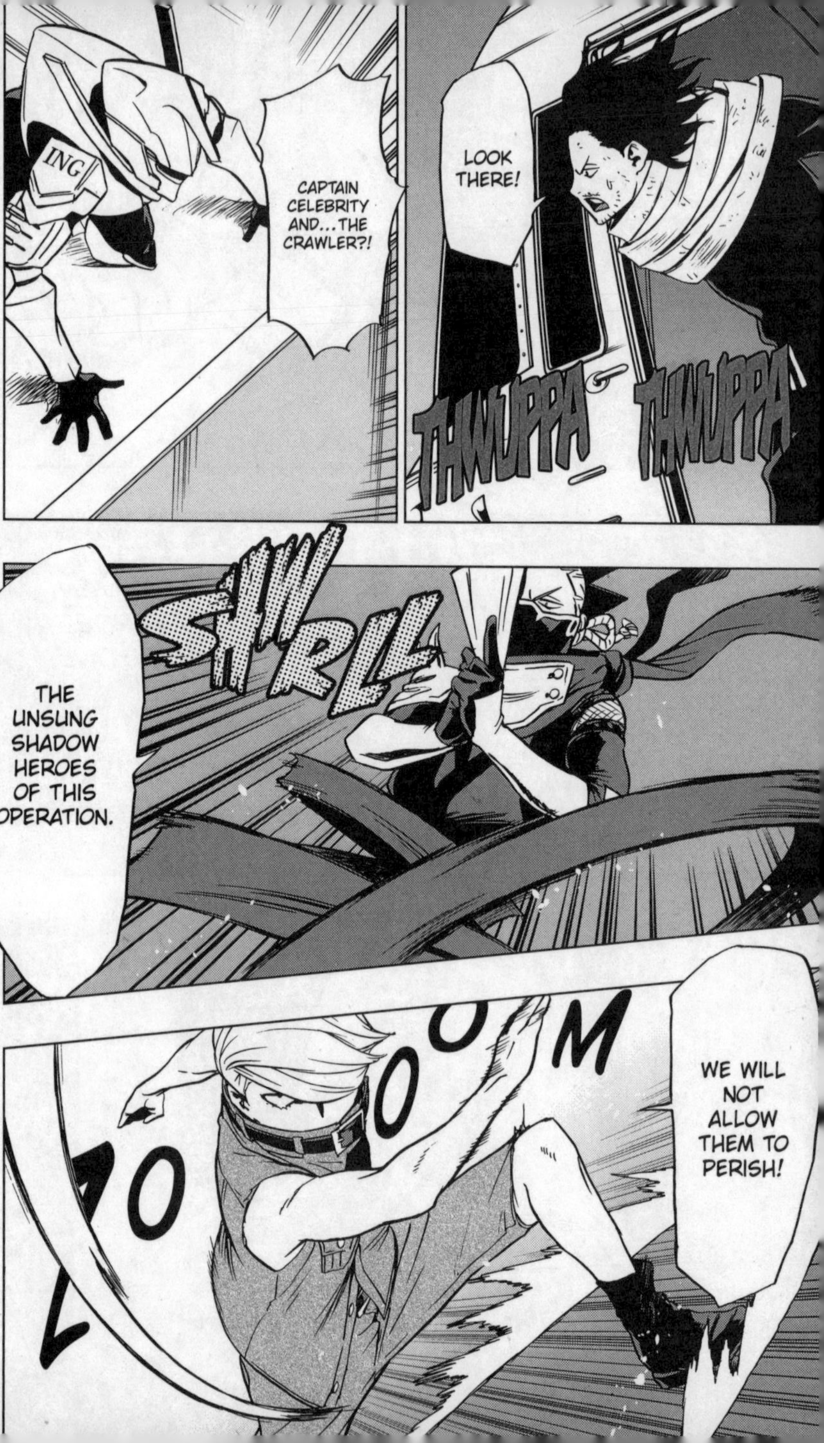
LOOK THERE!
THWUPPA THWUPPA
CAPTAIN CELEBRITY AND...THE CRAWLER?!
ING
SHRLL
THE UNSUNG SHADOW HEROES OF THIS OPERATION.
WE WILL NOT ALLOW THEM TO PERISH!
ZOOOOM

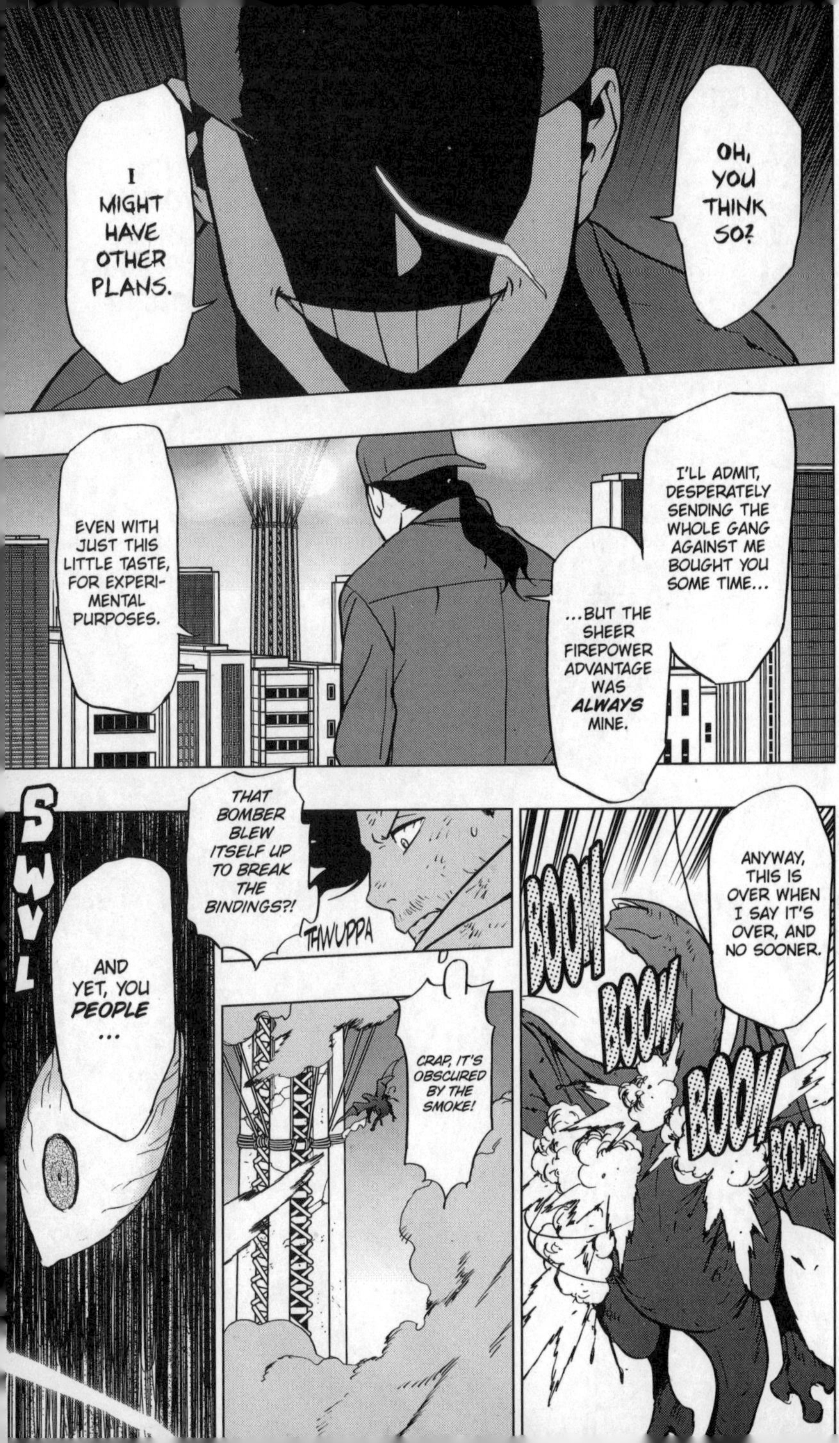
OH, YOU THINK SO?
I MIGHT HAVE OTHER PLANS.
I'LL ADMIT, DESPERATELY SENDING THE WHOLE GANG AGAINST ME BOUGHT YOU SOME TIME...
...BUT THE SHEER FIREPOWER ADVANTAGE WAS ALWAYS MINE.
EVEN WITH JUST THIS LITTLE TASTE, FOR EXPERI-MENTAL PURPOSES.
ANYWAY, THIS IS OVER WHEN I SAY IT'S OVER, AND NO SOONER.
BOOM
BOOM
BOOM
BOOM
THAT BOMBER BLEW ITSELF UP TO BREAK THE BINDINGS?!
THWUPPA
CRAP, IT'S OBSCURED BY THE SMOKE!
SWVL
AND YET, YOU PEOPLE ...

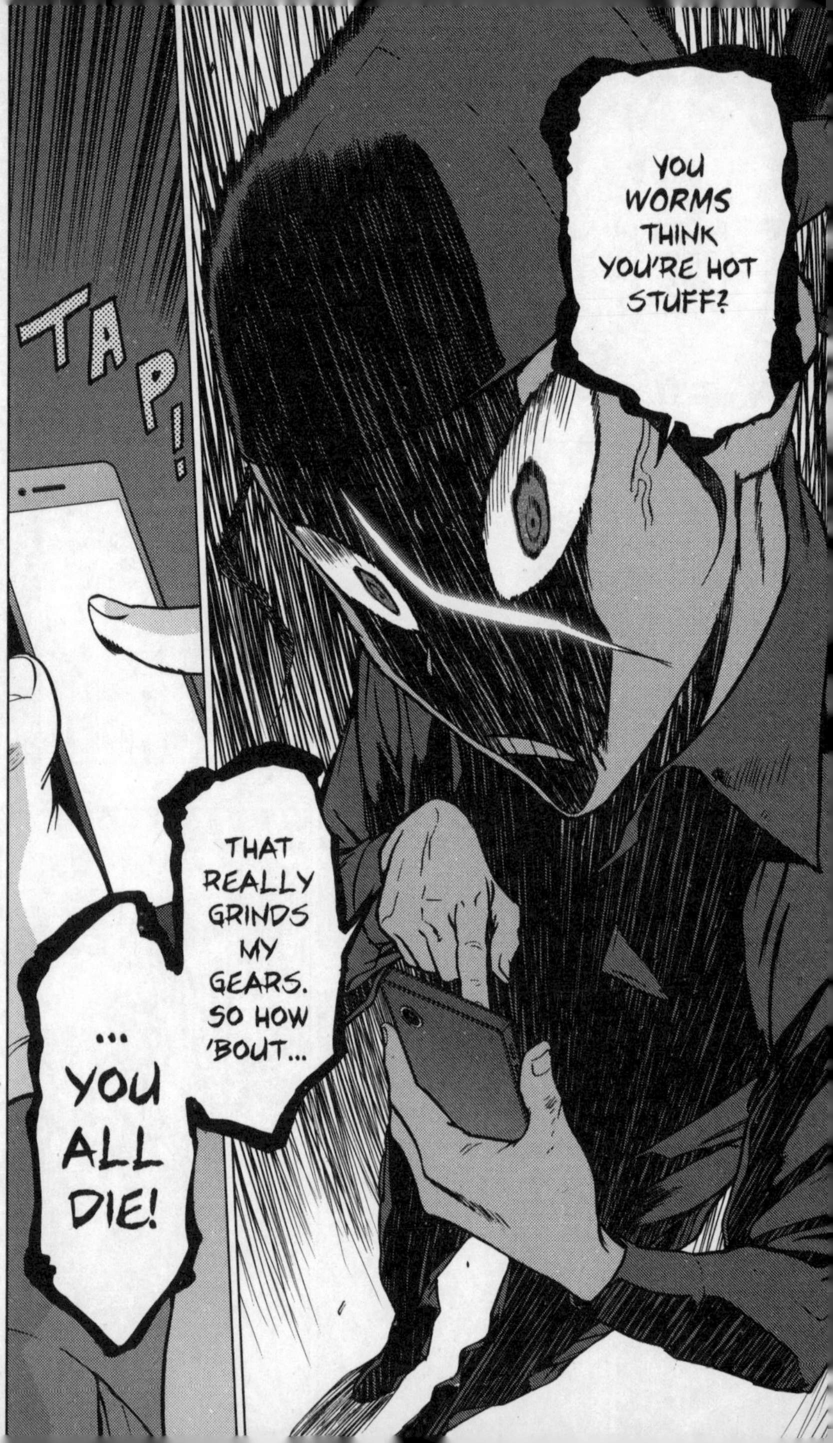

YOU WORMS THINK YOU'RE HOT STUFF?
TAP!!
THAT REALLY GRINDS MY GEARS. SO HOW 'BOUT...
... YOU ALL DIE!

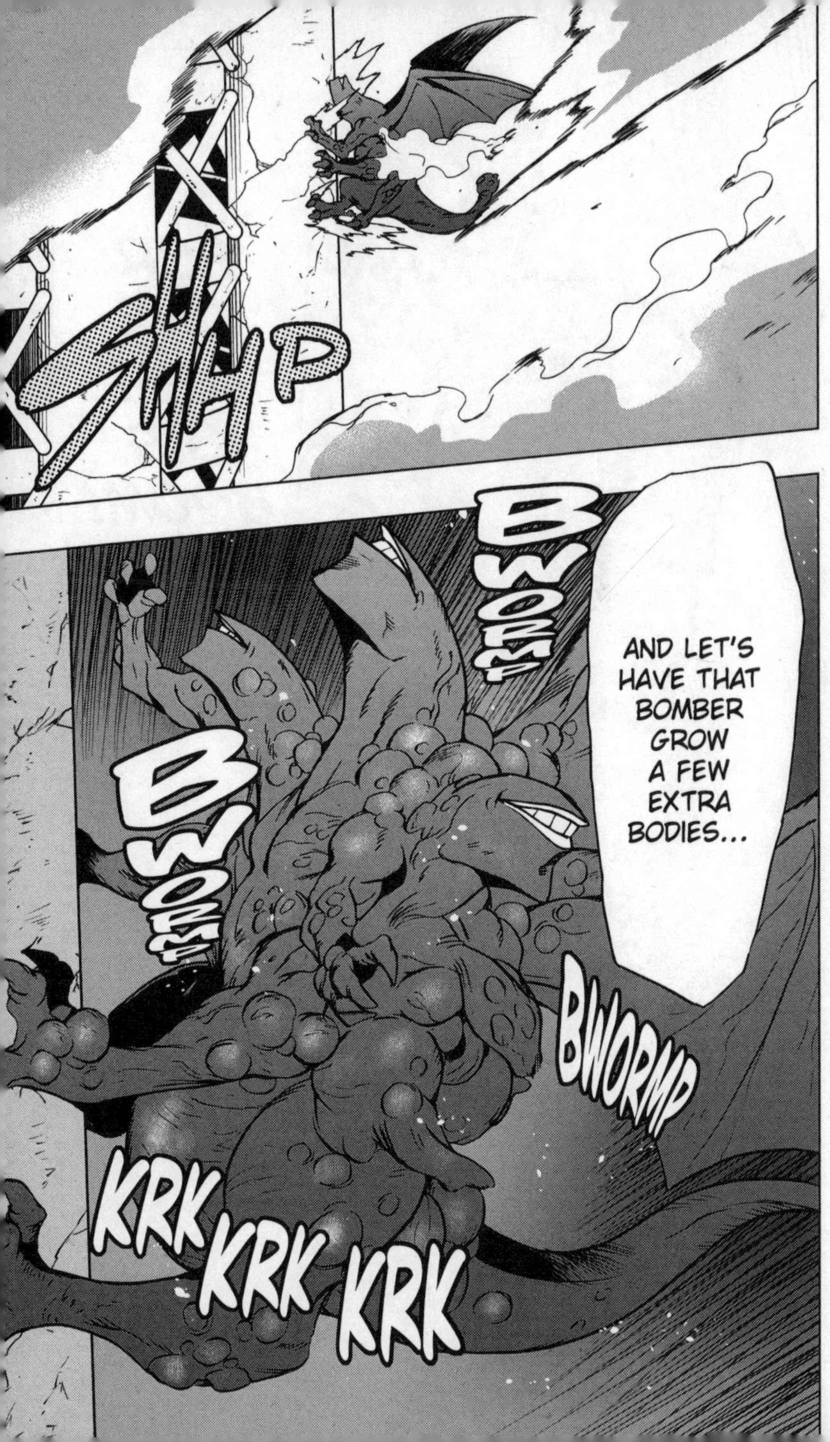
SHHP
AND LET'S HAVE THAT BOMBER GROW A FEW EXTRA BODIES...
BWORMP
BWORMP
BWORMP
KRK KRK KRK

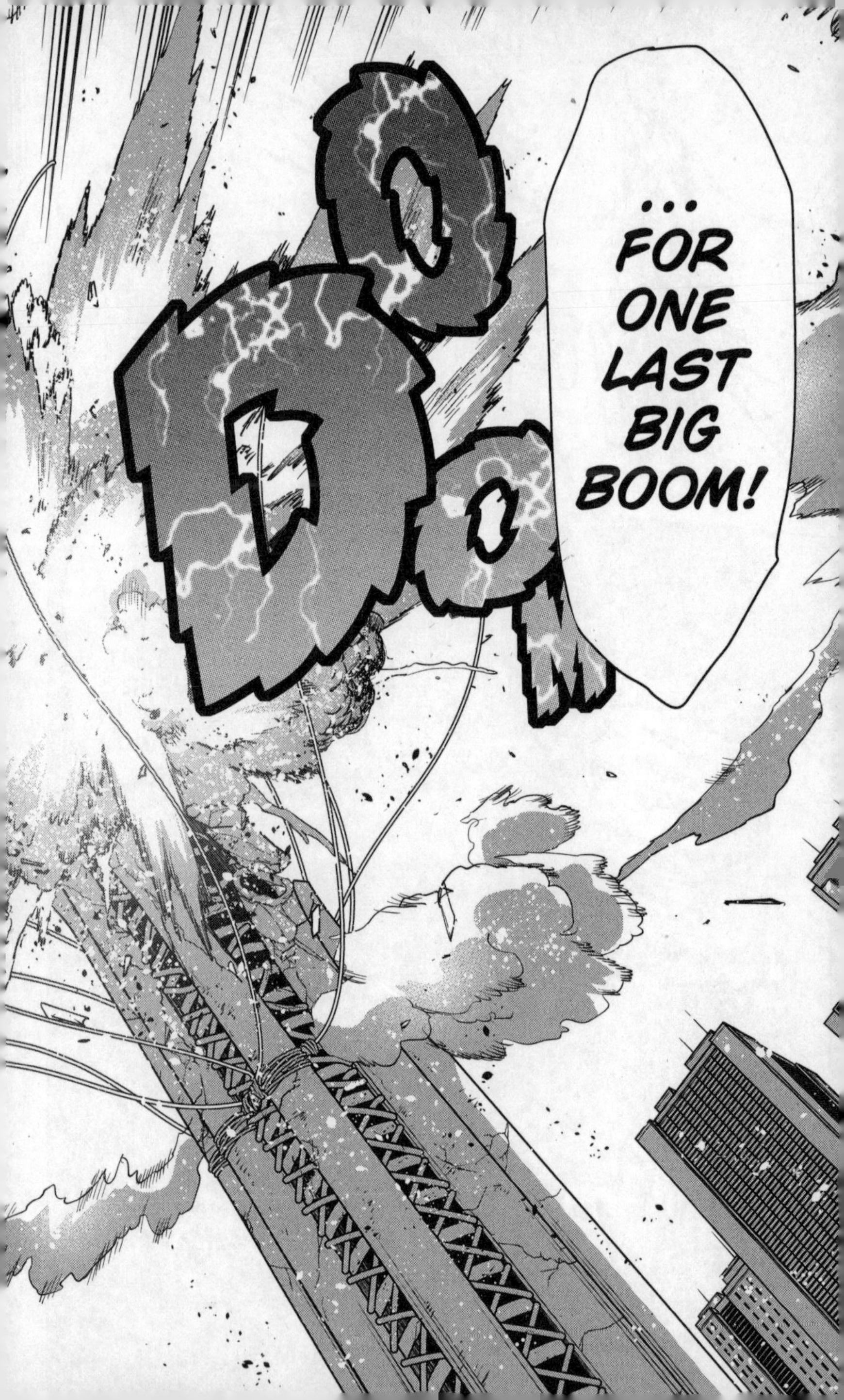
...FOR ONE LAST BIG BOOM!
DOOM

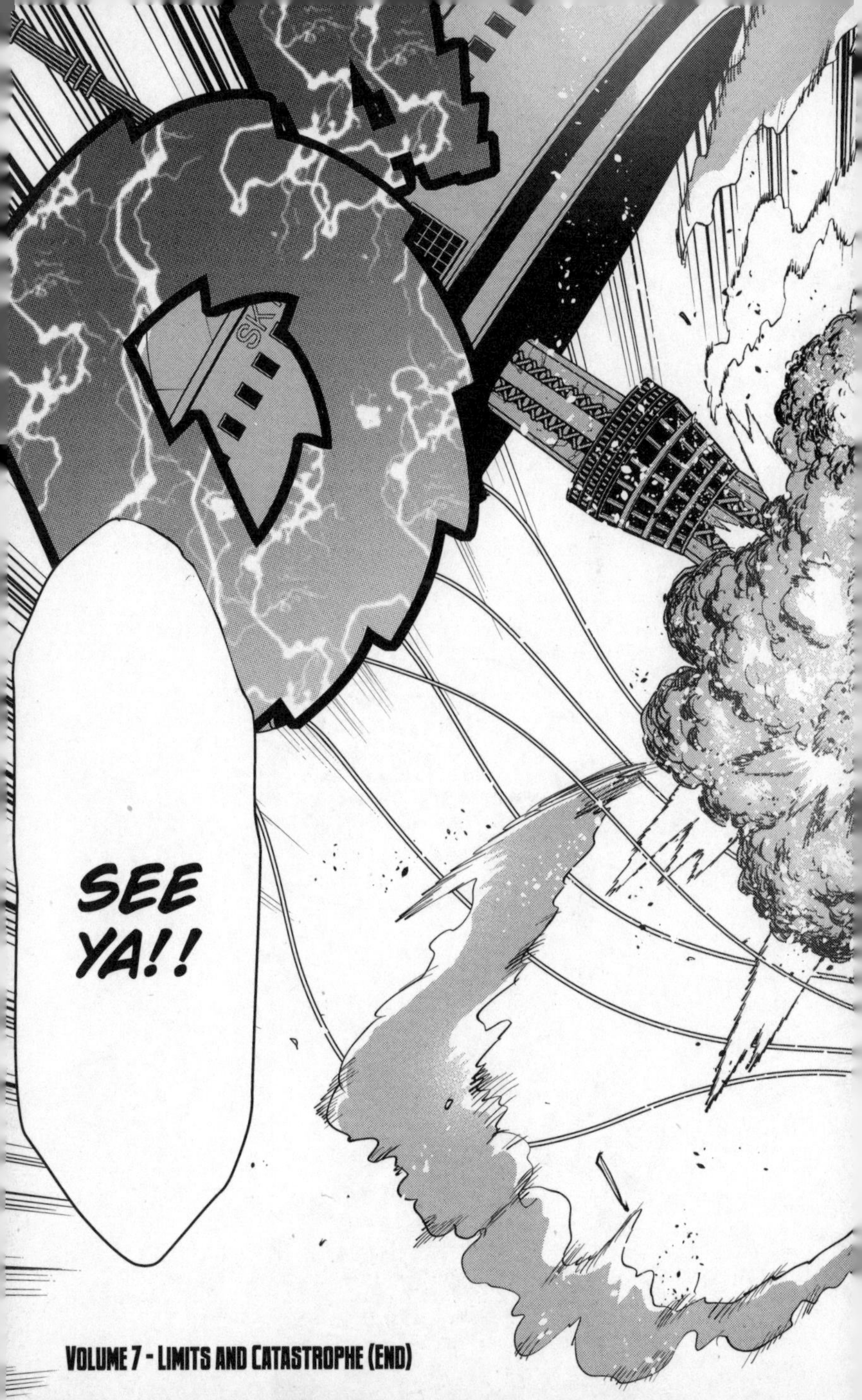
SEE YA!!

VOLUME 7 - LIMITS AND CATASTROPHE (END)

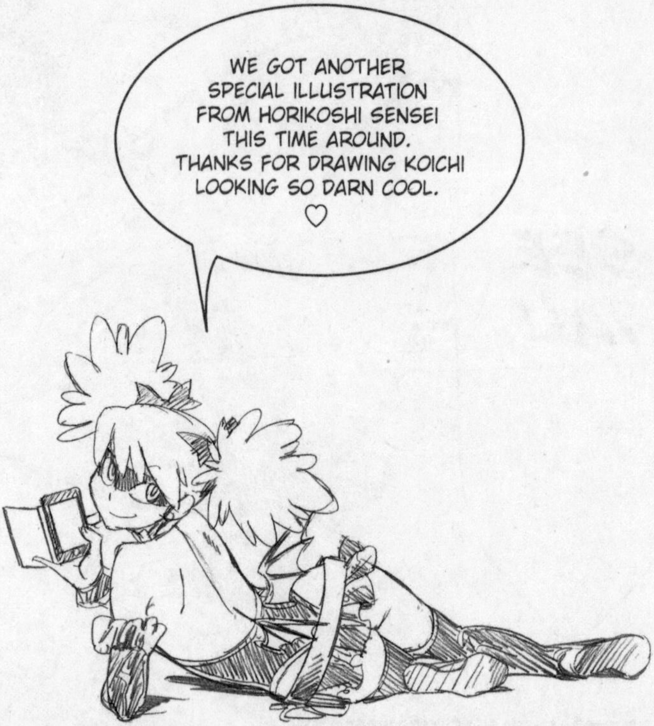
WE GOT ANOTHER SPECIAL ILLUSTRATION FROM HORIKOSHI SENSEI THIS TIME AROUND. THANKS FOR DRAWING KOICHI LOOKING SO DARN COOL. ♡

VIGILANTES 7

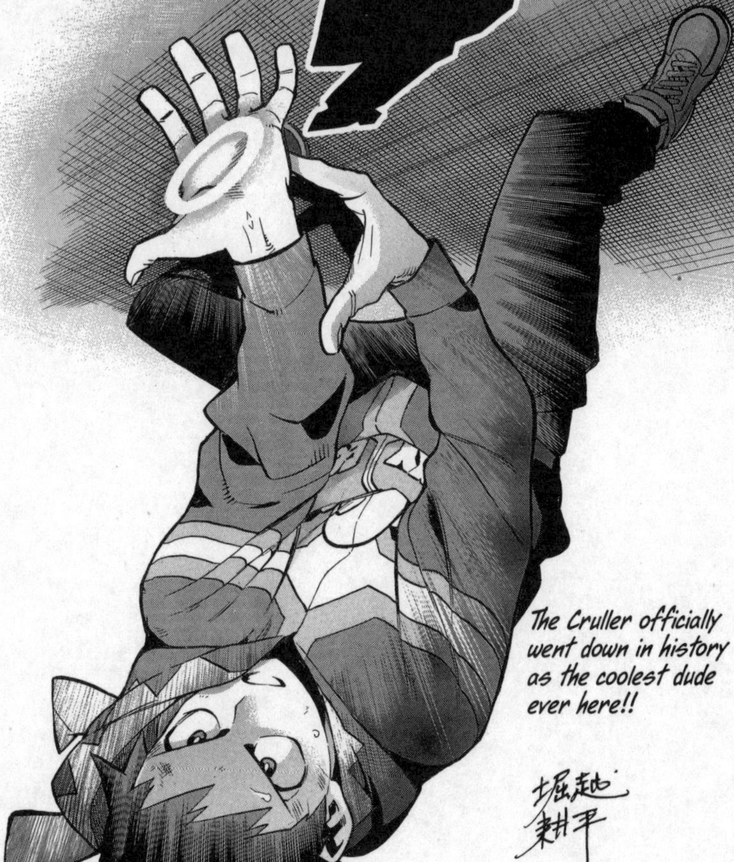

The Cruller officially went down in history as the coolest dude ever here!!

-Kohei Horikoshi

Message from KOHEI HORIKOSHI

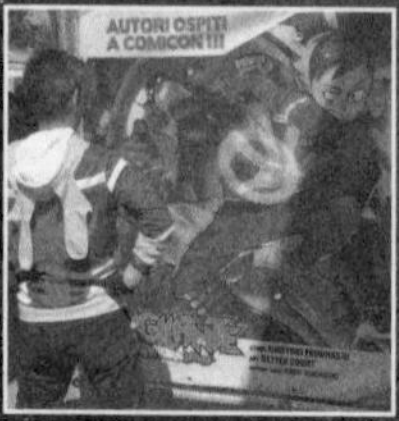
AUTORI OSPITI
A COMICON!!!

HIDEYUKI FURUHASHI

The week that chapter 52 was released (where we learn about Captain Celebrity's past), I was a guest at Napoli Comic-Con in Italy. It was so much fun!

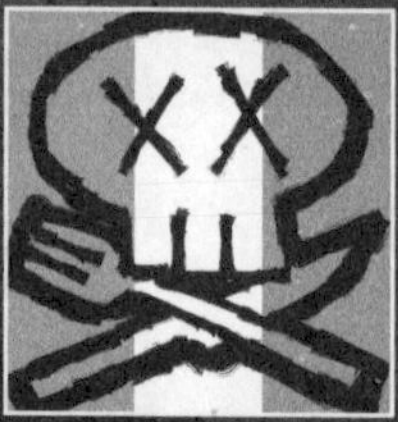

BETTEN COURT

I was invited to Napoli Comic-Con in Italy, and I had a blast. Ever since I got back, I've been in a daze and can't stop thinking about it.

VOLUME 7
SHONEN JUMP Manga Edition

STORY: HIDEYUKI FURUHASHI
ART: BETTEN COURT
ORIGINAL CONCEPT: KOHEI HORIKOSHI

Translation & English Adaptation/Caleb Cook
Touch-Up Art & Lettering/John Hunt
Designer/Julian [JR] Robinson
Editor/Mike Montesa

VIGILANTE -BOKU NO HERO ACADEMIA ILLEGALS-
© 2016 by Hideyuki Furuhashi, Betten Court, Kohei Horikoshi
All rights reserved.
First published in Japan in 2016 by SHUEISHA Inc., Tokyo.
English translation rights arranged by SHUEISHA Inc.

The stories, characters and incidents mentioned in this publication
are entirely fictional.

Printed in the U.S.A.

Published by VIZ Media, LLC
P.O. Box 77010
San Francisco, CA 94107

10 9 8 7 6 5 4 3 2 1
First printing, June 2020

viz.com

shonenjump.com

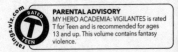

PARENTAL ADVISORY
MY HERO ACADEMIA: VIGILANTES is rated
T for Teen and is recommended for ages
13 and up. This volume contains fantasy
violence.

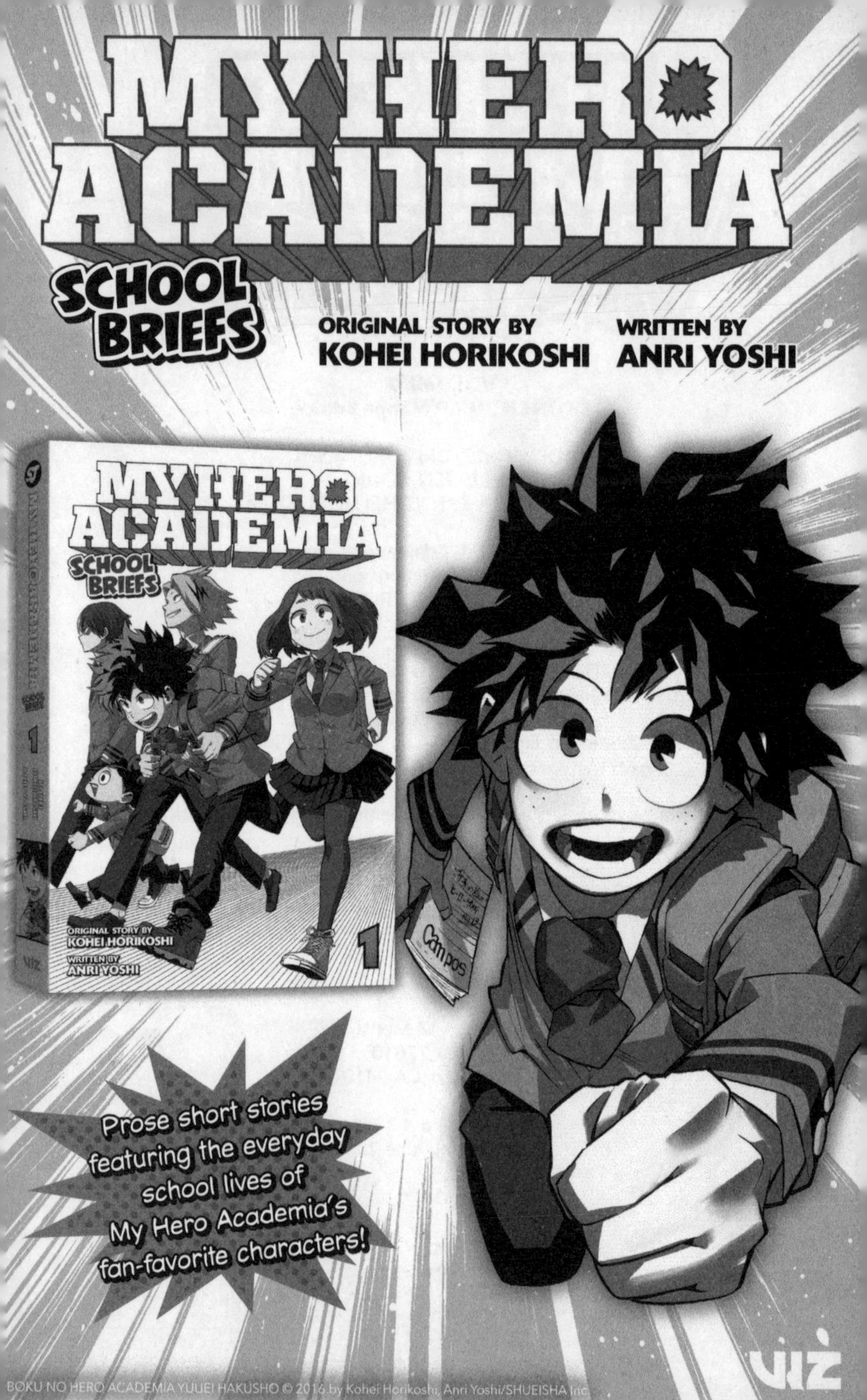
MY HERO ACADEMIA
SCHOOL BRIEFS
ORIGINAL STORY BY
KOHEI HORIKOSHI
WRITTEN BY
ANRI YOSHI
Prose short stories featuring the everyday school lives of My Hero Academia's fan-favorite characters!
VIZ

MY HERO ACADEMIA SMASH!!

Story and Art by Hirofumi Neda
Original Concept by Kohei Horikoshi

HILARIOUS HIJINKS
featuring the characters
and story lines of
MY HERO ACADEMIA!

The superpowered society of *My Hero Academia* takes a hilarious turn in this reimagining of the best-selling series! Join Midoriya, All Might and all the aspiring heroes of U.A. High, plus memorable villains, in an irreverent take on the main events of the series, complete with funny gags, ridiculous jokes and superpowered humor!

DRAGON
BALL
A Visual History

**AKIRA
TORIYAMA**

Featuring stunning full-color artwork, exclusive creator commentary and rarely seen sketches, *Dragon Ball: A Visual History* is the definitive journey through the artwork of one of the most influential and popular manga series of all time, Akira Toriyama's *Dragon Ball*.

**The Ultimate
DRAGON BALL
Art Collection!**

DEMON SLAYER

KIMETSU NO YAIBA

Story and Art by
KOYOHARU GOTOUGE

In Taisho-era Japan, kindhearted Tanjiro Kamado makes a living selling charcoal. But his peaceful life is shattered when a demon slaughters his entire family. His little sister Nezuko is the only survivor, but she has been transformed into a demon herself! Tanjiro sets out on a dangerous journey to find a way to return his sister to normal and destroy the demon who ruined his life.

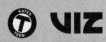

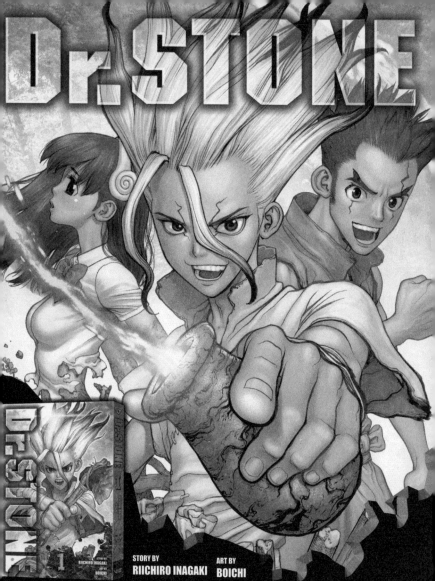

Dr. STONE

STORY BY
RIICHIRO INAGAKI

ART BY
BOICHI

One fateful day, all of humanity turned to stone. Many millennia later, Taiju frees himself from petrification and finds himself surrounded by statues. The situation looks grim—until he runs into his science-loving friend Senku! Together they plan to restart civilization with the power of science!

YOU'RE READING THE WRONG WAY!!

MY HERO ACADEMIA VIGILANTES

reads from right to left, starting in the upper-right corner. Japanese is read from right to left, meaning that action, sound effects and word-balloon order are completely reversed from English order.

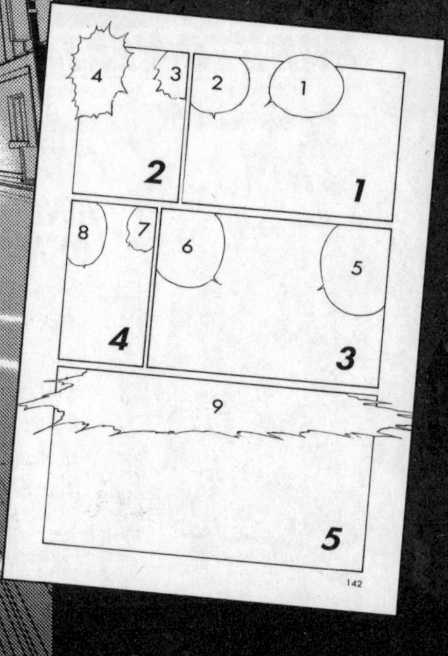

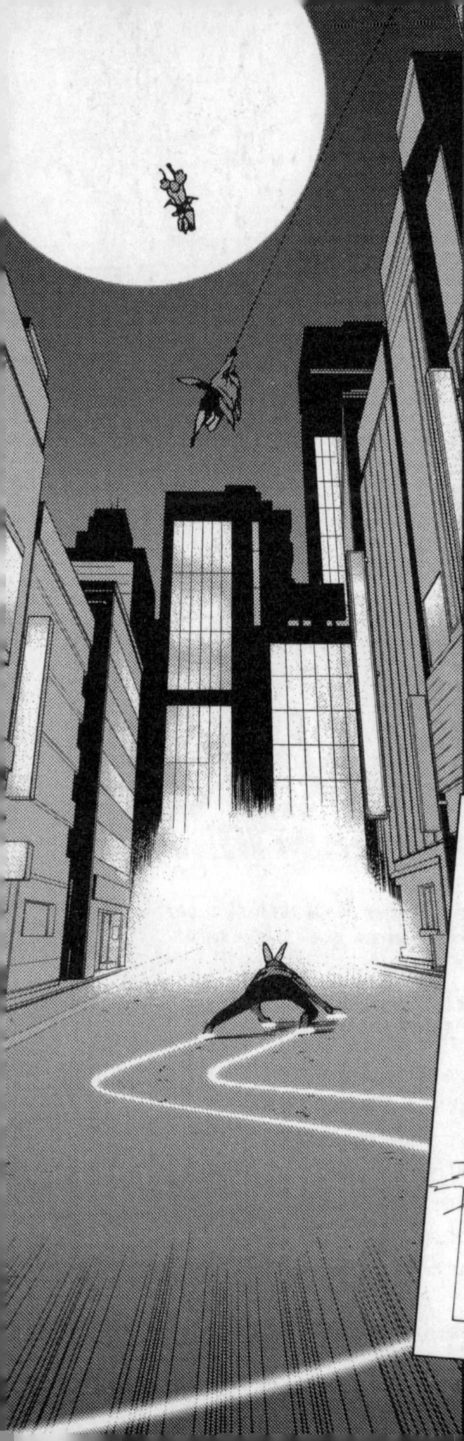